Uri Rubin (z"l)

Between Jerusalem and Mecca

Judaism, Christianity, and Islam – Tension, Transmission, Transformation

Edited by
Patrice Brodeur, Alexandra Cuffel, Assaad Elias Kattan, and Georges Tamer

Volume 22

Uri Rubin (z"l)

Between Jerusalem and Mecca

Sanctity and Redemption in the Qurʾān and the Islamic Tradition

DE GRUYTER MAGNES

This book is a translation from the Hebrew original, which was published under the title
בין ירושלים למכה : קדושה וגאולה בקוראן ובמסורת האסלאם
Jerusalem: Magnes 2019.

ISBN 978-3-11-221530-2
e-ISBN (PDF) 978-3-11-122231-8
e-ISBN (EPUB) 978-3-11-122297-4
ISSN 2196-405X

Library of Congress Control Number: 2023932881

Bibliographic information published by the Deutsche Nationalbibliothek
The Deutsche Nationalbibliothek lists this publication in the Deutsche Nationalbibliografie; detailed bibliographic data are available on the internet at http://dnb.dnb.de.

This volume is text- and page-identical with the hardback published in 2023.
Typesetting: Integra Software Services Pvt. Ltd.
Printing and binding: CPI books GmbH, Leck

www.degruyter.com

Preface

This book was first published in Hebrew by the Hebrew University Magnes Press (Jerusalem 2019). The present English version contains revised insights, additions, and further references to some Arabic sources as well as to more modern studies.

My thanks are due to Prof. Michael Lecker for his invaluable notes and comments on the present version. I also owe my thanks to Michael Guggenheimer, who prepared the initial English translation.

https://doi.org/10.1515/9783111222318-202

Contents

Preface — V

Introduction — 1
The Jerusalem-Mecca sanctity space and the plan of redemption — **3**
Methodology — **4**
The Qur'ān — **5**
The traditions and their transmitters — **7**
Sources on the internet — **7**
Terminology — **8**

Part One: **Navel of the Earth**

1 Muḥammad's journey to the "Farthest Mosque" — 13
The Farthest Mosque and the navel of the earth — **13**
The nocturnal journey and Jewish messianism — **18**
The nocturnal journey in extra-qur'ānic traditions — **22**
Muslims in al-Shām: al-Masjid al-Aqṣā and Īliyā' — **23**

2 Muḥammad's ascension to heaven — 25
Muḥammad's ascension and the Dome of the Rock — **25**
Muḥammad's ascension from Mecca — **30**
Mecca as the navel of the earth and the gate to Paradise — **31**
Between Jerusalem and Mecca: The issue of prayer and pilgrimage — **32**
Muḥammad's journey: The complete route — **35**

Part Two: **Land of Redemption**

3 Israel's redemption and "the Promise of the Latter Days" — 39
Pharaoh's defeat and the bequest of the land to the Children of Israel — **40**
Destruction of the Temple — **43**
The promise of the Latter Days (Q 17:103–104) — **45**
The evidence of the Jewish sources — **47**
Wa'd al-ākhira and the message to the qur'ānic audience — **51**
Redemption and resurrection: Exegesis and tradition — **52**
River of sand: Muqātil b. Sulaymān and the Apocalypse of Ezra — **53**

The promise of the Latter Days and Constantinople — 57
Sons of Moses — 58
The Mahdī — 59

Part Three: **Land of Resurrection**

4 **Resurrection in al-Shām — 63**
The Qurʾān: Resurrection upon the plain – *al-sāhira* — 63
Pre-Islamic Jewish apocalypse — 66
The traditions: The *sāhira* and the *baqīʿ* in al-Shām — 68
The merits of being buried in Bayt al-Maqdis and in al-Shām — 70
The merits of al-Shām and Umayyad interests — 74
God's descent to pass judgment in Jerusalem — 75
The Sde Boker inscription — 78
The mosaic inscription of the Dome of the Rock — 79

5 **Resurrection in Arabia — 84**
Obstructing the forces of evil: The Dajjāl and Gog and Magog — 84
Resurrection in Medina: The sanctity of Baqīʿ al-Gharqad — 86
The gathering of the resurrected in Medina: The Prophet's resurrection — 88
Al-sāhira and the merits of dying in Mecca — 90
Intercession by the sacred stones in Mecca — 91
Burial of the Muhājirūn in Mecca or in Medina — 92
Joint sanctity of Mecca and Medina — 93
Preserving Jerusalem's superiority: The Kaʿba will come to it — 93
The merits of burial elsewhere in the Muslim world — 95

Part Four: **Land of the Prophets**

6 **The Patriarchs in al-Shām — 99**
The three Patriarchs and al-Shām — 99
The land of the prophets at large and their graves — 101
The prophets and the defense of al-Shām — 106
In praise of traveling to al-Shām on the path of Abraham — 109
The Umayyads and the boundaries of Abraham's Promised Land — 111
The settlement of Bayt al-Maqdis is the ruin of Medina — 112

7 Ishmael and the progeny of Abraham — 114
The four patriarchs: Abraham, Ishmael, Isaac and Jacob — **114**
Abraham is neither a Jew nor a Christian — **115**
Violation of Abraham's covenant — **116**
The seed of Abraham in Christian theology — **118**
Ishmael in Christian theology — **119**
The qur'ānic response — **120**

8 Abraham and Ishmael build the Kaʿba — 121
Abraham in Mecca — **121**
Abraham prays by the Kaʿba — **123**
Raising the Kaʿba's foundations — **124**
The prayer of the Kaʿba's builders for Muḥammad and his nation — **125**
The Kaʿba's construction and Jubilees — **127**
The house of Abraham as *birah* — **134**
Appendix: Jubilees 22 — **135**

9 The attempted sacrifice between al-Shām and Mecca — 138
The qur'ānic version: Abraham goes to the place of the sacrifice — **138**
The traditions: The attempted sacrifice on the Rock in Bayt al-Maqdis — **140**
The ram's horns between Jerusalem and Mecca — **142**
The attempted sacrifice at Minā — **143**
Sozomen — **145**
Arabs and non-Arabs — **146**

10 The Kaʿba and the Prophets — 148
Adam in Mecca — **148**
The Kaʿba from Adam to Abraham — **149**
The number of prophets who came on pilgrimage to Mecca — **150**
The Children of Israel in Mecca — **151**
Jesus and Mecca — **152**
Mecca as a refuge for prophets — **152**
Medina and the prophets — **154**
Shared sanctity of the land of the prophets — **154**

Part Five: **Land of the Temple**

11 Solomon's Temple — 157
Solomon and the blessed land — **157**
The labor of the demons for Solomon — **158**
Solomon's Temple and the Dome of the Rock — **160**
The promise to Jacob and the Dome of the Rock — **162**
King David and ʿAbd al-Malik — **163**
The Jewish angle — **165**
The Temple and the prophets at large — **167**
Prayer niches in Solomon's Temple — **167**
Edifices in Bayt al-Maqdis from David's and Solomon's days — **168**

12 "The first House established for the people" — 170
The first-House passage — **170**
The biblical model: "exalted from the beginning" — **172**
Tafsīr of the first-House passage: Maqām Ibrāhīm and the pilgrimage — **173**
The stone of Maqām Ibrāhīm — **175**

13 The First House in Creation — 178
The Kaʿba and the Creation — **178**
The Kaʿba predated al-Masjid al-Aqṣā by forty years — **180**
Abraham's Kaʿba and Adam — **182**

14 The direction of prayer (*qibla*) within the sanctity space — 187
The Kaʿba as *qibla*: The qurʾānic data — **188**
The tradition: Circumstances of the change of *qibla* — **190**
After Muḥammad: Renewed tension between the two *qibla*s — **192**
The testimony of al-Farazdaq — **195**
The antiquity of the Kaʿba as *qibla* — **196**
The sanctity of the two *qibla*s — **198**

Part Six: **The Messianic Vision Inverted**

15 Romans (al-Rūm), Jews and Muslims — 203
The Roman victory and the inversion of the messianic vision — **203**
The chronology of the Rūm passage — **205**
The clash with the Jews of Medina: The *ḥashr* of the Naḍīr — **206**
The defeat of Qurayẓa — **208**

The victories in Arabia and the concept of *fatḥ* — **209**
Fatḥ versus Quraysh — **210**
"A nigh *fatḥ*" — **210**
Simultaneous Byzantine and Muslim victories — **213**
From persecuted in Mecca to triumphant in Medina — **215**
The conquest of al-Shām in the wake of the Children of Israel — **216**
Muḥammad and al-Shām — **217**

Summary — 219
Transition of sanctity patterns in the Qur'ān — **219**
Transition of sanctity patterns in the *ḥadīth* — **221**

Bibliography — 225

Index — 239

Introduction

The present study looks into the image of two cities, Jerusalem and Mecca, and examines the way in which they are depicted in early Muslim traditions. This topic has indeed already been addressed in numerous studies, including some that are devoted to a typological comparison between these two holy cities.[1] Heribert Busse, for example, showed that already in the Qur'ān the image of the Kaʿba was shaped according to the Jewish models of the Temple. He added that after Muḥammad's death, when the Muslims arrived in Palestine and Syria, Temple traditions of Jewish provenance began to migrate from the Islamic Jerusalem to Mecca. The process was accelerated due to the developing competition between the new political center in Syria and Palestine (the Umayyad dynasty) and conservative circles in Arabia, which set out to defend the position of the Ḥijāz as the cradle of Islam.[2]

While these are valid observations, the present study will endeavor to show that the competition over which is holier, Jerusalem or Mecca, which intensified during the Umayyad period, has its roots in the Qur'ān. Here one finds already the first intimations of Jerusalem's sanctity in Islam, unlike the opinion of scholars such as Amikam Elad, who argues that it was only in the Umayyad period that the process of Jerusalem's sanctification began.[3] Similarly, Ofer Livne-Kafri maintains that most Muslim traditions about the sanctity of Jerusalem arose after the Muslims established themselves on the Temple Mount, especially after the building projects carried out by the Umayyad rulers on that site.[4] Joseph Drory, too, writes that Jerusalem "aroused little interest during the reigns of the first Caliphs", and that it was the Umayyads who became active "in the creation of a web of adages and phrases in praise of Jerusalem (and al-Shām)".[5] Clearly the Umayyad role in the dissemination of traditions concerning the virtues of Jerusalem is undeniable, but the impression that the city's sanctity in Islam began only during their rule is wrong.

A number of scholars, including Yitzhak Hasson, have also argued that the identification of the well-known qur'ānic phrase *al-masjid al-aqṣā* (Q 17:1) with

1 See especially, Peters, *Jerusalem and Mecca*; Lazarus-Yafe, "Jerusalem and Mecca".
2 Busse, "Jerusalem and Mecca", pp. 243–244.
3 Elad, "The Status of Jerusalem", p. 23.
4 Livne-Kafri, "The Navel of the Earth", p. 72.
5 Drory, "A History of Early Islam", p. 64. See also Lassner, *Medieval Jerusalem*, p. 16: "By most accounts, medieval or modern, Jerusalem first became a Muslim *locus sacra* [*sic*] under Umayyad rule".

https://doi.org/10.1515/9783111222318-001

Jerusalem did not become generally accepted by the believers before the Umayyad period.[6] As Yitzhak Reiter, following Elad, Livne-Kafri and Hasson, puts it:

> From the end of the seventh century, [Muslims] began to associate the qur'ānic verse Q 17:1, which describes the Prophet Muḥammad's miraculous journey (*al-isrā'*) from Mecca to the Farthest Mosque (al-Masjid al-Aqṣā) and the traditions about his ascension to the heavens (*al-mi'rāj*), with Jerusalem.[7]

The same approach is reflected in Hasson's and Moshe Sharon's statements that Jerusalem is not mentioned in the Qur'ān at all, not even indirectly.[8] Furthermore, several researchers have argued that not only did Jerusalem come to be perceived as holy among Muslims only during the Umayyad period, but also that Mecca was always considered holier. As S.D. Goitein wrote:

> Despite all the admiration that the Holy Land acquired in Muslim pious circles, its status can in no way be compared to that of the Ka'ba, Mecca and associated sites. The Holy Land's sanctity was accepted into Islam due to Jewish and Christian influence. But after Islam had reached its full development, it was no longer prominent in its religious consciousness, and after the shocks of the Crusader period had been forgotten, it disappeared from the religious horizon almost completely.[9]

A number of scholars followed Goitein's attitude. They lowered the rank of Jerusalem's sanctity and denied its precedence over that of Mecca.[10] The more extreme deniers of the antiquity of Jerusalem's Islamic sanctity pointed out that compilations of traditions praising the city first appeared only in the fifth century AH, such as al-Wāsiṭī's (active *circa* 410/1019), from which they concluded that until then Jerusalem was not held in high esteem in Muslim thought.[11] But is this true? If we turn to Mecca, we find that the earliest collection of traditions concerning it was composed by al-Azraqī (d. 222/837). Should we conclude from this that for two-hundred years Mecca had little significance for the believers? Of

---

6 Hasson, "Jerusalem in the Muslim Perspective", pp. 288–289; Elad, "The Status of Jerusalem", p. 23, with references to further studies.
7 Reiter, "The Third in Sanctity", p. 164 (with reference to Elad, *Medieval Jerusalem*, p. 21).
8 Hasson, "Jerusalem in the Muslim Perspective", p. 285; Sharon, "The Praises of Jerusalem", p. 56. See also Havel, "Jerusalem", p. 126.
9 Goitein, "Sanctity", p. 126.
10 E.g. Sivan, *Political Myths*, p. 90: "It is possible to prove the extent to which Islam did not appreciate the sanctity of Jerusalem by the fact that Jerusalem was among the last cities to be conquered during the invasion to Syria". See also Reiter, *From Jerusalem to Mecca*, p. 14. However, I wonder since when the priorities in planning military movements are decided according to the sanctity of the targets in a given area and not in accordance with strategic considerations and tactics on the ground.
11 Sivan, "*Faḍā'il al-Quds*", p. 265.

course not. It is therefore necessary to distinguish between the history of a city's sanctity and the time when collections of traditions on its virtues first appeared. Far from signaling the flourishing of the idea of a city's sanctity, the act of collecting the relevant traditions implies a need to preserve them from possible neglect, due to changing circumstances.[12] That was the purpose of the books in which ancient traditions were collected. These traditions can be found in all ancient branches of Islamic literature, especially in works of qur'ānic exegesis and in biographies of the Prophet. These traditions never "remained as a dead letter" in *ḥadīth* (tradition) collections, nor were they cast "into oblivion", to use Reiter's expressions.[13] In our times these collections are constantly reprinted, and are also uploaded to the internet. It is from these sources that contemporary Muslims who write about the status of Jerusalem receive their inspiration. Reiter's argument that these Muslims invent "new myths" in their writings is thus not always justified. His sweeping claim that contemporary Muslims have "Islamized" and "Arabized" Jerusalem's pre-Islamic history is especially unwarranted.[14] In fact, already classical Muslim sources retell the history of the construction of Jerusalem from an Islamic perspective, beginning with Adam and Melchizedek king of Salem [Jerusalem], followed by Abraham and Jacob, down to David and Solomon.[15] All of these figures are without exception considered Muslims in every respect, not only by contemporary Muslim writers.

The Jerusalem-Mecca sanctity space and the plan of redemption

The antiquity of Jerusalem's holiness in Islam is evident from its qur'ānic roots. The point of reference for tracing these roots in the following chapters will be the observation that already in the Qur'ān both Jerusalem and Mecca belong to a common sanctity space in which God in every generation implements a plan of redemption for his believers.[16] The city of Medina, too, which is mentioned in the Qur'ān under its old name Yathrib (Q 33:13), is located in the same sanctity space. However, unlike Mecca, whose sanctity goes back to pre-Islamic times, Medina came to be considered a holy city only later, by virtue of Muḥammad's emigration to the city and the fact that he was buried there.

12 Cf. Hasson, "Jerusalem in the Muslim Perspective", p. 298.
13 Reiter, *From Jerusalem to Mecca*, pp. 16, 21.
14 *Ibid.*, pp. 51–58.
15 See below, Chapter 13.
16 See Rubin, "Between Arabia and the Holy Land".

Muslims over the centuries continued to be aware of this sanctity space and its two regions, but the relationship between the two regions within the space changed continuously. As we proceed below we shall show the internal movement of sanctity patterns from Jerusalem to Mecca. First intimations of this movement can already be perceived in the Qur'ān, and perhaps even earlier. At least this is what is implied by reports in some sources that the Ka'ba, which was rebuilt during Muḥammad's youth after having been damaged in a flood, was designed by a Christian architect and modeled after churches in Syria and Palestine (*al-Shām*).[17] The renovation included the addition of decorations inside the building, among them pictures of Abraham as well as of Jesus in his mother's lap.[18] As for the Qur'ān, in subsequent chapters we show how the transition of sanctity patterns from Jerusalem to Mecca is marked by the differences between verses about Jerusalem and Palestine and later verses, in which Mecca and the Ka'ba are highlighted, and their sanctity is shaped according to the models of Jerusalem and Palestine. The traditions that will be examined in subsequent chapters will demonstrate how the transition of sanctity patterns from Jerusalem to Arabia continued after the Qur'ān, and even accelerated.

The dynamics of the Jerusalem-Mecca sanctity space in the Qur'ān and in the *ḥadīth* will be examined under five parallel headings that reflect major aspects of the sanctity of Jerusalem, in the Qur'ān and in subsequent sources: (1) Navel of the Earth; (2) Land of Redemption; (3) Land of Resurrection; (4) Land of the Prophets; (5) Land of the Temple. These are five virtues ascribed to Jerusalem and Palestine whose components were at least partly taken up by Mecca and the Ka'ba – some already in the Qur'ān and others only in extra-qur'ānic tradition. Each of these topics reflects in one way or another the idea of the salvation which the believers will be granted in the sanctity space, as part of God's long-term plan. This signals the attention paid in the Qur'ān to the generations that preceded Muḥammad, whose history already foretells God's plan of salvation which is about to be implemented among Muḥammad's contemporaries.

Methodology

The study of the models of sanctity and their transition from one region to another will be based on a comparative examination of a variety of qur'ānic verses and traditions. This will be done in continuation with the method of M.J. Kister

17 Rubin, "The Ka'ba", p. 102.
18 Azraqī, *Akhbār Makka*, p. 113.

who paved the way for his students, including those whose studies on Jerusalem were mentioned above. However, Kister, too, like Goitein before him, argued that Jerusalem's status was lower than Mecca's, and refrained from discussing the qur'ānic background to the competition between the two cities. As he notes,

> Jerusalem could only be considered as a place of devotional prayer, a holy place endowed with special merits for pilgrims to Mecca but it could not be awarded the rank of Mecca and it never got it.[19]

At the same time, it was Kister who introduced the method of detailed textual analysis based on the greatest possible variety of texts into Islamic scholarship. He was also the first to have noticed a paragraph with a collection of traditions about the virtues of Jerusalem recorded in one of the earliest extant commentaries on the Qur'ān (*tafsīr*), by Muqātil b. Sulaymān (d. 150/767).[20] These traditions enumerate the virtues of Bayt al-Maqdis (Jerusalem) that distinguish it from all other places.[21] The very fact that the paragraph appears in Muqātil's *tafsīr* seems to testify to the early provenance of the venerated status of Jerusalem in the eyes of the Muslims.

The Qur'ān

Since the Qur'ān is the point of departure for the discussion below (unlike previous studies on the status of Jerusalem in Islam), a few words on it are in order. The Qur'ān according to Muslim tradition is the word of God as revealed to the Prophet Muḥammad through the angel Gabriel. The revelation began in Mecca, where Muḥammad was active for about ten years, until he emigrated to the city of Medina in 622. There he continued to receive revelations until his death in 632. According to tradition, Muḥammad's activity as prophet lasted ten years in Mecca and ten years in Medina.[22]

---

19 Kister, "Three Mosques", p. 182.

20 Kister, "A Comment on the Antiquity", p. 185.

21 In the printed edition of Muqātil's *Tafsīr*, the passage appears as an addendum in a footnote by the editor in vol. II, pp. 513–515 (Q 17:1). For the editor's reasons for expunging the passage from the main text of Muqātil, see Hasson, "Last Judgment". Quotations from this passage of Muqātil appear in various variants in Ibn al-Murajjā, *Faḍā'il*, pp. 258–261; Ibn al-Jawzī, *Ta'rīkh Bayt al-Maqdis*, pp. 70–74; Minhājī, *Itḥāf al-akhiṣṣā*, I, pp. 104–111; Ibn al-Faqīh, *Buldān*, pp. 145–146. For a Hebrew translation of this passage see Hasson, "Jerusalem in the Muslim Perspective", pp. 308–310.

22 Cf. Shnizer, "The Figure of Muḥammad", p. 36.

The Qurʾān was compiled mostly after the Prophet's death and received its definitive form during the reign of the third caliph, ʿUthmān b. ʿAffān (d. 35/656).[23] The divine revelations are arranged in chapters, *sūras*, of which there are 114. They are not arranged in the order in which they were revealed. In fact, the Qurʾān itself provides no details concerning the time when each *sūra* was revealed; our knowledge of the chronology of revelation comes from extra-qurʾānic sources, in which we find lists of the *sūras* arranged in order of their revelation, first those revealed in Mecca and then those revealed in Medina. In the following chapters I make use of a relatively early chronological list, reported on the authority of the Qurʾān exegete ʿAṭāʾ al-Khurāsānī, who was active towards the end of the Umayyad and at the beginning of the ʿAbbāsid period (d. 139/757). Interestingly enough, his list contains only 113 *sūras*; it is missing the opening *sūra* (*al-fātiḥa*), possibly because this prayer was not originally considered part of the canonical qurʾānic text.[24] Other lists beside al-Khurāsānī's also exist; whatever chronological list one uses needs to be approached with great caution, especially in view of the fact that modern scholars have proposed their own reconstructions of the "correct" order of revelation.[25] Still, the traditional lists can help us distinguish between Meccan and Medinan *sūras*, although the internal order within each period is quite doubtful. In any case, the distinction made in the traditional lists between the Meccan and the Medinan periods is consistent with formal and substantive differences between pre-*hijra* and later *sūras*.[26]

From the preceding discussion the reader will understand that I do not advocate the provocative thesis that was suggested in the second half of the last century, according to which the Qurʾān is not the earliest extant Muslim source, having been preceded by texts created during the first centuries AH. According to this thesis, Islam as we know it took shape outside of Arabia, and it was only later that traditions were created which retroactively placed its emergence in Mecca and Medina during the time of Muḥammad. This thesis was promoted by John Wansbrough (mainly in his *Quranic Studies*), on the one hand, and by Patricia Crone and Michael Cook (in their *Hagarism*), on the other. I mention it because it found its way also into studies on the beginnings of Islam in Palestine and on the evolution of its holiness in Islam.[27] It is for this reason that it is important for me to stress the difference between that thesis and the much less radical methodology adopted in

23 See Witztum, "The Qurʾān and Qurʾānic Research", pp. 135–142.
24 The list is found in Ibn al-Ḍurays (d. 293/906), *Faḍāʾil al-Qurʾān*, pp. 33–34.
25 See Robinson, *Discovering the Qurʾān*, pp. 60–96.
26 See also Witztum, "The Qurʾān and Qurʾānic Research", p. 158.
27 Especially Sharon, "The Cities of the Holy Land". And see criticism of Sharon's approach in Livne-Kafri, *Selected Essays*, pp. 107–109.

the present study. Nevertheless, the initial relationship between early Islam and Jewish messianism as proposed in the following chapters is already pointed out in the studies just mentioned.

The traditions and their transmitters

The traditions that will be examined below, in addition to the Qur'ān, are taken from *ḥadīth* collections, biographies of the Prophet (*Sīra*), commentaries on the Qur'ān (*Tafsīr*), history books (*Ta'rīkh*) and compilations devoted to the virtues (*Faḍā'il*) of Jerusalem and Mecca. These traditions contain utterances recorded on the authority of the Prophet as well as of his Companions and persons of the succeeding generations. Among contemporary *ḥadīth* researchers, there are those who examine the traditions not only according to their contents but mainly through careful scrutiny of their chains of transmission (*isnād*, pl. *asānīd*).[28] This applies also to the traditions about Jerusalem.[29] However, in the following chapters rather than expand on the chains of transmission, I shall let the traditions speak for themselves. Delving into the scrutiny of the chains of transmission will not only make it overly cumbersome, but could also divert attention from the message inherent in the tradition itself; furthermore, it is doubtful whether the chains, especially those that go back to the Prophet himself or to someone else of his generation, are reliable in all their links. In addition, Islamic scholars have for generations analyzed chains of transmission in order to distinguish between reliable and spurious transmitters, and determine which traditions are "correct" and which are not.[30] But in the present study the question of "correctness" does not arise, because every tradition that we read today in whatever source, whether "correct" or not, whether it is attributed to the Prophet or to someone from a later generation, and whether it is "authentic" or "fabricated", contributes to our knowledge of the varying and changing tendencies in play among the believers in every generation.

Sources on the internet

Nearly all the texts quoted in the present work can be found on the internet. Here are the main websites I used:

28 Cf. Landau-Tasseron, "Ḥadīth", pp. 205–215.
29 Elad, "An Early Arabic Source". See also *idem*, "The Status of Jerusalem", pp. 20–21.
30 Cf. Landau-Tasseron, "Ḥadīth", pp. 197–199.

Qur'ān exegesis: http://www.altafsir.com [Consulted online on 15.01.21].
Ḥadīth literature – *al-Mawsū'a al-shāmila*: http://islamport.com [Consulted online on 15.01.21].
Maktabat ahl al-bayt – https://ablibrary.net/#/ [Consulted online on 15.01.21].
Jewish sources: The Responsa Project: https://www.responsa.co.il/home.he.aspx [Consulted online on 15.01.21].

Although I used digital versions of these sources, in the footnotes I provide references (volume and page numbers) to printed editions of the Arabic sources. However, for commentaries on the Qur'ān, only the *sūra* and verse are given, for example: Ṭabarī, *Tafsīr* (Q 17:1).

Verses from the Qur'ān are quoted, with occasional changes, from Arthur J. Arberry, *The Koran Interpreted*. Biblical verses are quoted according to the *New Revised Standard Version* (https://www.biblestudytools.com/nrs/ [Consulted online on 15.01.21]).

Terminology

Before delving into our subject matter, I shall clarify some terms relating to the northern region of the Jerusalem-Mecca sanctity space (some of which already appeared above), which will accompany us throughout the book. In traditions about the life of Muḥammad the most common term for the region north of Arabia is *al-Shām* (الشام) or Greater Syria, an area that includes Palestine and Transjordan as well. Although the form *Sūriyā* (سوريا) does exist in Muslim texts that describe the Arab conquests outside of Arabia, it does not refer to the entire region encompassed by the term *al-Shām*, and will therefore not be used.

Another term used in the sources in addition to *al-Shām*, is *Filasṭīn* (فلسطين), the Arabic form of the name given to Palestine since the reign of the Emperor Hadrian (d. 138): *Syria Palaestina*.[31] The form *Filasṭīn* was known among Arabs already in the time of Muḥammad and it appears in traditions about his life. However, the most common term used for the region that encompasses both *Filasṭīn* and Transjordan (*al-Urdunn*, الأردن in Arabic) is *al-Shām*.

31 Tsafrir, "The Provinces in Palestine", pp. 352–353. Since the fifth century there were three provinces in Byzantine Palestine: Palaestina Prima ("First Palestine"), in the center of the land, Palaestina Secunda ("Second Palestine"), in the north, and Palaestina Tertia ("Third Palestine"), which was comprised of southern Transjordan, the Negev and part of the Sinai Peninsula. See Lewis, "Palestine", pp. 1–6; Gil, History of Palestine, pp. 110–111.

In the Qur'ān itself Palestine is referred to a number of times, although not by the form Filasṭīn. In one of these verses (Q 5:21), the land which Moses commanded the Children of Israel to enter is *al-arḍ al-muqaddasa* ("the Holy Land", or "the earth of holiness" [אדמת הקודש], as Goitein proposed).[32] The same ground is also called "the land that We have blessed" (*bāraknā fīhā*), that is, a land blessed by Allāh (Q 7:137); it is also the blessed land *(al-arḍ allatī bāraknā fīhā)* to which Abraham came after leaving his native land (Q 21:71). Solomon lived in it (Q 21:81) and it is also the land in which al-Masjid al-Aqṣā ("The Farthest Mosque") is located, in a region depicted as *alladhī bāraknā ḥawlahu*, "the precincts of which We had blessed" (Q 17:1). The Qur'ān also calls the same land *adnā l-arḍ* ("the nearest part of the land") (Q 30:3).

As for the name Jerusalem (Ūrshalīm), it is not widely current in the early Arabic sources, but we shall use it nevertheless for the sake of clarity. The sources themselves indicate that in the Prophet's time Jerusalem was known as Īliyā' (إيلياء). This form reflects the name *Aelia Capitolina*, by which the Romans called Jerusalem, also since Hadrian's reign. However, in texts on the life of Muḥammad the preferred name is Bayt al-Maqdis.[33] While some scholars have argued that this name only came into use after Muḥammad's death,[34] one should not ignore its prevalence in the earliest sources for the Prophet's biography. Especially significant is the fact that in traditions which state that at a certain stage Muḥammad prayed in the direction of Jerusalem, the term used is Bayt al-Maqdis[35] or *al-Shām*.[36] Furthermore, the form Bayt al-Maqdis stands not only for Jerusalem as a whole, but also occasionally refers to the Temple Mount or the Temple itself–Hebrew *Bet ha-Miqdash*–which is the origin of the form.[37] As we shall see below,[38] the form Bayt al-Maqdis is equivalent to the Arabic word *masjid* ("mosque"), which in the Qur'ān is used to describe the Temple (Q 17:7) as well as the Prophet's destination on his nocturnal journey, namely, al-Masjid al-Aqṣā (Q 17:1).

---

32 Goitein, "Sanctity", p. 121.

33 See, e.g. Yāqūt, *Mu'jam al-buldān*, V, p. 167 (s.v. *al-Maqdis*), a tradition stating that Īliyā' is the name of a woman who built the city, and therefore the place should not be thus named. The "woman" probably stands for Helena (248–329 CE), mother of Emperor Constantine I.

34 Gil, *History of Palestine*, p. 114: "Sometime after the conquest, also the name Bayt al-Maqdis began to come into use . . . ". See also Sharon, "The Cities of the Holy Land", p. 105. Cf. Lassner, *Medieval Jerusalem*, pp. 7, 56.

35 E.g. Ibn Sa'd, *Ṭabaqāt*, I, pp. 241–244.

36 E.g. Yūnus b. Bukayr, *al-Siyar wa-l-maghāzī*, p. 200.

37 See Livne-Kafri, "The Navel of the Earth", p. 63, note 93.

38 See below, Chapter 1.

Another term that will appear quite frequently in the following chapters is the Dome of the Rock (Qubbat al-Ṣakhra). This building was constructed on the Temple Mount during the reign of the Umayyad caliph ʿAbd al-Malik b. Marwān (d. 86/705) and stands there to this day, with its familiar golden dome. It is, of course, not mentioned in the Qurʾān, where we find only al-Masjid al-Aqṣā which denotes the Temple Mount.

Part One: **Navel of the Earth**

1 Muḥammad's journey to the "Farthest Mosque"

The destination of Muḥammad's nocturnal journey to the "Farthest Mosque" (al-Masjid al-Aqṣā) is the Temple Mount, the navel of the earth, where divine visions are revealed to him. The journey takes place at the height of messianic expectations that have swept throughout the entire region, especially among the Jews, due to the renewal of Jewish liturgy in Jerusalem following the Persian victory over Byzantium in 614. The vision of Muḥammad's journey to that place indicates identification with the messianic aspirations of redemption among the Jews; they are expected to join his cause and consummate their longed-for deliverance under his banner. After Muḥammad's death and the arrival of the first Muslims in Palestine, the latter revived the memory of their prophet's nocturnal journey and gave Īliyā', i.e. Jerusalem, the name al-Masjid al-Aqṣā. In other words, the Muslims identified this city as the destination of the Prophet's journey and the place where God's wondrous visions had been revealed to him.

One of the virtues of Jerusalem is its proximity to the upper worlds, which accords with its location around the navel of the earth, that is, around the point which connects all parts of the cosmos and from which the entire world was created.[1] The Qur'ān presents the Prophet Muḥammad as having been taken to this point and shown the wonders of heaven; this took place in his vision of a nocturnal journey (*isrā'*) to the Farthest Mosque.

The Farthest Mosque and the navel of the earth

Muḥammad's journey to the Farthest Mosque is described in the opening verse of Q 17:

> Glory be to him, who carried his servant by night from the Holy Mosque to the Farthest Mosque the precincts of which We had blessed, that We might show him some of our signs. He is the all-hearing, the all-seeing.

This verse which is from the Meccan period delineates the course of the nocturnal journey that runs through both regions of the Jerusalem-Mecca sanctity space. The point of departure is in Arabia, at a location called the Holy Mosque (al-Masjid al-Ḥarām). This is the usual name of the precinct in Mecca that contains

1 A detailed study of the idea of the navel of the earth in relationship to Jerusalem and Mecca is found in Livne-Kafri, "The Navel of the Earth". See also Speyer, *Die biblischen Erzählungen*, pp. 63–64.

https://doi.org/10.1515/9783111222318-002

the Kaʿba and adjoining sacred sites. Since the verse dates from the Meccan period, clearly the Prophet is still in that city, and from it he is taken to the Farthest Mosque.

The Farthest Mosque (al-Masjid al-Aqṣā) denotes the Temple Mount in Jerusalem.[2] This mosque (*al-masjid*) appears again a few verses later (Q 17:7–8):

> (7) . . . Then, when the promise of the latter came to pass, [We sent against you our servants] to discountenance you, and to enter the mosque (*al-masjid*), as they entered it the first time, and to destroy utterly that which they ascended to. (8) Perchance your Lord will have mercy upon you; but if you return, We shall return; and We have made Hell a prison for the unbelievers.

Clearly here the word *al-masjid* refers to the Temple. The Qur'ān hints at the fact that the Temple was destroyed twice, as God had promised, or warned, the Children of Israel. The use of the word "mosque" to denote the Temple is in conformity with the qur'ānic view, that the Temple was erected in order to worship God according to the true Islamic faith, which the Israelite prophets were sent to disseminate through the ages. The proximity of the verse mentioning the twice-destroyed *masjid* to the verse about the farthest *masjid* seems to indicate that both mosques are one and the same Temple.[3] Even though the building itself no longer existed in Muḥammad's time, its sanctity remained on the site on which it once had stood. Therefore, it continued to be considered a mosque, a word which applies not only to a specific building, but can represent any piece of land where God is worshipped. The same can be said of the Hebrew term *Har ha-Bayit* ("Temple Mount"), a phrase whose use has become independent of the existence of the

2 This stands in contrast to the view of scholars who maintain that Jerusalem is not mentioned in the Qur'ān under any name or appellation. On the arguments of the scholars in this respect see, e.g. Hasson, "Jerusalem in the Muslim Perspective", pp. 285–290; Busse, "Jerusalem and Mecca", p. 241. See also Lassner, *Medieval Jerusalem*, *passim*, and especially pp. 43–54 (arguing against Rubin's findings in the latter's "Muḥammad's Night Journey"). Lassner, however, does not seem to suggest any plausible answer of his own to the question, what is the Qur'ānic al-Masjid al-Aqṣā.

3 Some scholars who deny the relationship between the Qur'ānic al-Masjid al-Aqṣā and Jerusalem argue that the verses about the destruction of the Temple belong to a [Medinan] revelation different from that about the night journey [Meccan] (e.g. Busse, "Jerusalem and Mecca", p. 241; Lassner, *Medieval Jerusalem*, pp. 49, 53–54). Even so, this does not prove that the word *masjid* bears a different meaning in each revelation. The entire Qur'ān consists of separate revelations that have been put together when the text was committed to writing, and in many of them the same recurrent themes are treated from changing points of view. See also Rubin, "Between Arabia and the Holy Land", pp. 346–347.

Temple itself, destroyed ages ago. The Temple's destruction did not detract from the sanctity of the site.[4] Admittedly, one may wonder why the Qur'ān does not call the Temple by the overt name Bayt al-Maqdis which was in common use in Arabia in Muḥammad's time.[5] It would appear that the Arabic word *masjid* was preferred so as to preserve the symmetry between the two "mosques" at both ends of the night-journey's course.[6]

As for the reason why the Temple is given the epithet "Farthest", this can be explained through a pre-Islamic poetic verse ascribed to Abū Ṭālib, the Prophet's uncle. This is one of several verses that mention stations on the path followed by pilgrims during the rites of the *ḥajj* in Mecca and its surroundings. They are recorded in the *Sīra* (the Prophet's biography) by Ibn Isḥāq (d. 150/768), in Ibn Hishām's (d. 218/833) recension:[7]

وَبِالْمَشْعَرِ الْأَقْصَى إِذَا عَمَدُوا لَهُ

And by the farthest sacred site as they proceed towards it

Al-Suhaylī (d. 581/1185) in his commentary on Ibn Hishām explains that the "farthest sacred site" (*al-mash'ar al-aqṣā*) visited by the pilgrims to Mecca is 'Arafa.[8] His identification of the site is consistent with the fact that the latter is indeed the last station at the very eastern end of the course of *ḥajj* rites that begins at the Ka'ba; it is farther from the Ka'ba than the other stations of the *ḥajj* (Minā and Muzdalifa).[9] Likewise the Temple Mount may have been described as "Farthest" because it is the farthest sacred site from Mecca within the entire space that encompasses Arabia and al-Shām. Now some scholars who denied the connection between al-Masjid al-Aqṣā and Jerusalem asked how it was possible that a site located in what elsewhere in the Qur'ān (Q 30:3) is called "the nearest part of the land" (*adnā l-arḍ*), was called "Farthest".[10] But Berlin is also far from Paris, although they are located in neighboring countries.[11]

---

4 On the history of the phrase "Temple Mount", see Eliav, *God's Mountain*, pp. xxiii-xxv, 204–220.

5 See above, "Introduction".

6 See also Robinson, *Discovering the Qur'ān*, p. 192.

7 Ibn Hishām, *Sīra*, I, p. 293.

8 Suhaylī, *al-Rawḍ al-unuf*, II, p. 25.

9 On the stations of the *ḥajj* see Friedmann, "Pillars of Islam", pp. 270–271.

10 E.g. Gil, *History of Palestine*, p. 97.

11 Some scholars claimed also that the "Farthest Mosque" stands for a place within Arabia. E.g. Gil, "Political History", p. 3. But there is no real textual evidence to support this view, neither in the Qur'ān, nor in the extra-Qur'ānic sources.

Exegetes of the Qur'ān explain quite clearly why the Temple Mount is called "Farthest". Thus, for example, al-Qurṭubī (d. 671/1273) states:

> "To the Farthest Mosque": It is called "Farthest" because of the distance between it and the Holy Mosque; it was the Farthest (*ab'ad*) mosque on earth from the people of Mecca who would honor it by a [ritual] visit (*ziyāra*).[12]

Al-Qurṭubī's intimation that the Farthest Mosque was a site where a *ziyāra*, i.e. sort of little pilgrimage, used to be performed, evokes the possibility that already in the time of the Prophet journeys to the north were undertaken not only for trade, but also for religious rituals at the sacred sites of al-Shām. This confirms the status of this region as part of a shared sanctity space together with Mecca and the Kaʿba. As for the term *ziyāra* (literally: "visit"), contrary to the views of some scholars,[13] it does not imply that the status of Jerusalem was inferior to that of Mecca. Pilgrimage to Mecca is also called *ziyāra* numerous times in Muslim sources, which is equivalent to *ʿumra*, that is, a "minor" pilgrimage performed only in the immediate vicinity of the Kaʿba. Indeed, when Muḥammad planned on performing the *ʿumra* before the Ḥudaybiyya affair (6/628), during which he signed an armistice (*hudna*) agreement with the Quraysh, he is said to have intended to perform a *ziyāra* to the House (*bayt*) that is, to the Kaʿba.[14] Therefore, the difference between *ziyāra* and *ḥajj* does not signify a lesser degree of sanctity, only a limited scope of ritual framework.

A different exegetical explanation discerns in the term "Farthest" a celestial dimension and asserts that the phrase denotes the mosque "that is the farthest from the earth [from Mecca] and the closest to heaven, that is, the mosque of Bayt al-Maqdis".[15] In this manner a certain aspect of the holiness of the Farthest Mosque as the navel of the earth is revealed, that is, a location that connects the upper and the lower worlds. A more explicit expression of this status can be found in a tradition to the effect that the Jewish convert to Islam ʿAbdallāh b. Salām asked the Prophet what the meaning of the "the farthest" (*al-aqṣā*) was in the qur'ānic phrase *al-masjid al-aqṣā*. Muḥammad explained that it was named

12 Qurṭubī, *Aḥkām al-Qur'ān* (Q 17:1).
13 Elad, "The Temple Mount" p. 86; Reiter, *From Jerusalem to Mecca*, p. 14 (following Sivan). Cf. Sivan, "Faḍā'il al-Quds", pp. 267–268.
14 Ibn Hishām, *Sīra*, III, p. 322.
15 Fīrūzābādī, *Tanwīr al-miqbās* (Q 17:1). The celestial aspect is evinced mainly in the Shīʿī *Tafsīr* by al-ʿAyyāshī (third century AH). It contains the claim that al-Masjid al-Aqṣā is in heaven, which is a polemical argument designed to diminish the status of the earthly Jerusalem, as compared to that of al-Kūfa, in Iraq. See ʿAyyāshī, *Tafsīr* (Q 17:1). Modern scholars as well who denied the relationship between the night journey and Jerusalem argued that al-Masjid al-Aqṣā is the place where the angels worship God in heaven. See Goitein, "Arabic Names", p. 66, note 14.

so because it was "the center of the earth" (*wasaṭ al-dunyā*). Ibn Salām confirmed the Prophet's reply.[16] It would appear that the word "farthest" here is perceived as denoting an entity unique in its virtues, one whose location at the center of the world gives it the utmost of every merit upon earth. The status of al-Masjid al-Aqṣā as the center of the world is already hinted at in the way the Qur'ān describes the nocturnal journey's destination. It is stated here that God spread his blessing "around" al-Masjid al-Aqṣā (*bāraknā ḥawlahu*); the mosque thus lies in the center of the blessed region.

The purpose of the nocturnal journey to the Farthest Mosque is stated at the end of the verse: "that We might show him some of our signs". This conveys great intimacy with God who shows his prophet a sublime vision. No place is more fitting for such a revelation than the Temple Mount in Jerusalem. God's "signs" as seen by the Prophet are mentioned also in Q 53:13–18:[17]

> (13) Indeed, he saw him another time (14) by the lote-tree of the boundary (15) near which is the garden of the refuge, (16) when there covered the lote-tree that which covered; (17) his eye swerved not; nor swept astray. (18) Indeed, he saw some of the greatest signs of his Lord.

The signs here are divine visions of the wonders of Paradise; it is therefore conceivable that the visions he sees on his journey to al-Masjid al-Aqṣā are also of a divine nature.[18]

The divine visions revealed to Muḥammad are reminiscent of the prophet Ezekiel's journey, in which a wind carries him between heaven and earth from Babylonia to Jerusalem (Ezekiel 8:1–4):[19]

> (1) In the sixth year, in the sixth month, on the fifth day of the month, as I sat in my house, with the elders of Judah sitting before me, the hand of the Lord God fell upon me there. (2) I looked, and there was a figure that looked like a human being; below what appeared to be its loins it was fire, and above the loins it was like the appearance of brightness, like gleaming amber. (3) It stretched out the form of a hand, and took me by a lock of my head; and the spirit lifted me up between earth and heaven, and brought

16 Ibn al-Murajjā, *Faḍā'il*, p. 241 (no. 360). See also Minhājī, *Itḥāf al-akhiṣṣā*, I, p. 93; Livne-Kafri, "The Navel of the Earth", p. 49.

17 On Q 53, see e.g. Crone, "Problems in Sura 53", pp. 15–23; van Ess, "Vision and Ascension", pp. 47–62.

18 But Q 53 in itself does not contain any explicit mention of Muḥammad's ascension. The Qur'ān only attributes ascension to Idrīs (Q 19:56–57), Jesus (Q 3:55; 4:158), and to the angel who ascend to God (Q 70:4).

19 This was already noticed by several scholars. See Horovitz, "Muhammeds Himmelfahrt", p. 162; Nöldeke – Schwally, *Geschichte des Qorans*, I, p. 134, note 7; Wansbrough, *Quranic Studies*, p. 68; Rubin, "Between Arabia and the Holy Land", p. 347.

me in visions of God to Jerusalem, to the entrance of the gateway of the inner court that faces north, to the seat of the image of jealousy, which provokes to jealousy. (4) And the glory of the God of Israel was there, like the vision that I had seen in the valley.

Muḥammad's journey, like Ezekiel's journey, is a revelation designed to reveal for him the "visions of God" in the precinct of the Temple Mount, which is the navel of the earth. In this manner, the Prophet will be prepared to become the leader whose mission is to lead his followers in the path of redemption ordained for them.

The nocturnal journey and Jewish messianism

It appears that the qur'ānic vision of the Prophet's nocturnal journey to al-Masjid al-Aqṣā is contemporaneous with events that occurred in Jerusalem at the time when Muḥammad was active as a prophet in Mecca. In the year 614, about eight years before Muḥammad emigrated from Mecca to Medina, the Persians wrested control of Jerusalem from the Byzantines (the Rūm). The Jews aided the Persians during the latter's invasion of Palestine. Contemporary Christian sources relate that the Jews helped the Persians persecute the Christians in the city and destroy their holy sites.[20] Even if these reports are exaggerated,[21] they do point to a degree of Persian-Jewish cooperation in Jerusalem, as in other places at the time.[22]

The clash between the two mighty powers, Persia and Byzantium, began long before the emergence of Islam and gave rise to messianic expectations throughout the region. These expectations are reflected already in the words of the Amoraim, the Jewish Sages. For example: "R. Joshua b. Levi in the name of Rabbi said: Rome is designed to fall into the hands of Persia", and the contrary, in the same paragraph: "Rab said: Persia will fall into the hands of Rome" (Talmud Bavli, Yoma 10a).

These quotes represent two opposing groups among the Jewish Sages in the first half of the third century CE, one which yearns for the fall of Persia and the other for the fall of Rome.[23] A clear example of the interest which the Jews of

---

20 Stemberger, "Jerusalem in the Early Seventh Century", pp. 261–266. On the Christian reports about the Persian and Jewish aggression against the Christians in Jerusalem, see Bowersock, *Empires*, pp. 37–41.

21 Irshai, "Chronography and Apocalypse", p. xxxviii; Bowersock, *Empires*, pp. 41–48; Horowitz, "The Vengeance of the Jews", pp. 6–10.

22 Gil, *History of Palestine*, pp. 5–6. See further, Rubin Z., "History of Jerusalem", pp. 41–44; Safrai, "Jerusalem and the Jews", pp. 251–258; Bowersock, *Empires*, pp. 35–36.

23 See Irshai, "Chronography and Apocalypse", p. xi, note 20: ". . . It would be hard to assume that the sayings of these Sages were not at all influenced by the surrounding political reality – the rise of the Sasanians in Persia, or perhaps of the Parthians their predecessors, together with

Palestine showed in international affairs is the following statement by another Palestinian Amora, of the third generation (Midrash Rabbah, I, p. 346 [Genesis Rabbah 42: 6]):

> R. Eleazar b. Abina said: When you see the Powers fighting each other, look for the coming [lit. 'feet'] of the King Messiah . . .[24]

However, more important for our discussion are the events associated with the confrontation between Persia and Byzantium in Jerusalem at the time when Muḥammad was in Mecca, events which revived Jewish messianic hopes as reflected in contemporary Jewish writings.[25] One of these compositions is The Book of Zerubbabel,[26] which tells of the revival of the Jewish rites of sacrifice under the leadership of a man with the symbolic name Nehemiah Ben Ḥushiel.[27] From this text and others, some scholars surmised that Jews attempted to renew their liturgy on the Temple Mount under the auspices of the Persian occupation in 614.[28] If this was indeed the case, it meant the renewal of the Jewish rites that had been performed on the Temple Mount before the Byzantine period.[29] However, the Persian attitude towards the Jews worsened quite quickly, and in the year 617 they were expelled from Jerusalem. Subsequently, in 628, the Byzantines recaptured Jerusalem

---

the weakening of Rome in the East, which already in the third century led to the outbreak of skirmishes between these powers".

24 Irshai, "Chronography and Apocalypse", p. xxix, note 50: "It is quite possible that the inspiration for the saying of R. Eleazar b. Abina was the somewhat chaotic reality in the Eastern Empire in the third century".

25 Baras, "The Persian Conquest", p. 324. See also Stemberger, "Jerusalem in the Early Seventh Century", pp. 260, 266–270; Kaegi, *Heraclius*, p. 79.

26 See below, Chapter 3.

27 Reeves, "Sefer Zerubbabel", pp. 459–460: "The Lord's Messiah—Nehemiah ben Ḥushiel— will come five years after Hephsibah. He will collect all Israel together as one entity and they will remain for <four>" years in Jerusalem, (where) the children of Israel will offer sacrifice, and it will be pleasing to the Lord". See also Even-Shmuel, *Midrashei Geula*, pp. 77–78. And see Grossmann, "Jerusalem in the Jewish Apocalypse", pp. 238–240.

28 Reeves, "Sefer Zerubbabel", p. 460, note *b*. See further Avi-Yonah, *Rome and Byzantium*, p. 231; Sivan H., "From Byzantine to Persian Jerusalem", especially pp. 291–292; Baras, "The Persian Conquest", p. 334; Peters, *Jerusalem and Mecca*, pp. 87–88; Lassner, *Medieval Jerusalem*, pp. 25–26.

29 Eliav, *God's Mountain*, p. 228: ". . . during the first centuries after the destruction a steady stream of Jews regularly frequent the demolished compound of the Temple, interrupted only rarely by occasional local bans. These visitors were not mere tourists in the modern sense of the word, and such excursions took on a religious dimension that was accompanied by customs, prayers, and liturgical rituals".

from the Persians, depriving the Jews of the freedom to enter the city and of the ability to restore the ritual sanctity of the Temple Mount, then in ruins.[30]

But although the period when Jews had access to Jerusalem and the Temple Mount was short, the messianic atmosphere did not dissipate.[31] Moreover, the vision of Muḥammad's journey to al-Masjid al-Aqṣā predates the return of Byzantine rule to Jerusalem, and would therefore seem to be inspired by the same messianic fervor which peaked with the Persian occupation of Jerusalem and the freedom of worship on the Temple Mount granted to the Jews. Hence it can be assumed that through the vision of the nocturnal journey to the same site, the Prophet himself joined the swelling messianic hope which the Jews of Arabia shared. Indeed, a promise of redemption given to the Children of Israel is included quite explicitly in verse 8 in the Temple passage quoted above:

> Perchance your Lord will have mercy upon you; but if you return, We shall return; and We have made Hell a prison for the unbelievers.

This verse gives the Children of Israel some hope, despite the two-time destruction of the Temple described in the preceding verses. But the hope for renewing the Jewish rites in the Promised Land depends on their adherence to the straight path, that is, on their belief in Muḥammad. Furthermore, the vision of redemption in the Promised Land appears once again later in the same *sūra*, in a verse that promises the Children of Israel that they would return to their homeland in the Latter Days (Q 17:104).[32]

At this point we should note that the fact that the Temple Mount – the qur'ānic al-Masjid al-Aqṣā– was chosen as the destination of the Prophet's nocturnal journey reflects not only identification with Jewish hopes for redemption but also contradicts the Christian position which denied the Temple Mount's sanctity.[33] However, as we shall see in the subsequent chapters, this attitude soon changed, and the qur'ānic identification with Jewish messianic aspirations vanished.

The observation that Muḥammad's nocturnal journey to al-Masjid al-Aqṣā designates the path of the yearned-for redemption can be corroborated through the shared vocabulary of Muḥammad's journey and the journey of the Children of Israel upon their exodus from Egypt. Like Muḥammad's journey, that of the

---

30 Avi-Yonah, *Rome and Byzantium*, p. 233; Baras, "The Persian Conquest", pp. 334–336; Leder, "Attitude", pp. 64–65.

31 Baras, "The Persian Conquest", pp. 313–319.

32 See below, Chapter 3.

33 See Eliav, *God's Mountain*, p. 180: "Christian Jerusalem knew the Temple compound but avoided according it religious status".

Children of Israel under Moses' leadership takes place at night, as we read in the three verses in which God commands Moses to "go with my servants by night":

> Also We revealed unto Moses, 'Go with my servants *by night*; strike for them a dry path in the sea, fearing not overtaking, neither afraid' (Q 20:77).
>
> We revealed unto Moses, 'Go with my servants *by night*; surely you will be followed' (Q 26:52).
>
> Then go with my servants *by night*; surely you will be followed (Q 44:23).

The idea of an exodus by night is reminiscent of Exodus 12:31: "Then he [Pharaoh] summoned Moses and Aaron *in the night,* and said, 'Rise up, go away from my people, both you and the Israelites! Go, worship the Lord, as you said . . .'"

The Arabic verb used for denoting the exodus of the Children of Israel is *asrā* (= "make one travel by night"), the same verb used to describe the Prophet's nocturnal journey. In the qur'ānic setting, night was chosen for the Children of Israel's journey in order to allow them to escape Pharaoh, and the same is true of the Prophet in the first verse of Q 17; he is thus also a redeemer, a kind of new Moses, who on his nocturnal journey marks out the path of redemption towards the same land promised already to the ancient Israelites.[34]

Not only do Muḥammad's journey and the Children of Israel's exodus from Egypt share a common vocabulary, but, as already noted above, the Qur'ān describes the Prophet's destination, "the Farthest Mosque", as a place "the precincts of which We [i.e. God] had blessed" (*bāraknā ḥawlahu*). The divine blessing mentioned in this connection evokes an association with the land which the Qur'ān on several occasions calls the "land which We [i.e. God] had blessed" (*bāraknā fīhā*).[35] As we noted in the Introduction, this blessed land is the destination of Abraham (Q 21:71), the Children of Israel after their exodus from Egypt (Q 7:137), Solomon (Q 21:81) as well as the people of Sheba (Q 34:18). In all these cases, the blessed target land represents al-Shām; it is therefore more than likely that "the

---

34 On the link between Muḥammad's night journey and Moses, cf. Wansbrough, *Quranic Studies*, pp. 8, 68, 99. On the general messianic context of the relationship of Muḥammad to Moses, see Crone and Cook, *Hagarism*, pp. 16–20. The parallelism between the Egyptian exodus led by Moses and the nocturnal journey of Muḥammad invalidates the claims of scholars who have questioned the affinity between al-Masjid al-Aqṣā and Jerusalem, assuming that the nocturnal journey, the *isrā'*, was originally ascension to heaven. See Busse, "Jerusalem and Mecca", p. 242.

35 The relationship of al-Masjid al-Aqṣā to the blessed land was already noticed by several scholars. E.g. Schwarzbaum, *Folkloristic Aspects*, p. 146. See also Rubin, "Muḥammad's Night Journey", p. 152.

Farthest Mosque" whose surroundings God has blessed is located in the same blessed land or, more precisely, on the Temple Mount in Jerusalem.[36]

From the above we may conclude that Muḥammad's vision of his journey to the Farthest Mosque reflects identification with the messianic aspiration for redemption entertained by the Jews who would hopefully join his ranks and achieve their anticipated salvation under his leadership.

The nocturnal journey in extra-qur'ānic traditions

As for extra-qur'ānic traditions, these treat Muḥammad's nocturnal journey as a definite sign that he was part of the line of prophets who had preceded him, and who had operated mainly in the land to which his own journey took him. In one tradition, related on the authority of the Prophet's Companion Anas b. Mālik, Muḥammad tells what Gabriel instructed him to do as they were on their way on the flying steed al-Burāq:

> . . . [Gabriel] said: Descend and pray. This I did. [Gabriel then] said: Do you know where you prayed just now? You prayed in Ṭayba [Medina]. It is the destination of the *hijra* [*al-muhājar*]. [We continued on our way] and then Gabriel said: Descend and pray. I prayed, and then [Gabriel] said: Do you know where you prayed just now? You prayed on Mount Sinai [Ṭūr Sīnā']. This is the place where Allāh spoke with Moses, peace be upon him, face to face. [We continued on our way] and then [Gabriel] said: Descend and pray! I descended and prayed. [Gabriel then] said: Do you know where you prayed just now? You prayed in Bethlehem, Jesus' birthplace. Then I entered Bayt al-Maqdis, where the prophets had assembled in my honor. Gabriel placed me before them and I led them in prayer . . .[37]

In this narration, Muḥammad's first station after leaving Mecca is the city of Medina, in anticipation of the *hijra*, which will take place a number of years later. The journey then takes him beyond the borders of Arabia, to locations that witnessed key events in the lives of Moses and Jesus: Mount Sinai, where the Torah was handed down, and Bethlehem, where Jesus was born. The Prophet's prayers in these locations symbolize the sanctity which they all share equally. The journey's peak is Bayt al-Maqdis, where Muḥammad meets all the prophets and leads them in prayer.

---

36 During the Byzantine period, the southern Land of Israel was already called Palaestina Salutaris, namely the healthy, the useful, full of blessedness. This name was already used at the end of the fourth century but was still used in the fifth century, alongside the newer name of the same region, the Third Palestine (Palaestina Tertia). See Lewis "Palestine", p. 3; Dan, "Palaestina Salutaris", p. 134, note 4; Tsafrir, "The Provinces in Palestine", pp. 371–372.

37 Nasā'ī, *Sunan*, I, pp. 221–222 (no. 450).

The idea that Muḥammad's nocturnal journey was marked by his encounter with the prophets is also reflected in a tradition that states that one of the qur'ānic verses that was revealed to him during this journey was Q 43:45: "Ask those of our messengers We sent before you: Have We appointed, apart from al-Raḥmān, gods to be served?"[38] Of course, the journey presented Muḥammad with a good opportunity to ask questions of the prophets assembled in Bayt al-Maqdis, although some commentators maintain that in the end he did not ask, because he was fully aware that one should not worship any god but Allāh.[39]

Several traditions stress the miraculous element reflected not only in the journey itself and its distant destination, but also in the Prophet's lightning-quick return to Mecca in the same night. In one such tradition, reported in Ibn Isḥāq's book on the life of Muḥammad, Umm Hāni', the daughter of his uncle Abū Ṭālib, quotes the Prophet as saying that he entered Bayt al-Maqdis, prayed there and then returned to Mecca.[40] A more detailed version of the story of Umm Hāni' appears in Muqātil b. Sulaymān's (d. 150/767) *Tafsīr*.[41]

Muslims in al-Shām: al-Masjid al-Aqṣā and Īliyā'

Muḥammad's nocturnal journey to the Farthest Mosque is one of the qur'ānic themes that was uppermost in the minds of the first Muslims who advanced northward after the Prophet's death. When the armies of the Muslims first reached al-Shām, they felt that God was leading them on the same path as the Prophet's nocturnal journey. A clear indication of this is the fact that they used the qur'ānic phrase al-Masjid al-Aqṣā as their name for Jerusalem. This is evinced in poetic verses composed by a Muslim warrior by the name of Ziyād b. Ḥanẓala, a Companion of the Prophet who participated in the battles of the first Muslims in Palestine. In several verses he described the battles in which he had fought. One of these was the Battle of Ajnādayn,[42] a place in the vicinity of Beit Guvrin where the Byzantine forces suffered their first major defeat at the hands of the Muslims (13/634). In Muslim

38 See Maqdisī, *Muthīr al-gharām*, p. 261.
39 See Ṭabarī, *Tafsīr* (Q 43:45).
40 Ibn Hishām, *Sīra*, II, p. 43. Thus also in the version of Shaddād b. Aws: Ibn Kathīr, *Tafsīr* (Q 17:1).
41 Muqātil, *Tafsīr* (Q 17:1). On Muḥammad's return during the same night see also Qummī, *Tafsīr* (Q 17:1): Gabriel brings the Prophet to Bayt al-Maqdis mounted on al-Burāq, shows him the oratories of the prophets, and Muḥammad himself prays in them, and then Gabriel brings him back to Mecca that night.
42 Cf. Gil, *History of Palestine*, pp. 41–43.

sources the Roman commander is called Arṭabūn, a form reflecting the Roman title *Tribunus*. It is reported that after Arṭabūn had been defeated by the Muslim army, he fled to Īliyā' (Jerusalem), which was still in Byzantine hands.[43] This is told by the poet in the following line:[44]

وَنَحْنُ تَرَكْنا أَرْطَبونَ مُطَرِّدًا إلى المَسْجِدِ الأَقْصَى وفيه حُسورُ
We left Arṭabūn as he withdrew to al-Masjid al-Aqṣā in his exhaustion

Instead of Īliyā' which is used in the historical sources as Arṭabūn's refuge, the poet uses al-Masjid al-Aqṣā, a phrase he assuredly knew from the Qur'ān and which in his mind was associated with Jerusalem. Thus even before Īliyā' fell into Muslim hands it had been already identified by the believers as the destination of Muḥammad's nocturnal journey described in the Qur'ān and the place where God showed him his signs.

To summarize, the texts that describe the beginnings of the Muslim presence in Jerusalem testify to the preservation of the qur'ānic sanctity of al-Masjid al-Aqṣā as the place where God's sublime visions were revealed to Muḥammad. Indeed, these texts show how the Muslims in Jerusalem developed its image as the place where divine visions had been revealed, and added to the Prophet's nocturnal journey the scene of his miraculous ascension to heaven, as discussed in the next chapter.

43 Ṭabarī, *Ta'rīkh*, III, p. 606 (Brill: I, p. 2400).
44 Yāqūt, *Mu'jam al-buldān*, I, p. 104 (s.v. *Ajnādayn*). I thank my friend Prof. Michael Lecker for drawing my attention to these verses and to sources in which they appear.

2 Muḥammad's ascension to heaven

The first Muslims in al-Shām fostered the idea of Muḥammad's ascension to heaven from Bayt al-Maqdis, and concretized it by the construction of the Dome of the Rock. The Rock itself is described in Muslim tradition as the navel of the earth and as the point where heaven and earth are connected. Other traditions, however, maintain that the Prophet ascended to heaven directly from Mecca, independently of the nocturnal journey to al-Masjid al-Aqṣā. Still other traditions transfer the status of navel of the earth to the Kaʿba. However, this change of balance in favor of Mecca and the Kaʿba did not erase the nocturnal journey to al-Masjid al-Aqṣā from the believers' awareness. In the versions that took hold in their minds, the nocturnal journey to al-Masjid al-Aqṣā was the preliminary stage of Muḥammad's ascension to heaven, which began in Bayt al-Maqdis and nowhere else.

As we saw in the previous chapter, the Qurʾān asserts that the purpose of Muḥammad's journey to al-Masjid al-Aqṣā was to show him God's wondrous signs. But the first Muslims in al-Shām transformed the idea of seeing divine visions into an actual ascension of Muḥammad to heaven from Jerusalem, as a continuation of his nocturnal journey.

Muḥammad's ascension and the Dome of the Rock

The circumstances under which the idea of Muḥammad's ascension to heaven took shape are revealed in texts that deal with the construction of the Dome of the Rock (Qubbat al-Ṣakhra). This is described in al-Yaʿqūbī's (d. 283/897) *Taʾrīkh*:

> ʿAbd al-Malik prevented the people of al-Shām from performing the pilgrimage [to Mecca], because Ibn al-Zubayr forced the pilgrims to swear allegiance to him. When ʿAbd al-Malik saw this, he forbade them to leave for Mecca. The people were upset, and said: Will you prevent us from making the pilgrimage to Allāh's Holy House [= the Kaʿba] although it is a commandment given to us by Allāh? [ʿAbd al-Malik] said: Here is Ibn Shihāb al-Zuhrī, he relates a *ḥadīth* to you which says that the Messenger of Allāh said: "One should not saddle [the mounts] except for journeying to three mosques: The Holy Mosque [in Mecca], my mosque [in Medina] and the mosque of Bayt al-Maqdis". It will serve you instead of the Holy Mosque. And this rock [*al-ṣakhra*], of which it is told that Allāh's Messenger placed his foot on it when he ascended [*ṣaʿada*] to heaven, will replace the Kaʿba for you. He then built a dome [*qubba*] over the rock, hung silken covers over it, appointed doormen for it, and made the people perform circumambulations around it as they used to do around the Kaʿba.[1]

1 Yaʿqūbī, *Taʾrīkh*, II, p. 261.

https://doi.org/10.1515/9783111222318-003

In this tradition al-Yaʿqūbī ascribes to the builder of the Dome of the Rock, the Umayyad caliph ʿAbd al-Malik b. Marwān (d. 86/705), the announcement that the Rock on which he decided to build the dome was the spot from which Muḥammad had ascended to heaven. The reasons ʿAbd al-Malik gives for constructing the dome anchor this project in the rivalry that transpired with ʿAbdallāh b. al-Zubayr, who held sway in Mecca and challenged the Umayyad rulers. According to al-Yaʿqūbī, ʿAbd al-Malik's intention was to use the Dome of the Rock in order to attract pilgrims to Bayt al-Maqdis, as a substitute for the Kaʿba, which was controlled by Ibn al-Zubayr.[2] Whether this account of the facts is true or not,[3] what is important for our purpose is not only ʿAbd al-Malik's statement about the Prophet's ascent from the Rock, but also the tradition which he quotes on the authority of a respected Medinan scholar, Ibn Shihāb al-Zuhrī (d. 124/742).[4] This tradition enumerates three mosques which according to the Prophet were legitimate pilgrimage destinations, without defining the type of pilgrimage: One in Mecca, another in Medina and a third in Bayt al-Maqdis. This tradition is one reason why contemporary scholars have stated that Jerusalem is "the third place in religious importance for the Muslims".[5] However, at least with respect to the immediate context of the story of the Dome of the Rock's construction, this does not seem to be the case. ʿAbd al-Malik quotes the tradition concerning the three mosques on al- Zuhrī's authority in order to prove that Bayt al-Maqdis is just as legitimate a pilgrimage and worship destination as Mecca and Medina, thus justifying the construction of the Dome of the Rock. The order in which the three mosques appear in the tradition quoted by ʿAbd al-Malik says nothing about the relative importance of each mosque, but is purely chronological: Mecca was the first city in which the Prophet was active, Medina was the city where the Prophet lived after the *hijra*, and Bayt al-Maqdis was the place to which the Muslims arrived after the Prophet's death.

ʿAbd al-Malik's declaration that the Prophet's foot was put on the Rock as he ascended to heaven testifies to its sanctity. Muslim traditions attribute to it traits

---

2 See also Gil, *History of Palestine*, p. 102.

3 This issue was extensively debated among modern scholars. See e.g. Elad, "ʿAbd al-Malik and the Dome of the Rock"; *idem*, "The Temple Mount", pp. 73–76; *idem*, "The Status of Jerusalem", pp. 30–35. Cf. also Lassner, *Medieval Jerusalem*, pp. 126–150; Havel, "Jerusalem", pp. 143–149.

4 On the question whether this tradition is authentically al-Zuhrī's, see Elad, "The Status of Jerusalem", p. 50. On al-Zuhrī's relations with ʿAbd al-Malik a propos of the three-mosques-tradition, see Lecker, "Zuhrī", pp. 41–48.

5 Reiter, "The Third in Sanctity", p. 156.

similar to those of the Foundation Stone [Hebrew, *Even ha-Shtiyya*] known from Jewish tradition, although it is not certain whether the two stones are one and the same.[6] At any rate, according to the Jewish Sages, the Foundation Stone was the place where the Creation began or, "from it the world was founded" (העולם ממנה הושתת).[7] Therefore it is also considered to be the navel of the earth, that is, the point which connects heaven and earth, Paradise and Hell. Muslim sources contain indeed numerous traditions that retell the praises of Jerusalem as the navel of the earth.[8] The exegete Muqātil b. Sulaymān described the Rock as "the middle of the earth" (*awsaṭ al-arḍīn*).[9] As such, it is perceived as being of celestial origin or, in the words of one tradition, "one of the rocks of Paradise".[10]

Muqātil's statement reveals yet another significant aspect of the Rock's status as the navel of the earth. He says that "the Rock of Bayt al-Maqdis is linked [*mawṣūla*] to the rock which Allāh mentioned in the Qurʾān".[11] Hasson quite correctly notes that this is an allusion to Q 18:63,[12] which mentions "the rock" (*al-ṣakhra*) near which Moses and his page took rest on their journey to "the meeting of the two seas" (Q 18:60–61). The connection which Muqātil makes between the meeting of the two seas and the Rock of Bayt al-Maqdis accords with the fact that the "meeting of the two seas" can be understood as the cosmic origin of the world's water.[13] The Rock of Bayt al-Maqdis is also mentioned in some texts as the source of the world's sweet water.[14] One tradition, transmitted in the name of the Prophet's Companion Ubayy b. Kaʿb, states that "there is no sweet water [in the world] which does not spring from this Rock in Bayt al-Maqdis".[15] A more extensive ver-

6 Cf. Peters, *Jerusalem and Mecca*, p. 85.
7 E.g. Talmud Bavli, Yoma 54b. See also Eliav, *God's Mountain*, pp. 225–227.
8 Wensinck, *The Navel of the Earth*, pp. 24–25.
9 Muqātil, *Addendum*, p. 513. See also Ibn al-Murajjā, *Faḍāʾil*, p. 259; Minhājī, *Itḥāf al-akhiṣṣā*, I, p. 104. And see Livne-Kafri, "The Navel of the Earth", p. 49. It should be noted that other areas of the Muslim world also claimed to be the navel of the earth, such as Iraq. This was part of the rivalry between Syria and Iraq that originated in the Umayyad period. See Khaṭīb al-Baghdādī, *Taʾrīkh Baghdād*, I, pp. 22–23: The region of Iraq is the navel of the earth (*surrat al-dunyā*).
10 Ibn al-Jawzī, *Taʾrīkh Bayt al-Maqdis*, p. 70. See also Mujīr al-Dīn, *al-Uns al-jalīl*, I, p. 235; Minhājī, *Itḥāf al-akhiṣṣā*, I, p. 130; Livne-Kafri, "The Navel of the Earth", pp. 47, 56.
11 Muqātil, *Addendum*, p. 513.
12 Hasson, "Jerusalem in the Muslim Perspective", p. 308, note 1.
13 On this see Tesei, "Cosmological Notions", pp. 29–31.
14 Livne-Kafri, "The Navel of the Earth", pp. 54–56.
15 Ṭabarī, *Tafsīr* (Q 21:71). See also Ibn ʿAsākir, *Taʾrīkh Dimashq*, I, p. 204.

sion of this tradition adds that all the sweet water first descends from heaven to the Rock, whence it is then distributed throughout the earth.[16]

As the navel of the earth, Muslim tradition depicts the Rock as the point of departure for God's ascent to heaven during the Creation. This is one of several virtues ascribed to the Rock in a number of traditions, such as the following one, transmitted from Kaʿb al-Aḥbār (d. 32/652), a Jewish convert to Islam who was well-versed in the holy Scriptures and other Jewish traditions. The tradition begins as follows:

> In the name of Kaʿb the Muslim [Kaʿb al-Aḥbār[17]]. He said: Allāh in the Torah says to the Rock of Bayt al-Maqdis: You are the throne of mine that is the lowest [closest to the earth] [*ʿarshī l-adnā*], and from you I unfolded [*basaṭtu*] the earth and from you I ascended to heaven.[18]

The reference to the Torah indicates that Muslim tradition is aware of the Jewish origin of the Rock's sanctity as the navel of the earth in its various aspects. In this passage the Rock plays a two-way role: It is not only the point from where God ascends, but also the point of his landing, as it is his earthly throne, the place where he dwells when he descends from heaven. Several researchers have already noted the traditions about God's ascent from the Rock,[19] and a few also pointed out that the idea of God's ascent at the time of the Creation already appears in the Qur'ān.[20]

Muslim tradition asserts that Muḥammad ascended to heaven from precisely the same rock from which God had ascended (*ʿaraja*). This is what the angel Gabriel told him.[21] But there are also versions to the effect that Muḥammad ascended from

---

16 Suyūṭī, *al-Durr al-manthūr* (Q 21:71). For more traditions on the Rock's connection to the rivers of the world or to the four rivers of Paradise, see Ibn al-Jawzī, *Ta'rīkh Bayt al-Maqdis*, pp. 53–54; Livne-Kafri, "Jerusalem in Early Islam", pp. 389–390.

17 Aḥmad b. Ḥanbal, *ʿIlal*, II, p. 390 (no. 2741): Scholars such as Muḥammad b. Sīrīn (d. 110/729) refused to say Kaʿb al-Aḥbār (i.e. "of the Jewish Doctors"), but only Kaʿb al-Muslim. On Kaʿb al-Aḥbār see further, Reeves, "Jewish Apocalyptic".

18 Abū Nuʿaym, *Ḥilyat al-awliyā'*, VI, pp. 3–4. See also Levy-Rubin, "The Dome of the Rock", p. 456. Cf. Livne-Kafri, *Selected Essays*, pp. 49, 105.

19 E.g. Kister, "Three Mosques", p. 195; van Ess, "ʿAbd al-Malik and the Dome of the Rock", p. 98. See also Grabar, "The Meaning of the Dome of the Rock", pp. 117–118.

20 Q 41:11: "Then he lifted himself to heaven when it was smoke, and said to it and to the earth, 'Come willingly, or unwillingly!' They said, 'We come willingly'". God's ascension to the heavens occurs after he has already completed the creation of the earth. On the relationship of the traditions to this verse see Livne-Kafri, "The Navel of the Earth", p. 53, note 33.

21 E.g. Wāsiṭī, *Faḍā'il*, p. 72 (no. 117). See also Ibn Shaddād, *al-Aʿlāq al-khaṭīra*, p. 190.

another location on the Temple Mount.[22] At any rate, according to yet another version, the Rock is the place where the angel Gabriel tied al-Burāq,[23] in contrast to more widespread versions which have al-Burāq tied to a ring that had already been used by former prophets who had ridden that mount.[24] According to some other traditions, Gabriel placed a ladder (*miʿrāj*) on the Rock and elevated Muḥammad to heaven on it.[25]

Leaving aside the question of the precise location in Jerusalem whence the Prophet ascended to heaven, it would seem that the belief in his physical ascent emerged out of a desire to foster Muḥammad's image as savior and messiah, of equal standing, if not superior, to Jesus, who according to Christian belief ascended to heaven from Jerusalem, from the Mount of Olives. Christians even point to footprints of his that have remained there since his ascension.[26] Instead of the rock on the Mount of Olives from which Jesus ascended, the Muslims thus found an alternative rock with a sanctity of its own, namely the Rock on the Temple Mount.

But Islam's coping with Christianity is reflected not only in the idea of Muḥammad's ascension, but also in the construction of the Dome of the Rock itself. In addition to the struggle against Ibn al-Zubayr in Mecca, hinted at in al-Yaʿqūbī's account, and in addition to the rivalry with the Christians in Jerusalem, the Dome's construction also, and perhaps more than anything else, represented a desire to erect a holy site that would protect the status of Bayt al-Maqdis vis-à-vis the sanctity of Constantinople, the capital of the Byzantine Empire.[27]

---

22 See Elad, *Medieval Jerusalem*, pp. 49–50; *idem*, "The Temple Mount", pp. 78–79. Elad assumes that the tradition of Muḥammad's ascension from a point outside the Dome of the Rock is earlier than the one about his ascension from the Rock.

23 Ṭabarī, *Tafsīr* (Q 17:1). See also Ibn Kathīr, *Tafsīr* (Q 17:1).

24 E.g. ʿAbd al-Razzāq, *Tafsīr* (Q 17:1). See also Thaʿlabī, *al-Kashf wa-l-bayān* (Q 17:1); Ibn Kathīr, *Tafsīr* (Q 17:1); Qummī, *Tafsīr* (Q 17:1).

25 Thaʿlabī, *al-Kashf wa-l-bayān* (Q 17:1). See also Ṭabrisī, *Majmaʿ al-bayān* (Q 17:1).

26 Referring to what the Christian traveller Arculf records in his book *De Locis Sanctis*, Horovitz mentions that in the seventh century the footprints of Jesus were a sacred site on the Mount of Olives. See Horovitz, "Muhammeds Himmelfahrt", pp. 167–168. See also Peters, *Jerusalem and Mecca*, p. 41.

27 Levy-Rubin, "The Dome of the Rock", pp. 441–464. On the competition between Constantinople and Jerusalem in Christianity see also Livne-Kafri, *Selected Essays*, pp. 101–102.

Muḥammad's ascension from Mecca

Whatever the circumstances of the construction of the Dome of the Rock, this impressive building threatened to overshadow the ancient sanctity of Mecca and the Kaʿba and to undermine their position as pilgrimage destinations. As a result, the proponents of the status of the sacred Arabian city who were unhappy with Umayyad policies in al-Shām felt a need to disseminate traditions that would reinforce the virtues of the holy site in Arabia. As for Muḥammad's night journey, efforts were made to diminish its standing and, in particular, to isolate it from the scene of Muḥammad's ascension to heaven. In the following traditions the ascension is described as having taken place directly from Mecca.[28] One such tradition appears in al-Ṭabarī's (d. 310/932) *Taʾrīkh*:

> From Anas b. Mālik; he said: When the time came for the Prophet to be invested with prophethood, at which time he was in the habit of sleeping in the vicinity of the Kaʿba– Quraysh also used to sleep around it – two angels came to him, Gabriel and Michael . . . They found him asleep, turned him unto his back, opened his belly and then brought water from the Zamzam well and washed away any doubt, polytheism, *jāhiliyya* or going astray that was in his belly. Then they brought a golden basin that had been filled with faith and wisdom, and filled his belly and all his innards with faith and wisdom. Then [Gabriel] ascended with him to the first heaven . . .[29]

This tradition, ascribed to the Prophet's Companion Anas b. Mālik,[30] describes Muḥammad's initiation ceremony and how he was prepared for his role as prophet, a role that demanded that his body be completely purified and emptied of all doubt, idolatry and deviance from the right path. But the immediate aim of the rite was to prepare him for his ascension to heaven, where he would encounter the prophets in the different heavens, and also God himself. The location of the ceremony as well as the point of departure for his ascent was the Kaʿba's courtyard, whose sanctity derives from God's presence in his shrine, and therefore people would sleep there, in the hope of receiving prophetic dreams.

---

28 The significance of these versions was already noticed in Hirschberg, "The Place of Jerusalem", pp. 65–66. And see more about the various versions of the story of Muḥammad's ascension directly from Mecca in Rubin, "Muḥammad's Night Journey", pp. 162–163. Scholars advocating the view that the Islamic sanctity of Jerusalem was only formed during the Umayyad period maintain that the traditions of Muḥammad's ascension from Mecca are earlier than those about his ascension from Bayt al-Maqdis. See e.g. Busse, "Jerusalem and Mecca", p. 242. Cf. Elad, "The Temple Mount", p. 62.

29 Ṭabarī, *Taʾrīkh*, II, pp. 307–309 (Brill: I, pp. 1157–1159).

30 A similar version appears in Bukhārī, *Ṣaḥīḥ*, IX, p. 182 (*Tawḥīd* [97]: *Bāb wa-kallama llāu Mūsā* [37]). See also Huwwārī, *Tafsīr* (Q 17:1).

Another tradition also describes Muḥammad's ascension to heaven directly from Mecca, without any mention of the purification of his body. It appears in Ibn Saʿd (d. 230/845), who apparently took it from al-Wāqidī (d. 207/822):

> [The transmitters] said: God's Messenger, may God pray for him and give him peace, asked of his Lord to show him Paradise and Hell. When Saturday arrived, the 17th of Ramaḍān, eighteen months before the *hijra*, as God's Messenger was asleep in his home at noon, Gabriel and Michael came to him and said: Come to what you have asked of Allāh. So both went with him to a place between the [stone of] Maqām Ibrāhīm and the Zamzam well. Then they brought the ladder [*al-miʿrāj*], a most beautiful sight, and both ascended with him to the heavens, one heaven after the other, where he met the prophets. He reached "the Lote-Tree of the Boundary" [*sidrat al-muntahā*] and they showed him Paradise and Hell . . .[31]

In contrast to the previous version, in which the Prophet ascends to heaven in preparation for his career as prophet, here he ascends at a later stage, for the purpose of seeing Paradise and Hell. In both versions the ascent sets out from the courtyard in front of the Kaʿba's façade, between the Zamzam well and the sacred stone known as "Abraham's standing place" (Maqām Ibrāhīm), to which we shall return below.[32] As we see, the Kaʿba and its environs are perceived as a place that connects the upper and lower worlds, Paradise and Hell; in other words, this is the navel of the earth,[33] the local Arabian answer to the Rock of Bayt al-Maqdis.

Mecca as the navel of the earth and the gate to Paradise

Additional aspects of the status of the Kaʿba and its environs as the navel of the earth are revealed in traditions that appear in sources dedicated to the history of Mecca. In one such compilation by al-Fākihī (d. *circa* 272/885) we find a tradition that states that the Prophet once told his wife ʿĀʾisha that the most blessed piece of land on earth is that between the corner (*rukn*) of the Kaʿba (where the Black Stone is situated) and the stone of Maqām Ibrāhīm. According to the Prophet this is a garden (*rawḍa*) of Paradise; it is the place closest to Allāh and every prayer said there is accepted.[34] This is just one of a series of traditions in which the sacred stones near the Kaʿba are provided with a heavenly merit that is not inferior to that of the Rock in Bayt al-Maqdis. I will quote most of these from another collection devoted to Mecca by al-Azraqī (d. 222/837). Many of the traditions that he

---

31 Ibn Saʿd, *Ṭabaqāt*, I, p. 213.
32 See below, Chapter 12.
33 On this see Wensinck, *The Navel of the Earth*, pp. 23–24, 25; Livne-Kafri, "The Navel of the Earth", p. 48; Hawting, "Zamzam", pp. 50–54.
34 Fākihī, *Akhbār Makka*, I, p. 468 (no. 1032). See also Rubin, "The Kaʿba", pp. 108–109.

compiled maintain that the Black Stone originated in Paradise and descended to earth together with Adam.[35] This stone and that of Maqām Ibrāhīm are described as diamonds from Paradise,[36] although some traditions emphasize that the Black Stone is the only one that originated in Paradise. Its sheen has dimmed because of the sins of the people who touched it; otherwise it would have been able to heal anyone who touched it.[37] On the other hand, the southern corner (*al-rukn al-yamānī*) of the Kaʿba was also deemed especially sacred; it was called "one of the gates of Paradise".[38] These and similar traditions[39] caused Ibn Qutayba (d. 276/889) to declare that "the Holy Mosque [in Mecca] is superior [*afḍal*] to al-Masjid al-Aqṣā".[40]

Not only was Muḥammad's ascension to heaven linked to Mecca, but even the qur'ānic phrase al-Masjid al-Aqṣā was transferred from Bayt al-Maqdis to Arabia, this time to Medina, as we learn from the fact that al-Masjid al-Aqṣā appears in a list of that city's names and titles.[41] If not an undisguised attempt to shift the course of Muḥammad's nocturnal journey from al-Shām to Arabia, this at the very least implies the raising of Medina to a status which is no lower than that of Bayt al-Maqdis, the original site of al-Masjid al-Aqṣā.

Between Jerusalem and Mecca: The issue of prayer and pilgrimage

In addition to shifting the navel of the earth to Mecca and the Kaʿba, there is a clear tendency to minimize the importance of Bayt al-Maqdis in the scene of the nocturnal journey. A number of traditionists claimed that Muḥammad did not pray at all in Bayt al-Maqdis. One of these was the Prophet's Companion Ḥudhayfa b. al-Yamān who argued that had the Prophet prayed in Bayt al-Maqdis, the Qur'ān would have commanded the believers to do likewise. But the Qur'ān, he explains, does not instruct one to pray there, but only in the Holy Mosque (al-

---

35 Azraqī, *Akhbār Makka*, pp. 232, 233. See also Busse, "Jerusalem and Mecca", pp. 240–241.

36 Azraqī, *Akhbār Makka*, pp. 229, 232. See further, Kister, "Maqām Ibrāhīm", pp. 481–482.

37 Azraqī, *Akhbār Makka*, p. 232.

38 *Ibid.*, p. 240.

39 See also ʿAbd al-Razzāq, *Muṣannaf*, V, pp. 38–40.

40 Ibn Qutayba, *Mukhtalif al-ḥadīth*, p. 289. In the same chapter, Ibn Qutayba disproves the claim that the Black Stone is like the rest of the stones of which the Kaʿba was built and did not descend from heaven. See also Rubin, "The Kaʿba", p. 120, note 147.

41 Samhūdī, *Wafā'*, I, p. 23; Kister, "Sanctity Joint and Divided", p. 20.

Masjid al-Ḥarām) in Mecca.[42] Indeed, the only place in which the Qurʾān explicitly enjoins the believers to pray is Maqām Ibrāhīm (Q 2:125), in addition to the Holy Mosque, which is stated to be the sole direction of prayer for the believers (Q 2:144, 150).[43]

The same pro-Meccan tendency can be discerned in traditions concerning the pilgrimage. In one tradition the Prophet forbids one of the believers to fulfill a vow he took to pray in Bayt al-Maqdis and instructs him to fulfill it in Mecca instead. The Prophet is quoted as saying that praying in Mecca is worth a thousand times more than a prayer anywhere else.[44] In another tradition the caliph ʿUmar b. al-Khaṭṭāb (reigned 13–23/634–644) expresses a similar opinion and whips two people who had come from Bayt al-Maqdis to Medina because they had, so he claimed, performed *ḥajj* rites there that were identical to those which were customary in Mecca.[45] There are more traditions about Muslim scholars who reportedly expressed strong opposition to pilgrimage to Bayt al-Maqdis, stressing the virtues of Mecca as a more fitting destination.[46] Here and there traditions were disseminated that even remove al-Masjid al-Aqṣā from the list of the three mosques which the Prophet recommended as pilgrimage destinations according to al-Zuhrī's version as quoted by ʿAbd al-Malik (see above). These truncated versions state that the Prophet instructed the believers to journey for worship to only two mosques, the one in Mecca and the one in Medina.[47] Another version, which also removes al-Masjid al-Aqṣā from the list of three mosques, replaces it with the mosque of al-Khayf, located in the Minā region, east of Mecca, an important station on the *ḥajj* course.[48] Influenced by a variety of traditions that downplayed Jerusalem's importance, some modern Muslim scholars have argued that Medina is ten times as sacred as Jerusalem and that Mecca is one-hundred times as sacred.[49] However, this constitutes no more than a vain attempt to undermine an early tradition about three mosques situated in the two regions of the sanctity space, one which appears already in Muqātil's *Tafsīr*.[50]

42 ʿAbd al-Razzāq, *Tafsīr* (Q 17: 1); Ṭabarī, *Tafsīr* (Q 17:1); Māwardī, *Nukat* (Q 17:1).
43 See below, Chapter 14.
44 Azraqī, *Akhbār Makka*, p. 302. See also Kister, "Three Mosques", p. 180.
45 Azraqī, *loc. cit.* See also Kister, "Three Mosques", p. 180.
46 Kister, "Three Mosques", p. 183.
47 Kister, "Three Mosques", pp. 178–179. The tradition is recorded in ʿAbd al-Razzāq, *Muṣannaf*, V, p. 133 (no. 9161). See also Hasson, "Jerusalem in the Muslim Perspective", p. 291.
48 Kister, "Three Mosques", pp. 183–184.
49 Reiter, *From Jerusalem to Mecca*, p. 17 (with reference to the words of Abdul Hadi Palazzi).
50 Muqātil, *Addendum*, p. 513. Sharon's view that the version of the three mosques is a late extension of the "original tradition which allowed a pilgrimage only to Mecca" (Sharon, "The Cities of the Holy Land", p. 106) does not accord with the evidence of the texts before us.

Other traditions indeed retain Jerusalem's status as an appropriate pilgrimage destination and place of prayer. One of them relates the following:

> The Prophet's wife Maymūna said: O Messenger of Allāh, I made a vow that if Allāh would make Mecca yield to you I would pray in Bayt al-Maqdis. The Messenger of Allāh said: You cannot do so. The Romans [*al-Rūm*] stand between you and it. She said: If so, I will take with me a guard that will walk before me and behind me. He said: You cannot do so. Instead, send oil with which they will light candles in your name, and this will be deemed as if you went there. Since then, Maymūna would send money to Bayt al-Maqdis every year, with which they bought oil for lighting candles in Bayt al-Maqdis. When she was on her death bed she bequeathed [part of her property] so that this would continue.[51]

In this tradition, Maymūna wants to celebrate Muḥammad's conquest of Mecca (which occurred in the year 8/630) by praying in Jerusalem. The Prophet does not forbid this, but advises her what she should do if she should be unable to go and pray there. This version stands in contrast to a story in which Maymūna herself forbids a Muslim woman from traveling to Bayt al-Maqdis in order to fulfill the vow she had made to pray there in thanks for having recuperated from a serious illness. Maymūna tells her to fulfill her vow in Medina.[52]

Quite a few traditions commend Bayt al-Maqdis as a place of prayer. One tradition of the Prophet relates that Allāh had permitted Solomon to make various requests when he finished building the Temple. The king asked three things: Wisdom like the wisdom of Allāh, a reign which no one after him would deserve (Q 38:35), and absolute atonement of sins for all who would come to pray in the Temple. Allāh acceded only to the first two requests, and Muḥammad expressed his wish to his believers that the third would be answered as well.[53] According to the Prophet's Companion Abū Hurayra, Muḥammad declared: "Anyone who prays in Jerusalem will have all his sins forgiven".[54] Ka'b al-Aḥbār announced that all who come to Jerusalem and pray to the right and the left of the Rock and by the "place of the chain" (*mawḍiʿ al-silsila*) and who give alms there, will be as free of sin as a newborn baby.[55] Muḥammad himself is further quoted as stating that anyone who prays two *rakʿa*s in Jerusalem will have his sins forgiven.[56]

We thus see that the attempts to undermine the ritual balance in the Jerusalem-Mecca sanctity space and diminish the status of Bayt al-Maqdis in favor of the Ka'ba did not succeed. Further evidence for this is the great prevalence of the

51 Wāqidī, *Maghāzī*, II, p. 866. See also Goldziher, *Muslim Studies*, II, p. 45.
52 See Kister, "Three Mosques", p. 181; Livne-Kafri, "Christian Attitudes", p. 362.
53 Mujīr al-Dīn, *al-Uns al-jalīl*, I, pp. 228–229; Rubin, *Muḥammad the Prophet*, II, p. 250.
54 Mujīr al-Dīn, *al-Uns al-jalīl*, I, p. 229; Rubin, *Muḥammad the Prophet*, II, p. 250.
55 Ibid., p. 250.
56 Mujīr al-Dīn, *al-Uns al-jalīl*, I, pp. 240–241; Rubin, *Muḥammad the Prophet*, II, p. 250.

tradition of the three mosques as pilgrimage destinations, disseminated through a variety of transmission chains, and even included in al-Bukhārī's (d. 256/869) canonical *ḥadīth* collection.[57]

To this we should add the fact that a series of prominent personages chose Bayt al-Maqdis as the place where they entered the state of *iḥrām* ("sanctification"), in preparation for performing the pilgrimage to Mecca. It appears that this custom, praised also in early traditions, existed already before the Umayyad period.[58] One tradition that praises this custom appears in Abū Dāwūd's (d. 275/888) compilation of traditions, one of the six canonical *ḥadīth* collections. In it, the Prophet is quoted as saying: "Anyone who sanctifies himself [by pronouncing a certain formula] for the performance of the *ḥajj* or the *ʿumra* from al-Masjid al-Aqṣā to the Holy Mosque [in Mecca], all his former and latter sins will be forgiven, or [he said that] he will certainly go to Paradise".[59] This is an explicit recommendation to begin one's *ḥajj* in Jerusalem. Later on other cities also began to function as places from which pilgrim caravans to Mecca set out.[60]

Muḥammad's journey: The complete route

Indeed, despite the versions of the nocturnal journey and the ascension to heaven which try to move the center of the events from the Rock to the Kaʿba, the versions which enjoy the greatest currency and the most overwhelming recognition in available sources are those in which the journey as a whole is depicted in detail, including the Prophet's prayer in Bayt al-Maqdis, followed by his ascension to heaven. One such version, reported by the Prophet's Companion Mālik b. Ṣaʿṣaʿa, lists the following stages in the Prophet's journey: Opening of the chest and its purification in Mecca; riding al-Burāq to Bayt al-Maqdis; leading the prophets in prayer; ascension to heaven.[61] Similar traditions in which the ascension to heaven takes place from Bayt al-Maqdis after the nocturnal journey can be found in the exegetical literature, in commentaries on Q 17:1;

57 Bukhārī, *Ṣaḥīḥ*, II, p. 76 (*Faḍl al-ṣalāt fī masjid Makka wa-l-Madīna* [20]:1). See also Kister, "Three Mosques", pp. 184–188.

58 Elad, "The Temple Mount", p. 85 (with reference to Wāsiṭī, *Faḍāʾil*, pp. 58–59 [nos. 91, 92]). See also Kister, "Three Mosques", pp. 192–193; Rubin, *Muḥammad the Prophet*, II, p. 250.

59 Abū Dāwūd, *Sunan*, I, p. 404 (Manāsik [11]). See also Ibn al-Jawzī, *Taʾrīkh Bayt al-Maqdis*, p. 49.

60 On these towns see Peters, *Jerusalem and Mecca*, p. 47.

61 Ṭabarī, *Tafsīr* (Q 17:1).

detailed references are not needed.[62] We should only note here that Muslim scholars, when discussing the tradition of the direct ascension to heaven from Mecca do so with the intention of defending the idea of the ascension from Bayt al-Maqdis. For example, Ibn Ḥajar al-ʿAsqalānī (d. 852/1449) proposes two solutions to reconcile the two versions of the ascension: (a) the two versions refer to two distinct ascents of the Prophet to heaven, one from Mecca and the other from Bayt al-Maqdis; (b) both versions describe the same sequence of events, the nocturnal journey and the ascension to heaven, but in one version the journey from Mecca to Bayt al-Maqdis has, for some reason, been omitted, thus creating a shortened sequence in which the ascension to heaven *seems* to have taken place directly from Mecca.[63]

As for the traditions which describe the heavenly stage of the Prophet's complete itinerary, these can be found in all the earliest extant sources, including Ibn Isḥāq's *Sīra*.[64] Some of these use the vocabulary of Q 53 quoted above, especially when describing the Prophet's arrival in the seventh heaven and his approach to God's throne. Here "the Lote-Tree of the Boundary" (*sidrat al-muntahā*) is revealed to him and he approaches the throne to a distance of "two bows' length away, or nearer" (Q 53:9).

The virtues of al-Shām come up in the Qur'ān and in tradition not only through the image of Muḥammad being taken by night to the Farthest Mosque, but also through the Children of Israel's journey from Egypt to the blessed land, wherein their salvation lies. More on this in the next chapter.

---

62 In the version of Abū Saʿīd al-Khudrī, Muḥammad reaches Bayt al-Maqdis, prays, and then ascends to heaven. See ʿAbd al-Razzāq, *Tafsīr* (Q 17:1); Ṭabarī, *Tafsīr* (Q 17:1). According to other versions, Muḥammad ascended to heaven after leading the prophets in prayer. See Ṭabarī, *Tafsīr* (Q 17:1). See also Thaʿlabī, *al-Kashf wa-l-bayān* (Q 17:1). Here the names of all the prophets who prayed under Muḥammad's leadership are listed, then their conversation, and then his ascension.

63 Ibn Ḥajar, *Fatḥ al-bārī*, XIII, pp. 400–401 [on Bukhārī, *Ṣaḥīḥ*, *Tawḥīd* (97:37)].

64 Ibn Hishām, *Sīra*, II, pp. 44–50.

Part Two: **Land of Redemption**

3 Israel's redemption and "the Promise of the Latter Days"

The *sūra* which opens with Muḥammad's nocturnal journey contains in a subsequent passage the verse of *wa'd al-ākhira*, "the promise of the Latter Days" (Q 17:104). In it God promises the Children of Israel who are being delivered from the hands of Pharaoh that they would be "gathered together", *lafīfan*, at *al-ākhira*, i.e. in the Latter Days. A comparison with Jewish messianic texts leads to the conclusion that in this case, too, just as in the case of the passage of the nocturnal journey, the Qur'ān identifies with the Jewish vision of redemption. This time it is the displaced tribes of Israel who will return to their homeland from their places of exile and find their salvation there. Exegetical traditions have preserved the messianic framework of "the promise of the Latter Days" verse, as well as of another verse that refers to Moses' righteous nation, namely the Levites (Q 7:159).

The status of Jerusalem as the navel of the earth and the gate of heaven makes it the most appropriate location in which to be redeemed and protected by God. Redemption is the axis around which Muḥammad's prophetic message revolves, which especially in the Meccan *sūra*s aims at mobilizing the believers to take the path to Paradise and so avoid the fires of Hell. But redemption begins already here on earth, and the lesson which the Qur'ān draws from the past to demonstrate this lies in the history of the Children of Israel. We have already noted the verses that recount how Moses led the Children of Israel on a nocturnal journey to their Promised Land just like Muḥammad's own nocturnal journey to the same destination, as a sign of the latter's role as the redeemer of his generation.[1] Thus it is not surprising that the passage about the Prophet's nocturnal journey that opens Q 17 is followed by verses about Moses and the Children of Israel. These verses, which will be examined in this chapter,[2] are designed to present the reader with the main features of the vision of messianic redemption which was promised to the Children of Israel and which is about to be reenacted and implemented for Muḥammad's followers.

1 See above, Chapter 1.
2 For a previous version of this chapter see Rubin, "The Promised Land".

https://doi.org/10.1515/9783111222318-004

Pharaoh's defeat and the bequest of the land to the Children of Israel

Before looking at the verses about the Children of Israel in Q 17, let us examine verses in a number of other Meccan *sūras* which deal with the Children of Israel's journey to the land that God has given them (Q 7:137):

> And We bequeathed upon the people that were abased all the east and the west of the land that We had blessed; and perfectly was fulfilled the most fair word of your Lord upon the Children of Israel, for that they endured patiently; and We destroyed utterly the works of Pharaoh and his people, and what they had been building.

The destruction of Pharaoh's works is apparently an allusion to the plagues suffered by the Egyptians as described in the preceding verses (Q 7:130–133). God's good tidings, his promise of redemption to the Children of Israel, were fulfilled by bequeathing the land to them, the land that, like al-Masjid al-Aqṣā (Q 17:1), is in a region on which God has bestowed his blessing.

The area bequeathed to the Children of Israel extends over "all the east and the west of the land". It was given to them after Pharaoh drowned in the sea, as mentioned in the preceding verse (Q 7:136). The land's boundaries are reminiscent of the promise made by God to Abram in the Hebrew Bible (Genesis 13:14–15):

> (14) The Lord said to Abram, after Lot had separated from him, "Raise your eyes now, and look from the place where you are, northward and southward and eastward and westward; (15) for all the land that you see I will give to you and to your offspring forever. . . ".

The Children of Israel thus inherited the land as part of the same plan of redemption that God had promised to Abram.

In the following verse, immediately after the Qur'ān tells of the blessed land bequeathed to the Children of Israel, God scolds them for their adherence to idols after they had passed through the sea on their exodus from Egypt (Q 7:138). However, the fact remains that the bequeathing of the land signals God's power to carry out the plan of redemption for his persecuted believers. Indeed, we note that the redeemed Children of Israel are called *al-mustaḍʿafūn*, "those that were abased". In the same *sūra* this is the word used to describe other believers as well, who had been oppressed in previous generations and were eventually delivered from their enemies (Q 7:75). Furthermore, in other *sūras* the same adjective is used to denote even Muslims who are persecuted by the unbelievers (Q 4:75, 97–98; 8:26). The shared vocabulary is further evidence for the place of the Children of Israel in the same plan of redemption that applies also to the persecuted believers who follow the Prophet.

In other Meccan verses the area bequeathed to the Children of Israel after Pharaoh's defeat includes the latter's own land as well, a clear sign of his conclusive defeat. Thus in the following passage Moses comes to the Children of Israel who are then still under Pharaoh's yoke, and says to them (Q 7:128–129):

> (128) Said Moses to his people, 'Pray for succor to God, and be patient; surely the earth is God's and he bequeaths it to whom he will among his servants. The issue ultimate is to the godfearing.' (129) They said, 'We have been hurt before you came to us, and after you came to us.' He said, 'Perchance your Lord will destroy your enemy, and will make you successors in the land, so that he may behold how you shall do.'

Here the Children of Israel are the complainers who lack faith, who accuse Moses of having worsened their work conditions since the beginning of his mission.[3] But Moses brings them tidings of God's plan to overturn their fate: The Children of Israel will replace Pharaoh as the rulers of the land. This same plan is revealed in greater detail in Meccan verses that highlight the evil nature of Pharaoh, who is about to be defeated in his own land (Q 28:4–6):

> (4) Now Pharaoh had exalted himself in the land and had divided its inhabitants into sects, abasing one party of them, slaughtering their sons, and sparing their women; for he was of the workers of corruption. (5) Yet We desired to be gracious to those that were abased in the land, and to make them leaders, and to make them the inheritors, (6) and to establish them in the land, and to show Pharaoh and Haman, and their hosts, what they were dreading from them.

This passage is reminiscent of the account in Exodus 1 of the Children of Israel's oppression under Pharaoh and the latter's attempt to prevent them from multiplying and joining his enemies in time of war.[4] In this account (Exodus 1:15–21) Pharaoh commands the Hebrew midwives to kill all male newborn children. The midwives ignore this command and the Children of Israel proliferate. In the qur'ānic version, too, Allāh brings about what Pharaoh has feared: He lifts up the Children of Israel in

---

3 See Exodus 5:6–9 where Pharaoh imposes on the Children of Israel heavier tasks in their labor, in response to the demand of Moses and Aaron to let their people go, and especially verse 23 where Moses tells God: "Since I first came to Pharaoh to speak in your name, he has mistreated this people, and you have done nothing at all to deliver your people".

4 See Exodus 1:8–10: "(8) Now a new king arose over Egypt, who did not know Joseph. (9) He said to his people, Look, the Israelite people are more numerous and more powerful than we. (10) Come, let us deal shrewdly with them, or they will increase and, in the event of war, join our enemies and fight against us and escape from the land" [lit.: "will go up from the land"]. The expression "go up from the land" (וְעָלָה מִן הָאָרֶץ) is explained in the Jewish Midrash in the meaning of rising up from the level of lowliness. See Midrash Rabbah, III, p. 12 (Exodus Rabbah 1:9): "Another explanation of 'And he will go up from the land' is, that Israel will always ascend from the lowest degradation . . . ".

Pharaoh's own land and makes them masters. In this manner, the fear of Pharaoh and his people, including Haman,[5] lest the Children of Israel would dispossess them of their land, comes true.[6] Some Muslim exegetes explain that the Children of Israel who became masters of the land were Joseph and his offspring.[7] In a similar vein, the Mishna states that Joseph foresaw this change.[8]

As for the "sects" (*shiya*ʿ) into which Pharaoh divided his people, Muslim commentators explain that Pharaoh separated the Children of Israel from the rest of the Egyptians.[9] This explanation is in line with one of the earliest Jewish Apocrypha, Jubilees 46:16: "The Egyptians considered the Israelites detestable". The Biblical account may be of relevance, too, in this connection. There we read that the Children of Israel resided separately, in the Land of Goshen, although in this case the separation was done at their own behest, on Joseph's advice to his brothers.[10]

In other Meccan verses, Pharaoh suffers a double defeat, first in his own land and then on the sea (Q 26:57–66):

> (57) So We expelled them from gardens and fountains, (58) and treasures and a noble station; (59) even so, and We bequeathed them upon the Children of Israel. (60) Then they followed them at the sunrise; (61) and, when the two hosts sighted each other, the companions of Moses said, 'We are overtaken!' (62) Said he, 'No indeed; surely my Lord is with me; he will guide me.' (63) Then We revealed to Moses, 'Strike with your staff the sea'; and it clave, and each part was as a mighty mount. (64) And there We brought the others on, (65) and We delivered Moses and those with him all together; (66) then We drowned the others.

5 Modern scholars point to the similarity in the Hebrew Bible between the descriptions of Ahasuerus and his deeds and Pharaoh's descriptions, so that the figure of Haman could wander from the court of Ahasuerus to that of Pharaoh. See Silverstein, "Hāmān", pp. 285–308. Haman is mentioned together with Pharaoh (and Koraḥ) also in Q 29:39; 40:24.

6 See also Q 7:110; 20:57, 63; 26:35.

7 E.g. Māwardī, *Nukat* (Q 28:5–6).

8 *Abot de Rabbi Nathan Version B*, p. 255 (Chapter 43): "Joseph prophesied and did not know what he was prophesying, as Scripture says: 'For the best of all the land of Egypt is yours' (Gen. 45:20). He prophesied that they were destined to despoil Egypt". This Midrash alludes to what is told in Exodus 12:35–36: "(35) The Israelites had done as Moses told them; they had asked the Egyptians for jewelry of silver and gold, and for clothing, (36) and the Lord had given the people favor in the sight of the Egyptians, so that they let them have what they asked. And so they plundered the Egyptians". As for Joseph's prophesying, this too is perhaps reflected in the Qur'ān, where Moses, or the believer of the house of Pharaoh, says to the Children of Israel, or to Pharaoh: Joseph brought you the clear signs before, yet you continued in doubt concerning what he brought you (Q 40:34).

9 Māwardī, *Nukat* (Q 28:4).

10 Genesis 46:34: You shall say, "Your servants have been keepers of livestock from our youth even until now, both we and our ancestors' – in order that you may settle in the land of Goshen, because all shepherds are abhorrent to the Egyptians".

However, in the following passage, Pharaoh's double defeat takes place in reverse order: First the Egyptians drown in the sea and then they lose their estates (Q 44:23–28):

> (23) Then go with my servants by night; surely you will be followed. (24) And leave the sea becalmed; they are a drowned host.' (25) They left how many gardens and fountains, (26) sown fields, and how noble a station, (27) and what prosperity they had rejoiced in! (28) Even so; and We bequeathed them upon another people.

In this passage Allāh commands Moses to bring his people out of Egypt at night. The pursuing Egyptians who are about to drown leave their estates unprotected and Allāh bequeaths them to "another people", that is, to the Children of Israel. Muslim exegetes explain that the Children of Israel returned to Egypt after Pharaoh had drowned.[11]

Pharaoh's double defeat can also be explained with the help of Jubilees. In chapter 46 we read of two journeys of the Children of Israel from Egypt to Canaan. First they make the journey in order to bury the bones of Jacob's sons. Then they return to Egypt, which closes its gates before the enemy outside. Pharaoh persecutes this group, but it multiplies.[12] Perhaps this is the source of the qurʾānic account of Pharaoh's defeat inside Egypt and the Children of Israel's seizure of his estates—all of this apart from the story of the Egyptians' drowning in the sea.[13]

Destruction of the Temple

Bequeathing Pharaoh's land to the Children of Israel is the first stage in the process of redemption, which is destined to continue in days to come. That redemption will take place after the greatest disaster to befall the Jewish people, the destruction of the Temple. This takes us back to the passage immediately following the account of Muḥammad's nocturnal journey in Q 17. We discussed part of this passage already in the chapter "Muḥammad's Journey to the Farthest Mosque". Here it is in full (Q 17:4–7):

> (4) And We decreed for the Children of Israel in the Book: 'You shall do corruption in the earth twice (*marratayn*), and you shall ascend exceeding high.' (5) So, when the promise of the first of these came to pass, We sent against you servants of ours, people of great might, and they went through the habitations, and it was a promise performed. (6) Then We gave back to you the turn to prevail over them, and We succored you with wealth and children, and We made you a greater host. (7) 'If you do good, it is your own selves you do good to, and

11 Ibn ʿAṭiyya, *Tafsīr* (Q 44:28).
12 Cf. the notes in Werman, *Jubilees*, pp. 520–525.
13 For the entire issue see Sinai, "Inheriting Egypt", pp. 198–214.

> if you do evil it is to your selves likewise.' Then, when the promise of the latter came to pass, [We sent against you our servants] to discountenance you, and to enter the Mosque [*al-masjid*], as they entered it the first time, and to destroy utterly that which they ascended to.

This is the qur'ānic version of the destruction of the first and second Temples (586 BCE and 70 CE, respectively). The destruction of the First Temple is "the promise of the first of these" (*wa'd ūlāhumā*) and that of the Second Temple is "the promise of the latter" (*wa'd al-ākhira*). In other words, both destructions are part of a preordained plan which God promised to implement as punishment for the Children of Israel's sins. The plan was written in advance already in the Book given to Moses.

The Qur'ān does not provide details about the nature of the sin committed by the Children of Israel which resulted in the enemy entering "the Mosque", that is, the Temple, and destroying it. According to Muslim exegetes, the Children of Israel's sin was to persecute and kill the prophets that were sent to them. According to some commentators, the first sin was committed when they killed Isaiah[14] and the second or last sin was committed when they killed John the Baptist and his father Zacharias.[15]

But in the qur'ānic version destruction is only one part of the divine plan; there is still hope for the Children of Israel, as we read in the next verse (Q 17:8):

> Perchance your Lord will have mercy upon you; but if you return [to do evil], We shall return . . .

In other words, the second destruction, *wa'd al-ākhira*, which has already been inflicted on the Children of Israel, is neither final nor absolute. God will show mercy towards the Children of Israel, if they do not return to their evil ways. The idea of redemption after destruction in fact already appears in Jewish sources. For example, in the apocryphal Testament of Moses 9:2 we read of "a second punishment" (i.e. the second destruction), which is "cruel, impure, going beyond all bounds of mercy — even exceeding the former one".[16] This is followed in the next chapter by a depiction of the future redemption of Israel, in which God will appear and establish his encompassing kingdom in the Latter Days.[17] A clear expression of the idea that in the destruction inheres redemption is found in the assertion that the Messiah was born on the day the Temple was destroyed.[18] But in the Qur'ān there is a condition: The Children of Israel will be redeemed only if they

---

14 Cf. Talmud Bavli, Yevamoth 49b: . . . and in it was also written, "Manasseh slew Isaiah"'.

15 Ṭabarī, *Tafsīr* (Q 17:4), from Ibn Isḥāq.

16 Cf. Busse, "The Destruction of the Temple", p. 3.

17 Testament of Moses 10:1–10.

18 E.g. Midrash Zuta p. 73 (on *Lamentations*, version 2): "On the day when enemies entered the city and destroyed the Temple . . . at that hour a Messiah was born". See more details in Schwarzbaum, *Folkloristic Aspects*, pp. 130–131.

believe in Muḥammad's prophetic message. Therefore, in the verse immediately following the promise of divine mercy, God states (Q 17:9):

> Surely this Qur'ān guides to the way that is straightest and gives good tidings to the believers who do deeds of righteousness, that theirs shall be a great wage.

The promise of the Latter Days (Q 17:103–104)

The promise to the Children of Israel reappears later in Q 17, separately from the passage about the destruction of the Temple (Q 17:103–104):

> (103) [Pharaoh] desired to startle them from the land; and We drowned him and those with him, all together. (104) And We said to the Children of Israel after him, 'Dwell in the land; and when the promise of the Latter Days (*wa'd al-ākhira*) comes to pass, We shall bring you gathered together [*lafīfan*]'.

In this passage the locution *wa'd al-ākhira* appears for the second time and is discussed below. First it should be noted that in the present passage the consequence of Pharaoh's defeat is the bequeathing of the land from which Pharaoh wanted to uproot the Children of Israel that is, Egypt. This is also how some exegetes interpreted the passage, for example Fakhr al-Dīn al-Rāzī (d. 607/1210):

> Pharaoh wanted to drive Moses out of Egypt so that these districts would be an inheritance for himself only. But Allāh destroyed Pharaoh and gave Pharaoh's kingdom as a bequest to Moses and his people alone, and said to the Children of Israel: 'Dwell in the land, and it will be an endowment only for you and empty of your enemy [*khāliṣa lakum khāliya min 'aduwwikum*].[19]

We note that al-Rāzī perceives Pharaoh's plan against the Children of Israel as aimed at expelling them from his land rather than at annihilating them. Yet he preserves the idea of bequeathing Egypt to the Children of Israel. Other commentators explained that the land to be bequeathed was al-Shām, either in addition to Egypt,[20] or alone.[21] However, the qur'ānic text appears to speak about bequeathing the land from which Pharaoh wanted to expel the Children of Israel, that is, Egypt itself.

Pharaoh's failed plot against the Children of Israel is described with the Arabic verb *istafazza*, which in the same *sūra* is also used when relating the failed plot of the Prophet's enemies in Arabia (Q 17:76). In both cases, the plotters suffer

---

19 Rāzī, *Tafsīr* (Q 17:104). See also Wāḥidī, *Wasīṭ* (Q 17:104).

20 Tha'labī, *al-Kashf wa-l-bayān* (Q 17:104).

21 Ṭabarī, *Tafsīr* (Q 17:104). According to other traditions, the "land" that was bequeathed to the Israelites was Transjordan (al-Urdunn) and Palestine. See Fīrūzābādī, *Tanwīr al-miqbās* (Q 17:104); Ibn al-Jawzī, *Zād al-masīr* (Q 17:104).

utter defeat,[22] but the passage under discussion here (Q 17:104) adds an eschatological dimension to the Children of Israel's redemption; it will be achieved "when the promise of the Latter Days comes to pass" [*wa-idhā jā'a wa'd al-ākhira*]. Modern scholars thought this was a promise for the afterworld,[23] an interpretation that cannot be ruled out. However, it should be noted that the qur'ānic term *al-ākhira* refers to the afterworld usually when it is contrasted with *al-dunyā*, the temporal world.[24] But here the word *al-ākhira* stands alone, and should be compared to other cases in which it is not contrasted with *al-dunyā*. In the latter cases it is contrasted with *al-ūlā* ("the first"),[25] and at least in some of these occurrences it can be understood as denoting a future on earth, contrasted with the past on earth, in which case it can be translated as "the latter", as in Q 93:4:

وَلَلْآخِرَةُ خَيْرٌ لَكَ مِنَ الْأُولَى

. . . and the latter [*al-ākhira*] shall be better for you than the first [*al-ūlā*].

Exegetes explain that the promised improvement will happen when the Prophet's troops will defeat his enemies.[26] In other words, it is a promise relating to a future on earth.

The Arabic *ākhira* in the sense of a future on earth (and not in the next world) is cognate with the Biblical אַחֲרִית (*aḥarīt*), as used for example in Job 42:12:

וה' בֵּרַךְ אֶת אַחֲרִית אִיּוֹב מֵרֵאשִׁתוֹ

The Lord blessed the Latter Days (אַחֲרִית) of Job more than his beginning.

Therefore, we can translate *wa'd al-ākhira* in the passage under discussion as "the promise of the Latter Days". It must be added that as already noted above, the phrase *wa'd al-ākhira* appears already at the beginning of the *sūra*, in the passage on the Temple's destruction (Q 17:7). There it is used to describe the second stage of destruction following the first stage (Q 17:5), for which the word *al-ūlā* is used (*wa'd ūlāhumā*). Therefore, *wa'd al-ākhira* was translated there as "the

---

22 The similarity between Pharaoh's plot and defeat and the plot of Muḥammad's enemies was also noted in the commentaries of the Qur'ān. See e.g. Tha'labī, *al-Kashf wa-l-bayān* (Q 17:104).

23 E.g. Paret, *Der Koran: Kommentar und Konkordanz*, p. 308; Ambros, *A Concise Dictionary*, p. 22.

24 E.g. Q 2:86, 114, 130, 200, 201, 217, 220; 4:77; 6:32, etc. In Q 17 itself, *al-ākhira* also appears as the opposite of this world (v. 72), including verses in which the people who do not believe in *al-ākhira* are warned of the punishment that awaits them in the next world (vv. 10, 45), in contrast to the reward that awaits the righteous there (vv. 19, 21).

25 E.g. Q 53:24–25; 92:13.

26 This is suggested, for example, by the exegete Ibn 'Aṭiyya (d. 546/1152). See Ibn 'Aṭiyya, *Tafsīr* (Q 93:4). See also Paret, *Der Koran: Kommentar und Konkordanz*, p. 513.

promise of the latter". In Q 17:104, however, the fulfillment of *wa'd al-ākhira* is given as a forecast for the future ("when . . . comes to pass"), already announced as early as Pharaoh's time; therefore, "the promise of the Latter Days" is a more fitting translation in the present context.

God's promise to the Children of Israel that is about to materialize in the Latter Days continues with God's undertaking to bring them "gathered together", in Arabic, *lafīfan*. This word, which appears only in Q 17:104, denotes a mixture of different tribes or of people from different places who have gathered in one place. Muḥammad's army contained a unit consisting of a mixture of tribes, mentioned during the distribution of the booty following the Battle of Khaybar (6/628). There a special portion was set aside as *sahm al-lafīf*, that is, the part given to the mixed group consisting of the tribe of Aws, joined by the Juhayna tribe and others who participated in the Battle of Khaybar.[27] Also in the direct exegesis of the *wa'd al-ākhira* passage, some exegetes explain the word *lafīf* using military imagery, i.e. armies (*juyūsh*) that clash and intermix (*ikhtilāṭ*).[28] Such an interpretation may perhaps be taken to imply that the return of the Children of Israel at the time of *wa'd al-ākhira* will involve a war against the forces of evil in their holy land.

The evidence of the Jewish sources

The conceptual background of the Children of Israel's return to their homeland at the time of *wa'd al-ākhira* is illuminated by a number of messianic Jewish sources. We begin with a work known as the Book of Zerubbabel, mentioned briefly above (Chapter 1). It reflects the proliferation of messianic hopes in Palestine at a time when the Byzantine Empire showed weakness in its war against Persia.[29] Like similar compositions, the Book of Zerubbabel contains eschatological visions

27 Ibn Hishām, *Sīra*, III, p. 365. See also Wāqidī, *Maghāzī*, II, p. 690.

28 Ṭabarī, *Tafsīr* (Q 17:104). See also Thaʿlabī, *al-Kashf wa-l-bayān* (Q 17:104); Rāzī, *Tafsīr* (Q 17:104).

29 As noted in Reeves, "Sefer Zerubbabel", p. 451: "Most modern scholars accept the persuasive arguments advanced by Israel Levi for locating the work during the first quarter of the seventh century in Palestine within the context of the fierce struggles of Persia and Rome for control of the Holy Land". See also Himmelfarb, "Sefer Zerubbabel", p. 67. See more about the book of Zerubbabel and its early provenance and probable relationship to the Persian conquest of Jerusalem, in Grossmann, "Jerusalem in the Jewish Apocalypse", pp. 238–243; Rubin Z., "History of Jerusalem", p. 44; Shoemaker, "The Reign of God", pp. 550–555. See further Newman, "Methodological and Historical Criticism", pp. lxiii–lxxiv; *idem*, "Dating Sefer Zerubavel", pp. 324–336; Irshai, "Chronography and Apocalypse", p. xxx.

about the return of the Jews to their homeland from their places of dispersion in the Latter Days, the defeat of the false Messiah and the redemption of Israel in Jerusalem. The work is extant in a number of versions.[30] The part that is relevant to our discussion contains a vision of events that are to take place in the Latter Days, 990 years after the destruction of the Second Temple. At that time, God will descend to earth and fight against the nations, and the Messiah of the House of David and the Children of Israel will kill the false Messiah Armilos and his hosts. These events will pave the way for Israel's redemption in Jerusalem. The description of the return of the Children of Israel to their homeland appears, with insubstantial differences, in all the manuscripts of the Book of Zerubbabel. It is related there that the dead of the wilderness (מֵתֵי מִדְבָּר), that is, the generation that sinned in the affair of the twelve spies and were condemned to die out while wandering in the desert for forty years (Numbers 13–14), will be resurrected, as will be the congregation of Koraḥ, who was swallowed up by the earth (Numbers 16:31–32). They will all gather around Moses and will together enter the land. This is the passage of relevance to us:

> in the second month; i.e. Iyyar, the congregation of Koraḥ will reemerge upon the plains of Jericho near the Wādī Shiṭṭim. They will come to Moses (*sic.*!). Asaph (the biblical choirmaster) was a member of the cohort of the Koraḥites. On the eighteenth day of it (the second month) the mountains and hills will quake, and the earth and everything on it will shake, as well as the sea and its contents. On the first day of the third month those who died in the desert will revive and will come with their families to the Wādī Shiṭṭim.[31]

The gathering of the lost groups of the tribes of Israel will take place after a tremendous earthquake that will shake both land and sea. Shiṭṭim, according to Joshua 2:1, is the name of the place where the Children of Israel camped before they crossed the Jordan River to the Land of Canaan. It became the valley of Shiṭṭim in the Book of Zerubbabel following Joel 3 [4]:18: נַחַל הַשִּׁטִּים.[32]

Two groups will gather at the valley of Shiṭṭim, Koraḥ's congregation and the dead of the wilderness. While the Jewish Sages rejected the notion that these two groups would return,[33] the Book of Zerubbabel expresses the fervent hope that

30 Himmelfarb, "Sefer Zerubbabel", pp. 67–90; Reeves, *Trajectories*, pp. 40–51; *idem*, "Sefer Zerubbabel". On the Geniza versions of the book, see Gil, "The Apocalypse of Zerubbabel", pp. 1–98. Cf. Lassner, *Medieval Jerusalem*, pp. 65–66.

31 Reeves, "Sefer Zerubbabel", p. 463. See also *idem*, *Trajectories*, pp. 61–62; Wertheimer, *Batei Midrashos*, II, pp. 500–501; Eisenstein, *Ozar Midrashim*, I, p. 160; Even-Shmuel, *Midrashei Geula*, p. 87.

32 Himmelfarb, "Sefer Zerubbabel", p. 88, note 92.

33 Talmud Yerushalmi, XII, pp. 377–378 (Sanhedrin 10:4–5): "The generation of the desert has no part in the World to Come . . . The band of Koraḥ will not be resurrected in the future".

they will return to their holy land, thus signaling the beginning of the messianic age. The dead of the wilderness will come "with their families",[34] or, according to another version, ". . . the dead of the wilderness will come and assemble in groups [חֲבוּרוֹת חֲבוּרוֹת] together with their brethren at the valley of Shiṭṭim".[35] It should also be noted that the dead of the wilderness will come after having revived [וְיִחְיוּ].[36]

The Book of Zerubbabel proceeds to describe how the returning Israelites will witness redemption in Jerusalem at the hand of God who will stand on the Mount of Olives:

> In Tammuz, the fourth month, the Lord God of Israel will descend upon the Mount of Olives, and the Mount of Olives will split open at His rebuke. . . The Lord will kill all their plunderers, and He will battle those nations like a warrior fired with zeal. The Lord's Messiah—Menaḥem b. ʿAmiel—will come and breathe in the face of Armilos and thereby slay him. . . The saintly people will come out to witness the Lord's deliverance: all of Israel will actually see Him (equipped) like a warrior with the helmet of deliverance on His head and clad in armor. . . All of Israel will then issue forth and [despoil] their despoilers, looting those who previously plundered them for seven months.[37]

This description elaborates on several biblical passages, including Zechariah 14:3–4 which is also used in other sources for the scene of the Day of Judgement (see below, Chapter 4).

Israel's redemption culminates with the renewed Temple:

> Then the Lord will lower the celestial Temple which had been previously built to earth, and a column of fire and a cloud of smoke will rise to heaven. The Messiah and all of Israel will follow them to the gates of Jerusalem.[38]

Apart from the Book of Zerubbabel, the idea that the dead—or the generation—of the wilderness will return together with the congregation of Koraḥ also appears in another text which is part of a collection known as *Pirkei Mashiach*. Here we read that Elijah and the King Messiah will come to the Children of Israel, and Elijah will encourage them and perform seven miracles for them, the first two being:

---

34 Yassif, *The Book of Memory*, p. 432 [ויבואו בבתיהם].

35 Wertheimer, *Batei Midrashos*, II, p. 501.

36 Eisenstein, *Ozar Midrashim*, I, p. 160. See also Himmelfarb, "Sefer Zerubbabel", p. 78 ("will come to life").

37 Reeves, "Sefer Zerubbabel", pp. 463–464.

38 Reeves, "Sefer Zerubbabel", p. 464.

> The first miracle: He will bring to them Moses and his generation from the wilderness, for it is said (Psalms 50: 5): "Gather to me my faithful ones". The second miracle: He will bring up for them Koraḥ and all his congregation, for it is said (Psalms 71: 20): "[You] will revive me again; from the depths of the earth you will bring me up again".[39]

We see here that the return of the redeemed involves their resurrection as well ("[You] will revive me again"). The passage subsequently presents a midrashic interpretation of Isaiah 52:7: "How beautiful upon the mountains are the feet of the messenger":

> Why upon the mountains? This only means: How beautiful are Moses and his generation who come from the wilderness.

Moses himself is described in a number of other Jewish sources as the future leader of the generation of the wilderness returning to their homeland.[40]

To the evidence in the Book of Zerubbabel and Pirkei Mashiach we may add the following quote from the Talmud Yerushalmi:

> On that day, a great ram's horn will be blown, and those lost in the land of Assyria will come — these are the ten tribes, and those displaced in the land of Egypt, that is the generation of the desert. These and those — will bow down before the Eternal on the Holy Mountain in Jerusalem.[41]

This is a midrashic exegesis on Isaiah 27:13:

> And on that day a great trumpet will be blown, and those who were lost in the land of Assyria and those who were driven out to the land of Egypt will come and worship the Lord on the holy mountain at Jerusalem.

The Talmudic conception that the generation of the wilderness will return from Egypt provides support for the conjecture that the *wa'd al-ākhira* passage alludes to them. This is due to the fact that the promised return of the Children of Israel, who have been "gathered together" is about to occur after they inhabit the land from which Pharaoh wanted to remove them, to wit, Egypt.

In light of these Jewish texts we may surmise that in Q 17:104 the Qur'ān reflects the messianic idea of the redemption of the generation of the wilderness, which is resurrected and brought to their holy land and Jerusalem, perhaps in

---

39 Jellinek, *Bet Ha-Midrasch*, III, pp. 72–73; Even-Shmuel, *Midrashei Geula*, pp. 336–337.
40 E.g. Midrash Rabbah, III, p. 51 (Exodus Rabbah 2:4): "In the wilderness wilt thou leave them, and from the wilderness wilt thou bring them back in the Messianic times . . .".
41 Talmud Yerushalmi, XII, p. 379 (Sanhedrin 10:4).

combination with the myth of the expected return of the ten lost tribes.[42] Just as in the Book of Zerubbabel the dead of the wilderness and Koraḥ's congregation are expected to return in groups or families, so does the Qur'ān expect their return all together, as *lafīf*, at the time of *wa'd al-ākhira*.

Wa'd al-ākhira and the message to the qur'ānic audience

The qur'ānic "promise of the Latter Days" is designed to signal to Muḥammad's contemporaries that they are the community for which this ancient promise will be fulfilled, and that through them the plan of redemption will be carried out. This is confirmed by the following verses, which come immediately after the passage of *wa'd al-ākhira* (Q 17:105–109):

> (105) With the truth We have sent it down, and with the truth it has come down; and We have sent you not, except good tidings to bear, and warning; (106) and a Qur'ān We have divided, for you to recite it to people at intervals, and We have sent it down successively. (107) Say: 'Believe in it, or believe not; those who were given the knowledge before it when it is recited to them, fall down upon their faces prostrating, (108) and say, 'Glory be to our Lord! Our Lord's promise [*wa'du rabbinā*] is performed.' (109) And they fall down upon their faces weeping; and it increases them in humility.

The keyword in this passage is God's "promise" (*wa'd*), with which the believers who received divine knowledge before Muḥammad's appearance are acquainted. In other words, they read about it in the Scriptures that preceded the Qur'ān. These believers express their joy at being witnesses to the fulfillment of the promise through the words of a prophet who brings them Allāh's word in a Qur'ān that has descended from heaven. In this manner an idea is conveyed which is familiar from other places in the Qur'ān, namely that Muḥammad's emergence fulfills a divine plan of salvation that is mentioned already in the Torah and in other scriptures. This idea comes up mainly in verses in which the Prophet and the Qur'ān "confirm" the Scriptures revealed before the Qur'ān (for example, Q 2:89, 101 and elsewhere). By this are meant not only the Bible but the entire pre-Islamic Jewish and Christian literature that contains various messianic tidings. The promise of Q 17:104 concerning the Latter Days thus can, by its very nature, also be counted among the ancient promises of redemption that are fulfilled through the Prophet and the community of his believers. This community includes all pagans, Jews and Christians who take

42 On the other hand, some Sages denied the idea of the return of the ten tribes. See Talmud Bavli, Sanhedrin, 110b: "Mishna: The ten tribes will not return [to Palestine] for it is said, 'and cast them into another land, as is this today.' [Deut. 29:27]. Just as the day goes and does not return, so they too went and will not return: This is R. Akiba's view".

it upon themselves to believe in Muḥammad. The promise will be fulfilled wherever this community will reestablish Allāh's true religion, whether in Arabia or in al-Shām; any one of these places will be the land of redemption.

Redemption and resurrection: Exegesis and tradition

In the Jewish sources mentioned above, the return of the Israelites to their land involves their resurrection. The thin line separating between a return preliminary to a messianic redemption and resurrection is also noticeable in Muslim traditions pertaining to the qur'ānic *wa'd al-ākhira* (Q 17:104). These traditions corroborate the observation that the promise of the Latter Days implies the return of the displaced Israelites to their homeland, but they also combine the idea of messianic aspect with the idea of resurrection. An example of this is the employment of the term *lafīf*. A tradition of the Prophet addressed to his Companions says:

> . . . the people will be resurrected [*yuḥsharu*] assembled in groups [*fawjan lafīfan*], a believer will not join an unbeliever, nor an unbeliever a believer. Then the angel of the trumpet [*al-ṣūr*] will descend and stand on the Rock [al-Ṣakhra] of Bayt al-Maqdis . . .[43]

This tradition preserves the idea of *lafīf* as various groups going together to their holy land. However, here they consist not of the redeemed Children of Israel but of all people, believers and unbelievers alike. All will gather to be judged by God on the Day of Resurrection at the Rock on the Temple Mount. They will be summoned there by the blast of a trumpet blown by an angel.[44] In direct exegesis of the qur'ānic *wa'd al-ākhira*, too, some traditions link the notion of *lafīf* to the scene of resurrection. For example, we read in al-Ṭabarī's (d. 310/923) commentary:

> . . . when the Hour [of Judgment] will come, which is the promise of the Latter Days, We will bring you gathered together (*lafīfan*), that is, We will gather you [*ḥasharnākum*] out of your graves to the place of the resurrection [*mawqif al-qiyāma*].[45]

Another interpretation in the same vein is found in al-Māwardī's (d. 450/1058) *Tafsīr*:

43 Wāsiṭī, *Faḍā'il*, p. 88 (no. 142).
44 On the blowing of the trumpet see below, Chapter, 4.
45 Ṭabarī, *Tafsīr* (Q 17:104).

> The promise of the last return [*al-karra al-ākhira*], when you will be transferred to the land of al-Shām.[46]

Here al-Shām is mentioned explicitly as the Children of Israel's destination, although in this case —yet again— it is for the purpose of resurrecting them.

River of sand: Muqātil b. Sulaymān and the Apocalypse of Ezra

Further details concerning the return of the Children of Israel to their land at the time of *wa'd al-ākhira* are provided in the words of the exegete Muqātil b. Sulaymān (d. 150/767) on Q 17:104:

> "And We said to the Children of Israel after (Pharaoh)": They were seventy thousand settled beyond the river of the land of China, with the Torah. "Dwell in the land": This was after Moses and after Joshua son of Nun. "And when the promise of the Latter Days (*wa'd al-ākhira*) comes to pass": That is, the time (*mīqāt*) of *al-ākhira*, that is, the Day of Resurrection (*yawm al-qiyāma*). "We shall bring you": As well as the people of Moses (*wa-bi-qawm Mūsā*). "*lafīfan*": That is, all together (*jamīʿan*). They reside beyond the land of China. They went from Bayt al-Maqdis for a year and a half six thousand leagues, and between them and the other people there was a river of flowing sand; its name was Ardaf. It used to cease to move on the Sabbath. All this happened because the Children of Israel killed the prophets and worshipped idols, and then the believers among them said: O God, do separate us from them. So then God dug a tunnel in the ground, from Bayt al-Maqdis till beyond the land of China. They began to walk in it, while he opened the way before them and cut it off behind them. Allāh made a pillar of fire for them and made manna and quails descend on them, as they were on their way. It is these whom Allāh mentioned in *Sūrat al-Aʿrāf* [Q 7:159]: "Of the people of Moses there is a group (*umma*) [whose people are] guided by the truth, and by it act with justice". When the Prophet was taken at night [Q 17:1], he came to them that night and taught them the call to prayer, the prayer and some *sūra*s from the Qur'ān. Then they embraced Islam. These are the believers; they have no sins and they come to their wives at night. [The angel Gabriel] came to them with the Prophet. They greeted him before he greeted them, and said to the Prophet: Were it not for the sins that there are among the sons of your nation, the angels would have shaken their hands.[47]

Muqātil states here that the time of the fulfillment of *wa'd al-ākhira* is the Day of Resurrection, and then immediately identifies those who will come at that time as the Children of Israel who had separated themselves from their sinful brethren and settled by a remote river of sand beyond the land of China. While saying this he mentions Q 7:159, which praises a group of the people of Moses. We shall return

46 Māwardī, *Nukat* (Q 17:104).
47 Muqātil, *Tafsīr* (Q 17:104). Cf. Rubin, *Between Bible and Qur'an*, pp. 27–29.

to this verse later in this chapter, but right now let us look at Muqātil's direct commentary on it:

> "Of the people of Moses": That is, the Children of Israel. "There is a group (whose people are) guided by the truth": That is, a group that calls to others to come to the truth. "And by it act with justice": That is, those who now reside beyond the land of China. These are the people whom [Allāh] transported at night under the ground and drew out for them a river out of the Jordan, a river of sand, called Ardaf [printed: *ardaq*]. It is located beyond the land of China and it flows like water. Allāh transported them at night under the ground for a year and a half. When Jesus son of Mary descends to the earth, Joshua son of Nun will be with him. These are the ones among the People of the Book who believed.[48]

Other commentators, too, repeatedly mention the river in connection with the qur'ānic group of the people of Moses.[49] In one version, reported in the name of the Kūfan al-Suddī (d. 128/746) the river consists of silt (*sihl*);[50] in another version, on the authority of al-Kalbī (d. 146/763) and others, it is a river of sand (*raml*);[51] still others maintain that it is a river of honey (*shuhd* شُهْد);[52] but the latter version is in all likelihood an orthographical error for *sihl* (سهل), influenced by the rivers of honey (*'asal* عسل) that flow in Paradise according to Q 47:15.

Muqātil's commentary raises a number of topics whose origins can be traced back to one of the books of the Jewish Apocrypha, the Apocalypse of Ezra (= 4 Ezra).[53] It is ascribed to Ezra the Scribe and was composed not long after the destruction of the Second Temple. The original Jewish text is lost; it survives in translations to a number of languages, including Syriac and Latin.

In the sixth vision, Ezra is told of the Messiah who will come and stand on the summit of Mount Zion, destroy the evil nations and gather to him a multitude of the redeemed:

> (39) And as for your seeing him gather to himself another multitude that was peaceable, (40) these are the ten tribes which were led away from their own land into captivity in the days of King Hoshea, those whom Shalmaneser king of the Assyrians led captive; he took them across the river, and they were taken into another land. (41) But they formed this plan for themselves, that they would leave the multitude of the nations and go to a more distant region, where people had never lived, (42) that there at least they might keep their statutes which they had not kept in their own land. (43) And they went in by the narrow passages of the Euphrates River. (44) For at that time the Most High performed signs for them and

48 Muqātil, *Tafsīr* (Q 7:159).
49 See Epstein, *Works*, I, pp. 45–46.
50 Ibn Abī Ḥātim, *Tafsīr* (Q 7:159).
51 Tha'labī, *al-Kashf wa-l-bayān* (Q 7:159); Suyūṭī, *al-Durr al-manthūr* (Q 7:159).
52 Ṭabarī, *Tafsīr* (Q 7:159); Ibn Kathīr, *Tafsīr* (Q 7:159).
53 On the connection between Muqātil and the Apocalypse of Ezra see Reeves, *Trajectories*, pp. 201–202.

> stopped the channels of the river until they had passed over. (45) Through that region there was a long way to go, a journey of a year and a half; and that country is called Arzaret. (46) Then they dwelt there until the last times; and now, when they are about to come again, (47) the Most High will stop the channels of the river again, so that they may be able to pass over. Therefore you saw the multitude gathered together in peace. (48) But those who are left of your people, who are found within my holy borders, shall be saved. (49) Therefore when he destroys the multitude of the nations that are gathered together, he will defend the people who remain. (50) And then he will show them very many wonders.[54]

In this passage the ten tribes (in the Syriac version: nine and a half tribes) decide to separate themselves from those of their nation who were exiled to Babylonia, and to seek a distant place where they could keep the Torah's commandments. They cross the Euphrates whose flow God has stopped, and reach their isolated destination after a journey of a year and a half. In the Latter Days they will return to their homeland in the same way.

Muqātil's commentary provides the same details given in the Apocalypse of Ezra about the year and a half journey of the ten tribes to a region where they are isolated from their brethren. In Muqātil's version they make their way underneath the ground and then arrive at a river of sand called Ardaf. The origin of the latter form becomes clear in light of the above passage from the Apocalypse of Ezra, in which the abode where the people dwell is called "another land", following Deuteronomy 29:28 [27] in which the Hebrew form is *ereẓ aḥeret* (אֶרֶץ אַחֶרֶת). But in the Latin version of the apocalypse the name of the land was distorted into Arzaret, while in the Syriac translation the name is Arzaf (ܐܪܙܦ).[55] In all likelihood this is the origin of the form Ardaf in Muqātil's version.[56]

As for Muqātil, he presents the people residing beyond the river as the chosen few who separated themselves from their sinful brethren. Their journey from Bayt al-Maqdis (which here denotes their entire land) to their remote destination is depicted with biblical symbols gleaned from the Israelite exodus (the pillar of fire, manna and quails). Muqātil also highlights the Muslim faith of those who reside beyond the river and describes how Muḥammad visited them during his nocturnal journey (to al-Masjid al-Aqṣā), and how they learnt the basic tenets of Islam and pledged allegiance to the Prophet. The reference to the nocturnal journey (Q 17:1) connects the *wa'd al-ākhira* passage with the verse that opens the *sūra* in which it appears.

54 Apocalypse of Ezra 13:39–50. For the various versions of the translations of this passage, see Licht, *Apocalypse of Ezra*, p. 102.
55 See English translation of the section from the Syriac version in Reeves, *Trajectories*, pp. 201–202.
56 Reeves, *Trajectories*, p. 202, note 6.

Hence we see that Muqātil's commentary associates the *wa'd al-ākhira* passage with the Jewish myth of the ten lost tribes, who, according to the Apocalypse of Ezra, reside in "another land", where they will remain until the Latter Days, when they will be gathered and return to their homeland. In Muqātil's account it is the righteous among the Children of Israel who reside beyond the river of sand. This is the river Sambaṭyon of Jewish tradition.[57] This connection corresponds with the relationship already noted above, between the *wa'd al-ākhira* passage and the myth of the future return of the ten tribes together with the dead of the wilderness. However, it must be remembered that for Muqātil their return is not necessarily for the purpose of fulfilling the vision of redemption implied in the Apocalypse of Ezra, but rather for the resurrection. Redemption and resurrection are thus intertwined once more.

Another notable point in Muqātil's account, in addition to the details concerning the *wa'd al-ākhira* passage, is his comment on Q 7:159, where he refers to the return of Jesus and Joshua. Their names are almost identical. In this commentary, Joshua is a warrior who defeats the unbelievers and drives them out of the Promised Land. The idea of Jesus' descent in the Latter Days is one which Islam shares with Christianity. In the Islamic outlook, when he descends to earth, he will defeat the forces of evil in al-Shām, who are represented by the false Messiah, the Antichrist, who in Arabic is called *al-masīḥ al-dajjāl* ("the deceiver").[58] This idea has its counterpart in the Book of Zerubbabel, according to which the Messiah Menaḥem b. ʿAmiel will defeat Armilos (see above); but in the traditions under discussion here Jesus appears instead of the (Jewish) Messiah.[59] The concept of messianic redemption which is also inherent in the *wa'd al-ākhira* passage is preserved here completely.

Jesus is also mentioned in a number of commentaries on Q 17:104. Thus in the *Tafsīr* ascribed to the Prophet's Companion ʿAbdallāh b. ʿAbbās, known as the founder of Qur'ān exegesis, we read:

> "And when the promise of the Latter Days comes to pass": That is resurrection [*al-ba'th*] after death. And some say: The descent of Jesus son of Mary.[60]

57 See e.g. Talmud Yerushalmi, XII, p. 383 (Sanhedrin 10:6): "Israel was exiled to three diasporas: one inside the river Sanbation, one to Daphne of Antiochia, and one on whom the Cloud descended and covered them".
58 See below, Chapter 5.
59 See also Thaʿlabī, *al-Kashf wa-l-bayān* (Q 17:104); Māwardī, *Nukat* (Q 17:104); Qurṭubī, *Aḥkām al-Qur'ān* (Q 17:104).
60 Fīrūzābādī, *Tanwīr al-miqbās* (Q 17:104).

The promise of the Latter Days and Constantinople

Other traditions which preserve the idea of Israel's return in order to fulfill the vision of redemption link "the promise of the Latter Days" in Q 17:104 to the vision of the redemption of the Muslims themselves. These traditions contain the eschatological vision of the fall of Constantinople, the fortified city that remained unconquered during the first centuries of Islam and only fell in the middle of the fifteenth century (1453 CE). Constantinople's endurance was not only a source of frustration for Muslims, but also raised fears of a counter-attack and conquest of the territories which had been taken from the Christians. Apart from these fears there was also hope for an apocalyptic victory that would bring that city, too, under the aegis of Islam. Constantinople thus became the new Promised Land which the believers did not yet inherit. Its hoped-for takeover was perceived as an event that would signal fulfillment of the vision of the return of the tribes of Israel in the Latter Days. This comes out in a number of traditions concerning the promise of the Latter Days.[61] One of these appears in a work devoted to apocalyptic traditions by Nuʿaym b. Ḥammād (d. 229/843):[62]

> . . . in the name of Kaʿb [al-Aḥbār] concerning the verse (Q 17:104), "And when the *waʿd al-ākhira* comes to pass. . .".: He said: Two tribes [*sibṭān*] of the Children of Israel that will fight on the day of the Great Battle [*al-malḥama al-ʿuẓmā*] and help Islam and its people.

Kaʿb al-Aḥbār (d. 32/652), to whom this tradition is attributed, was, as already noted previously, a Jewish convert to Islam who acquainted his Muslim colleagues with Jewish traditions. It preserves the basic meaning of *waʿd al-ākhira* as a prediction that the tribes of Israel would be brought back from their places of exile as warriors who would enter their holy land in the Latter Days. But now this land also includes Byzantine territories that had not yet been conquered by the Muslims. While the name of Constantinople is not mentioned explicitly, the term *al-malḥama*, or *al-malḥama al-ʿuẓmā*, in works that deal with the apocalyptic future denotes the fierce battle at the end of which that city would fall.[63] According to Kaʿb al-Aḥbār, two of the tribes of Israel would participate in that battle.[64]

---

61 Cf. Rubin, *Between Bible and Qur'an*, p. 24.

62 Nuʿaym b. Ḥammād, *Fitan*, p. 336 (no. 1260).

63 E.g. Ibn Kathīr, *al-Nihāya fī l-fitan*, p. 42.

64 There may be a reflection here of the two and a half tribes (Reuven, Gad, and the half-tribe of Manasseh) that formed a group of their own whose estate was to the east of Jordan rather than in Canaan itself. Their mission was to go armed before the Israelites and to assist them in the conquest of the land (Numbers 32:17–22). On the other hand, it should be noted that in other traditions, which are not related to Qur'ān exegesis, the participants in the Islamic campaign against

Sons of Moses

Another verse about the Children of Israel that was adapted to the fall of Constantinople in the messianic future was mentioned briefly in the discussion above (Q 7:159):

> Of the people of Moses (*qawm Mūsā*) there is a group (*umma*) [whose people are] guided by the truth, and by it act with justice.

The verse itself is very reminiscent of the biblical phraseology in Moses' blessing of the tribe of Levy (Deuteronomy 33:10):

> They teach Jacob your ordinances, and Israel your law.

We may surmise from this that the Qur'ān, too, when praising the *umma* of the people of Moses, alludes to the tribe of Levy.[65] The Qur'ān calls them *qawm Mūsā*, that is, people of the progeny of Moses' sons Gershom and Eliezer, and their numerous descendants of the tribe of Levy.[66] In Jewish tradition they are said to reside beyond the river Sambaṭyon.[67] Now we understand why Muqātil, too, associates the people of Moses of Q 7:159 with the same myth, as seen above.

In any event, the qur'ānic people of Moses are connected with the vision of Constantinople in the following tradition:

> . . . Ṣafwān b. ʿAmr said: "Of the people of Moses there is a group [whose people are] guided by the truth": By this are meant two tribes [*sibṭayn*] of the tribes of Israel on the day of the Great Battle [*al-malḥama al-ʿuẓmā*]. They will help Islam and its people.[68]

Constantinople are not the Children of Israel, but the children of Isaac. Rubin, *Between Bible and Qur'an*, pp. 30–31. This variant is recorded in Muslim, *Ṣaḥīḥ*, VIII, pp. 187–188 (*al-Fitan wa-ashrāṭ al-sāʿa* [52]). It takes the Israelites out of the picture and brings the children of Isaac into it, namely, the Rūm, descendants of Esau son of Isaac, who are destined to believe in Muḥammad in the Latter Days. For this meaning of the variant see Ibn Kathīr, *al-Nihāya fī l-fitan*, p. 46.

65 On the relationship between Q 7:159 and the sons of Levi in the blessing of Moses, see Rubin, "Children of Israel".

66 1 Chronicles 23:14–17: (14) but as for Moses the man of God, his sons were to be reckoned among the tribe of Levi. (15) The sons of Moses: Gershom and Eliezer. (16) The sons of Gershom: Shebuel the chief. (17) The sons of Eliezer: Rehabiah the chief; Eliezer had no other sons, but the sons of Rehabiah were very numerous.

67 In the Targum Pseudo-Jonathan (pp. 558–559, on Exodus 34:10), God decides to generate from Moses (i.e. from the Levites) "a multitude of the righteous" who will "go into captivity by the rivers of Babylon". See also *Bereshit Rabbati*, p. 124 (on Gen. 30:24): "The Levites sons of Moses, they are encamped beyond the river Sabaṭyon [Sambaṭyon]".

68 Ibn Abī Ḥātim, *Tafsīr* (Q 7:159).

This commentary is ascribed to a Syrian from Homs (*Ḥimṣ*), Ṣafwān b. ʿAmr (d. 100/718). He uses the accepted term Great Battle for the future war at Constantinople, and once again it is "two tribes" of the Children of Israel who will participate in it. Another tradition, again in Kaʿb al-Aḥbār's name, gives more details of this future battle against the Rūm, i.e. the Byzantines, including the following:

> Kaʿb: . . .The Muslims will pursue [the Rūm] and kill them on every plain and mountain. No shelter and no city will withstand them until they will come to Constantinople. Then a group (*umma*) of the people of Moses will join the Muslims and participate with them in the conquest. The Muslims will shout *Allāhu akbar* from one wing, and then the wall will crack and fall down, and the people will climb and enter Constantinople . . .[69]

We cannot ignore the similarity of this scene to the motif of the fall of the walls of Jericho at the gate of the Promised Land. Thus the scene is an apocalyptic version of the first conquest of that land. The tribes of Israel take part in the battle at Constantinople together with the Muslims, for the sake of Islam. In other words, the Muslim holy war fulfills the ancient task of the Children of Israel entering the Promised Land.

The Mahdī

Outside the exegetical context, the idea of the return of the Children of Israel in order to fulfill a messianic mission under the flag of Islam has also been preserved in traditions about the Mahdī, the Islamic Messiah. A tradition transmitted on the authority of Qatāda (d. 117/735) describes the Mahdī as follows: "A forty-year-old man who will seem as if he were a man of the Children of Israel" (*ka-annahu rajul min Banī Isrāʾīl*).[70] In another tradition, also in Qatāda's name, the Mahdī's advent is perceived as having already taken place, in the form of the caliph ʿUmar b. al-Khaṭṭāb (d. 24/644), during whose reign the Muslims first took control of Jerusalem:

> It used to be said that the Mahdī would be forty years old and would follow the conduct (*yaʿmalu bi-aʿmāl*) of the Children of Israel. If this was not ʿUmar, I do not know who it was.[71]

ʿUmar here seems to be perceived as the savior, who already accomplished in full the role assigned to the Children of Israel in the Islamic conquests.[72] Alternatively,

---

69 Nuʿaym b. Ḥammād, *Fitan*, p. 319. See also Rubin, *Between Bible and Qur'an*, p. 25.
70 Nuʿaym b. Ḥammād, *Fitan*, p. 258 (no. 1008).
71 Dānī, *Fitan*, V, p. 1074 (no. 588).
72 Another messianic title given to ʿUmar is "Iron Horn" (*Qarn min Ḥadīd*). See a comprehensive discussion in Hakim, "Biblical Annunciation", pp. 139–145.

in other traditions which present the Mahdī as a valiant man of the Children of Israel, it is stated that he will appear in Mecca, where all those residing in the Muslim world will pledge their allegiance to him.[73]

The foregoing discussion indicates that al-Shām's virtues as the land of redemption are discernable both in qur'ānic verses about the Israelites and in traditions about them. In the Qur'ān, the *wa'd al-ākhira* passage is consistent with the Messianic background of Muḥammad's nocturnal journey which we have already discussed in a previous chapter.[74] These verses — all in Q 17, which belongs to the Meccan period — illuminate the qur'ānic identification with the vision of the redemption of the Israelites. The contemporary Jews of the Prophet are thus expected to see him as the new redeemer and to join his ranks.

Moreover, we have already seen above that the idea of redemption is not confined to the framework of this world. Redemption is also expected to continue during the resurrection phase and Judgment Day. This idea, too, reveals aspects of al-Sham's sanctity. More about this in the next chapter.

73 Rubin, *Between Bible and Qur'an*, p. 44. See also Rubin, "The Ka'ba", p. 109.
74 See above, Chapter 1.

Part Three: **Land of Resurrection**

4 Resurrection in al-Shām

The Messianic Jewish vision of redemption in Palestine is also reflected in the Qur'ān, in the depictions of the resurrection and the Day of Judgment. These descriptions are based on pre-Islamic apocalyptic themes of the redemption of the displaced Israelites in Jerusalem. These themes were transformed in the Qur'ān into a vision of resurrection for all of God's creation. Traditions disseminated after the Muslims had arrived in al-Shām employed the qur'ānic resurrection motifs to establish and strengthen the status of Jerusalem and the Rock on the Temple Mount as the site where the resurrected would gather, and as the gate to heaven. The status of al-Shām as the arena of the resurrection is also revealed in two inscriptions, the Sde Boker inscription and the mosaic inscription in the Dome of the Rock.

A very thin line separates redemption from resurrection. The promise of *wa'd al-ākhira* to the Children of Israel, discussed in the previous chapter, can be understood not only as a promise of earthly redemption in their holy land, or al-Shām, in the Latter Days, but also as a promise of resurrection in the same land on the Day of Resurrection. Indeed, al-Shām's status as the place where the resurrected will gather is implicit in other qur'ānic verses and is made explicit in early Muslim tradition as well as in two early Islamic inscriptions. In the Qur'ān, the descriptions of the resurrection of the dead occupy a prominent place.[1] In what follows, we shall survey the resurrection process that these descriptions reveal and discuss their connection to al-Shām.

The Qur'ān: Resurrection upon the plain – *al-sāhira*

Several qur'ānic descriptions of the Day of Resurrection tell of a change in the situation of the earth in preparation for the rise of the dead from their graves. For example, in Q 18:47 we read:

> And on the day We shall set the mountains in motion, and you see the earth coming forth [*bāriza*], and We muster them [*wa-ḥasharnāhum*] so that We leave not so much as one of them behind.

The gathering of the resurrected is described with the verb *ḥashara*. Indeed, the root *ḥ-sh-r* serves elsewhere in the Qur'ān to describe the gathering of the dead

1 See Borrmans, "Resurrection"; Smith, "Eschatology"; Hasson, "Last Judgment"; Leemhuis, "Apocalypse".

https://doi.org/10.1515/9783111222318-005

who have arisen from their graves and are taken to be judged by God.[2] The root *n-sh-r* is also used in the context of bringing the dead out of their graves (Q 35:9; 67:15). In the present passage God promises to gather every one of the resurrected and leave no one in his grave. The in-gathering will take place on a plain from which God has removed the mountains. The following passage states the same (Q 20:105–108):

> (105) They will question you concerning the mountains. Say: 'My Lord will scatter them as ashes, (106) then leave them a plain, smooth level (*qāʿ ṣafṣaf*), (107) wherein you will see no crookedness neither any curving.' (108) On that day they will follow the crier (*al-dāʿī*), not straying from him; voices will be hushed to the all-merciful, so that you hear nothing but a murmuring.

In this passage, the resurrected dead who will follow the "crier" (see below) will pass through leveled ground which God will create after crushing the mountains there. The transformation of the surface leads to the creation of a new earth (Q 14:48):

> (48) Upon the day the earth shall be changed [*tubaddal*] to other than the earth, and the heavens as well, and they shall come uncovered [*wa-barazū*] before God, the one, the omnipotent. (49) And you shall see the sinners that day coupled in fetters . . .

The exegete Muqātil b. Sulaymān (d. 150/767) explains that when the dead rise from their graves they will not be able to hide from God, because the ground will be level (*mustawiya*) and stretched out (*mamdūda*), with no mountains, vegetation or anything else on it.[3] A similar explanation is offered on the authority of Ibn ʿAbbās:

> [The land] will be stretched like skin [*adīm*], its mountains, hills, trees and everything on it will disappear, until "you will see no crookedness neither any curving" (Q 20:107).[4]

The changed land may perhaps echo Isaiah 65:17: "For I am about to create new heavens and a new earth". A number of scholars have also pointed to the following passage in the New Testament:[5]

> (1) Then I saw a new heaven and a new earth; for the first heaven and the first earth had passed away, and the sea was no more. (2) And I saw the holy city, the new Jerusalem, coming down out of heaven from God, prepared as a bride adorned for her husband. 3 And I

2 E.g. Q 19:85; 50:44. And see Hasson, "Last Judgment".
3 Muqātil, *Tafsīr* (Q 14:48).
4 Abū Ḥayyān, *al-Baḥr al-muḥīṭ* (Q 14:48)
5 Speyer, *Die biblischen Erzählungen*, p. 454.

> heard a loud voice from the throne saying, "See, the home of God is among mortals. He will dwell with them; they will be his peoples, and God himself will be with them".[6]

Here the idea of a new earth is associated with that of a new Jerusalem that will descend from heaven and represent God's throne that will dwell among the people. However, it is doubtful whether the changed earth in the above-quoted qur'ānic passage is connected to the idea of the new earth descending from heaven.

In the following passage the flat, desolate and exposed plain created by the removal of the mountains receives a special name, *al-sāhira* (Q 79:6–14):

> (6) Upon the day when the quaking one *(al-rājifa)* quakes (7) and the second one *(al-rādifa)* follows it, (8) hearts upon that day shall palpitate (9) and their eyes shall be humbled. (10) They shall say, 'What, are we being restored as we were before? (11) What, when we are bones old and wasted?' (12) They shall say, 'That then were a losing return!' (13) But it shall be only a single cry, (14) and behold, they are upon the *sāhira*.

As in previous passages, here, too, the process of resurrection begins with a change in the form of the earth, through two earthquakes, followed by a single "cry".[7] Some exegetes interpret the first two "quakes" as sounds of the trumpet, separated by forty years; in other words, the trumpet is blown three times.[8] On the other hand, Q 6:73 mentions only a single trumpet blast.[9]

In the present passage the new earth that will be formed is called *al-sāhira*, a word derived from the root *s-h-r*, whose basic meaning is wakefulness.[10] In this spirit, the exegete Qatāda (d. 117/735) explains that *al-sāhira* is an epithet of Hell, where the unbelievers will remain awake forever.[11] However, the same exegete maintains elsewhere that it is the surface of the earth, where those resurrected from death will arise from their graves.[12] Muqātil refines this observation, explaining that *al-sāhira* is the name of the new earth (*al-arḍ al-jadīda*) "which will be extended over this earth, and Allāh will yank (the old earth) from under it, like one yanks off an old, worn garment".[13] According to a different interpretation, *al-sāhira* in Arabic is a desert or a prairie (*falāt*).[14] In line with the basic meaning of the root *s-h-r*, wakefulness, the latter interpretation explains that

---

6 Revelation 21:1–3.
7 In Arabic, *zajra*; lit. "the driving away with a cry".
8 See Muqātil, *Tafsīr* (Q 79:14).
9 On the blast of the trumpet, see Smith, "Eschatology"; Hasson, "Last Judgment"; Leemhuis, "Apocalypse".
10 See Ambros, *A Concise Dictionary*, p. 140.
11 E.g. Ṭabarī, *Tafsīr* (Q 79:14); Ibn ʿAṭiyya, *Tafsīr* (Q 79:14).
12 Ṭabarī, *Tafsīr* (Q 79:14).
13 Muqātil, *Tafsīr* (Q 79:14).
14 Ṭabarī, *Tafsīr* (Q 79:14).

such land is called *sāhira* because there is no sleep there (*dhāt sahar*) and because it frightens those who traverse it by night.[15] According to Mujāhid (d. 104/722), one of the earliest commentators of the Qur'ān, *al-sāhira* is a level place (*al-makān al-mustawī*).[16]

Pre-Islamic Jewish apocalypse

The scene of resurrection associated with a change in the contours of the land reflects pre-Islamic themes that revolve around Jerusalem. First of all, already in the Book of Zerubbabel, discussed in the previous chapter, the return of the generation of the wilderness and Koraḥ's congregation to their holy land is accompanied by a great earthquake that smites the land and the sea. A transformation of the earth's surface is already described in the Hebrew Bible, in the following depiction of God's arrival in Jerusalem in the Latter Days, in order to redeem His people (Isaiah 40:3–4):

> (3) A voice cries out: In the wilderness prepare the way of the Lord, make straight in the desert a highway for our God. (4) Every valley shall be lifted up, and every mountain and hill be made low; the uneven ground shall become level, and the rough places a plain.

God's path to Jerusalem passes through a plain that was formed after the mountains were removed from it and its valleys became level. Such process is also described in Zechariah 14:3–4:

> (3) Then the Lord will go forth and fight against those nations as when he fights on a day of battle. (4) On that day his feet shall stand on the Mount of Olives, which lies before Jerusalem on the east; and the Mount of Olives shall be split in two from east to west by a very wide valley; so that one half of the Mount shall withdraw northward, and the other half southward.

And later in the same chapter:

> (9) And the Lord will become king over all the earth; on that day the Lord will be one and his name one. (10) The whole land shall be turned into a plain . . .

Zechariah describes two stages in the transformation of the land's surface when God appears on earth: First the Mount of Olives will be split into two parts, with a broad valley between them, and then the land will become a plain. Zechariah's vision of the splitting of the Mount of Olives reappears in early Jewish apocalyptic

15 Qurṭubī, *Aḥkām al-Qur'ān* (Q 79:14).
16 Mujāhid, *Tafsīr* (Q 79:14).

literature, where it is joined to the idea of the redemption of the tribes of Israel and their return to their homeland. According to one such work, *Pesikta Rabbati*, the people of Israel will return from their places of exile via tunnels that God will make for them. They will journey along those tunnels until they rise out of the ground in the valley that will be formed after the splitting of the Mount of Olives:[17]

> . . . the Holy One, blessed be He, will make passageway after passageway for them, and they will find their way underground through them, until they arrive under the Mount of Olives which is in Jerusalem. And the Holy One, blessed be He, will stand upon the mount, and after it is cleaved open for the exiles, they will come up out of it. As Zechariah says, *and His feet shall stand in that day upon the Mount of Olives, which is before Jerusalem on the east, and the Mount of Olives shall be cleft in the midst thereof toward the east and toward the west*, etc. (Zechariah 14:4).[18]

According to the Talmud Bavli, tunnels will also be the means whereby the resurrected will reach the Land of Israel.[19] An early expression of the aspiration for resurrection in the Land of Israel can be found in Ezekiel 37:12:

> Therefore prophesy, and say to them, Thus says the Lord God: I am going to open your graves, and bring you up from your graves, O my people; and I will bring you back to the land of Israel.

In line with this verse, it is said about "our teachers in the diaspora" that "the Holy One, praised be He, makes the earth erode before them and they roll like wine barrels. When they arrive at the land of Israel their souls return to them".[20] Hence the benefit of being buried in the Land of Israel which saves the need to "roll" through the tunnels.[21]

All of the above leads us to conclude that the qur'ānic depiction of the transformation of the face of the earth in preparation for the resurrection of the dead, who will rise from their graves onto level ground, constitutes a reshaping of the pre-Islamic Jewish apocalypse. The latter revolves around Israel's redemption in

17 On the early date of the core material of the *Pesikta Rabbati* (from the fifth or sixth century Palestine), see Ulmer, *Pesiqta Rabbati*, I, pp. xv-xviii; Grossmann, "Jerusalem in the Jewish Apocalypse", pp. 242–243; Hoyland, *Seeing Islam*, pp. 312–313.

18 *Pesikta Rabbati*, II, p. 617 (Piska 31). See also Eisenstein, *Ozar Midrashim*, I, p. 91. The scene of the opening of the Mount of Olives and the coming out of the exiles is found also in one of the versions of the Book of Zerubbabel. Grossmann, "Jerusalem in the Jewish Apocalypse", p. 239. Cf. Even-Shmuel, *Midrashei Geula*, p. 84.

19 Talmud Bavli, Kethuboth 111a: . . . R. Elai replied: [They will be revived] by rolling [to the Land of Israel] . . . Abaye replied: Cavities will be made for them underground.

20 Talmud Yerushalmi, III, p. 312 (Kilaim 9:4).

21 For studies about the bringing of the dead from the diaspora for burial in the land of Israel see Oppenheimer/Lecker, "Boundaries of Babylonia", p. 182, note 51.

Jerusalem, specifically on the Mount of Olives, where the dispersed of Israel will come from their places of exile by rolling through tunnels. In the qur'ānic version redemption is universal and is retold in order to foster the idea of resurrection and promote the general argument for reward and punishment that will be applied in the world to come. Thus the qur'ānic scene of resurrection testifies to the presence of the underlying Jewish idea of messianic redemption in Jerusalem.

Here we may add that the blowing of the trumpet which in the Qur'ān signals the resurrection (see above), marks in the Hebrew Bible the return of the dispersed of Israel to their homeland, as we read in Isaiah 27:13:

> And on that day a great trumpet will be blown, and those who were lost in the land of Assyria and those who were driven out to the land of Egypt will come and worship the Lord on the holy mountain at Jerusalem.

This time the culmination is on the Temple Mount, and in the previous chapter we saw that this verse was also associated with the future return of the ten tribes and the generation of the wilderness. However, in the New Testament the blowing of trumpet is associated with the resurrection:

> . . . in a moment, in the twinkling of an eye, at the last trumpet. For the trumpet will sound, and the dead will be raised imperishable . . .[22]

From this it is a short distance to associating the trumpet with the Day of Resurrection, as the Qurān does.

Furthermore, it would seem that when the pre-Islamic apocalyptic themes of redemption in the Latter Days were appropriated, the place of the events remained unchanged. Admittedly, the Qur'ān does not provide an explicit location for the resurrection, but it must be remembered that opacity is a feature that is typical of qur'ānic style. Therefore, the possibility cannot be ruled out that the implicit qur'ānic place of resurrection is Jerusalem.

The traditions: The *sāhira* and the *baqīʿ* in al-Shām

Traditions disseminated after the Muslims' arrival in Jerusalem strengthen the link between the qur'ānic resurrection and sites in that city. We refer mainly to traditions to the effect that the *sāhira* is in Bayt al-Maqdis.[23] In one of these traditions,

22 1 Corinthians 15:52.

23 See Schwarzbaum, *Folkloristic Aspects*, pp. 25–27; Livne-Kafri, *Selected Essays*, pp. 53–54; Elad, *Medieval Jerusalem*, pp. 141–144.

from which we quoted in the previous two chapters, the Prophet predicts to several of his Companions that on the Day of Resurrection the people will be gathered (*yuḥsharu*) in groups (*fawjan lafīfan*) and will come to a region called *al-sāhira* in the vicinity of Bayt al-Maqdis. The area will be vast enough to contain all the people.[24] This tradition accords with the explanation that *sāhira* is a wide open plain (*al-arḍ al-ʿarīḍa al-basīṭa*).[25] The *sāhira* is associated with Jerusalem already in Mujāhid's *Tafsīr*, where a tradition is quoted about Wahb b. Munabbih (d. 110/728), an expert on biblical traditions. He was in Bayt al-Maqdis and he reportedly announced that this was the location of the *sāhira*.[26] In another version, Wahb declares that the *sāhira* is a mountain in al-Shām, which Allāh will stretch and level for the gathering (*ḥashr*) of the resurrected.[27] Other traditions maintain that the *sāhira* is "in the region between Mount Ḥassān and Mount Jericho, and God will stretch it (*yamudduhu*) as much as he will want".[28]

A particularly precise identification is provided by the Jerusalemite Ibrāhīm b. Abī ʿAbla al-Maqdisī (d. 152/769). He states that the *sāhira* is the *baqīʿ* ("the broad area") located at the side of the Mount of Olives.[29] In the same vein, Mujīr al-Dīn al-Ḥanbalī (d. 928/1522) reports that the *sāhira* is the *baqīʿ* to the west of the mountain,[30] although he also relates that "*al-baqīʿ* known as al-*sāhira* is outside of al-Quds, to the north, and in it is a cemetery in which the Muslim dead are buried". This cemetery is on a high hill, above a cave that is used by a Ṣūfī order as a site for its rites.[31] Al-Minhājī (d. 880/1475), on the other hand, says that on the Mount of Olives itself, on the side that faces the *sāhira*, there are pilgrimage sites (*mazārāt*) which the people visit, such as the tomb of the ascetic woman (*zāhida*) Rābiʿa bint Ismāʿīl al-ʿAdawiyya (d. 135/753) on the summit of the mountain.[32]

24 Wāsiṭī, *Faḍā'il*, p. 88 (no. 142). See also Ibn al-Murajjā, *Faḍā'il*, pp. 234–235 (no. 347). Minhājī, *Itḥāf al-akhiṣṣā*, I, pp. 221–222.

25 Minhājī, *Itḥāf al-akhiṣṣā*, I, p. 222.

26 Mujāhid, *Tafsīr* (Q 79:14).

27 Ibn ʿAṭiyya, *Tafsīr* (Q 79:14). See also Abū Ḥayyān, *al-Baḥr al-muḥīṭ* (Q 79:14). Cf. Ṭabarī, *Tafsīr* (Q 79:14). See also Livne-Kafri, "Jerusalem in Early Islam", p. 391.

28 Ṭabarī, *Tafsīr* (Q 79:14).

29 Wāsiṭī, *Faḍā'il*, p. 48 (no. 71). See also Ibn al-Jawzī, *Ta'rīkh Bayt al-Maqdis*, p. 65; Ibn al-Murajjā, *Faḍā'il*, p. 235 (no. 348); Livne-Kafri, "Jerusalem in Early Islam", p. 391. In this version of Ibn Abī ʿAbla, the Baqīʿ, which is identified with the *sāhira*, is located "under the monastery on the road that leads to Bayt al-Maqdis".

30 Mujīr al-Dīn, *al-Uns al-jalīl*, II, p. 62.

31 *Ibid.*, pp. 63, 64.

32 Minhājī, *Itḥāf al-akhiṣṣā*, I, pp. 222–223. Cf. Gil, History *of Palestine*, p. 629.

The merits of being buried in Bayt al-Maqdis and in al-Shām

The identification of the Mount of Olives or its close vicinity with the *sāhira* preserves that mountain's role in the messianic future as depicted in Jewish sources. The Muslims did indeed preserve the memory of the Mount of Olive's sanctity, including its status as the place from which Jesus ascended to heaven.[33] But the area in which the resurrection was to take place eventually spread beyond the Mount of Olives itself to encompass the entire holy city and its cemeteries, the largest of which was the cemetery (*maqbara*) of Māmillā (Mamilla), located outside the city and to the west of Jerusalem. An early name for this site was Zaytūn al-Milla,[34] and al-Ḥasan [al-Baṣrī?] (d. 110/728) is quoted as saying that anyone who is buried in Bayt al-Maqdis in Zaytūn al-Millā is considered as if he was buried in the first heaven (*al-samāʾ al-dunyā*).[35] The scholar ʿAbd al-Razzāq (d. 211/827) declared that he had heard that Zaytūn al-Millā was a garden (*rawḍa*) of Paradise.[36] Moshe Gil, in a discussion of Muslim pilgrimage to Jerusalem in the eleventh century and of Muslim sources from that period came to the conclusion that the traditions quoted above show that Muslim tradition "adopted the [Jewish] idea of the preference of being buried in Jerusalem".[37] However, as we can now see, this idea has much older roots, going back to the first century AH, not to speak of the fact that the Jewish view on the merits of burial in the Land of Israel (which saves the dead the trouble of rolling through the tunnels upon their resurrection) is much older than the emergence of Islam.[38]

As for the entire area of Bayt al-Maqdis, the traditions that speak highly of burial there are also early, appearing already in Muqātil's *Tafsīr*. One such tradition states that whoever dies in Bayt al-Maqdis "is as if he died in heaven, and whoever dies in the region surrounding Bayt al-Maqdis is as if he died within it".[39] In the name of Kaʿb al-Aḥbār (d. 32/652), it was related that whoever was

33 E.g. Ibn al-Murajjā, *Faḍāʾil*, p. 236 (no. 349). See also Elad, *Medieval Jerusalem*, p. 144. And see *ibid.*, note 334, references to studies about the sanctity of the Mount of Olives in Judaism and Christianity as appropriated in Islam.

34 Mujīr al-Dīn, *al-Uns al-jalīl*, II, p. 64. Cf. Gil, *History of Palestine*, p. 634.

35 Mujīr al-Dīn, *al-Uns al-jalīl*, II, p. 64.

36 Ibn al-Jawzī, *Taʾrīkh Bayt al-Maqdis*, pp. 65–66.

37 Gil, History of Palestine, p. 633.

38 Oppenheimer/Lecker, "Boundaries of Babylonia", p. 182.

39 Muqātil, *Addendum*, p. 513. See also Ibn al-Murajjā, *Faḍāʾil*, p. 259; Ibn al-Jawzī, *Taʾrīkh Bayt al-Maqdis*, p. 65 (in the name of Kaʿb al-Aḥbār), pp. 70–71 (from Muqātil); Rubin, *Muḥammad the Prophet*, II, p. 251; Livne-Kafri, *Selected Essays*, p. 60.

buried in Bayt al-Maqdis was sure to traverse "the bridge" (*al-ṣirāṭ*) safely.[40] The *ṣirāṭ* leads the righteous from Bayt al-Maqdis to Paradise and the wicked to Hell.[41] Crossing this bridge safely is a test of one's piety and ensures entrance to Paradise. A tradition in Wahb b. Munabbih's name also extols the merits of burial in Bayt al-Maqdis and states that whoever is buried there will be spared "the trials and tribulations of the grave" (*min fitnat al-qabr wa-ḍīqihi*).[42] By the latter are meant the torments of the grave (*ʿadhāb al-qabr*), i.e. the punishments meted out by the angel of death and the two interrogating angels (Munkar and Nakīr) who awaken the dead in the grave and put them through a variety of trials and torments.

Even just being in Jerusalem was declared praiseworthy in connection with the resurrection and the world to come. Thus Muḥammad stated that "Whoever visits Jerusalem, desiring nothing else (*muḥtasiban*), Allāh will grant him the recompense of a thousand martyrs (*shahīd*)".[43] According to another version "Allāh will forbid the fire of Hell to harm the flesh of his body".[44] It was also said that whoever manages to patiently bear the hardships of living in Jerusalem for one year, Allāh will provide for his livelihood and he will enter Paradise.[45] Kaʿb al-Aḥbār states that Allāh said of Jerusalem that it was His garden, His holiness and His chosen place, and that whoever resides in it will enjoy His mercy and whoever leaves it will suffer His anger.[46] According to Wahb, the residents of Jerusalem are God's "neighbors" (*jīrān*), whom He is obliged to protect.[47]

In addition to the virtues of death and burial in Jerusalem as the site of the resurrection, there are traditions that praise other burial sites throughout al-Shām as ensuring full redemption on the Day of Resurrection for those who are buried there. Some of these traditions mention the typological number seventy thousand to indicate the huge number of resurrected people who will be redeemed. This number is commonly encountered in traditions that deal with the merits of various groups in Islam (such as the Shīʿīs) who will enter Paradise

---

40 Ibn al-Jawzī, *Taʾrīkh Bayt al-Maqdis*, p. 65. See also Rubin, *Muḥammad the Prophet*, II, p. 251; Livne-Kafri, *Selected Essays*, p. 60.

41 Muqātil, *Addendum*, p. 514. See also Ibn al-Murajjā, *Faḍāʾil*, p. 261; Minhājī, *Itḥāf al-akhiṣṣā*, I, p. 107.

42 Ibn al-Jawzī, *Taʾrīkh Bayt al-Maqdis*, p. 65. See also Livne-Kafri, *Selected Essays*, p. 60.

43 Mujīr al-Dīn, *al-Uns al-jalīl*, I, p. 229; Rubin, *Muḥammad the Prophet*, II, p. 251.

44 Mujīr al-Dīn, *al-Uns al-jalīl*, I, p. 229; Rubin, *Muḥammad the Prophet*, II, p. 251.

45 Mujīr al-Dīn, *al-Uns al-jalīl*, I, p. 240; Rubin, *Muḥammad the Prophet*, II, p. 251.

46 Mujīr al-Dīn, *al-Uns al-jalīl*, I, p. 228. Rubin, *Muḥammad the Prophet*, II, p. 251.

47 Mujīr al-Dīn, *al-Uns al-jalīl*, I, p. 232. The same is said about the people of Mecca. See Rubin, *Muḥammad the Prophet*, II, p. 251.

directly.[48] However, here we will concentrate on the seventy thousand motif as used for ranking the degree of sanctity of the various resurrection sites. For example, Kaʿb al-Aḥbār is quoted as saying that in the cemetery of Bāb al-Farādīs (in Damascus) seventy thousand martyrs will be resurrected (*yubʿathu*), each of whom will intercede (*yashfaʿūn*) for another seventy thousand.[49] ʿUmar b. al-Khaṭṭāb related that the Prophet had said that in the vicinity of the city of Homs in Syria seventy thousand people would be resurrected and would not be interrogated on the Day of Judgment. ʿUmar himself intended to settle in this city with his family, at a time when all of Syria suffered from a plague epidemic.[50] Concerning the cemetery of Ashkelon (ʿAsqalān) the Prophet is quoted as saying that seventy thousand martyrs will be resurrected there, each of whom will be able to intercede for as many people as are in the Arab tribes of Rabīʿa and Muḍar.[51]

About Bāniqyā (in the Kūfa region), a site on Abraham's route from Babylonia to the Promised Land, it was said that Abraham had informed his companion that Allāh would in the future resurrect seventy thousand on that location, that they would enter Paradise without being interrogated or judged, and that each of them would intercede for an unspecified number of people.[52] Bāniqyā was located west of the Euphrates river, in a place called Tarbiqna, which in the Talmudic period was deemed to belong to the Land of Israel; therefore already at that time being buried there was considered a virtue.[53]

As for the city of Kūfa near Bāniqyā, it was reported that the Jews believed that seventy thousand of their dead in the local Jewish cemetery on the outskirts of the town would be resurrected and would enter Paradise without being interrogated. When ʿAlī b. Abī Ṭālib heard this from the Exilarch (*raʾs al-jālūt*) he decided that this was a merit due to Muslim (i.e. Shīʿī) believers only, and therefore purchased the area from the local owners.[54]

Some traditions mention slightly different numbers. Of the city of Homs it was said that the Prophet had declared that Allāh would resurrect ninety thousand of its inhabitants and that they would be exempt from judgment.[55]

---

48 For details see Rubin, *Muḥammad the Prophet*, II, pp. 253–256, 274–275.

49 Ibn ʿAsākir, *Taʾrīkh Dimashq*, II, p. 410. See also Rubin, *Muḥammad the Prophet*, II, p. 255.

50 Ḥākim, *Mustadrak*, III, pp. 88–89; Rubin, *Muḥammad the Prophet*, II, p. 255.

51 Suyūṭī, *Laʾāliʾ*, I, p. 460; Rubin, *Muḥammad the Prophet*, II, p. 255.

52 Ṣadūq, *ʿIlal*, p. 585 (no. 30); Rubin, *Muḥammad the Prophet*, II, p. 255.

53 Oppenheimer/Lecker, "Boundaries of Babylonia", p. 182.

54 Kister, "Sanctity Joint and Divided", p. 33. The owner may have been the Exilarch himself. For properties in the area of al-Kūfa, owned by the Exilarch at the beginning of Islam, see Lecker, "The Exilarch's Dams".

55 Haythamī, *Majmaʿ al-zawāʾid*, X, p. 411; Rubin, *Muḥammad the Prophet*, II, pp. 255–256.

The merits of burial sites in al-Shām were promoted in traditions that do not contain numerical motifs. Thus the Prophet is quoted as saying that the people who were buried in the cemetery of Ashkelon would hurry to Paradise, like a bride who hurries to her groom.[56] In another tradition the Prophet reportedly stated that whoever stays in Ashkelon for the task of *ribāṭ* (being stationed on the enemy's frontier), even if he were to spend all his time there asleep, Allāh would appoint angels who would pray in his stead, and he would be resurrected together with those who did pray and would enter Paradise.[57] The Prophet also reportedly declared that whoever stayed in Ashkelon for only one day and died within sixty years of that day, would be considered a *shahīd*, even if he died in the land of the unbelievers.[58] The same is said of those who visit Abraham's tomb in Hebron (al-Khalīl), where God will gather the resurrected and protect them from the tribulations of the Day of Judgment.[59] Those buried in Ramla will also enjoy a special status on the Day of Resurrection.[60]

Jerusalem's status as the arena of the resurrection is mentioned explicitly in other traditions as well.[61] The tradition quoted below gives Jerusalem the name *arḍ al-maḥshar wa-l-manshar* ("land of gathering and resurrection"):[62]

> From Maymūna the Prophet's freed-slave. She said: Give us a ruling concerning [pilgrimage] to Bayt al-Maqdis. He [the Prophet] said: That is the land of gathering and resurrection. Come to it and pray there, for one prayer there is worth a thousand prayers elsewhere. [Maymūna said]: I said: What do you think I should do if I cannot bear the hardship of the journey there? He said: Send a gift of oil to light a lamp there. Anyone who does so, is counted as if he were there.[63]

In Muḥammad's dialogue with Maymūna, one version of which was discussed in a previous chapter,[64] the status of Bayt al-Maqdis as the locus of the resurrection is presented as the main feature that justifies pilgrimage to it. This status is also reflected in the epithet "resurrection zone" (*'arṣat al-qiyāma*) given to Bayt al-Maqdis.[65]

---

56 Suyūṭī, *La'āli'*, I, p. 460; Rubin, *Muḥammad the Prophet*, II, p. 251.
57 Suyūṭī, *La'āli'*, I, p. 462; Rubin, *Muḥammad the Prophet*, II, p. 251.
58 Suyūṭī, *La'āli'*, I, p. 462; Rubin, *Muḥammad the Prophet*, II, p. 251.
59 Kister, "Sanctity Joint and Divided", pp. 28–29.
60 Kister, "Sanctity Joint and Divided", p. 22.
61 See Livne-Kafri, "The Navel of the Earth", pp. 49, 61, 65.
62 On this title see Kister, "Three Mosques", p. 185.
63 Ibn Māja, *Sunan*, I, p. 451 (5:196), no. 1407. See also Livne-Kafri, *Selected Essays*, p. 48; *idem*, "In Praise of Jerusalem", pp. 182–183.
64 See above, Chapter 2. In the present version Maymūna who is identified as Muḥammad's freed-slave (*mawlāt al-nabī*) is Maymūna bint Sa'd. Muḥammad's wife was Maymūna bint al-Ḥārith.
65 See Yāqūt, *Mu'jam al-buldān*, V, p. 169 (s.v. al-Maqdis).

The merits of al-Shām and Umayyad interests

Jerusalem's status as the place where the resurrected will be gathered was especially useful to the Umayyad rulers, who sought to encourage the believers to come to al-Shām. A clear example of this can be found in the following story about Muʿāwiya b. Abī Sufyān (d. 60/680), the first Umayyad caliph. Here he is presented as taking pride in the merits of al-Shām, although he was also sharply criticized by his detractors. One of the latter was a Shīʿī supporter of ʿAlī named Ṣaʿṣaʿa b. Ṣūḥān (d. 44/666):

> . . . A delegation of people from Iraq came to Muʿāwiya, among them Ṣaʿṣaʿa b. Ṣūḥān. Muʿāwiya said to them: Welcome. You have come to the best of places; you have come to the best caliph, and he is a shield (*junna*) over you; you have come to the Holy Land (*al-arḍ al-muqaddasa*), and you have come to the land of the gathering and resurrection (*arḍ al-maḥshar wa-l-manshar*); you have come to a land containing the graves of the prophets. Ṣaʿṣaʿa said: You said, 'You have come to the best of places', but this is said only to whoever comes to Allāh and Allāh is pleased with him [in Paradise]. You said, 'You have come to your caliph, who is your shield'. What kind of shield will this be for us when it is consumed by fire? You said, 'You have come to the holy land', but the land does not make its inhabitants holy, only its inhabitants make it holy. You said, 'You have come to the land of the gathering and the resurrection', but being far from it will not help the unbeliever, nor will it harm the believer. You said, 'you have come to the land of the prophets, which contains the graves of the prophets', but more Pharaohs [i.e. wicked unbelievers] have been buried there than prophets. Muʿāwiya said, Be silent, may you not have a land! [Ṣaʿṣaʿa] said, Nor you, Muʿāwiya. The land belongs to Allāh and he will bequeath it to whomever he desires from among his servants. Muʿāwiya said, I have always hated you as an orator. [Ṣaʿṣaʿa] said, And I always hated you as caliph.[66]

The merits which Muʿāwiya enumerates constitute the essence of the traditions concerning al-Shām as the land of the resurrection. The Shīʿī however, does not share his views. As a Shīʿī, he must have held that other places, like al-Kūfa in Iraq, surpassed the earthly Jerusalem in sanctity (see above, Chapter 1, note 15).

---

66 Ibn al-Faqīh, *Buldān*, p. 164. See also Ibn ʿAsākir, *Taʾrīkh Dimashq*, XXIV p. 93. See a shorter version in Balādhurī, *Ansāb*, V, p. 38. Cf. Hasson, "Last Judgment". See also Livne-Kafri, "In Praise of Jerusalem", p. 184; *idem*, *Selected Essays*, pp. 47–48, 97–98; Elad, "The Status of Jerusalem", pp. 27–28.

God's descent to pass judgment in Jerusalem

Jerusalem is not only the site of the resurrection, but also of God's descent to earth on the Day of Judgment. Signs of this can already be found in the Qurʾān itself (Q 39:68–69):[67]

> (68) For the trumpet shall be blown, and whosoever is in the heavens and whosoever is in the earth shall swoon, save whom God wills. Then it shall be blown again, and lo, they shall stand, beholding. (69) And the earth shall shine with the light of its Lord, and the book shall be set in place, and the prophets and witnesses shall be brought, and justly the issue be decided between them, and they not wronged.

The resurrection here is accompanied by two blows of the trumpet. According to some commentators, the first will cause those who emerge from their graves to faint or to die again. Then a second blow of the trumpet will revive everyone. After the trumpet blows the book of everyone's deeds on earth will be presented.[68] God's descent from on high is hinted at by the light that He will bring to the earth. His descent marks the opening of the trial itself, in which everyone will be judged by what is inscribed in the book of that person's deeds. Then the prophets and the other witnesses will come forth, and finally a just ruling will be pronounced over every one of the resurrected.

A further intimation of the idea of God's descent can be discerned in the words of the exegete Muqātil about the verse just quoted. He states that the light that will shine on the earth will come out of God's leg. God's leg, Muqātil points out, is also mentioned in Q 68:42: "Upon the day when the leg shall be bared (*yukshafu ʿan sāq*), and they shall be summoned to bow themselves, but they cannot".[69] In his commentary on the latter verse, Muqātil quotes an exegetical tradition related on the authority of the Prophet's Companion ʿAbdallāh b. Masʿūd (d. 32/652), according to which the leg that will be bared is God's right leg, which will throw its light upon the face of the earth.[70] Of course, this rather crude anthropomorphism is rejected by most exegetes of the Qurʾān, who offer metaphorical interpretations of the leg that will be bared.

The theme of light caused by the descent of heavenly figures can also be found in pre-Islamic sources. In the New Testament the earth is lit when an angel

---

67 On this passage, see Smith, "Eschatology".

68 On the book in which the deeds are recorded see Smith, "Eschatology"; Hasson, "Last Judgment".

69 Muqātil, *Tafsīr* (Q 39:69).

70 Muqātil, *Tafsīr* (Q 68:42).

descends from heaven.[71] God's descent from heaven in order to pass judgment on earth is described in Joel 3 [4]: 1–2:

> (1) For then, in those days and at that time, when I restore the fortunes of Judah and Jerusalem, (2) I will gather all the nations and bring them down to the valley of Jehoshaphat, and I will enter into judgment with them there, on account of my people and my heritage Israel, because they have scattered them among the nations. They have divided my land.

In this description God descends to Jerusalem in order to avenge Himself on Israel's enemies and redeem His nation. The site to which God descends has the symbolic name Jehoshaphat (Hebrew: "God judged"). There He will put the nations on trial. The trial will take place after God gathers all the world's nations there. In view of this description, it is quite possible that in the Qur'ān, too, God's descent as judge is meant to be in Jerusalem, although not in order to save Israel from its enemies but in order to judge all of his creation on the Day of Judgment.

While the Qur'ān is opaque with respect to the place where God will spread His light when He descends to earth, traditions very explicitly maintain that it is Jerusalem. These traditions assign a special standing to the Rock (al-Ṣakhra), due to its status as the navel of the earth. Previously we saw its role as the point from where the Prophet and God Himself ascended to heaven.[72] The traditions we discuss now tell us that on the Day of Resurrection the Rock will also be the place where God will descend and on which He will pass judgment on the resurrected. One such tradition appears in Yāqūt's (d. 626/1229) geographical lexicon (*Mu'jam al-buldān*) in the entry on Jerusalem (al-Maqdis). This version quotes Abū Mālik al-Quraẓī, a Medinan Jew and a contemporary of Muḥammad, who was known for his command of Jewish scripture:[73]

> Abū Mālik al-Quraẓī said: In the book of the Jews [the Torah] which has not been perverted it is noted that Allāh created the earth, looked at it and said: I will now set foot (*wāṭi'*) on your face. Then the mountains rose but the Rock lowered itself (*tawāḍa'a*). God thanked it and said: This is the place where I will stand, the place of my scales, my Paradise and my Hellfire, and the gathering place of my creatures (*wa-maḥshar khalqī*), and I am the judge of the Day of Judgment.[74]

In this tradition the Rock is called *maḥshar*, that is, the place of gathering of the resurrected. It also features as the navel of the earth, where Paradise and Hell are

71 See Revelation 18:1: "(1) After this I saw another angel coming down from heaven, having great authority; and the earth was made bright with his splendor".

72 See above, Chapter 2.

73 See Lecker, "Abū Mālik".

74 Yāqūt, *Mu'jam al-buldān*, V, p. 167 (s.v. al-Maqdis). Another version is traced back to Wahb b. Munabbih. See Ibn al-Jawzī, *Ta'rīkh Bayt al-Maqdis*, p. 53.

located and to which God will descend and judge His creatures with the scales of justice, each one according to his deeds,[75] to be sent either to Paradise or to Hell. This function of the Rock is stated already in the Torah and was determined at the time when the world was created. Other traditions relate that the people will be dispersed (*yaftariqu*), either to Paradise or to Hell. The traditions find hints for this dispersal in two qur'ānic verses, Q 30:14 ("Upon the day when the hour is come, that day they shall be divided") and Q 30:43 ("on that day they shall be sundered apart").[76]

Another tradition about God's descent also quotes the Torah. Nawf al-Bikālī, a nephew of Ka'b al-Aḥbār, the Jewish convert to Islam, told the Umayyad caliph 'Abd al-Malik the following story about Bayt al-Maqdis:

> In Allāh's book that was sent down from heaven [the Torah] it is written that Allāh says: In you [in Bayt al-Maqdis] there are six qualities [*khiṣāl*]: In you will be the place where I will stand (*maqāmī*), [in you] I will settle accounts [with the resurrected], and [in you] is the place where I will gather them, and [in you] are my Paradise, my Hellfire and my scales.[77]

Yet other traditions report that the heavenly entity that will descend onto the Rock on the Day of Resurrection is the angel assigned to blow the trumpet. This is the angel mentioned in a tradition discussed above, where the Prophet predicts to several of his Companions that when the people are gathered in groups (*fawjan lafīfan*), the angel of the trumpet (*malak al-ṣūr*) will descend and stand on the Rock of Bayt al-Maqdis.[78]

The name of the angel of the trumpet is Isrāfīl.[79] He appears in traditions where he precedes the angel Gabriel in bringing down prophetic revelations to Muḥammad.[80] Isrāfīl's role on the Day of Resurrection is described by Muqātil, among others. In his commentary on the series of quakes in the *sāhira* passage he explains that the Rock of Bayt al-Maqdis is the place where the angel Isrāfīl will sound the trumpet and call out, "O rotting bones; O severed arteries (*al-'urūq al-*

75 On the scales of justice in the Qur'ān, see Smith, "Eschatology"; Hasson, "Last Judgment".

76 Muqātil, *Addendum*, p. 515. See also Ibn al-Murajjā, *Faḍā'il*, p. 261; Ibn al-Jawzī, *Ta'rīkh Bayt al-Maqdis*, p. 72.

77 Wāsiṭī, *Faḍā'il*, p. 23 (no. 28). See also Livne-Kafri, *Selected Essays*, pp. 48, 104–105; Hasson, "Last Judgment". Another version of these words of God defines al-Shām as *arḍ al-manshar wa-l-maḥshar* ("the land where the dead will rise from the graves and the resurrected will be assembled"). See Ibn 'Asākir, *Ta'rīkh Dimashq*, I, p. 153, XVI, pp. 459–460.

78 Wāsiṭī, *Faḍā'il*, p. 88 (no. 142). Cf. above, Chapter 3.

79 On this see Hasson, "Last Judgment"; Leemhuis, "Apocalypse".

80 Rubin, *The Eye of the Beholder*, pp. 111–112. And see an extensive study of the image of Isrāfīl in Shnizer, *The Qur'ān*, pp. 54–68.

munqaṭiʿa); O torn flesh. Come out of your graves so that you will be given recompense for your deeds".[81] The same Muqātil associates Isrāfīl's standing on the Rock with the following qurʾānic passage (Q 50:41–44):

> (41) And listen you for the day when the crier (*al-munādī*) shall cry (*yunādī*) from a near place. (42) On the day they hear the cry in truth, that is the day of coming forth. (43) It is We who give life, and make to die, and to us is the homecoming [from the grave]. (44) Upon the day when the earth is split asunder from about them as they hasten forth [from their graves]; that is a mustering easy for us.

Muqātil explains:

> "The day when the crier shall cry": . . . that is Isrāfīl peace be upon him, when he stands on the Rock of Bayt al-Maqdis, which is the nearest place to heaven, at a distance of eighteen miles. All of God's creation will hear and gather in Bayt al-Maqdis. This city is the center of the earth (*wasaṭ al-arḍ*) and [the Rock] is the closest place . . .[82]

Here Muqātil identifies the Rock on which Isrāfīl stands with the "near place" (*makān qarīb*) from which the crier will summon the resurrected.[83] His statement that the Rock, as the "near place", is located eighteen miles from heaven is reminiscent of a Jewish midrash, already noted by Livne-Kafri, according to which the distance between the terrestrial and the heavenly Temples is eighteen miles.[84]

The Sde Boker inscription

In addition to traditions, we are also in possession of an early Islamic inscription which mentions Jerusalem as the site of the resurrection and the scene of the Day of Judgment. The inscription was incised into the natural rock in the vicinity of Kibbutz Sde Boker in the Negev. It was discovered and analyzed by Moshe Sharon, who dated it to the beginning of the eighth century CE.[85] The six visible lines run as follows:

---

81 Muqātil, *Tafsīr* (Q 79:14).
82 Muqātil, *Tafsīr* (Q 50:41). See also Sharon, "The Praises of Jerusalem", p. 57; Livne-Kafri, *Selected Essays*, pp. 52–53; *idem*, "Jerusalem in Early Islam", pp. 388–389.
83 See more traditions identifying the "near place" with the Rock of Bayt al-Maqdis in Wāsiṭī, *Faḍāʾil*, pp. 88–89 (nos. 143–145). See also Livne-Kafri, "The Navel of the Earth", p. 58; Leemhuis, "Apocalypse".
84 Midrash Rabbah, II, p. 634 (Genesis Rabbah 69:7): "R. Simeon b. Yoḥai said: The celestial Temple is higher than the terrestrial one only by eighteen miles". See Livne-Kafri, "The Navel of the Earth", pp. 58–59. Cf. *idem*, "Christian Attitudes", p. 371.
85 Sharon, "Shape of the Holy", pp. 298–299.

1 بسم الله 2 رب موسى 3 ومحمد يوم يدعو يوم [يدعو] 4 المناد من إيليا يوم يناد [من] إيليا يوم ... 5 ... الله رب عيسى
وموسى 6 حتى يوم يدعو المناد من إيليا يوم ...

In the name of Allāh. The Lord of Mūsā and Muḥammad. In the day whereon the crier shall cry (*yad'ū*) from Īliyā; the day whereon he shall call [*yunādī*] from Īliyā the day . . . Allah the Lord of 'Īsā and Mūsā. Until the day whereon the crier shall cry (*yad'ū*) from Īliyā. . .

As observed by Sharon, the inscription repeats several times part of Q 50:41 with a minor change. Instead of "the near place" the inscription twice states (lines 4 and 6) that the crier will call from Īliyā, that is, from Jerusalem. Besides, the verb denoting his call is not just *yunādī* (line 4) as in Q 50:41, but also *yad'ū* (lines 3 and 6), as in a parallel qur'ānic verse (Q 54:6) where the crier is called *al-dā'ī*. The Sde Boker inscription constitutes evidence of the early date of the awareness that the qur'ānic scene of resurrection will take place in Jerusalem.

Apart from the issue of the crier, God's image as portrayed in the inscription deserves attention, too. He is called the Lord of Mūsā and Muḥammad, and also the Lord of 'Īsā and Mūsā. This accords with the Qur'ān, in which God is often mentioned as Lord (*rabb*), including the Lord of Moses, Jesus, Muḥammad, as well as other prophets who called on their respective generations to believe in their Lord.[86] Moses and Jesus were prophets of the Children of Israel, and both urged their audiences to believe in Muḥammad. The Qur'ān asserts that in Moses' Torah Muḥammad is called *al-nabī al-ummī* (the prophet of the nations)[87] and that Jesus foretold his coming under the epithet of Aḥmad.[88] Therefore, the inclusion of Moses and Jesus in the inscription seems to have been designed to underline the necessity of believing in Muḥammad particularly in the land of the Israelite prophets. This close adherence of the inscription to the qur'ānic message reinforces the impression that the identification of Īliyā as the site where the crier of the resurrection will stand also reflects the spirit of the Qur'ān.

The mosaic inscription of the Dome of the Rock

Another early inscription that preserves the status of Jerusalem as the site of the resurrection and the venue of the Day of Judgment is the mosaic inscription in the Dome of the Rock. We have already discussed the circumstances of the

86 Lord of Moses: E.g. Q 7:121–122; 26:47–48. Lord of Jesus: E.g. Q 3:51; 5:72, 117. Lord of Muḥammad: E.g. Q 6:57, 161.
87 Q 7:157. On the significance of *al-nabī al-ummī* and its function in Muslim tradition, see Rubin, *The Eye of the Beholder*, pp. 23–28.
88 Q 6:61.

construction of the dome in the chapter on Muḥammad's ascent to heaven, and we shall return to it below.[89] For now we shall focus on the inscription itself. The shrine's builders placed it on the outer face and inner face of each of the eight parts of the octagonal arcade that surrounds the Rock (al-Ṣakhra).[90] In addition to the mosaic inscription, there were also copper inscriptions, still extant, which were originally attached to two of the structure's doors.[91]

The inscription, mainly on the arcade's outer face, consists of a number of repetitive passages that contain the two parts of the *shahāda*, belief in Allāh and belief in Muḥammad as the Messenger of Allāh.[92] The *shahāda* is always preceded by the *basmala*, that is, the formula *bi-smi llāhi al-raḥmān al-raḥim* ("in the name of Allāh the merciful the compassionate"). The text of both parts of the *shahāda* as it appears in one passage (outer face, east and south-east side) runs as follows:

بسم الله الرحمن الرحيم لا اله الا الله وحده لا شريك له محمد رسول الله صلى الله عليه

> In the name of Allāh the merciful the compassionate; there is no god but Allāh alone. He has no associate. Muḥammad is Allāh's Messenger. May Allāh's prayer be on him.

An identical version of both parts of this *shahāda* appears on the coins of ʿAbd al-Malik, who built the Dome of the Rock, as well as on buildings and milestones which ʿAbd al-Malik placed on the roads leading from Damascus to Jerusalem.[93] The *shahāda* in the mosaic inscription is expanded with qurʾānic as well as non-qurʾānic statements about Allāh and Muḥammad.[94] Of particular significance is the following non-qurʾānic passage (outer face, northwest and north side):

محمد رسول الله صلى الله عليه وملائكته ورسله والسلام عليه ورحمة الله.

> Muḥammad is the Messenger of Allāh. May Allāh's prayers be on him and [the prayer of] his angels and messengers, peace be upon him and Allāh's mercy.

---

89 See below, Chapter 11.

90 For the inscriptions of the Dome of the Rock and the studies of their historical context and of the Dome of the Rock itself, see Milwright, *The Dome of the Rock*, pp. 214–250; Elad, "ʿAbd al-Malik and the Dome of the Rock", pp. 184–187; *idem*, "The Status of Jerusalem", pp. 45–48; Sharon, "Shape of the Holy", p. 299.

91 See Milwright, *The Dome of the Rock*, pp. 51–55.

92 The text of the passages quoted here is according to Kessler, "ʿAbd al-Malik's Inscription", pp. 2–64. See also Milwright, *The Dome of the Rock*, pp. 66–82. The inscription is shaped in a Kūfi script with no diacritics.

93 See Sharon, "Shape of the Holy", p. 293.

94 On the issue of the relationship between the inscription and the "official" Qurʾān, see Whelan, "Forgotten Witness", pp. 1–14; Robinson Ch., *Abd al-Malik*, pp. 100–104.

The prayer of Allāh and His angels for Muḥammad is also mentioned in the Qur'ān (Q 33:56), but only in the above-quoted passage are His messengers (*rusul*) added to those who pray for him. The interpolation of the messengers in the list of those praying for the Prophet in an inscription placed in an edifice located in the midst of the city where Israel's prophets were active, emphasizes Muḥammad's status as an intrinsic link in the chain of prophets and as the one who establishes God's true faith on earth. We also note that here Muḥammad is presented as superior to other prophets, unlike the Sde Boker inscription in which, as we saw above, Muḥammad is listed on a par with Moses and Jesus.

The only other prophet mentioned in the mosaic inscription is Jesus. The Dome of the Rock's planners included a number of qur'ānic verses in the inscription that define Jesus as a flesh-and-blood human being, who was born and who died like any other mortal.[95] The purpose of these quotes is to undermine the Christian view of Christ as the son of God.[96] The inscription also contains a qur'ānic verse that declares that Allāh never had any progeny (Q 17:111). The need to outline the image of Jesus was due to the fact that most of Jerusalem's inhabitants at the time were Christians. The inscription's aim was thus to thwart any possible Christian influence on the newly-arrived Muslims who, it was feared, could be influenced by the Christian view of Jesus as divine, a view that contradicted the qur'ānic view, according to which there was nothing of the divine about him.

But the passage that is of interest here, in connection with the topic of the present chapter, is the following, which mentions the Day of Resurrection (outer face north and northeast side):

بسم الله الرحمن الرحيم لا اله الا الله وحده لا شريك له ... محمد رسول الله صلى الله عليه ويقبل شَفاعَتَهُ يومَ القيامة في أمّته.

> In the name of Allāh the merciful the compassionate; there is no god but Allāh alone. He has no associate . . . Muḥammad is the Messenger of Allāh, may Allāh's prayer be on him, and [Allāh] will accept [Muḥammad's] intercession for his nation on the Day of Resurrection.

Here, too, the idea of praying for the Prophet is present, although it is only Allāh and no one else who prays. The passage continues with a declaration that on the Day of Judgment Allāh will accept Muḥammad's intercession (*shafāʿa*), a right

---

95 On the possible significance of the Dome of the Rock in the context of Islam-Christianity relations, see especially Grabar, *The Dome of the Rock*; *idem*, "The Umayyad Dome of the Rock", pp. 33–62; *idem*, "The Meaning of the Dome of the Rock". On the Christians and their holy places in Jerusalem on the eve of Islam, see Sharon, "Shape of the Holy", pp. 287–288.

96 The Qur'ānic verses dealing with Jesus which appear in the inscription are: Q 4:171, 172; 19:34–36. A verse relating to John (Q 19:15) also appears in the inscription, but here it alludes to Jesus.

which he does not have in the Qur'ān itself.[97] To the contrary, there we read that even if *shafāʿa* is possible on the Day of Judgment, it is the exclusive prerogative of God (Q 32:4; 39:44) and cannot exist without His permission (Q 10:3; 20:109; 34:23; 2:255). The Qur'ān does here and there grant the angels the possibility to intercede, with the prophets as witnesses, but even the angels require Allāh's permission to do so (Q 53:26).[98] The Prophet himself is allowed to intercede for himself and for the believers (Q 47:19), as well as to pray for their wellbeing (Q 9:103),[99] but this does not apply to *shafāʿa* on the Day of Judgment. The inscription thus adds a new dimension to Muḥammad's image as a redeemer through whom the believers will achieve redemption and enter Paradise. The same declaration concerning divine acceptance of Muḥammad's *shafāʿa* for his believers is found on the copper inscriptions that covered the Dome of the Rock's doors.[100]

The idea expressed in the inscription that God will accept Muḥammad's intercession for his nation marks another very significant aspect of the elevation of the Prophet's qur'ānic figure. It is not only Muḥammad's superiority that is avowed here, but also the superiority of his Arab nation (*umma*) vis-à-vis the nations of non-Arab prophets. Of all nations, only Muḥammad's *umma* will enjoy the intercession of its Arab prophet with Allāh, and so will attain everlasting life in the world to come. The inscription thus further develops the qur'ānic declaration that the community of believers are the best nation (*khayr umma*) that has ever existed (Q 3:110).

Muḥammad's right of intercession signals a diminution of Jesus' status. According to accepted Christian dogma, Jesus was resurrected three days after his death and ascended to heaven. Since then he intercedes for his believers, as reflected in the following verse: "It is Christ Jesus, who died, yes, who was raised, who is at the right hand of God, who indeed intercedes for us" (Romans 8:34). Similarly, elsewhere in the New Testament (Hebrews 7:25) we read that Jesus "is able for all time to save those who approach God through him, since he always lives to make intercession for them". In contrast to the Christian view, the inscription declares that the right of *shafāʿa* belongs to Muḥammad, but will only be exercised on the Day of Resurrection, when Muḥammad will be resurrected together with the rest of the people who will rise after him.

To sum up, the declaration about resurrection in the Dome of the Rock inscription indicates that its designers viewed Jerusalem as the place where the resurrection would take place and where God would judge the resurrected. Here

---

97 Cf. Smith, "Eschatology"; Hasson, "Last Judgment".
98 On the intercession of angels in apocryphal sources, see e.g. Testament of Levi 5:6.
99 Cf. Hoffman, "Intercession".
100 See Whelan, "Forgotten Witness", pp. 6–7.

Muḥammad will be the first to rise from the dead and he will intercede with God to ensure for his *umma* safe entrance into Paradise. The mosaic inscription thus adds to the evidence provided by the Sde Boker inscription, although, unlike the latter, it has no direct or explicit connection to the qurʾānic scene of the resurrection.

The virtue of being the land of resurrection and the site of the Day of Judgment is a major component in Jerusalem's sanctity. However, Jerusalem never possessed this merit exclusively. Mecca and Medina, the two holy cities in the Arabian region of the sanctity space, demanded a considerable share of this merit. More on this in the next chapter.

5 Resurrection in Arabia

> The models of resurrection and the merit of being the gate to Paradise were transferred from Jerusalem to Mecca in traditions that promote the status of the latter in the Jerusalem-Mecca sanctity space. Medina, too, where Muḥammad was buried, was praised in traditions that promise those buried there the Prophet's intercession (*shafāʿa*), thus making the promise of redemption in al-Shām superfluous. This city, too, attained the status of the place of gathering (*ḥashr*) of those who will rise from the grave. However, other traditions render the position of the Kaʿba subsidiary in comparison with that of Bayt al-Maqdis as the place of the resurrection and the gate to Paradise.

Like the idea of the navel of the earth, the virtue of al-Shām as the land of redemption and resurrection wandered to Arabia. Before considering the traditions that demonstrate the process, we should note that the status of a region as the locus of the resurrection is closely associated with its immunity to various forces of evil that can endanger the resurrected. This immunity is discussed in apocalyptic traditions which also reflect the move of sanctity patterns from Jerusalem to Mecca.

Obstructing the forces of evil: The Dajjāl and Gog and Magog

A number of traditions tell of Jesus' expected appearance in the messianic future, when he will descend to earth and defeat the forces of evil.[1] The Islamic recognition of the idea of Jesus' expected return does not contradict the Islamic view, noted already in the previous chapter, that the one who will intercede for the believers on the Day of Resurrection is Muḥammad, not Jesus. Thus the exegete Qatāda b. Diʿāma (d. 117/735) explains the merits of the blessed land (al-Shām) in his commentary on a qurʾānic verse (Q 21:71) about Abraham and Lot who escaped to that land:

> Some say that this land is the place of gathering and the rise of the dead from their graves (*arḍ al-maḥshar wa-l-manshar*), where the people will gather, where Jesus son of Mary will

1 The future descent, or the "second coming", of Jesus, as it is referred to in Christian sources, is told in a series of Islamic traditions about *nuzūl ʿĪsā*. On the various traditions of Jesus and the Dajjāl, see Livne-Kafri, *Selected Essays*, pp. 67–70; Cook, "Dajjāl". For the Christian perspective see e.g. 1 Thessalonians 4:16–17: "(16) For the Lord himself, with a cry of command, with the archangel's call and with the sound of God's trumpet, will descend from heaven, and the dead of Christ will rise first. (17) Then we who are alive, who are left, will be caught up in the clouds together with them to meet the Lord in the air; and so we will be with the Lord forever". See also Busse, "Jerusalem and Mecca", p. 241.

https://doi.org/10.1515/9783111222318-006

> descend, and where Allāh will destroy the Dajjāl, the master of deviation, the impostor (*shaykh al-ḍalāla al-kadhdhāb*).[2]

This tradition indicates that the representative of the forces of evil is the false messiah, the Dajjāl, and the region which is immune to him, thanks to Jesus, is al-Shām or, more precisely, Bayt al-Maqdis.[3] An expanded version of Qatāda's commentary has the Prophet himself describe Jesus' good works after his eventual descent:

> . . . and he will kill the pig and abolish the *jizya* tax. Money will flow with abundance and he will do battle against the people for the sake of Islam, until Allāh will annihilate in his time all the congregations [*al-milal*] except for Islam. And Allāh will destroy in his time the Dajjāl, the false messiah of deviation, the impostor (*masīḥ al-ḍalāla al-kadhdhāb*). . .[4]

But not only al-Shām is said to be immune to the Dajjāl. Some traditions assign to the land of Arabia the merit of being immune to him. This comes out in a tradition recorded in Aḥmad b. Ḥanbal's (d. 241/855) compilation, which contains a huge number of early traditions about the Prophet and his Companions. The tradition attributes to Muḥammad the declaration that the Dajjāl will tarry for forty days in the world and will rule over every "watering and halting place" (*manhal*), although "he will not reach four mosques: the Kaʿba, the Prophet's mosque (in Medina), the Farthest Mosque (*al-masjid al-aqṣā*) and Mount Sinai [*al-Ṭūr*].[5] The Jerusalem-Mecca sanctity space that is immune to the Dajjāl appears here in its full dimensions, covering all the sacred sites in both of its regions. But in another version of the Prophet's declaration, the region that is immune to the Dajjāl is restricted to Arabia. This version appears in the *Ṣaḥīḥ* ("genuine") compilation by al-Bukhārī (d. 256/870), a contemporary of Aḥmad b. Ḥanbal:

> There is no city in which al-Dajjāl will not tread, except for Mecca and Medina. He will find no breach [*naqb*] through the mountains that surround them without ranks of angels rallying there to protect them . . .[6]

---

2 Ṭabarī, *Tafsīr* (Q 21:71).
3 On Jesus' descent in Bayt al-Maqdis, see also Muqātil, *Addendum*, p. 514; Ibn al-Jawzī, *Taʾrīkh Bayt al-Maqdis*, p. 72. See further Robinson, "Antichrist".
4 Ṭabarī, *Tafsīr* (Q 4:159).
5 Aḥmad b. Ḥanbal, *Musnad*, V, p. 364. See more sources in Kister, "Sanctity Joint and Divided", p. 37. And see also Ibn al-Jawzī, *Taʾrīkh Bayt al-Maqdis*, p. 74; Livne-Kafri, *Selected Essays*, p. 67.
6 Bukhārī, *Ṣaḥīḥ*, III, p. 28 (*Faḍāʾil al-Madīna* [29]: *Bāb lā yadkhulu l-dajjāl al-Madīna*).

These two versions of Muḥammad's statement are recorded with equally reliable chains of transmission,[7] but al-Bukhārī's version places the ancient holy site in Mecca and the Prophet's tomb in Medina above Jerusalem.

The same fluctuation in the defined boundaries of the area which will enjoy divine protection in the messianic future is discerned in traditions concerning the appearance of Gog and Magog.[8] Thus in the following tradition recorded in Muqātil's *Tafsīr* we read:

> Gog and Magog will extend their rule over the entire earth, except for Bayt al-Maqdis. Allāh will destroy Gog and Magog in Bayt al-Maqdis.[9]

Yet in a later quote from Muqātil, which appears in Ibn al-Jawzī's (d. 597/1201) *Ta'rīkh Bayt al-Maqdis*, it is said that "Gog and Magog will extend their rule over the entire earth, except for Mecca, Medina and Bayt al-Maqdis. Allāh will destroy them on the land of Bayt al-Maqdis".[10] The addition of Mecca and Medina to the protected region yet again reflects the effort to restore their ancient status in the Jerusalem-Mecca sanctity space as against the holiness of Bayt al-Maqdis, which persisted since the beginning of the Muslim presence there.

Resurrection in Medina: The sanctity of Baqīʿ al-Gharqad

The struggle to defend the sanctity of the holy places in Arabia is also reflected in the theme of the resurrection. Medina, in particular, enjoys a prominent status in Muslim eschatology, due to the fact that the Prophet Muḥammad died and was buried there. The tomb's sanctity affected the entire space in which it is located, especially Medina's main graveyard, al-Baqīʿ, whose full name is Baqīʿ al-Gharqad. *Gharqad* is the box-thorn (genus *Lycium*), a bush that had grown there before the area was turned into a Muslim cemetery. It is located just to the southeast of the Prophet's mosque and tomb. A Jewish cemetery used to be in this vicinity as well. Al-Baqīʿ in Medina is an active cemetery to this day, although it underwent alterations and demolitions over the centuries.[11] Among Muḥammad's contemporaries who were buried there were members of his family as well as martyrs, *shuhadā'*, who were killed fighting against Muḥammad's enemies, especially in the Battle of

7 See al-Haythamī's comment on Ibn Ḥanbal's version (Haythamī, *Majmaʿ al-zawā'id*, VII, p. 346): رواه أحمد، ورجاله رجال الصحيح. See more sources in Kister, "Sanctity Joint and Divided", p. 36.

8 Cf. Livne-Kafri, *Selected Essays*, p. 65.

9 Muqātil, *Addendum*, p. 514. See also Ibn al-Murajjā, *Faḍā'il*, p. 260; Minhājī, *Itḥāf al-akhiṣṣā*, I, p. 106.

10 Ibn al-Jawzī, *Ta'rīkh Bayt al-Maqdis*, p. 71.

11 See Ende, "Baqīʿ al-Gharqad"; Lecker, *Muḥammad and the Jews*, p. 218.

Uḥud (3/625), in which the Muslims suffered heavy losses. After Muḥammad's death other venerable figures were buried there such as Shīʿī Imāms and Ṣūfī ascetics. As a result, the site became an important pilgrimage destination, including for Shīʿīs.

The special merits of al-Baqīʿ are fostered in a series of traditions about the Prophet. One of them relates that a few days before his death, God commanded Muḥammad to visit al-Baqīʿ and pray for the martyrs buried there.[12] A unique aspect of the site's sanctity is revealed in a tradition quoted by Ibn Shabba (d. 262/876) in his book on the history of Medina. The tradition speaks of Muṣʿab b. al-Zubayr (d. 72/691), brother of Mecca's ruler ʿAbdallāh b. al-Zubayr. Muṣʿab, who had been appointed to the post of governor of Iraq by his brother, came to Medina on his way to perform the pilgrimage to Mecca. He entered the city through al-Baqīʿ, accompanied by the son of the Jewish Exilarch from Babylonia. There the Exilarch's son exclaimed: This is the place! Muṣʿab asked him what he meant, and the Exilarch's son explained that in the Torah there is a description of a cemetery surrounded by date palms and residential quarters, a description that perfectly matched the surroundings of al-Baqīʿ in Medina. He added that in the Torah it is also written that seventy thousand would be resurrected in this place and their faces would shine like the full moon. The name of the cemetery in the Torah is Kafta.[13] As we saw in the previous chapter, in al-Kūfa there was a cemetery concerning which the Exilarch declared that seventy thousand would be resurrected while here we have a tradition in which the Exilarch's son ascribes the same merit to al-Baqīʿ in Medina. Beyond the question about the historical authenticity of the visit of the Exilarch's son in Medina, the tradition reflects the transfer of sanctity pattern from al-Kūfa to Medina. We can conclude therefore that the boundaries of the sanctity space outside of Arabia are not always limited to al-Shām, but can also encompass other locations, such as Bāniqyā, which Jews considered part of the Land of Israel (see above), and from which sanctity models spread also to the Arabian part of that space.

The relationship between al-Baqīʿ in Medina and other places in the sanctity space is retained in the tradition according to which the Prophet declares that two cemeteries will in future shine for the residents of the heavens just like the sun and the full moon shine for those on earth: al-Baqīʿ in Medina and the cemetery of Ashkelon.[14] As

12 Ibn Hishām, *Sīra*, IV, p. 291; Ibn Saʿd, *Ṭabaqāt*, II, pp. 203–205. See Rubin, *Muḥammad the Prophet*, II, p. 312.

13 Ibn Shabba, *Taʾrīkh al-Madīna*, I, p. 93. For more versions see Samhūdī, *Wafāʾ*, III, pp. 887, 889–890. The form *Kafta* being the name of Baqīʿ al-Gharqad, was explained in various ways, some in the spirit of Q 77:25, where the form *kifāt* indicates the ground that is closing in (*taḍummu*) on the dead. This is also how *Kafta* was explained. See Ibn ʿAṭiyya, *Tafsīr* (Q 77:25).

14 Samhūdī, *Wafāʾ*, III, p. 889.

we saw in the previous chapter, the traditions about the merits of Ashkelon also contain the motif of the seventy thousand who will be resurrected.

The gathering of the resurrected in Medina: The Prophet's resurrection

The motif of the seventy thousand reappears in traditions about the resurrection in Medina. These traditions depict Medina as the site where the dead will be resurrected and gathered (*ḥashr*), a status inspired in all likelihood by the fact that the Prophet's tomb and the tomb of some of his most prominent Companions are in this city. One tradition quotes the Prophet himself as saying that from the cemetery of Baqīʿ al-Gharqad seventy thousand will be gathered (*yuḥsharu*) and that they will enter Paradise without being interrogated or judged, and their faces will shine like the full moon.[15] Another cemetery in Medina that has been associated with the gathering of the resurrected is that of the Banū Salima (of the Khazraj). The Jewish convert to Islam Kaʿb al-Aḥbār is quoted as saying that it is written in the Torah that "from the graveyard [*maqbara*] in the west of Medina, on the banks of a stream [*ḥāfat sayl*], seventy thousand will be gathered [*yuḥsharu*] who will not be interrogated or judged".[16] The same declaration, albeit without the number, is also quoted on the Prophet's authority.[17] In this context it is often mentioned that some of those killed in the Battle of Uḥud were buried in the cemetery of the Banū Salima.[18]

The idea that the gathering of the resurrected will take place in Medina is especially prominent in traditions that identify this city as the location where the dead will arise from their graves. The traditions unanimously agree that Muḥammad, who is buried in Medina, will be the first to rise from the dead; in this respect, he is superior to all people, including all the other prophets. The order in which everyone else would be resurrected became a bone of contention among various groups in Islam. One tradition states that Muḥammad will be the first one for whom the earth will split (*tanshaqqu*), followed by the caliphs Abū Bakr and ʿUmar. The Prophet will then come to al-Baqīʿ, and those buried there will be gathered (*fa-yuḥsharūn*) with him. He will then wait for the people of Mecca and then will be gathered [with everyone] from the area between the two holy places [*bayna l-ḥaramayn*], that is,

15 Ibn ʿAṭiyya, *Tafsīr* (Q 79:14). See also Abū Ḥayyān, *al-Baḥr al-muḥīṭ* (Q 79:14); Samhūdī, *Wafāʾ*, III, p. 886. And see Rubin, *Muḥammad the Prophet*, II, p. 255.
16 Ibn Shabba, *Taʾrīkh al-Madīna*, I, p. 92. See also Samhūdī, *Wafāʾ*, III, p. 887.
17 Ibn Shabba, *Taʾrīkh al-Madīna*, I, pp. 92–93, 94; Samhūdī, *Wafāʾ*, III, p. 887–888.
18 Samhūdī, *Wafāʾ*, III, p. 888.

between Mecca and Medina.[19] According to other versions, the Prophet will rise from the grave with his right hand placed on Abū Bakr and his left hand on ʿUmar or on his Companions from among the Muhājirūn and the Anṣār.[20] In one version the Prophet declares that when people will be gathered (*ḥushira*) on the Day of Judgment, he himself will be resurrected together with the people buried in al-Baqīʿ.[21]

These traditions present Mecca, and especially Medina, as an alternative to al-Shām as the site of the resurrection, thanks to the exalted status of Muḥammad, the first caliphs and the rest of the first Muslims buried in Medina.

Furthermore, Jesus was also made part of the resurrection scene in Medina. A tradition related on the Prophet's authority by his Companion Abū Hurayra states that when Jesus will descend from heaven he will perform a *hijra* to Medina and will live there until he dies. Then he will be buried next to the grave of ʿUmar b. al-Khaṭṭāb: "How happy are the lots of Abū Bakr and ʿUmar; they will be gathered [*yuḥsharān*] on the Day of Resurrection between two prophets [Jesus and Muḥammad]".[22]

As we can see, al-Shām's virtues as the land of the resurrection found their way to Arabia and were incorporated into traditions about Medina. In the following tradition about the Meccan scholar ʿAbdallāh b. ʿUmar (d. 73/692) Medina is explicitly mentioned as an alternative to al-Shām. The tradition is found in the *ḥadīth* compilation of al-Tirmidhī (d. 279/892):

> [ʿAbdallāh] Ibn ʿUmar related that a slave girl came to him and said: The troubles of the times lie heavy on me and I would like to go to Iraq. [Ibn ʿUmar] said: Why not to al-Shām, the land of the resurrection [*arḍ al-manshar*]? But be patient [*iṣbirī*], silly one, for I heard the Messenger of Allāh say: Whoever remains steadfast in the face of [Medina's] hardships and tribulations, I will intercede for him on the Day of Resurrection.[23]

For Ibn ʿUmar the status of al-Shām as the land of the resurrection (*arḍ al-manshar*) is thus not unique, and there is no need to go there; dying in Medina also ensures one redemption on the Day of Resurrection, thanks to the intercession of Muḥammad, who is buried there. This message is also conveyed in the following tradition:

> The Jews came to the Prophet and said: If you are truly a prophet, move to al-Shām, for al-Shām is the land of the gathering of those who will be resurrected [*al-maḥshar*] and the land

19 Mubārakfūrī, *Tuḥfat al-aḥwadhī*, X, p. 181 (no. 3775) (= Tirmidhī, *Sunan*, *Manāqib* [46]). See also Fākihī, *Akhbār Makka*, III, p. 70 (no. 1814); Rubin, *Muḥammad the Prophet*, II, p. 218.
20 Ḥākim, *Mustadrak*, III, p. 68; Rubin, *Muḥammad the Prophet*, II, p. 218.
21 ʿAbd al-Razzāq, *Muṣannaf*, III, p. 580 (no. 6736).
22 Zamakhsharī, *Rabīʿ al-abrār*, I, p. 248. See also Busse, "Jerusalem and Mecca", p. 241.
23 Mubārakfūrī, *Tuḥfat al-aḥwadhī*, X, pp. 417–418 (no. 4011) (= Tirmidhī, *Sunan*, *Manāqib* [46]: *Faḍl al-Madīna* [67]).

> of the prophets. The Messenger of Allāh believed them and set out to participate in the raid on Tabūk. His intention was to enter al-Shām. When he reached Tabūk Allāh revealed to him verses from Q 17 after it had already been sealed: "Indeed they were near to startling you from the land, to expel you from it . . .". (Q 17:76). God then commanded him to return to Medina and said: There is your life, there is your death, and there you will be resurrected [*wa-fīhā tubʿathu*].[24]

In this tradition the Jews try to persuade the Prophet to move to al-Shām, because, so they claim, that is the land of the resurrection. However, when the Prophet arrives at the southern border of al-Shām and subdues the Arabs in the vicinity of Tabūk (9/630), God tells him not to proceed further north, for his resurrection will be in Medina and nowhere else.

Al-sāhira and the merits of dying in Mecca

Mecca, too, is mentioned in traditions that foster Arabia as the site of the resurrection. These traditions, too, demonstrate the transfer of sanctity patterns from Jerusalem to Mecca. Thus, while in the previous chapter, we saw traditions that identify the qurʾānic *al-sāhira* with Bayt al-Maqdis, a tradition attributed to Ibn ʿAbbās states that it is "the land of Mecca" (*arḍ Makka*).[25] In other words, the place where the dead will rise from the grave is in Mecca rather than in al-Shām.

The same trend can be seen in traditions that transfer the status of a preferred burial place to Mecca. Of particular interest is a tradition quoting the Prophet himself as saying that God will resurrect any pilgrim who passes away between the two sacred enclaves (*bayna l-ḥaramayn*) of Mecca and Medina, and will spare him the need to account for his deeds, for which he will not be punished. Furthermore, the Prophet says, whoever dies in Mecca is counted as if he died in the first heaven; if someone runs between the hills of al-Ṣafā and al-Marwa [across from the Kaʿba], God will make his legs stand firm on the *ṣirāṭ* [bridge].[26] In the same spirit it is reported that the Prophet stated that whoever is buried in Mecca as a Muslim will be resurrected safely on the Day of Resurrection.[27] The Shīʿīs took the same view, as reflected in a tradition according to which the sixth Imām Abū ʿAbdallāh (Jaʿfar al-Ṣādiq, d. 148/765) reportedly says

---

24 This tradition is transmitted in the name of ʿAbd al-Raḥmān b. Ghanm (Syrian, d. 78/697). See Ibn Abī Ḥātim, *Tafsīr* (Q 17:76); Suyūṭī, *al-Durr al-manthūr* (Q 17:76).

25 Ibn ʿAṭiyya, *Tafsīr* (Q 79:14). See also Abū Ḥayyān, *al-Baḥr al-muḥīṭ* (Q 79:14).

26 Fākihī, *Akhbār Makka*, III, p. 160 (no. 1918). See also Ibn al-Jawzī, *Taʾrīkh Bayt al-Maqdis*, p. 72; Rubin, *Muḥammad the Prophet*, II, p. 249.

27 Muḥibb al-Dīn, *Qirā*, p. 654; Suyūṭī, *al-Durr al-manthūr* (Q 3:96); Rubin, *Muḥammad the Prophet*, II, p. 249.

that whoever dies on the way to or from Mecca will be spared the great fright (*al-faza' al-akbar*) on the Day of Resurrection.[28]

One tradition relates that the Prophet stood in front of the cemetery of Mecca and declared that from this place as well as from the entire *ḥaram* seventy thousand would be resurrected and would enter Paradise without being interrogated and that each of them would intercede for another seventy thousand.[29] We thus see that the motif of the seventy thousand examined in the previous chapter found its way from al-Shām to Mecca.

The merit ascribed to burial in Mecca is perceived as an act of divine grace, granted to the city in Adam's lifetime. It is related that Adam asked of Allāh that any man who believed in Allāh as the only god and performed the pilgrimage to Mecca would be permitted to join him in Paradise. Allāh promised Adam that anyone who died in the *ḥaram* (of Mecca) and believed in God's unity would be resurrected and would not be sent to Hell.[30]

Even just being in Mecca has its own sanctity. Muḥammad said:

> Whoever bears one hour of Mecca's heat during daytime, the fire of Hell moves away from him a distance of a hundred year's march, and Paradise approaches him by a distance of a hundred year's march.[31]

Intercession by the sacred stones in Mecca

In addition to the merits of being buried in Mecca, the trial before God on the Day of Judgment was associated with this city. This can be seen in traditions according to which the sacred stones of Mecca have the power to intercede on the Day of Resurrection on behalf of the pilgrims who visited them. One tradition, transmitted by the Meccan scholar Mujāhid (d. 104/722), states that "On the Day of Resurrection the Black Stone and the stone of Maqām Ibrāhīm, both of which will be the size of Mount Abū Qubays [which faces the Ka'ba], will come to testify in favor of all those who visited them faithfully".[32] According to this tradition, their testimony will guarantee entry into Paradise. In a particularly picturesque declaration, ascribed to the Prophet himself, it is stated that on the Day of Resurrection God will bring the Black Stone to life, and "it will have two eyes with which to see and a tongue with which to speak. It

28 Rubin, *Muḥammad the Prophet*, II, p. 249.
29 Fākihī, *Akhbār Makka*, IV, p. 51 (no. 2370). See also Rubin, *Muḥammad the Prophet*, II, p. 255.
30 Khargūshī, *Sharaf al-Muṣṭafā*, II, p. 232 (no. 430); Rubin, *Muḥammad the Prophet*, II, p. 249.
31 Khargūshī, *Sharaf al-Muṣṭafā*, II, p. 252 (no. 460); Rubin, *Muḥammad the Prophet*, II, p. 249.
32 Azraqī, *Akhbār Makka*, p. 230. See also Kister, "Maqām Ibrāhīm", p. 482.

will testify in favor of anyone who touched it in true faith".[33] Touching the stone is a common custom during the circumambulation (*ṭawāf*) of the Kaʿba. Another tradition states that whoever touches the Black Stone is considered to have fulfilled the ancient covenant that Allāh made with humanity, which committed itself to believe in him and to arrive as believers to their judgment on the Day of Resurrection (Q 7:172). God placed the covenant document inside the Black Stone.[34]

Burial of the Muhājirūn in Mecca or in Medina

In addition to the rivalry for preeminence between Mecca and al-Shām, a similar struggle took place between Mecca and its sacred sister city in Arabia itself, Medina.[35] A number of traditions reflect the rivalry between these two cities over the status of being the best place in which to be buried. The problem arose with respect to the Muhājirūn, Muslims from Mecca who had adopted Islam and emigrated to join the Prophet in Medina. The question was whether a Muhājir who had returned to Mecca after the *hijra* for whatever reason and died in the latter city could be buried there, that is, in a city that he had left when he abandoned idolatry. Was there not a risk that he would lose his status as a Muhājir? Despite such doubts, not everyone was afraid of being buried in Mecca, as proven by the existence there of a special cemetery (*maqbara*) for Muhājirūn.[36] A tradition in praise of those buried in this cemetery is related by the Tābiʿī (a member of the second generation of Muslim scholars) Yaḥyā b. ʿAbdallāh b. Ṣayfī. He states that whoever dies and is buried in this cemetery will be resurrected. In addition, he transmitted a tradition which says that whoever dies in the *ḥaram* (of Mecca) will be resurrected in the same way.[37]

However, there were also Muhājirūn who did not want to be buried in Mecca. One of these was the Prophet's Companion Saʿd b. Abī Waqqāṣ, who lay on his deathbed in Mecca, after this city had already come under the Prophet's control. The dying man was afraid he would be buried in the city from which he had emigrated after having turned from idolatry to Islam. The Prophet ordered that if

---

33 Azraqī, *Akhbār Makka*, p. 228.
34 Azraqī, *Akhbār Makka*, pp. 228–229. See also Busse, "Jerusalem and Mecca", p. 241.
35 On the competition between Mecca and Medina see Arazi, "Matériaux"; Lazarus-Yafe, "Jerusalem and Mecca", pp. 202–203.
36 One of those buried there was the Muhājir Abū Wāqid al-Bakrī. See ʿAbd al-Razzāq, *Muṣannaf*, III, p. 578 (no. 6730); Fākihī, *Akhbār Makka*, IV, p. 65 (no. 2387). Cf. Rubin, *Muḥammad the Prophet*, II, p. 249.
37 ʿAbd al-Razzāq, *Muṣannaf*, III, p. 578 (no. 6731); Fākihī, *Akhbār Makka*, IV, p. 66 (no. 2387). Cf. Rubin, *Muḥammad the Prophet*, II, p. 249.

he would indeed die in Mecca, he should be brought to burial in Medina, even if the transfer would pose difficulties.[38]

Joint sanctity of Mecca and Medina

The preceding section presents one inner-Arabian aspect of the struggle between different sites over special status on the Day of Resurrection. But there were also attempts to maintain solidarity and attain equality regarding the virtues ascribed to Mecca and Medina. A tendency towards combining the sanctity of the two cities is reflected in a tradition that we already mentioned above and according to which the Prophet declares that whoever dies in one of the two *ḥarams* will be resurrected and will be immune from divine punishment.[39] Another slightly different version states that if someone dies in one of the two *ḥarams* during the performance of the *ḥajj* or the *ʿumra*, God will resurrect him without this person being interrogated and punished.[40]

Some traditions testify to an attempt to divide the merits of resurrection equally among different places throughout the regions of the sanctity space. For example, a tradition quotes the Prophet as saying that there are four cities of Paradise: Mecca, Medina, Damascus and Jerusalem.[41] But this equality between sites is not maintained in all traditions. Some retain the tendency to prefer the Arabian region, as in the version that states that four gates of Paradise are open on earth: The first three are is Alexandria, Ashkelon and Qazwīn but the superiority of Jedda (in Arabia) over all these cities is like the superiority of the Kaʿba over all other shrines.[42]

Preserving Jerusalem's superiority: The Kaʿba will come to it

Finally, let us point out that, in contrast to the many traditions in praise of Mecca as the place of resurrection, there are traditions that reflect the efforts of the champions

38 ʿAbd al-Razzāq, *Muṣannaf*, III, pp. 577–578 (nos. 6728–6729); Ibn Saʿd, *Ṭabaqāt*, III, p. 146; Fākihī, *Akhbār Makka*, IV, pp. 64–65 (nos. 2385–2387). Cf. Rubin, *Muḥammad the Prophet*, II, p. 248.
39 ʿAbd al-Razzāq, *Muṣannaf*, IX, p. 267 (no. 17166); Fākihī, *Akhbār Makka*, III, pp. 68–69 (no. 1811); Rubin, *Muḥammad the Prophet*, II, p. 249.
40 Fākihī, *Akhbār Makka*, III, p. 68 (no. 1810). And see *ibid.*, p. 69 (no. 1813), a tradition emphasizing that even unbelievers who perish between the two *ḥarams* are guaranteed this reward subject to God's verdict on the Day of Judgement. Cf. Rubin, *Muḥammad the Prophet*, II, p. 249.
41 Mujīr al-Dīn, *al-Uns al-jalīl*, I, p. 228; Rubin, *Muḥammad the Prophet*, II, p. 252.
42 Suyūṭī, *Laʾāliʾ*, I, p. 460; Rubin, *Muḥammad the Prophet*, II, p. 252.

of the superior status of al-Shām to defend the position of Bayt al-Maqdis as the ultimate site of resurrection. The following tradition, also recorded in Muqātil's *Tafsīr*, reflects this aspiration. One of the virtues of Bayt al-Maqdis enumerated there is that on the Day of Resurrection, "the Holy House [al-Bayt al-Ḥarām], i.e. the Kaʿba, and the Black Stone, will be taken [from Mecca] to Bayt al-Maqdis as a bride is conducted to her bridegroom (*yuzaffu*)." [The Stone] will testify in favor of whoever touched it in sincere loyalty, and those who sanctified themselves in preparation for the pilgrimage will rise from their graves, uttering the call of the *talbiya* [a formula uttered during the pilgrimage] in the direction of Bayt al-Maqdis".[43]

In contrast to the above traditions which praise the touching of the Black Stone because that ensures redemption in Paradise, this tradition subordinates the Black Stone to the sanctity of Bayt al-Maqdis and to its status as a pilgrimage destination. A shorter version, transmitted on the authority of Kaʿb al-Aḥbār, clearly states that on the Day of Resurrection, the Kaʿba "will surely be gathered" [*la-tuḥsharanna*] to Bayt al-Maqdis,[44] while a solemn formulation, also in Kaʿb's name, declares: "The Hour of Judgment will not arrive until the Holy House visits [*yazūr*] Bayt al-Maqdis, and then both will be led together to Paradise, with their inhabitants".[45] This scene was so cherished that it was depicted in other picturesque versions, which describe how the pilgrims hang on to the cloth cover of the Kaʿba as it makes its way to Bayt al-Maqdis and how the Rock in Bayt al-Maqdis welcomes its visitors.[46] According to more ambitious traditions, other cities, for example, Alexandria, will arrive in Bayt al-Maqdis with their inhabitants in the Latter Days.[47]

Furthermore, the bones of Muḥammad himself, so it is said, will be transferred to Bayt al-Maqdis on the Day of Resurrection,[48] clearly an attempt to counter the status of the Prophet's grave in Medina as the place where he will be resurrected.

---

43 Muqātil, *Addendum*, p. 514. See further, Kister, "Three Mosques", p. 191; Livne-Kafri, "The Navel of the Earth", p. 66. For more versions see *idem*, "Christian Attitudes", pp. 365–366; *idem*, "In Praise of Jerusalem", pp. 180–181; *idem*, "Jerusalem in Early Islam", pp. 392–395; Busse, "The Sanctity of Jerusalem", pp. 467–468.

44 Nuʿaym b. Ḥammād, *Fitan*, p. 425.

45 Ibn Shaddād, *al-Aʿlāq al-khaṭīra*, p. 189.

46 Fākihī, *Akhbār Makka*, I, pp. 436–438; Sharon, "The Cities of the Holy Land", p. 106.

47 Livne-Kafri, *Selected Essays*, pp. 116–117.

48 Wāsiṭī, *Faḍāʾil*, p. 102 (no. 165); Livne-Kafri, *Selected Essays*, pp. 62, 106.

The merits of burial elsewhere in the Muslim world

Not only Arabia appropriated the merits of al-Shām as the land of the resurrection. Pilgrims to the mosque in the city of al-Kūfa, mentioned above, will, so it is said, enjoy the mosque's intercession on the Day of Resurrection.[49] About the mosque of the city of Ubulla (east of Baṣra, on the banks of the Tigris) it is said that the Prophet declared that from that place Allāh would resurrect (*yabʿathu*) martyrs (*shuhadāʾ*) who alone deserve to stand together with the martyrs of the Battle of Badr.[50] As for the city of Qazwīn, it is related in Muḥammad's name that whoever stays there for forty days will have a golden post in Paradise on which to prop his tent.[51] Of the city of Bukhārā it is said that its people will be spared the tribulations of the Day of Judgment and that every night Allāh forgives the sins of any of its people who asks for forgiveness.[52] The people of Samarqand, too, will be spared the tribulations of the Day of Judgment; their sins will be forgiven, and every night a herald cries out to them and gives them tidings of Paradise.[53]

Al-Shām is not only the site of redemption and resurrection in the eschatological future, but is also a region in which people live out their earthly lives under God's blessing and protection, which are promised to the worthiest of them, especially prophets. The most prominent of these is Abraham, in whose biography the transition of sanctity patterns from al-Shām to Mecca and Medina is also presented in the Qurʾān itself. More on this in the following chapters.

49 Kister, "Sanctity Joint and Divided", p. 32.

50 The mosque is called Masjid al-ʿAshshār. See Muḥibb al-Dīn, *Qirā*, pp. 699–700; Rubin, *Muḥammad the Prophet*, II, p. 251.

51 Suyūṭī, *Laʾāliʾ*, I, p. 463; Rubin, *Muḥammad the Prophet*, II, pp. 251–252. See also Kister, "Sanctity Joint and Divided", p. 43.

52 Suyūṭī, *Laʾāliʾ*, I, p. 467; Rubin, *Muḥammad the Prophet*, II, p. 252.

53 Suyūṭī, *Laʾāliʾ*, I, p. 467; Rubin, *Muḥammad the Prophet*, II, p. 252.

Part Four: **Land of the Prophets**

6 The Patriarchs in al-Shām

The qur'ānic view of al-Shām as a longed-for destination for the prophets and their pilgrimages is reflected in the verses describing Abraham's wanderings away from his homeland and his being blessed with progeny in the land where he found shelter. These are Meccan verses, which connect with the verses that describe the Children of Israel's arrival at the same desired destination and Muḥammad's nocturnal journey to it. All these verses reflect the qur'ānic identification with the Jewish messianic vision of redemption in the Promised Land. Exegetical traditions about Abraham's journey to al-Shām testify to this land's continued sacred status in the first century AH as a destination for prophets and as the place where they operated, which they defended and where they were buried. Abraham figures prominently in these traditions as a model for believers who showed them the path of *hijra* to that coveted destination. The ancient sanctity of the Cave of the Patriarchs (Hebrew: מערת המכפלה), where Abraham (al-Khalīl), Isaac and Jacob are buried, was also preserved and fostered, in addition to other sites throughout al-Shām where numerous other prophets (including Moses) are believed to be buried. It was the Umayyad rulers who strove to promote the status of al-Shām as the foremost region in the Islamic state that one must come to, thus following in the footsteps of the prophets. That region was the place where the territories of Islam had to be defended against Byzantine encroachment. On the other hand, concern about the future of the dwindling population in Arabia arose, following the mass emigration to the territories that were conquered after the Prophet's death.

Apart from the traditions that praise al-Shām as the land of redemption and resurrection in the Latter Days there are traditions that praise it as the land where those whom God chose in the past were active. For the most part, these are prophets whose life and career are considered a model for Muḥammad's activity among his own contemporaries. Abraham is one of the most prominent of these prophets.

The three Patriarchs and al-Shām

A number of Meccan verses describe Abraham's journey from his homeland to the land that God has given him, al-Shām, where he is blessed with Isaac and Jacob. Before we examine these verses, we should note that already in the Hebrew Bible we find the three Patriarchs — Abraham, Isaac and Jacob — in the land which God promised to bequeath to them, and where they were about to play their part in the plan of redemption.[1] In the Qur'ān, the three Patriarchs are mentioned in several passages, including the one about the angels' visit to Abraham on their

1 The promise to Abraham: Genesis 12:7; 13:14–15. The promise to Isaac and Jacob: Genesis 26:3–4; 28:13.

https://doi.org/10.1515/9783111222318-007

way to punish Lot's people. On that occasion they inform Abraham and his wife Sarah of the expected birth of Isaac and Jacob (Q 11:69–71). The same three are mentioned in the story of Joseph when Jacob reminds his son that the three enjoy God's grace, and Joseph himself declares his belief in them (Q 12:6,38). But the most significant verses are those which tell of Abraham's journey from his homeland to the land destined for him, where he finds redemption and is blessed with Isaac and Jacob. In one of the Meccan verses Abraham's departure begins with a "withdrawal" (Q 19:49–50):

> (49) So, when he withdrew from them (*iʿtazalahum*) and what they worshipped apart from God, We gave him Isaac and Jacob, and each We made a prophet; (50) and We gave them of our mercy, and We left (behind them) a truthful mention of eminence for them.

In the passage that precedes these verses (Q 19:41–48), Abraham comes into conflict with his father, who refuses to put a stop to his people's idolatry. Abraham is thus forced to leave his homeland after having discovered that God is the only deity. His withdrawal from the unbelievers brings Abraham to the land in which he is blessed with Isaac and Jacob, who continue to be the bearers of God's plan of redemption, and the Qurʾān praises their memory and their heritage. However, the place to which the withdrawing Abraham goes is not specified.

In another passage Abraham's destination is mentioned with precision. This time his departure towards it is depicted as deliverance from his enemies (Q 21:71–73):

> (71) And We delivered (*najjaynāhu*) him [Abraham], and Lot, unto the land that We had blessed for all beings. (72) And We gave him Isaac and Jacob in superfluity, and every one made We righteous (73) and appointed them to be leaders guiding by our command, and We revealed to them the doing of good deeds, and to perform the prayer, and to pay the alms, and us they served.

In this passage, God defines Abraham's destination as the land "that We had blessed" (*bāraknā fīhā*). As noted above,[2] the Qurʾān reserves this expression for the blessed land, which is al-Shām and which was the destination of the Children of Israel following their exodus from Egypt. This blessed land appears in the passage just quoted as the place where Abraham found shelter after God saved him from those who pursued him. Abraham found refuge there together with Lot, in keeping with the biblical account of their arrival in Canaan (Genesis 11:31). The reason why Abraham needed shelter is explained in the preceding verses of the same *sūra*, where it is related that when still a youth (*fatā*), Abraham smashed his

2 See above, Chapter 1.

people's idols, and Allāh saved him from the furnace in which his enemies intended to burn him as punishment for his deed (Q 21:51–70). These are also familiar themes in Jewish midrashic literature.[3]

Upon arrival in the blessed land, God blesses Abraham with two children: Isaac and Jacob. Their faith revolves around prayer and the giving of alms (*zakāt*), two of the pillars of Islam. It follows that, from the qurʾānic point of view, the Patriarchs of the Jewish people were good Muslims. The message to the Jews of Muḥammad's time is clear: They, too, must adhere to the fundamental principles of Islam if they are to preserve their forefathers' heritage faithfully.

In the following Meccan account, Abraham's arrival at his destination constitutes a *hijra* (Q 29:26–27):

> (26) But Lot believed him; and [Abraham] said, 'I will set out [*muhājir*] to my Lord; he is the all-mighty, the all-wise.' (27) And We gave him Isaac and Jacob, and We gave the prophecy and the book to his seed; We gave him his wage in this world, and in the world to come he shall be among the righteous.

In this verse the target of Abraham's *hijra* is God himself, which is yet another sign that his destination is a region placed under God's blessing and guidance. In a commentary attributed to Ibn ʿAbbās, a Companion of the Prophet who is considered the father of Qurʾān exegesis, it is stated that Abraham "left Ḥarrān for Filasṭīn".[4] The assertion that prophecy and the Book were given to Isaac's and Jacob's progeny alludes to the prophets of Israel; all of them thus followed the righteous path of Islam.

The various Meccan verses that describe Abraham's arrival in the land promised him and his descendants link up with the verses depicting the arrival of the Children of Israel at the same destination,[5] as well as with the verse about Muḥammad's nocturnal journey there.[6] All these passages emphasize the qurʾānic identification with the Jewish messianic vision of redemption in the Promised Land.

The land of the prophets at large and their graves

Extra-qurʾānic traditions, especially the ones that interpret the verses that hint at al-Shām, expand on the number of prophets who lived and operated in that land until

3 See e.g. Talmud Bavli, Pesachim 118a.
4 Fīrūzābādī, *Tanwīr al-miqbās* (Q 29:26).
5 See above, Chapter 3.
6 See above, Chapter 1.

they died there. The exegete Mujāhid (d. 104/722) summarizes the virtues of al-Masjid al-Aqṣā, to which God led Muḥammad on his nocturnal journey (Q 17:1):

> Mujāhid said: [Allāh] called [al-Masjid al-Aqṣā] blessed, because it is the abode [*maqarr*] of the prophets and the place where the angels and prophetic revelation descend; it is the Rock, and from it people will be summoned to gather [*yuḥshar*] on the Day of Resurrection.[7]

Al-Shām is thus not only the place where the resurrection will take place; it is also the land of prophets, a status implied in the traditions seen above about the course of Muḥammad's nocturnal journey that took him through key sites in the lives of Moses and Jesus.[8] Indeed, not only Muḥammad came to this land, and not only the three Patriarchs before him. Kaʿb al-Aḥbār (d. 32/652), the Jewish convert to Islam who introduced Muslims to traditions about holy scriptures and holy places, says: "All the prophets came on pilgrimage [*zārū*] to Bayt al-Maqdis, for its glorification [*taʿẓīman*]".[9]

The prophets' presence is the source of the blessing that suffuses the land. The exegete al-Thaʿlabī (d. 427/1035), when speaking of the land in which Abraham found refuge from his enemies, summarizes its merits as follows: "It was blessed in this that most of the prophets came from there. It is a fertile land, with plenty of trees, rivers and fruits; there the lives of the poor and the rich are good".[10]

The prophets' blessed presence in al-Shām is continuous, for they are also buried there. This point is explicitly stated in commentaries on Q 7:137, in which God bequeaths to the Children of Israel their blessed ground. Kaʿb al-Aḥbār explains this blessing: "It is written in the Torah that al-Shām is Allāh's treasure [*kanz*], and his treasure that resides in it is his servants, that is, the graves of the prophets, peace be upon them, Abraham, Isaac and Jacob".[11]

The fact that the tradition focuses on the tombs of the Patriarchs as the source of the blessing of the land given to the Children of Israel testifies to the preservation of the ancient sanctity of the Cave of the Patriarchs, where they are buried. According to this tradition, the sanctity of that site is the main source of the sanctity of the entire land. Indeed, the first Muslims who came to the land as Islam expanded beyond the borders of Arabia were no doubt exposed to the

---

7 Thaʿlabī, *al-Kashf wa-l-bayān* (Q 17:1).

8 See above, Chapter 1.

9 Yāqūt, *Muʿjam al-buldān*, V, p. 167 (s.v. al-Maqdis). On the relationship between the prophets and Bayt al-Maqdis see also Livne-Kafri, "The Navel of the Earth", p. 70.

10 Thaʿlabī, *al-Kashf wa-l-bayān* (Q 21:71). See also Ibn al-Jawzī, *Zād al-masīr* (Q 21:71); Qurṭubī, *Aḥkām al-Qurʾān* (Q 21:71); Abū Ḥayyān, *al-Baḥr al-muḥīṭ* (Q 21:71).

11 Suyūṭī, *al-Durr al-manthūr* (Q 7:137). See also Ibn ʿAsākir, *Taʾrīkh Dimashq*, I, p. 123. Cf. Kister, "Sanctity Joint and Divided", p. 22.

sacred site in Hebron and to the structure built over it, and especially to the site's connection to Abraham. They would have especially remembered Abraham's status in the Qur'ān (Q 4:125) as Allāh's friend [*khalīl*]. This title reflects the latter's merit as a "lover of God", a status granted to Abraham in pre-Islamic sources, for example, the Jewish Apocrypha.[12] The first Muslims who came to Palestine applied the qur'ānic version of this title to the city of Hebron as a whole.[13] However, Muslim scholars never forgot the biblical basis for Hebron's Abrahamic sanctity, as we can see in the geographical lexicon of the Muslim world composed by Yāqūt (d. 626/1229). He notes that the city's name is al-Khalīl and that it originally was called Hebron. He goes on to report that in the Torah it is related that al-Khalīl (Abraham) bought a plot of land from ʿAfrūn b. Ṣūḥār [Ephron son of Zohar] the Hittite for four hundred dirhams, and buried Sarah there.[14] The Muslims had no qualms about adopting the biblical connection between Hebron and Abraham and the other Patriarchs since in the Qur'ān itself they are all deemed good Muslims.[15]

The sanctity of Abraham's tomb in Hebron was incorporated in scenes of Muḥammad's nocturnal journey. In a tradition ascribed to the Prophet's Companion Abū Hurayra, it is related that on their way to Bayt al-Maqdis Gabriel brought Muḥammad to Abraham's tomb in Hebron and commanded him to descend and pray, because "here is the tomb of your father Abraham, peace be upon him".[16] The merit of Abraham's tomb is also implied in traditions that refer to the value of visiting the site and to the sanctity of the mountain of Hebron as a place of refuge for persecuted believers. Legends also arose that associated Abraham's tomb with Solomon, the builder of the Temple: Demons helped him erect a structure to mark the site of the tomb. In addition, stories were told about how God chose the mountain of Hebron out of all places on earth to be Abraham's burial site, and how He sanctified it for those who would visit it. The traditions emphasize the sanctity of the tombs of Sarah, Isaac and Jacob, which are located there as well. Muslim scholars linked the sanctity of this site to that of Joseph's tomb and spoke of the merits of pilgrimage to the latter site.[17]

---

12 E.g. Jubilees 19:9; Apocalypse of Abraham 10:5. See also Talmud Bavli, Menachoth 53b, Shabbath 137b.

13 On the Islamic conquest of Hebron see Gil, *History of Palestine*, pp. 57–58. On its sanctity in Islam: Sharon, "The Cities of the Holy Land", pp. 102–105.

14 Yāqūt, *Muʿjam al-buldān*, II, pp. 387–388 (s.v. al-Khalīl). See also Ibn al-Jawzī, *Ta'rīkh Bayt al-Maqdis*, pp. 75–76. Cf. Genesis 23:3–20.

15 See more on the Islamic sanctity of Hebron in Kister, "Sanctity Joint and Divided", pp. 27–29.

16 Ibn al-Jawzī, *Ta'rīkh Bayt al-Maqdis*, p. 75.

17 Kister, "Sanctity Joint and Divided", pp. 27–29. See also Ibn al-Jawzī, *Ta'rīkh Bayt al-Maqdis*, pp. 75–80; Mujīr al-Dīn, *al-Uns al-jalīl*, I, pp. 55–56.

On the other hand, Muslim scholars who opposed the veneration of saints and graves — most prominent among whom was Ibn Taymiyya (d. 728/1328) — strongly disapproved of the mass of traditions and popular customs that had developed around Abraham's tomb.[18] Of course, such opposition does not mean that the belief in the merits of sacred sites in Hebron or anywhere else throughout al-Shām ever became less powerful among the believers. To the contrary, even such a respected scholar as Mujīr al-Dīn al-Ḥanbalī (d. 928/1522), author of a monumental work on the virtues of Jerusalem and Hebron, testifies that his pilgrimage to Abraham's tomb and his prayer there helped him extricate himself from a great hardship whose details he does not divulge.[19]

Other traditions about Abraham's tomb create a sanctity axis connecting Hebron and Jerusalem. These traditions can be found in the voluminous compilation of Ibn ʿAsākir (d. 570/1175), which contains traditions about Syria and Palestine throughout history. One of these traditions maintains that "Abraham's body is located in a cave [*maghāra*] that extends between the Rock and Abraham's mosque, that is, the Cave of the Patriarchs; his legs are lying underneath the mosque [in Hebron] and his head underneath the Rock [on the Temple Mount]".[20] The Rock (al-Ṣakhra) is the one above which the Dome of the Rock was erected. The idea that underneath it lies a cave may hint at the site's function as the navel of the earth, which connects the upper and lower worlds. The connection with Hebron might indicate that this ancient city shares the merit of the navel of the earth. A similar sanctity formula is used to describe Adam's tomb, said to be "located in a cave that extends between Bayt al-Maqdis and Abraham's mosque. His legs are located beside the Rock and his head is in Abraham's mosque. The distance between them is eighteen miles".[21] It was Noah who buried Adam in Bayt al-Maqdis. He took his body with him on the Ark, and after the Flood brought the body out of the Ark.[22] Adam himself, according to another tradition, died in India, but requested to be buried in Bayt al-Maqdis. Abraham, Isaac, Jacob, and Joseph asked before their death to be buried in Bayt al-Maqdis.[23] This implies that the term Bayt al-Maqdis could signify al-Shām as a whole.

---

18 Kister, "Sanctity Joint and Divided", pp. 29–30.

19 Mujīr al-Dīn, *al-Uns al-jalīl*, I, p. 56–57. Cf. Sharon, "The Cities of the Holy Land", p. 104–105.

20 Ibn ʿAsākir, *Taʾrīkh Dimashq*, I, p. 256.

21 Ibn ʿAsākir, *Taʾrīkh Dimashq*, VII, p. 458. See also Wāsiṭī, *Faḍāʾil*, p. 77 (nos. 125, 126, 127); Livne-Kafri, *Selected Essays*, p. 62. On Adam's burial under the Foundation Stone in Jewish tradition, cf. Eliav, *God's Mountain*, pp. 78–79.

22 Suyūṭī, *al-Durr al-manthūr* (Q 11:44).

23 Muqātil, *Addendum*, p. 514. See also Ibn al-Murajjā, *Faḍāʾil*, p. 260; Ibn al-Jawzī, *Taʾrīkh Bayt al-Maqdis*, p. 72.

A special site for the burial of prophets is the Mount of Olives:

On the Mount of Olives seventy thousand prophets died, killed by famine, nakedness and lice. The mountain overlooks the [Aqṣā] Mosque, and between them lies the Valley of Hinnom (*wādī jahannam*). From it Jesus was taken up to heaven and there the bridge [*al-ṣirāṭ*] will be placed [on the Day of Judgment]. There ʿUmar b. al-Khaṭṭāb prayed, and there the tombs of the prophets are located.[24]

Here we find allusions to Jewish and Christian traditions about pilgrims and prophets (such as Haggai, Zechariah and Malachi) who were buried on the Mount of Olives. The stress which this tradition places on the fact that they died hungry and destitute serves to highlight their asceticism and the risks they were willing to take as pilgrims to the Holy Land. Indeed, Muslim ascetics, *zuhhād* or Ṣūfīs, who were devoted to the sanctity of al-Shām, contributed greatly to traditions about the merits of visiting it, and some also journeyed there themselves,[25] thus preserving an ancient Christian monastic tradition.[26] In the above tradition, the caliph ʿUmar b. al-Khaṭṭāb (ruled 13–23/634–644), under whom the Muslims gained control over Jerusalem, is also one of these devoted pilgrims.[27] The mention of Jesus' ascension from the Mount of Olives conforms to the Christian tradition on this matter; the Qurʾān, too, mentions Jesus' ascension, without naming a location (Q 3:55; 4:158).

In addition to the Mount of Olives, traditions also mention the "Mountain of al-Shām". The Prophet himself is quoted as saying: "Allāh took it upon himself to vouch [*takaffala*] for al-Shām and its inhabitants on my behalf. Iblīs [Satan] came to Iraq, lay his eggs there and hatched his chicks. Then he came to Egypt, where he spread his rug and sat on it. [The Prophet] said: The Mountain of al-Shām is the mountain of the prophets".[28] The meaning of the "Mountain of al-Shām" (*jabal al-Shām*) is somewhat obscure. It is probably the mountain range known as Mount Lebanon, or more likely the mountain cluster called Mount Hermon. The inviolability of the latter was compared to that of Mount Sinai, and it was respected in Late Antiquity as a sanctuary.[29]

24 Yāqūt, *Muʿjam al-buldān*, IV, p. 47–48 (s.v. Ṭūr Zaytā).

25 Goitein, "Sanctity", pp. 122–126; Livne-Kafri, *Selected Essays*, pp. 85, 88–98,118–123.

26 Goitein, "Sanctity", p. 126; *idem*, *Studies*, pp. 142–146.

27 Ṣafiyya, the Jewish wife of Muḥammad who converted to Islam, also prayed on the Mount of Olives. See Ashtor, "Arabic Book", p. 213; Bashear, "*Qibla Musharriqa*", p. 273; Livne-Kafri, *Selected Essays*, pp. 54–55; *idem*, "Christian Attitudes", p. 371.

28 Ibn ʿAsākir, *Taʾrīkh Dimashq*, I, p. 99.

29 See Myers, *The Ituraeans*, p. 65. As for the entire tradition, ʿAbdallāh b. Wahb (d. 197/813) explains that it alludes to events connected with the murder of ʿUthmān which the people of al-

The prophets and the defense of al-Shām

A series of traditions magnifies the number of prophets who were interred at various sites in al-Shām, as an indication of the great sanctity of these sites.[30] Thus, parallel to the tradition we discussed above about the seventy thousand prophets who died on the Mount of Olives, we have another one, transmitted in the name of ʿAbdallāh b. Salām, a convert from Judaism and a Companion of the Prophet. This tradition states that the number of the graves of prophets in al-Shām is two thousand seven hundred.[31] Another tradition, again quoting Kaʿb al-Aḥbār, enumerates many tombs of prophets in frontier regions located on the front with the Byzantines:

> In the name of Kaʿb, he said: In Ṭarsūs there are ten tombs of prophets, in al-Maṣṣīṣa there are five . . . in Ḥimṣ there are thirty tombs, in Damascus there are five-hundred tombs and in the district of al-Urdunn there is the same number . . . [according to another version Kaʿb said:] On the frontiers [*al-thughūr*] and on the shores of al-Shām there are a thousand tombs of prophets . . . in the district of al-Urdunn there is the same number, in Filasṭīn there is the same number, in Bayt al-Maqdis there are a thousand tombs, and in al-ʿArīsh there are ten. And Moses' tomb is in Damascus.[32]

Ṭarsūs and Maṣṣīṣa were near the frontiers (*al-thughūr*), on the conflict line with the Christians in northwestern Syria.[33] The coasts of Syria and Filasṭīn were also considered a frontier that had to be protected from the navies of the unbelievers. In all these regions the Muslims performed *ribāṭ*, i.e. maintaining a presence for defense and for raids into the territory of the unbelievers.[34] The statement attributed to Kaʿb about the many tombs of prophets meant to serve as a model for generations of believers, who are thus encouraged to come to the front and engage in *ribāṭ*. The tombs in other regions of al-Shām, Damascus, al-Urdunn and Filasṭīn, emphasize the land's merit as a place that must be protected and settled in order to prevent it from falling into non-Muslim hands.

As for Moses' tomb, in a number of traditions about Muḥammad's nocturnal journey through key sites in the lives of the prophets who preceded him,[35] he sees Moses standing in prayer in his tomb. This was near the Red Sand Dune

---

Shām did not take part in (among those who did participate in the murder were ʿAlī's supporters, residents of Iraq). See Ibn ʿAsākir, *Taʾrīkh Dimashq*, I, p. 317.

30 Cf. Kister, "Sanctity Joint and Divided", p. 22.

31 Suyūṭī, *al-Durr al-manthūr* (Q 21:71).

32 Ibn ʿAsākir, *Taʾrīkh Dimashq*, II, p. 410–411. See also Kister, "Sanctity Joint and Divided", p. 42.

33 See Grossmann E., *The Concepts of ribāṭ*, p. 184: "Ṭarsūs was then considered 'the *thaghr* of the Muslims' in the full sense of the term, whence the Muslims set out for the *jihād*".

34 On the importance of the *ribāṭ* along the sea shores see *ibid.*, p. 207. See also Goitein, *Studies*, p. 146; Elad, "The Coastal Cities"; Livne-Kafri, *Selected Essays*, pp. 113–114.

35 See above, Chapter 1.

(*al-kathīb al-aḥmar*).[36] According to some traditions, the Red Sand Dune that marks Moses' tomb is located on the summit of Mount Sinai (*al-Ṭūr*) or in Jericho, as opposed to Kaʿb's tradition which locates it in Damascus.[37]

The military context of the Muslim presence in al-Shām comes up in a statement ascribed to the Prophet himself in a version transmitted by the Baṣran exegete Qatāda (d. 117/735). It is recorded in the commentary on the verse that mentions Abraham's land of refuge (Q 21:71):

> There will in future be an army [*jund*] in al-Shām, an army in Iraq, and an army in Yemen. Then one of the people asked: O Messenger of Allāh, choose for me [which army to join]. [The Prophet] said: You should go to al-Shām [*ʿalayka bi-l-Shām*], for Allāh pledged to me to vouch for al-Shām and its inhabitants . . .[38]

The Arabic term *jund* ("army") can also mean a military district, such as the five districts established in the reign of the caliph ʿUmar b. al-Khaṭṭāb in Palestine and Syria (Filasṭīn, Urdunn, Qinnasrīn, Dimashq, Ḥimṣ).[39] However, in the present tradition the term refers to al-Shām in general as a *jund* by itself, in addition to the districts of Iraq and Yemen.[40] The Prophet's statement here to the effect that of all the districts one should strive to go to al-Shām is designed to reinforce the Muslim presence in a region where Abraham and Lot found shelter from their pursuers.

The call to settle al-Shām is also attributed to the Prophet in other traditions according to which he places special emphasis on the preferred status of al-Shām over Yemen as a land of refuge: "Whoever refuses [to come to al-Shām], let him sit in his Yemen [*fa-l-yalḥaq bi-Yamanihi*] and water [his flocks] from its springs. Allāh, may he be exalted, pledged to me to vouch for al-Shām and its inhabitants".[41] The Prophet also declares that those who reside in al-Shām are in a constant state of readiness and are to be considered as *murābiṭūn*. The territory covered by their *ribāṭ* extends until the end of the *Jazīra*. This definition applies also to civilians, women and children included. Those who reside on the shores of the Mediterranean Sea are *mujāhidūn* (that is, they have the status of full-fledged warriors); in Jerusalem they

---

36 E.g. Muslim, *Ṣaḥīḥ*, VII, p. 102 (*Faḍāʾil* [44]).

37 See Schwarzbaum, *Folkloristic Aspects*, pp. 47, 50–51. See also Sadan, "The Tomb of Moses", pp. 22–38. A later tradition, originating in the Occult and the Kabbalah, places the tomb of Moses in the Cave of the Patriarchs. See Ish-Shalom, "The Cave of Machpela".

38 Ṭabarī, *Tafsīr* (Q 21:71). See also Ibn ʿAṭiyya, *Tafsīr* (Q 21:71).

39 See Gil, *History of Palestine*, pp. 110–111.

40 Other versions mention two or four regions including al-Shām. See Bashear, "Yemen in Early Islam", pp. 354–358.

41 Aḥmad b. Ḥanbal, *Musnad*, V, pp. 33–34 (*awwal musnad al-Baṣriyyīn, ḥadīth ʿAbdallāh b. Ḥawāla*).

have the status of performers of *ribāṭ*.[42] In another version, the Prophet assigns to the coastal settlements first priority. Whoever stays in them will receive a recompense equal to that given to all those who make the pilgrimage to the Kaʿba.[43]

The traditions that call for enhancing the Muslim presence throughout al-Shām reflect the Muslim fear of a Byzantine *Reconquista*. But not everyone supported this approach. The contrary position is taken in a tradition concerning ʿAbdallāh b. Salām, a Companion of the Prophet and a convert from Judaism. In a reply to his son who was eager to participate in the war, he said: "My son, do not make me distressed by losing you (*lā tafjaʿnī bi-nafsika*). The call to come to the aid of al-Shām (*ṣarīkh al-Shām*[44]) will in any case come to every believer".[45] However, in light of the Muslim fear of the enemies lying in wait on the borders of the lands of Islam, al-Shām remained the first priority as a destination for the believers, as in the above traditions that were disseminated during the first centuries AH.

On the other hand, the idea of *ribāṭ* did not remain restricted to the territory of al-Shām over time. Various cities throughout the Muslim world, from Khurāsān (Qazwīn), through Iraq (ʿAbbādān) and al-Shām itself (Ashkelon), to Egypt (Alexandria), vied for the status of the blessed *ribāṭ*, as part of the local-patriotic campaign of each of these cities.[46] Of particular significance in the present context is the following statement ascribed to the Prophet: "Mecca is a *ribāṭ* and Jedda is a *jihād*".[47] Mecca and its port city of Jedda thus join inland cities of al-Shām such as Jerusalem and the coastal towns of the land which are defined as regions of *ribāṭ* and *jihād*. This expansion of the bounds of *ribāṭ* and *jihād* to cities that are not on the frontlines of the direct confrontation with the unbelievers does not clearly distinguish between the two concepts, and is mainly of a symbolic nature.[48]

---

42 Ibn ʿAsākir, *Taʾrīkh Dimashq*, I, p. 283. See also Livne-Kafri, *Selected Essays*, p. 112.
43 Ibn ʿAsākir, *Taʾrīkh Dimashq*, I, p. 348.
44 I.e. "the crying out for help of al-Shām". Cf. Cook, *Muslim Apocalyptic*, pp. 310–311. See also Q 36:43.
45 Nuʿaym b. Ḥammād, *Fitan*, p. 427.
46 Livne-Kafri, *Selected Essays*, p. 113–123; *idem*, "In Praise of Jerusalem", pp. 174–181.
47 Fākihī, *Akhbār Makka*, II, pp. 312–313 (no. 1570).
48 See Livne-Kafri, *Selected Essays*, p. 113. On the designation of Medina as *ribāṭ* zone in Muḥammad's time, see Grossmann E., *The Concepts of ribāṭ*, pp. 178–181 (in Ibn Taymiyya's discussion).

In praise of traveling to al-Shām on the path of Abraham

Beyond the military context, there are traditions according to which setting forth to al-Shām is conceived as an ideal embedded in the divine plan of redemption that is written in the holy Scriptures:

> It has been reported that Wahb al-Dhimārī said: Allāh wrote [in the Torah] to al-Shām: I have sanctified you and blessed you. I placed my dwelling [*maqāmī*] in you. You are the one I chose [*ṣafwatī*] of all my lands. I shall lead the chosen among my servants to you. Be expansive for them in the livelihood and the places of residence that you contain, just as the womb expands: If two will be placed within it, it will contain them, and if three, it will do so as well. I have put my eye on you in dew and rain, since the beginning of years until the end of time. I will not forget you until I forget my right arm, and until she who possesses the womb will forget what is in it.[49]

In this tradition, reported on the authority of the Yemeni traditionist Wahb al-Dhimārī — who was also a well-versed scholar in the holy Scriptures[50] — allusions to a number of biblical verses can be discerned that deal with Jerusalem (for example, Psalm 137:5: "If I forget you, O Jerusalem, let my right hand wither!"). We see that as far as the merits of al-Shām are concerned, this tradition, like others that we will not quote here, finds them in scriptures revealed to all the prophets, thus giving this region priority in the enactment of God's preordained plan of redemption.

One of the ideas on which the campaign to encourage the believers to move to al-Shām was based was that of *hijra*. Already in the Qur'ān, the term *hijra* is used to describe not only Abraham's departure from his unbelieving compatriots, but also the withdrawal of the believers in Muḥammad's time, who removed themselves from the zone of unbelief. Of particular importance is the following verse, from the Medinan period, that is, after Muḥammad himself performed *hijra* (Q 4:100):

> Whoso emigrates in the way of God will find in the earth many refuges and plenty; whoso goes forth from his house an emigrant to God and his Messenger, and then death overtakes him, his wage shall have fallen on God; surely God is all-forgiving, all-compassionate.

The emigrant's recompense, according to this verse, is redemption on earth, but also possibly a place in Paradise, if one dies in the course of the act of *hijra*. The boundaries of the region in which redemption is promised to those who emigrate to their God are thus not limited to this world, but encompass the world to come as well.

49 Ibn ʿAsākir, *Taʾrīkh Dimashq*, I, pp. 152–153.
50 See about him Ibn Saʿd, *Ṭabaqāt*, V, p. 537.

In post-qurʾānic tradition the image of Abraham as an emigrant was reintroduced and raised to the rank of a model which the believers must follow. This is demonstrated in a tradition of Qatāda recorded in commentaries on Q 21:71 that tells of Abraham's land of refuge: "Both [Abraham and Lot] were in the land of Iraq and were rescued to the land of al-Shām. Al-Shām used to be called the pillar of the *hijra* abode [*ʿimād dār al-hijra*] . . . ".[51] In other words, no other region is more fit as the place in which to implement the model of Abraham's *hijra*.

Another verse that has been interpreted in light of the idea of *hijra* is Q 37:99:

> He [Abraham] said, I am going to my Lord; he will guide me.

This verse alludes to Abraham's journey to the place of his attempted sacrifice of his son. We shall get back to it in the following chapters. For now, we will only look at what the exegete Muqātil b. Sulaymān (d. 150/767) says in his commentary on this verse. He states that Abraham was the first *muhājir* on earth.[52] Although some scholars maintain that Abraham's "going" to God in this verse is metaphorical, as when one places one's trust completely in God — like Abraham's state of mind before he was cast into the flames[53] — most exegetes are of the opinion that Abraham's journey in the present verse is real, that he cut off his ties with the unbelievers and went away, to a destination that was better suited for worshipping God. The verse is thus presented as a "fundamental precedent [*aṣl*] for the principle of *hijra* and withdrawal [*al-ʿuzla*]".[54]

But the most explicit verse is of course the one that defines Abraham's departure from his homeland as *hijra* (Q 29:26). One tradition relating to this verse is again of Qatāda:

> In the name of Qatāda . . . it was reported to us that the Prophet used to say: There will be *hijra* after *hijra* and the people will move in the direction of Abraham's place of emigration [*muhājar*]. In the land only the worst of its inhabitants will remain, until it will throw them up and abhor them and the fire will gather them [*taḥshuruhum*] together with the monkeys and the pigs.[55]

In this tradition, the Prophet asserts that the most appropriate destination for the people's *hijra* is al-Shām, as it was for Abraham.[56] The fire which will pursue those who refuse to come to al-Shām symbolizes a flood of enemies who trample

---

51 Ṭabarī, *Tafsīr* (Q 21:71).
52 Muqātil, *Tafsīr* (Q 37:99).
53 Ibn ʿAṭiyya, *Tafsīr* (Q 37:99).
54 Qurṭubī, *Aḥkām al-Qurʾān* (Q 37:99).
55 Ṭabarī, *Tafsīr* (Q 29:26).
56 Cf. Goitein, *Studies*, pp. 144–145.

upon everything that stands in their way.[57] The recalcitrants, according to this tradition, will share the same horrible fate as the most inferior animals, namely, the monkeys and the pigs. The Qur'ān depicts these animals as lowly creatures, in whose image Allāh transformed the Jews and the Christians (Q 2:65; 5:60). In this manner Abraham's *hijra* marks al-Shām's special merit as the land imbued with God's blessing, and hence the most appropriate place for whoever is forced to leave his home and seek God's protection elsewhere.[58] In light of the above, the position of Bayt al-Maqdis as a *hijra* destination in the Latter Days is one of al-Shām's virtues as recorded in Muqātil's *Tafsīr*.[59]

The Umayyads and the boundaries of Abraham's Promised Land

The idea of Abraham's *hijra* was conscripted for the promotion of the idea of *ribāṭ* and *jihād*. This can be seen in a tradition according to which God informed Abraham that in the Latter Days. He will bring His best people to the land of Abraham's *hijra*, namely, "Filasṭīn and Bayt al-Maqdis", in order that they may do battle on that land's shores against the children of Esau, i.e. the Romans.[60] This is an apocalyptic vision that expresses hope for a definitive victory over the Rūm (the Byzantines) who threatened to reconquer al-Shām. The most eager ones to mobilize the believers for defending the land against the Rūm were the Umayyads. Therefore, they disseminated traditions that enumerated al-Shām's virtues as a longed-for destination. This interest is reflected in traditions about Muʿāwiya, the first of the Umayyad caliphs. In one of these he is presented as evoking the model of the biblical promise to Abraham, that his seed would inherit the land "from the river of Egypt to the great river, the river Euphrates" (Genesis 15:18). In the spirit of this promise, Muʿāwiya said that God commanded Abraham: "Reside [*uʿmur*] in the land, from al-ʿArīsh to the Euphrates, this is the blessed land".[61]

57 In another tradition attributed to Muḥammad himself, the fire that is to pursuit the people until Muhājar Ibrāhīm is about to emerge from Aden. See Nuʿaym b. Ḥammād, *Fitan*, p. 428. In another version the fire will come from Ḥaḍramawt. See Mubārakfūrī, *Tuḥfat al-aḥwadhī*, VI, pp. 463–464 (no. 2314) (= Tirmidhī, *Sunan*, *Fitan* [31]). In yet other versions the origin of the fire that will pervade the people is in other zones of the Muslim world such as the Mashriq and the Maghrib. See e.g. Nuʿaym b. Ḥammād, *Fitan*, p. 425.

58 On the notion of Abraham's *hijra* to al-Shām see also Livne-Kafri, *Selected Essays*, p. 85.

59 Muqātil, *Addendum*, p. 514. See also Ibn al-Murajjā, *Faḍā'il*, p. 260.

60 Ibn al-Murajjā, *Faḍā'il*, p. 160 (no. 212). Quoted in Livne-Kafri, *Selected Essays*, p. 47.

61 Suyūṭī, *al-Durr al-manthūr* (Q 7:137). Suyūṭī gleaned this tradition from Ibn ʿAsākir, *Ta'rīkh Dimashq*, I, p. 141.

Wādī al-ʿArīsh is the largest stream in the Sinai Peninsula that flows into the Mediterranean Sea. In Muʿāwiya's rendering it corresponds to the biblical "river of Egypt". Elsewhere it is called "the Wādī of Egypt" [נַחַל מִצְרַיִם] (1 Kings 8:65).[62] We thus see that Islam's sanctification of the blessed land, the land given to Abraham, is based on the biblical outline of the borders of the Promised Land. Kaʿb al-Aḥbār, a rich source of supposedly reliable information about holy scriptures and Israelite history, is also quoted as having testified that "Allāh, may he be blessed and exalted, blessed al-Shām, the region extending from the Euphrates to al-ʿArīsh".[63] Kaʿb himself resided in the city of Homs (Ḥimṣ) in Syria, which explains why he narrated so many traditions about the merits of al-Shām, which were ostensibly already foretold in the Torah.

The same borders of the Promised Land recur in a tradition that uses imagery taken from nature, again in the name of Kaʿb al-Aḥbār: "Soon the thunder and the lightning will emigrate to al-Shām, until there will be no thunder and no lightning anywhere except in the region between al-ʿArīsh and the Euphrates".[64]

What better proof is there that al-Shām is superior to all other places on earth?

The settlement of Bayt al-Maqdis is the ruin of Medina

But the call to settle al-Shām is only one side of the coin. There are other traditions, which oppose the rush to leave Arabia for the territories that came under Islamic rule after the Prophet's death. These traditions express a desire to retain the populace of Medina, the Prophet's city, which was abandoned by the believers who were seeking a better life outside of Arabia:

> The Messenger of Allāh said: The settlement [*ʿumrān*] of Bayt al-Maqdis is the ruin [*kharāb*] of Yathrib [Medina]; the ruin of Yathrib is the beginning of the war [*al-malḥama*] [between Muslims and Romans]; the war is the conquest [*fatḥ*] of Constantinople; the conquest of Constantinople is the emergence of the Dajjāl.[65]

62 As for the river Euphrates, it appears as the border of the Promised Land in more instances in the Hebrew Bible, e.g. Deuteronomy 11:24: "Every place on which you set foot shall be yours; your territory shall extend from the wilderness to the Lebanon and from the River, the river Euphrates, to the Western Sea".

63 Suyūṭī, *al-Durr al-manthūr* (Q 7:137). See also Ibn ʿAsākir, *Taʾrīkh Dimashq*, I, p. 144.

64 Ibn ʿAsākir, *Taʾrīkh Dimashq*, I, p. 227.

65 Abū Dāwūd, *Sunan*, II, p. 425 (*Malāḥim* [36]:3 [*Bāb amārat al-malāḥim*]. See also Ibn Abī Shayba, *Muṣannaf*, XV, pp. 135–136 (no. 19323); Aḥmad b. Ḥanbal, *Musnad*, V, p. 232, 245; Daylamī, *Firdaws*, III, p. 50 (no. 4127). The tradition is quoted in Kister, "A Comment on the Antiquity", p. 185. See also Livne-Kafri, *Selected Essays*, p. 66.

This apocalyptic vision depicts the dismal situation of Medina along the lines of the literary model of the Portents of the Hour (*ashrāṭ al-sāʿa*). The first portent is the settlement of Bayt al-Maqdis. This is explained as a prediction of the excessive nature of its settlement or as a scenario where it will be settled by unbelievers who will rebuild it according to their self-centered ambitions after they will have conquered it.[66] The vision continues with the apocalyptic war between the believers and the Rūm at the end of which Constantinople, which was not conquered during the period of the caliphate, will fall. Thereupon the Dajjāl, the false Messiah, will appear (eventually to be defeated by Jesus, son of Mary).

Abraham's journey to al-Shām is only one aspect of his wanderings, as described both in Meccan verses of the Qurʾān and in various traditions. In other *sūra*s, most of them Medinan, a new path for his journey is discerned-one that does not end in al-Shām but instead brings him to Mecca and the Kaʿba. The redefined course marks a reinforcement of the Ishmaelite identity of Abraham's descendants, alongside with the renunciation of the Jewish messianic vision of redemption in the Promised Land. More on this in the next two chapters.

66 See Dānī, *Fitan*, IV, pp. 887–888, the comment of the editor which pertains to traditions that regret the settlement in the new territories outside of Arabia at the expense of Medina. See also Livne-Kafri, "Jerusalem in Early Islam", p. 399.

7 Ishmael and the progeny of Abraham

The group of three Patriarchs-Abraham, Isaac and Jacob—which is described in Meccan verses about Abraham's arrival in the blessed land that God promised him (al-Shām), is expanded in Medinan verses in which Ishmael joins it and takes his place before Isaac. This expanded group has no connection to the blessed land. The verses in which it is mentioned signal the growth of the Ishmaelite identity of the community of believers, and stress that Abraham and his descendants were neither Jews nor Christians. These verses form part of the disputation with Judaism and Christianity and represent the qur'ānic response to the Christian view that Isaac, "son of the promise", is to be preferred over Ishmael, "son of the flesh".

In contrast to the Meccan *sūra*s examined in the previous chapter, in which the three Patriarchs are mentioned in connection with the land blessed by God (al-Shām), the verses that we shall examine in the present chapter add Ishmael to Abraham's descendants. At first, he is placed next to Isaac and Jacob, but eventually he replaces them. The growth of the Ishmaelite identity of Abraham's progeny has its roots in Islam's dispute with Judaism and Christianity.

The four patriarchs: Abraham, Ishmael, Isaac and Jacob

Evidence for the addition of Ishmael to the Patriarchs is provided in the following verse, which appears in a Medinan *sūra* (Q 2:133):

> Why, were you witnesses, when death came to Jacob? When he said to his sons, 'What will you serve after me?' They said, 'We will serve your God and the God of your fathers Abraham, Ishmael and Isaac, one God; to him we surrender [*muslimūn*].

This is the scene of Jacob on his deathbed which appears in the Talmud, where his sons commit themselves to the worship of the One God (Talmud Bavli, Pesachim 56a):

> Jacob wished to reveal to his sons the 'end of the days', whereupon the Shechinah departed from him. Said he, 'Perhaps, Heaven forfend! there is one unfit among my children, like Abraham, from whom there issued Ishmael, or like my father Isaac, from whom there issued Esau.' [But] his sons answered him, 'Hear O Israel, the Lord our God the Lord is One.[1]

1 This passage as well as some parallel ones was already noted by Speyer, *Die biblischen Erzählungen*, p. 222.

https://doi.org/10.1515/9783111222318-008

In this midrash Ishmael is a link that impairs the lineage of Abraham, Isaac and Jacob. The Qurʾān, however, gives him pride of place, as Abraham's first-born son, placing him before Isaac and Jacob. This signals the growing Ishmaelite identity of the bearers of the divine plan of redemption who are now four: Abraham, Ishmael, Isaac and Jacob.

In other verses all of Muḥammad's contemporaries are commanded to believe in the group of four, as well as in the other prophets whose heritage represents Islam (Q 2:136; 3:84). All of them were granted a divine revelation of the same kind as was given to Muḥammad himself (Q 4:163).

Abraham is neither a Jew nor a Christian

The group of four is also mentioned along with the statement that none of them and none of their descendants was a Jew or a Christian (Q 2:140):

> Or do you say, 'Abraham, Ishmael, Isaac and Jacob, and the Tribes [= sons of Jacob] — they were Jews, or they were Christians'? Say: 'Have you then greater knowledge, or God? And who does greater evil than he who conceals a testimony received from God? And God is not heedless of the things you do'.

Not only are the four patriarchs and Jacob's sons presented here as Muslims, with no relationship to the people of Israel, but the Qurʾān even declares that this is a fact which was already written in the "testimony", that is, in the Torah, possessed by the Jews and Christians themselves. Perhaps this is an allusion to the passages in the Pentateuch that relate that Abraham was born and raised in Ur of the Chaldeans (Genesis 11:27–29), and that Jacob was of Aramean origin before he became a "great nation".[2]

Of the group of four patriarchs, other Medinan verses focus on Abraham alone and further promote the idea that he was neither a Jew nor a Christian. This is achieved through the argument that he preceded in time both Moses and Jesus, i.e. he lived before the Torah was given to the Jews or the Gospel to the Christians (Q 3:65–68):

2 Deuteronomy 26:5: "A wandering Aramean was my ancestor; he went down into Egypt and lived there as an alien, few in number, and there he became a great nation, mighty and populous". Peshiṭta (Deuteronomy), p. 145: "My father was taken to Aram, and he went down to Egypt . . . ". This is a formula God commands a person to say when firstfruits are brought to the Temple. It portrays Jacob as a lost Aramean, meaning that he was of Aram and was a wanderer. The Sages changed the meaning of "A wandering Aramean was my ancestor", and maintained that it says: "An Aramean [i.e. Laban] tried to kill my ancestor". See e.g. Midrash Tanḥuma (Buber), Deuteronomy, Parashat Ekev 5.

> (65) People of the Book! Why do you dispute concerning Abraham? The Torah was not sent down, neither the Gospel, but after him. What, have you no reason? (66) Ha, you are the ones who dispute on what you know; why then dispute you touching a matter of which you know not anything? God knows, and you know not. (67) No; Abraham in truth was not a Jew, neither a Christian; but he was a *ḥanīf*, a Muslim; certainly he was never of the idolaters. (68) Surely the people standing closest to Abraham are those who followed him, and this Prophet, and those who believe; and God is the protector of the believers.

In this passage the Qur'ān states not only that Abraham was neither a Jew nor a Christian, but also that his entire conduct was that of a *ḥanīf*, that is, one who does not belong to any established religion. In a Meccan *sūra* the Qur'ān severs Abraham from any institutional religion that preceded Islam (Q 16:120):

> Surely, Abraham was a nation [unto himself] obedient unto God, a *ḥanīf*, and no idolater.

By calling Abraham a "nation" (*umma*), the Qur'ān tells us that he did not belong to any community, neither Jewish nor Christian; he was a *ḥanīf*, an individual believer in God's unity.

The message these passages convey is that Abraham's true legacy has been preserved only among Muḥammad's Muslim *umma*, the one nation that has not failed to maintain Abraham's monotheistic heritage, in contrast to the Jews and the Christians. It is the Prophet who redeems people from idolatry, who is the sole guide in his generation to the true path, and who implements the plan of redemption in all its aspects. Therefore, it is incumbent upon the Jews and the Christians to join him as Muslims, if they truly wish to preserve Abraham's heritage. This is stated explicitly in the verse that precedes the passage about Abraham the *ḥanīf* (Q 3:64):

> Say: 'People of the Book! Come now to a word common between us and you, that we serve none but God, and that we associate not aught with him, and do not some of us take others as Lords, apart from God.' And if they turn their backs, say: 'Bear witness that we are Muslims.'

In other words, only by joining the Prophet can the People of the Book, the Jews and the Christians, ensure their redemption, for only Muḥammad's supporters are the true Muslims.

Violation of Abraham's covenant

The Qur'ān not only severs any connection which Abraham and his descendants might have with Judaism and Christianity, but in other verses it also accuses the Jews and the Christians of having violated Abraham's covenant. A hint of this can be found at the end of the qur'ānic version of the story of Abraham's attempted sacrifice of his son to which we shall return below. It appears in a Meccan *sūra* (Q 37:113):

> And We blessed him, and Isaac; and of their seed some are good-doers, and some manifest self-wrongers.

The "self-wrongers" whom the Qur'ān condemns here are of the seed of Isaac, that is, Jews and Christians. The same can be seen in other verses, most of them from later Medinan *sūras* (Q 2:130–132):

> (130) Who therefore shrinks from the religion of Abraham, except he be foolish-minded? Indeed, We chose him in the present world, and in the world to come he shall be among the righteous. (131) When his Lord said to him, 'Surrender,' he said, 'I have surrendered me to the Lord of all being.' (132) And Abraham charged his sons with this and Jacob likewise: 'My sons, God has chosen for you the religion; see that you die not save as Muslims'.

Here, too, the condemnation of the "foolish-minded" who did not adhere to the path of Islam is most probably aimed at groups among the descendants of Abraham himself. This is clearly the case in the following verse (Q 57:26):

> (26) And We sent Noah, and Abraham, and We appointed the prophecy and the book to be among their seed; and some of them are guided, and many of them are ungodly.

The many "ungodly" among the progeny of Noah and Abraham are those who did not obey the commandments of the prophets and the holy Scriptures which they gave them, that is, who did not accept Islam, as required by their prophets' words. The intended objects of this condemnation are almost certainly the non-Muslim descendants of Abraham in Muḥammad's time, namely, the Jews and the Christians. An indirect criticism of these groups is repeated in the following Medinan verse (Q 2:124):

> And when his Lord tested Abraham with certain words, and he fulfilled them. He said, 'Behold, I make you a leader [*imāman*] for the people.' Said he, 'And of my seed?' He said, 'my covenant shall not reach the evildoers.'

The "evildoers" mentioned here are those who did not remain loyal to Abraham's heritage. Abraham himself had become an *imām* for the people, that is, an origin of guidance and blessing. Perhaps there is a connection here to Genesis 12:3: "I will bless those who bless you, and the one who curses you I will curse; and in you all the families of the earth shall be blessed". In other words, people will find in Abraham a source of blessing and guidance, but only those who do not curse him. In fact, whoever curses him will be cursed by God. The same message is contained in the qur'ānic verse just quoted: God will expel the evildoers among Abraham's descendants from his covenant. Here the identity of the evildoers is not made explicit, but we may conjecture that, again, the reference is to the Jews and

Christians of Muḥammad's time. This observation is explicit in the words of the exegete Muqātil b. Sulaymān (d. 150/767) on Q 2:124:

> God says (to Muḥammad): Among your seed there are evil doers (*ẓalama*), namely the Jews and the Christians.

The seed of Abraham in Christian theology

The need to detach Abraham from both Judaism and Christianity, as discerned in the Qur'ān, stems from the fact that not only Jews, but also Christians, claimed that they were his exclusive heirs and progeny. One clear example of this can be found in Paul's Epistle to the Galatians (3:15–17):

> (15) Brothers and sisters, I give an example from daily life: once a person's will has been ratified, no one adds to it or annuls it. (16) Now the promises were made to Abraham and to his offspring; it does not say, 'And to offsprings,' as of many; but it says, 'And to your offspring,' that is, to one person, who is Christ. (17) My point is this: the law, which came four hundred thirty years later, does not annul a covenant previously ratified by God, so as to nullify the promise.

The idea here is that the covenant with Abraham relates to "an offspring" (in the singular), that offspring being Jesus Christ. The covenant had been made four hundred and thirty years before the Law was given at Sinai, and it therefore takes precedence. In other words, only Christ and his followers are the true seed of Abraham, and the Jews, who rely on Moses' reception of the Law, are not to be counted as such.[3] Indeed, in the Christian view the promise to Abraham, the covenant which God made with him, applies only to the Christians, as we read in Acts 3:25–26:

> (25) You are the descendants of the prophets and of the covenant that God gave to your ancestors, saying to Abraham, 'And in your descendants all the families of the earth shall be blessed.' (26) When God raised up his servant, he sent him first to you, to bless you by turning each of you from your wicked ways.

The sentence "And in your descendants all the families of the earth shall be blessed" is a combination of the two formulations of the covenant in Genesis 12.

---

3 The same idea recurs later in the epistle (Galatians 3:26–29): "(26) For in Christ Jesus you are all children of God through faith. (27) As many of you as were baptized into Christ have clothed yourselves with Christ. (28) There is no longer Jew or Greek, there is no longer slave or free, there is no longer male and female; for all of you are one in Christ Jesus. (29) And if you belong to Christ, then you are Abraham's offspring, heirs according to the promise".

At this point it is worth noting that already in the Hebrew Bible the people of Israel is depicted as having betrayed the divine covenant made at Sinai:

Jeremiah 31:31–33 [30–32]

> (31) The days are surely coming, says the Lord, when I will make a new covenant with the house of Israel and the house of Judah. (32) It will not be like the covenant that I made with their ancestors when I took them by the hand to bring them out of the land of Egypt – a covenant that they broke, though I was their husband, says the Lord. (33) But this is the covenant that I will make with the house of Israel after those days, says the Lord: I will put my law within them, and I will write it on their hearts; and I will be their God, and they shall be my people.

It here follows that the covenant of the giving of the Torah in Sinai has expired, and has been replaced by a new covenant that will come into force in days to come. This passage from Jeremiah is quoted in the New Testament (Hebrews 8:9–10), where the conclusion is as follows: (verse 13): "In speaking of 'a new covenant', he has made the first one obsolete. And what is obsolete and growing old will soon disappear".

Ishmael in Christian theology

As for Ishmael, Paul draws a distinction between the sons of Ishmael, whom he defines as "the children of the flesh", and the progeny of Isaac, who are "the children of the promise", alluding to the divine promise given to Abraham when Isaac was born (Genesis 18:10).[4] This implies that it is Isaac's seed that will partake of God's promised plan of redemption, rather than the children of Hagar and Ishmael. Indeed, Paul highlights the biblical verse (Genesis 21:10) in which, according to his paraphrase, Sarah demands of Abraham to "Drive out the slave and her child; for the child of the slave will not share the inheritance with the child of the free woman" (Galatians 4:30). In other words, the Christians are among the children of Isaac, the sons of the free woman (Sarah), and they are the heirs chosen to be included in God's plan of redemption.

4 Romans 9:6–13. See also Galatians 4:22–31.

The qur'ānic response

It would appear that the Qur'ān is aware of the idea of the covenant with Abraham's seed in its Christian form, since it denies its validity in the following verse (Q 5:14):

> And with those who say 'We are Christians' We took compact; and they have forgotten a portion of that they were reminded of. So We have stirred up among them enmity and hatred, till the Day of Resurrection; and God will assuredly tell them of the things they wrought.

God's covenant with the Christians that is mentioned in this verse stands apparently for Abraham's covenant. Not only does the Qur'ān condemn the Christians for having violated that covenant, it also condemns both them and the Jews for the enmity between them, or perhaps for the enmity between the various Christian denominations. As for Ishmael, the Qur'ān rehabilitates him and joins him to the Patriarchs, thus giving preference to those whom the Christians call "the children of the flesh". In the Qur'ān Ishmael's status is even superior to that of Isaac's progeny, whom the Christians view as "the children of the promise". The genealogical consideration, that Muḥammad is a descendant of Ishmael, constitutes the foundation for the rehabilitation of this patriarch in the Qur'ān.

We thus see that in the Medinan verses the tone of criticism of the Jews and Christians sharpens and they are deprived of the true, Islamic, heritage of the Ishmaelite seed of Abraham. Abraham's, Isaac's and Jacob's connection to the blessed land mentioned in the Meccan verses disappears, a sign of the changing attitude towards the Jewish vision of redemption in their Promised Land. Furthermore, the Medinan verses place the Ishmaelite seed of Abraham in the Arab environment of Mecca and the Kaʿba instead of in the blessed land, and at the same time make Isaac disappear completely, replacing him with Ishmael. More on this in the next chapter.

8 Abraham and Ishmael build the Kaʿba

In the Medinan *sūras*, the Qur'ān not only attaches Ishmael to the three Patriarchs, thus reasserting the Ishmaelite identity of Abraham's seed, but eventually pushes Isaac and Jacob aside, so that Ishmael is left alone with Abraham. Both appear in Mecca, where together they build the walls of the Kaʿba on its ancient foundations. The description of the work of construction reflects the model of the construction of Abraham's house in Hebron as found in the Book of Jubilees. The glorification of the Ishmaelite character of the Arabian temple is designed to shape it as a worthy arena for the appearance of Muḥammad, the redeeming Arab Messenger, scion of Abraham and Ishmael. The appearance of this Messenger is presaged in Abraham's and Ishmael's joint prayer after having completed the Kaʿba's construction. In their prayer, Muḥammad is the one who will bring the true faith to the seed of Abraham and Ishmael and will disseminate it among his Muslim community.

The growth of the Ishmaelite identity of Abraham's progeny reaches its clearest manifestation in Medinan verses in which Abraham's journey does not end in the land that God has blessed (al-Shām), as it does in the Meccan verses, but continues on to Mecca and the Kaʿba, where he is accompanied only by Ishmael. In what follows we look at the verses which describe Abraham's arrival at the site of the Kaʿba, which he constructs with Ishmael's help. These descriptions are loaded with models that can be traced to Jewish sources.

Abraham in Mecca

One of the Medinan verses in which Abraham appears at the Kaʿba is the following (Q 22:26):

> And when We pointed for Abraham at the place of the House: 'You shall not associate with me anything. And purify my House for those that shall go about it and those that stand, for those that bow and prostrate themselves'.

The "place of the House" is the site where the Kaʿba is to be built, as described in a verse to which we will come below (Q 2:127). Exegetical sources contain the following episode in connection with the present verse, for example al-Samarqandī's (d. 375/985) *Tafsīr*:

https://doi.org/10.1515/9783111222318-009

> Allāh sent a cloud (*saḥāba*) possessing the dimensions of the House, with a talking head. It said: O Abraham, build according to my dimensions opposite me. So he founded the House accordingly, and the cloud disappeared.[1]

The theme of the cloud appears in pre-Islamic sources, in connection with the attempted sacrifice of Isaac (Midrash Rabbah, I, p. 491 [*Genesis Rabbah* 56:1]):

> 'And saw the place afar off' (22: 4): What did he see? He saw a cloud enveloping the mountain, and said: It appears that that is the place where the Holy One, blessed be he, told me to sacrifice my son.[2]

The tradition about Abraham being directed to the site of the House by a cloud thus constitutes an adapted version of Abraham's journey to the place of Isaac's attempted sacrifice. The version in the Qur'ān may already contain elements of the story of the attempted sacrifice, since in the biblical account of this episode which unfolds on Mount Moriah, the word "place" (*maqōm*) appears no less than four times (Genesis 22:3, 4, 9, 14). It may thus be surmised that the Medinan verse above, in which Abraham's destination is "the place (*makān*) of the House", redefines Abraham's path, which this time takes him not to the place of Isaac's attempted sacrifice but to the site of the Kaʿba.

Another biblical model which may also be contained in the qur'ānic version of Abraham's journey is the following: Genesis 12:9 reads: "And Abram journeyed on by stages towards the Negeb [הַנֶּגְבָּה = 'towards the south']". The Jewish Sages explained that "He drew a course and journeyed towards the [future] site of the Temple (Midrash Rabbah, I, p. 325 [*Genesis Rabbah* 39:16])".[3] In the qur'ānic version Abraham travels to "the place of the House", which is indeed in the south. The Temple in Jerusalem has thus been replaced by the Arabian shrine in Mecca.

Whatever the biblical-midrashic model, Abraham's guidance towards "the place of the House" as described above includes the command not to "associate" anything with God. Abraham is thus the founder of monotheism. This account differs from the one in the Meccan passage (Q 6:75–79) in which it is the young Abraham's observation of the heavenly bodies that led him to realize that Allāh was

---

1 Samarqandī, *Tafsīr* (Q 22:26). See also Busse, "Jerusalem and Mecca", p. 240; Witztum, "The Foundations of the House", pp. 34–35.

2 Witztum, "The Foundations of the House", pp. 34–35.

3 This midrash is based on two verses in Ezekiel and one in Psalms, in which the words *negeb* and *darom* ["south"] are seemingly synonymous with the Temple: Ezekiel 21:2 [20:46]: "Mortal, set your face toward the south, preach against the *south* [lit. אֶלדָּרוֹם], and prophesy against the forest land in the Negeb"; Ezekiel 21:7 [21:2] "Mortal, set your face toward *Jerusalem* and preach against the sanctuaries; prophesy against the land of Israel"; Psalms 126:4: "Restore our fortunes, O Lord, like the watercourses in the *Negeb*".

the one and only God. This is a model that appears already in pre-Islamic Jewish literature.[4] But in the present Medinan verse, the belief in monotheism is presented to Abraham as a divine commandment that is linked to the establishment of the Kaʿba as a shrine of the one God.

After Abraham is commanded to believe in one God, Allāh tells him to purify the House. He is instructed to do so presumably after he himself has built the actual house over the place to which God led him. The act of purification is intended to protect the Kaʿba from any trace of polytheism and make it fit to serve as a place where pilgrims can worship God. Here, too, Abraham emerges not only as the father of monotheism, but also as the founder of the pilgrimage to Mecca.

The instruction to purify the Kaʿba is repeated in a Medinan *sūra* in a passage that also deals with Abraham's connection to the Kaʿba (Q 2:125–129). Let us follow the sequence of events described in it, beginning with the command of purification. This time God gives it jointly to Abraham and Ishmael (Q 2:125):[5]

> . . . And We made covenant with Abraham and Ishmael: 'Purify my House for those who shall circumambulate it, and those who cleave to it, to those who bow and prostrate themselves'.

Ishmael's presence at the Kaʿba with Abraham indicates that he arrived there on the same road as the one taken by Abraham, whom God had directed to the place of the House. Here, too, the command to purify the site is given in connection with the establishment of the Kaʿba as a pilgrimage destination, where various rites are to be performed, such as circumambulation (*ṭawāf*).

Abraham prays by the Kaʿba

Ishmael appears next to Abraham by the Kaʿba in a Meccan *sūra*, although there he is not the only son present; Isaac is there, too (Q 14:35–40):

> (35) And when Abraham said, 'My Lord, make this land secure, and turn me and my sons away from serving idols; (36) my Lord, they have led astray many people. Then whoso follows me belongs to me; and whoso rebels against me, surely you are all-forgiving, all-compassionate. (37) Our Lord, I have made some of my seed to dwell in a valley where is no sown land by your Holy House; Our Lord, let them perform the prayer, and make hearts of people yearn towards them, and provide them with fruits; haply they will be thankful. (38) Our Lord, you know what we keep secret and what we publish; from God nothing whatever is hidden in earth and heaven. (39) Praise be to God, who has given me, though I am old,

4 See e.g. Jubilees 12:16–20; Jellinek, *Bet Ha-Midrasch*, I, p. 26, II, p. 118.
5 On this verse cf. Sinai, *Fortschreibung*, pp. 135–138.

> Ishmael and Isaac; surely my Lord hears the petition. (40) My Lord, make me a performer of the prayer, and of my seed. Our Lord, and receive my petition.[6]

Here Abraham appears as the founder of the Meccan hallowed region, whose livelihood is provided by the pilgrims to the Ka'ba. He is also the defender of monotheism who asks God to protect him and his sons from idolatry. In addition, he asks his Lord to make Mecca a "secure" (in Arabic: *āmin*) abode, thus establishing the *ḥaram* of Mecca, i.e. its sacred enclave in which bloodshed is forbidden, both of humans and animals (Q 28:57; 29:67).

What matters for our purpose is that already in this Meccan *sūra* Ishmael joins Abraham at the Ka'ba, but he is mentioned together with Isaac who has not been completely dismissed yet. Nevertheless, Ishmael is the senior brother, whose name appears first.

Raising the Ka'ba's foundations

As we return to the Medinan passage that illuminates Abraham's image in his relation to the Ka'ba, we find here, too, Abraham's prayer, but in a shorter version.[7] On the other hand, the curse which God pronounces over the unbelievers in his response to Abraham's prayer is particularly harsh. He promises that they will be punished in the fire of Hell (Q 2:126):

> And when Abraham said, 'My Lord, make this a secure land, and provide its people with fruits, such of them as believe in God and the Last Day'. He [God] said, 'And whoso disbelieves, to him I shall give enjoyment a little, then I shall compel him to the chastisement of the Fire – how evil a homecoming!'

Abraham institutes the pilgrimage and implores God to grant livelihood to the people of Mecca. Here he is referring to the trading activity of the pilgrims in the markets that were open during the *ḥajj* season.

Throughout this Medinan passage Isaac's name has disappeared completely, while Ishmael is mentioned again as the passage continues (Q 2:127):

> And when Abraham, and Ishmael with him, raised up the foundations of the House. . .

Scholars have suggested the likely possibility that the image of Abraham building the Ka'ba in Mecca is a transformation of his experience in the Binding of Isaac

---

6 See the discussion of this prayer in Beck, "Die Gestalt des Abraham", pp. 77–84. On the wider context of the prayer see Sinai, *Fortschreibung*, pp. 129–144

7 On the versions of Abraham's prayer see also Busse, "Jerusalem and Mecca", pp. 238–239.

(Hebrew: עֲקֵידַת יִצְחָק) on the Temple Mount, as described in pre-Islamic sources.[8] However, the qur'ānic version contains other layers as well that deserve close examination, in addition to the general framework shared by the Binding of Isaac and the construction of the Kaʿba. First of all, the statement that Abraham and Ishmael "raised up" the foundations (*al-qawāʿid*)[9] indicates that the foundations themselves already existed before the act of "raising".[10] The exegete al-Zamakhsharī (d. 538/1143) explains this as follows: "Raising up the foundation means building over it, since when one builds over it, it changes from a state of lowness [*hay'at al-inkhifāḍ*] to a state of highness [*hay'at al-irtifāʿ*], and it extends [upwards] after it was short".[11] A similar conclusion may be drawn from the commentary of an earlier exegete, ʿAbd al-Razzāq (d. 211/827). "He quotes a tradition in the name of Ibn ʿAbbās to the effect that the "foundations of the House [that were raised] stand for the foundations that had been the foundations of the House before that [*al-qawāʿid allatī kānat qawāʿida l-bayti qabla dhālika*]".[12]

The idea that the foundations of the House existed before Abraham and Ishmael is in keeping with the verse we saw above (Q 22:26), in which God directs Abraham to the "place" (*makān*) of the House. In light of this verse, it would appear that in the qur'ānic view the "place" of the House was the site where its foundations waited beforehand in order to ultimately be raised up by Abraham and Ishmael, i.e. to have walls built over them.

The prayer of the Kaʿba's builders for Muḥammad and his nation

As we continue our examination of the Medinan passage about Abraham and the Kaʿba, we encounter another prayer which he says immediately after the construction. This time Ishmael also participates in it, after having joined his father in the construction itself (Q 2:127–128):

8 Busse, "Jerusalem and Mecca", p. 238. See also Witztum, "The Foundations of the House", pp. 25–40. Witztum points to Syriac homilies depicting the construction of the altar of the Binding by Abraham and Isaac, and suggests seeing in these descriptions a model on which the building of the Kaʿba by Abraham and Ishmael is based.

9 The word *qawāʿid* (sing. *qāʿida*) also appears in Sura 16:26. There, it describes the foundations of the building that God brought down on the unbelievers who had founded it in ancient generations, perhaps partially on the model of the Tower of Babylon.

10 See also Beck, "Die Gestalt des Abraham", p. 78

11 Zamakhsharī, *Kashshāf* (Q 2:127).

12 ʿAbd al-Razzāq, *Tafsīr* (Q 2:127).

> (127) And when Abraham, and Ishmael with him, raised up the foundations of the House: 'Our Lord, receive this from us; you are the all-hearing, the all-knowing. (128) and, our Lord, make us submissive to you [*muslimayni laka*], and of our seed a nation submissive to you [*muslima laka*]; and show us our holy rites, and turn towards us; surely you turn, and are all-compassionate'.

The prayer of the two begins with a wish that the act of construction will succeed in its sacred objective, which depends on God's willingness to accept the builders' blessed enterprise and to make the building into his temple. Solomon, too, said a prayer of supplication of this kind when he completed the Temple's construction (1 Kings 9:1–5). It would thus seem that the Qur'ān presents Abraham's and Ishmael's prayer after having constructed the Kaʿba as having preceded Solomon, who prayed after having completed the Temple. Below we will discuss the tension between Abraham's and Solomon's shrines in greater detail.[13]

The joint prayer of Abraham and Ishmael continues with a request that God's blessing apply to their progeny and the Islamic faith which they both have undertaken to follow. Their request concerning the rites (*manāsik*) pertains to the pilgrimage (*ḥajj*) rites at Mecca. Once again, it is implied that Abraham established these rites, this time together with Ishmael. The Islamic faith which Abraham and Ishmael refer to is intended to be embraced not only by them but also by the "nation" that will emerge from their progeny. In this way the Qur'ān defines the *raison d'être* of Abraham's Ishmaelite progeny.

The joint prayer ends as follows (Q 2:129):

> 'And, our Lord, send among them a messenger, one of them, who shall recite to them your signs, and teach them the book and the wisdom, and purify them; you are the all-mighty, the all-wise.'

This verse focuses the virtue of the Ishmaelite nation on the messenger that will appear within it. He is Muḥammad, whose task it is to recite God's signs to the people of his generation and to teach them the "book", that is, the Qur'ān, which faithfully represents all preceding holy scriptures. The statement that the messenger will be "one of them" (*rasūl minhum*), that is, of the progeny of Ishmael, accords with the idea that the prophet and his audience are of identical descent. This assertion is repeated in other verses about Muḥammad, as well as about some of the prophets who preceded him.[14] Muḥammad, as a descendant of Abraham and Ishmael, is thus the ultimate redeemer who will lead his generation

13 See below, Chapters 12, 14.

14 Muḥammad: Q 2:151; 3:164. And so also about Hūd who was sent to ʿĀd (Q 23:32). In other cases, the prophet is the "brother" of the people to whom he was sent. Hūd: Q 7:65; 11, 50. Ṣāliḥ: Q 7:73; 11:61; 27:45. Shuʿayb: Q 11:84; 29:36

towards the right path. Conversion to Islam is therefore the only option for whoever wishes to be redeemed, whether one is an idolater, a Jew or a Christian.

The Ka'ba's construction and Jubilees

A significant aspect of Abraham's image is his role as the Ka'ba's builder. A precedent for this can be found in one of the books of the Jewish Apocrypha, the Book of Jubilees. We refer mainly to chapter 22, which is devoted to the events on the last day of Abraham's life. The chapter begins with a visit by Isaac and Ishmael to Abraham in Hebron to celebrate the "Festival of Weeks" [Pentecost]. Abraham is happy that his two sons have come to see him as he lies on his deathbed. Isaac slaughters a sacrifice on the altar that Abraham built in Hebron. Rebecca makes fresh bread out of new wheat. She gives it to her son Jacob to bring to Abraham some of the firstfruits of the land, so that he will eat it and bless the Creator of everything before he dies. Isaac, too, sends through Jacob an excellent peace offering together with wine to his father Abraham for him to eat and drink. Abraham eats and drinks. Then he blesses God who created the heavens and the earth, who made all the fatness of the earth, and who gave them to humanity to eat, drink, and say a blessing over them in praise of its Creator. Abraham then summons Jacob and blesses him and his progeny.[15]

A number of key issues in this chapter can be identified in various locations throughout the two qur'ānic versions of Abraham's sojourn in Mecca, the Meccan (Q 14:35–40) and the Medinan (Q 2:126–129). The following comparative table is arranged according to the order of events in Jubilees 22 (see Appendix at the end of this chapter):

	Jubilees 22	Q 14:35–40 [Meccan]	Q 2:126–129 [Medinan]
A. Isaac and Ishmael	(1) . . . Isaac and Ishmael came from the well of the oath [Beersheba] to their father Abraham to celebrate the festival of weeks—this is the festival of the firstfruits of the harvest. Abraham was happy that his two sons had come.	(39) Praise be to God, who has given me in old age Ishmael and Isaac.	

15 Jubilees 22:1–24. Cf. van Ruiten, "Abraham's Last Day".

(continued)

	Jubilees 22	Q 14:35–40 [Meccan]	Q 2:126–129 [Medinan]
B. A chosen nation	(9) May your kindness and peace rest on your servant and on the descendants of his sons so that they, out of all the nations of the earth, may be your acceptable people and heritage from now until all the time of the earth's history throughout all ages. (10) He summoned Jacob and said to him: 'My son Jacob, may the God of all bless and strengthen you to do before him what is right and what he wills. May he choose you and your descendants to be his people for his heritage in accord with his will throughout all time.		(128) . . . Our Lord, make us both submissive (Muslims) to you and make out of our offspring a (Muslim) nation (*umma*) submissive to you, and show us how to exp;ress devotion and turn to us mercifully. You are the oft-returning (to compassion) merciful.
C. Blessed offspring	(11) May my son Jacob and all the sons be blessed to the Most High God throughout all ages. May the Lord give you righteous descendants, and may he sanctify some of your sons in the entire earth. May the nations serve you, and may all the nations bow before your descendants.	(37) Make the hearts of people yearn towards them and provide them with fruits, that they may be grateful.	(126) provide its people with fruits for sustenance.

(continued)

	Jubilees 22	Q 14:35–40 [Meccan]	Q 2:126–129 [Medinan]
D. Dissociation from impure idols	(19) As for you, my son Jacob, may the Most High God help you and the God of heaven bless you. May he remove you from the impurity [of the idolaters] and from all their errors . . . (22) There is no hope in the land of the living for all who worship idols and for those who are odious. For they will descend to sheol, and will go to the place of judgment. There will be no memory of any of them on the earth. As the people of Sodom were taken from the earth, so all who worship idols will be destroyed.	(35) . . . and keep me and my sons away from worshipping idols (*aṣnām*). (36) My Lord, surely they have caused many people to go astray (*aḍlalna*).	(126) . . . And whoever disbelieves, I will grant him enjoyment for a short while, then I will drive him to the chastisement of the Fire; and it is an evil destination.
E. The building of the house	(24) This house I have built for myself to put my name on it upon the earth. It has been given to you and to your descendants forever. It will be called Abraham's house. It has been given to you and your descendants forever because you will build my house and will establish my name before God for all eternity. Your descendants and your name will remain throughout all the history of the earth.'		(127) And when Abraham, and Ishmael with him, raised up the foundations of the House: Our Lord, receive this from us; you are the all-hearing, the all-knowing.

The five themes compared in this table show a connection between the Qur'ān and Jubilees:

A. Isaac and Ishmael

In Jubilees 22 Isaac and Ishmael come to Abraham in Hebron on the Festival of Weeks. Since this is one of the three pilgrimage holidays, their visit to Abraham in Hebron constitutes a ritual pilgrimage. Indeed, the text subsequently mentions the altar that Abraham built in Hebron, to which Isaac comes from Beersheba and on which he slaughters a sacrifice.[16] Already in the Hebrew Bible Abraham is presented as having established places of worship through the building of altars. One of these he sets up in Hebron or at the oak of Mamre near Hebron,[17] and another in the Land of Moriah, for the purpose of Isaac's Binding (Genesis 22:9). Hebron's status as a pilgrimage destination in which there is an altar to God is therefore a clear hallmark, one with which we are familiar from the position of Mecca and the Kaʿba as pilgrimage destinations and as sites where sacrificial rites are performed.

As for Abraham's joy at Isaac's and Ishmael's visit as described in Jubilees 22, this seems to be the basis of the qur'ānic passage in which Abraham expresses his joy at God having granted him Ishmael and Isaac when he was already an old man. This passage appears in the Meccan version of Abraham's prayer, and therefore some modern scholars considered it a later interpolation, since Ishmael's connection with Abraham is evident mainly in the Medinan *sūras*.[18] However, in view of the text in Jubilees 22, we may now assert that the names of both Ishmael and Isaac in the Meccan version of Abraham's prayer are an inseparable component of the narrative framework. In the Qur'ān, however, Ishmael's name comes before Isaac's, as is the case in the later Medinan *sūras*, in which, as we saw in the previous chapter, Ishmael is counted among the four patriarchs. The priority given to Ishmael's name hides the active role which Jubilees 22 assigns to Isaac – the sacrifice on Abraham's altar in Hebron.

16 Werman, *Jubilees*, pp. 342, 345.
17 Genesis 12:7 (at the oak of Moreh); Genesis 13:18 (by the oaks of Mamre, which are at Hebron).
18 Cf. Beck, "Die Gestalt des Abraham", pp. 80–83; Sinai, *Fortschreibung*, pp. 111–112.

B. A chosen nation

In Jubilees 22 Abraham beseeches God to bless his progeny so that they, out of all the nations of the earth, may be God's "acceptable people and heritage throughout all ages". This idea continues in Abraham's direct address to Jacob, in which he wishes that God will choose Jacob and his descendants "to be his people for his heritage in accord with his will throughout all time". In the qur'ānic Medinan version of Abraham's prayer, this virtue is shifted to Ishmael who, together with Abraham, hopes that a (Muslim) nation (*umma*) submissive to God will emerge from his own seed.

The inspiration for the transfer of the virtue of the nation to Ishmael can be traced to the Hebrew Bible, where Ishmael enjoys a special status (Genesis 17:18–20):

> (18) And Abraham said to God, "O that Ishmael might live in your sight!" (19) God said, "No, but your wife Sarah shall bear you a son, and you shall name him Isaac. I will establish my covenant with him as an everlasting covenant for his offspring after him. (20) As for Ishmael, I have heard you; I will bless him and make him fruitful and exceedingly numerous; he shall be the father of twelve princes, and I will make him a great nation".

Here God declares that Abraham's son Isaac is the one who will continue the divine covenant that was made with Abraham, but God also grants a certain status to Ishmael, Abraham's first-born. God blesses his seed, which, He promises, will become "exceedingly numerous" and develop into a "great nation".[19] This promise to Ishmael is repeated in Genesis 21:13: "As for the son of the slave woman, I will make a nation of him also, because he is your offspring". In the qur'ānic version, the nation that comes out of Ishmael's progeny is Muḥammad and his Muslim nation.

C. Blessed offspring

In Jubilees 22, after Abraham finishes his thanksgiving prayer, he blesses Jacob and asks God to make the nations serve him and bow before his descendants. This blessing is inspired by Isaac's blessing of Jacob (Genesis 27:28–29):

19 In later literature, this idea was corroborated through Gematria. With 92 being the identical sum of the name "Muḥammad" [*m*+*ḥ*+*m*+*d*] as well as of the Hebrew words *bi-me'od me'od* ("exceedingly") [*b*+*m*+*a*+*d*+*m*+*a*+*d*], Muslim exegetes maintained that the latter (in their rendering, Mād or Mūd Mūd) stood for the name of the Prophet. See Lazarus-Yafeh, *Intertwined Worlds*, pp. 107–108

> . . . (28) May God give you of the dew of heaven, and of the fatness of the earth, and plenty of grain and wine. (29) Let peoples serve you, and nations bow down to you. Be lord over your brothers, and may your mother's sons bow down to you. Cursed be everyone who curses you, and blessed be everyone who blesses you![20]

However, in the Meccan version of Abraham's prayer, the blessing of Isaac's and Jacob's seed, whom the other nations are supposed to worship, is exclusively transferred to the branch of Abraham's progeny that resides in Mecca. The Qurʾān describes this branch as the one for whom all people yearn, meaning especially the pilgrims who come to visit the Kaʿba and who consider the tribe of Quraysh as a holy community. Extra-qurʾānic sources tell us that the Quraysh tribe was considered *ahl Allāh* ("people of God") who are not to be harmed.[21] In addition, just as in Genesis 27 God gives Jacob "of the dew of heaven, and of the fatness of the earth, and plenty of grain and wine", in the Qurʾān, too, in both Meccan and Medinan versions of Abraham's prayer, the merit of Abraham's progeny in Mecca is associated with economic wellbeing or, in the Qurʾān's words, with the fact that Allah will "provide them with fruits".

D. Dissociation from impure idols

According to Jubilees 22, Abraham goes on to bless Jacob and asks God to remove him from the impurity of the idolaters and from all their errors. Abraham tells Jacob that there is "no hope in the land of the living for all who worship idols and for those who are odious. For they will descend to sheol, and will go to the place of judgment". Earlier, when still in Haran, before arriving in Canaan, Abraham asks of his God:

> Save me from the power of evil spirits who rule the thoughts of peoples' minds. May they not mislead me from following you, my God. Do establish me and my posterity forever. May we not go astray from now until eternity.[22]

In the Meccan version of Abraham's prayer, his blessing of his seed focuses on the *aṣnām*, the "idols" that lead the people astray. Abraham asks God to keep him and his sons away from them. In the Medinan version, God answers Abraham and declares that he will bring the unbelievers "to the chastisement of the Fire".

---

20 In another chapter of *Jubilees* (16:17–18) Isaac himself is destined to be a father to holy progeny that will become "the share of the Most High". See also Werman, *Jubilees*, pp. 302, 346.
21 "Mecca and Tamīm", p. 139; Rubin, "The Īlāf of Quraysh", p. 179.
22 Jubilees 12:20.

E. The building of the House

In Jubilees 22 Abraham continues to address Jacob and mentions the house that he built, which will be called "the house of Abraham". It will be given to Jacob and his descendants; Jacob, too, will build it and establish Abraham's name before God for all eternity. This declaration about the combined construction of the house by Abraham and Jacob has its parallel in the qur'ānic passage that immediately follows the Medinan version of Abraham's prayer, in which Abraham and Ishmael raise up together the Kaʿba's foundations, that is, raise its walls (see above). A closer examination of the meaning of the building of the "house of Abraham" in Jubilees will clarify the connection between it and Abraham's and Ishmael's activities at the Kaʿba.

To begin with, in her Hebrew critical edition of Jubilees, Cana Werman explains that Abraham, in his words about the "house of Abraham", establishes Jacob's standing as the first-born in the family. Abraham bequeaths the house to him in accordance with the ancient inheritance law that gives the first-born son the father's house. Jacob, Abraham's grandson, is thus the sole heir among the latter's progeny (Isaac and Ishmael), and is granted the legal standing of a first-born son.[23] From Jacob the "house" will pass on as an inheritance to his seed for all generations. As Werman explains: "The law of inheritance that states that Jacob inherits the house of Abraham is supported by a metaphor: Jacob follows in Abraham's footsteps and through his action he constructs a memorial to him".[24]

The house of Abraham is also a shrine of sorts, as can be understood from another passage in Jubilees, where God commands Jacob, through an angel who comes to him in Bethel, to continue to reside in the house of Abraham his father, and forbids him to construct a shrine in Bethel or anywhere else (Jubilees 32:22):

> [The angel said to him]: 'Do not build up this place, and do not make it an eternal temple. Do not live here because this is not the place. Go to the house of your father Abraham and live where your father Isaac is until the day of your father's death'.

When one reads this passage together with Abraham's testament to Jacob in Jubilees 22, one understands the status of Abraham's house not only as the place fit for Jacob to dwell in, but also as the only sacred precinct in which he will be able to establish Abraham's name "before God for all eternity".

---

23 Werman, *Jubilees*, p. 349.
24 *Loc. cit.*

The house of Abraham as *birah*

The house of Abraham is mentioned in Jubilees also by another name. A comparison of the extant non-Hebrew versions of this work has led scholars to the conclusion that in the book's original Hebrew version the name was *birah* [25](בִּירָה). These findings led Werman to explain that Abraham's *birah* is a square manor house built around a courtyard, which Jacob is to inherit according to Abraham's will (Jubilees 22:24).[26]

In Werman's Hebrew rendering of the Jubilees text, *birah* recurs several times. It is related that Jacob went to his father Isaac and to his mother Rebekah, "in the house of his father Abraham". He took two of his sons with him—Levi and Judah. Rebekah went out of the *birah* [מהבירה] into the gate of the *birah* [אל שער הבירה] to kiss Jacob (Jubilees 31:5–6). Here Abraham's *birah* and Abraham's house are one and the same. In another passage, Jacob is said to have sent goods to Isaac and Rebekah who lived in Abraham's *birah* [בבירה אשר לאברהם] four times a year. Isaac himself had gone up "to the *birah* of his father Abraham [בירת אביו אברהם], and had settled there away from his son Esau". He settled in the "*birah* of Abraham his father" [בבירת אברהם אביו] which was in the mountain of Hebron (Jubilees 29:16–17, 19). In accordance with Abraham's testament, Isaac bequeathed to Jacob the larger portion of his property "along with the *birah*" [ואת הבירה], and everything around it (Jubilees 36:12). After Isaac's death, Jacob "lived on the mountain of Hebron, in the *birah* [בבירה] in the land of Canaan, in the land of his father Abraham. He worshipped the Lord wholeheartedly and in line with the revealed commands according to the divisions of the times of his generation" (Jubilees 36:20). In this *birah* Jacob waged his war against Esau, who attacked it with his people in order to avenge himself on Jacob for having stolen the birthright (Jubilees 37–38).

It should also be noted that the word *birah* occurs frequently in rabbinic literature in association with the Temple Mount and the Temple. There it generally refers to the walled Temple courtyard, which contained a variety of buildings.[27] It would thus appear that the author of Jubilees intentionally chose this word to describe Abraham's manor, alluding to the sanctity which the site shared with the Temple that Solomon would in future build elsewhere. Indeed, already in the Hebrew Bible we read that Solomon built "the fortress [*birah*]" on the Temple Mount.[28]

---

25 Mandel, "'Birah'", pp. 200–203.

26 Werman, *Jubilees*, p. 405.

27 Mandel, "'Birah'", pp. 209–210.

28 1 Chronicles 29:19: "Grant to my son Solomon that with single mind he may keep your commandments, your decrees, and your statutes, performing all of them, and that he may build the

In light of the evidence of Jubilees, it is feasible to surmise that Abraham's house in Hebron is reflected in the Qur'ān in the image of the Kaʿba that Abraham builds.[29] The description of Abraham's building activity is attached to the Medinan version of his prayer by the Kaʿba. Like the house of Abraham in Jubilees, in whose "construction" Jacob also participates for the sake of the succeeding generations, in the Qur'ān, too, Abraham is not the sole builder. However, instead of Jacob's metaphorical construction, the Qur'ān has Ishmael participating in the actual construction ("raising up the foundations"), once again revealing the special merit of the Ishmaelite branch of Abraham's seed.[30]

Lastly, it should be noted that the fact that the Qur'ān shapes the construction of the Kaʿba by Abraham and Ishmael in the spirit of Jubilees does not mean that Abraham's image as the builder of the Kaʿba was not known already in pre-Islamic times. Evidence for the antiquity of the association between Abraham and the Kaʿba can be found in Arabic texts that relate the history of Mecca in pre-Islamic times. We shall come to them later on. However, as seen above, the Qur'ān reshapes the Kaʿba's Abrahamic sanctity in accordance with the polemic aims connected with its dispute with Judaism and Christianity.

Appendix: Jubilees 22

(1) In the first week in the forty-fourth jubilee, during the second year [2109] – it was the year in which Abraham died – Isaac and Ishmael came from the well of the oath [Beersheba] to

temple (lit. הַבִּירָה) for which I have made provision". VanderKam rejects Werman's explanation according to which the "house" of Abraham in Jubilees 22:24 is a literal building. He rather insists that in the context of Jubilees 22:24, "house" is not being used in its literal sense (VanderKam, *Jubilees*, II, p. 667 n. 73). Furthermore, he holds that Abraham's "Tower" was "an impressively strong and high structure from which one could keep an eye on the surrounding territory for any approaching danger" (VanderKam, *Jubilees*, II, p. 811). But if Abraham's "tower" is indeed the Hebrew *birah*, then Abraham's house can well be a literal house, as is indicated in Jubilees 31:5–6 where *birah* and "house" stand for the same place.

29 Researchers have noted the affinity between the "House of Abraham" that Abraham builds in *Jubilees*, and his construction of the Kaʿba as described in the Qur'ān. See e.g. Rubin, "Ḥanīfiyya and Kaʿba", pp. 107–108. Witztum's reluctance to accept this link is based on the (wrong) argument that in *Jubilees* Abraham does not build an "actual house or temple in his lifetime". See Witztum, "The Foundations of the House", p. 28.

30 But Jacob did not completely disappear as Abraham's partner in the legacy of faith. A few verses below in the same *sūra* it is said (Q 2:132): "And Abraham charged his sons with this and Jacob [likewise . . .]". Jacob's name appears in the same unusual syntactic position as Ishmael's name in verse 127: "And when Abraham raised up the foundations of the House, and Ishmael [with him]".

their father Abraham to celebrate the festival of weeks—this is the festival of the firstfruits of the harvest. Abraham was happy that his two sons had come. (2) For Isaac's possessions in Beersheba were numerous. Isaac used to go and inspect his possessions and then return to his father. (3) At that time Ishmael came to see his father, and both of them came together. Isaac slaughtered a sacrifice for the offering; he offered (it) on his father's altar that he had made in Hebron. (4) He sacrificed a peace offering and prepared a joyful feast in front of his brother Ishmael. Rebecca made fresh bread out of new wheat. She gave it to her son Jacob to bring to his father Abraham some of the firstfruits of the land, so that he would eat (it) and bless the Creator of everything before he died. (5) Isaac, too, sent through Jacob (his) excellent peace offering and wine to his father Abraham for him to eat and drink. (6) He ate and drank. Then he blessed the Most High God who created the heavens and the earth, who made all the fatness of the earth, and gave it to humanity to eat, drink, and say a blessing over it in praise of its Creator. (7) 'Now I pay homage to you, my God, because you have shown me this day. I am now 175 years of age, old and satisfied with (my) days. All of my days have proved to be peace for me. (8) The enemy's sword has not subdued me in anything at all that you have given me and my sons during all my lifetime until today. (9) May your kindness and peace rest on your servant and on the descendants of his sons so that they, out of all the nations of the earth, may be your acceptable people and heritage from now until all the time of the earth's history throughout all ages.' (10) He summoned Jacob and said to him: 'My son Jacob, may the God of all bless and strengthen you to do before Him what is right and what He wills. May He choose you and your descendants to be His people for His heritage in accord with His will throughout all time. Now you, my son Jacob, come close and kiss me.' (11) So he came close and kissed him. Then he said: 'May my son Jacob and all the sons be blessed to the Most High God throughout all ages. May the Lord give you righteous descendants, and may He sanctify some of your sons in the entire earth. May the nations serve you, and may all the nations bow before your descendants. (12) Be strong before people, and exercise power among all of Seth's descendants. Then your ways and the ways of your sons will be justified so that they may be a holy people. (13) May the Most High God give you all the blessings with which He blessed me and with which He blessed Noah and Adam. May they come to rest on the sacred head of your descendants throughout each and every generation and forever. (14) May He purify you from all filthy pollution so that you may be pardoned for every sin you have committed in ignorance. May He strengthen and bless you; may you possess the entire earth. (15) May He renew His covenant with you so that you may be for Him the people of His heritage throughout all ages. May He truly and rightly be God for you and your descendants throughout all the time of the earth. (16) Now you, my son Jacob, remember what I say, and keep the commandments of your father Abraham. Separate from the nations, and do not eat with them. Do not act as they do, and do not become their companion; for their actions are something that is impure, and all their ways are defiled and something abominable and detestable. (17) They offer their sacrifices to the dead and they worship demons. They eat in tombs, and everything they do is empty and worthless. (18) They have no mind to think, and their eyes do not see what they do, and how they err in saying to (a piece of wood): 'You are my god,' or to a stone: 'you are my lord, you are my deliverer.' They have no mind. (19) As for you, my son Jacob, may the Most High God help you and the God of heaven bless you. May He remove you from their impurity and from all their error. (20) Be careful, my son Jacob, not to marry a woman from all the descendants of Canaan's daughters because all of his descendants are (meant) to be uprooted from the earth. (21) For through Ham's sins Canaan erred. All of his descendants and all of his (people) who remain will be destroyed and will be removed from the earth; on the day of judgment there will be no one (descended) from him who will be saved. (22) There is no hope in the land of the living for all who worship idols and for those who are odious. For they will descend to sheol, and will go to the place of judgment. There will be no memory of any of them on the earth. As the people of Sodom were taken from the earth, so all who worship idols will be destroyed. (23) Do not be afraid, my son Jacob, and do not be upset, son of Abraham. May the Most High God keep you from corruption; and from every erroneous way may He rescue you. (24) This house I have built for myself to put my name on it upon the earth. It has been given to you and to your descendants forever. It will be called Abraham's house. It has been given to you and your descendants forever because you will build my house and will establish my name before God for all eternity. Your descendants and your name will remain throughout all the history of the earth'.

(25) Then he finished commanding him and blessing him. (26) The two of them lay down together on one bed. Jacob slept in the bosom of his grandfather Abraham. He kissed him seven times, and his feelings and mind were happy about him. (27) He blessed him wholeheartedly and said: 'The Most High God is the God of all and Creator of everything who brought me from Ur of the Chaldeans to give me this land in order that I should possess it forever and raise up holy descendants so that they may be blessed forever.' (28) Then he blessed Jacob: 'My son, with whom I am exceedingly happy with all my mind and feelings – may your grace and mercy continue on him and his descendants for all time. (29) Do not leave or neglect him from now until the time of eternity. May your eyes be open on him and his descendants, so that they may watch over them and so that you may bless and sanctify them as the people of your heritage. (30) Bless him with all your blessings from now until all the time of eternity. With your entire will renew your covenant and your grace with him and with his descendants throughout all the generations of the earth'.

After the first Muslims arrived in Jerusalem, and in the wake of the city's increasing sanctity and prestige, which culminated with the construction of the Dome of the Rock, there arose a need to preserve and foster the ancient Abrahamic sanctity of Mecca and the Kaʿba. The promotion of Mecca's Abrahamic sanctity is focused on the attempted sacrifice of Abraham's son. More on this in the next chapter.

9 The attempted sacrifice between al-Shām and Mecca

The competition of Mecca and the Kaʿba with Jerusalem, as reflected in traditions disseminated after the arrival of the Muslims in al-Shām, revolves also around the location of the attempted sacrifice, or the Binding (Hebrew: עֲקֵידָה) of Abraham's son. In the qurʾānic version the event apparently takes place in al-Shām, the land to which Abraham arrives after leaving his homeland. In extra-qurʾānic tradition this location is preserved in reports about the Dome of the Rock. But, on the other hand, traditions were disseminated which located the attempted sacrifice in Arabia. The latter gained wide circulation thanks to the incorporation of the story in the rites of the pilgrimage to the holy sites in Mecca.

The changes in the course of Abraham's journeys between the two shrines of the Jerusalem-Mecca sanctity space brought about a parallel change in the location of Abraham's attempted sacrifice of his son in this space. The Islamic version of the attempted sacrifice has been much discussed by scholars,[1] but still deserves further examination, first in its qurʾānic version and then in the traditions concerning it.

The qurʾānic version: Abraham goes to the place of the sacrifice

The scene of Abraham's attempted sacrifice of his son appears in the Qurʾān, in a Meccan *sūra*. It begins when Abraham takes flight from his idol-worshiping countrymen who threaten to kill him. His flight into the domain of redemption is also mentioned in other verses, discussed above.[2] We saw that in these verses his departure is described as a "withdrawal" (Q 19:49–50), as "deliverance" (Q 21:71–73) and also as a *hijra* ("emigration") (Q 29:26–27). In another passage, Abraham's parting with his evil compatriots and the ensuing events is described in Q 37:99–101:

> (99) [Abraham] said, 'I am going to my Lord; he will guide me. (100) My Lord, give me one of the righteous.' (101) Then We gave him the good tidings of a prudent boy.

Abraham's departure from his homeland and his redemption by God is here described by the word "going". This wording is reminiscent of the biblical verses Gen. 12:1–2:

1 See e.g. Busse, "Jerusalem and Mecca", p. 238.
2 See above, Chapter 6.

https://doi.org/10.1515/9783111222318-010

> (1) Now the Lord said to Abram, "Go from your country and your kindred and your father's house to the land that I will show you. (2) I will make of you a great nation, and I will bless you, and make your name great, so that you will be a blessing. . .".

But the instruction to "go" is given to Abraham another time as well, in preparation for the sacrifice of his son (Gen. 22:2):

> He said, "Take your son, your only son Isaac, whom you love, and go to the land of Moriah, and offer him there as a burnt offering on one of the mountains that I shall show you".

It would appear that in the Qur'ān the two divine commands to "go" were combined into a single "going": Abraham leaves his people and God guides him, not to the blessed land as a whole, but specifically to the place of the intended sacrifice. The fact that in the Qur'ān Abraham's going at God's behest is mentioned immediately before the story of the attempted sacrifice, testifies to this amalgamation.

The story of the attempted sacrifice itself appears right after Abraham goes to his Lord (Q 37:102–113):

> (102) and when he had reached the age of running with him, he said, 'My son, I see in a dream that I shall sacrifice you; consider, what you think?' He said, 'My father, do as you are bidden; you shall find me, God willing, one of the steadfast.' (103) When they had surrendered, and he flung him upon his brow, (104) We called unto him, 'Abraham, (105) you have confirmed the vision; even so We recompense the good-doers. (106) This is indeed the manifest trial.' (107) And We ransomed him with a mighty sacrifice, (108) and left for him among the later folk (109) 'Peace be upon Abraham!' (110) Even so We recompense the good-doers; (111) he was among our believing servants. (112) Then We gave him the good tidings of Isaac, a prophet, one of the righteous. (113) And We blessed him, and Isaac; and of their seed some are good-doers, and some manifest self-wrongers.

As for the identity of the intended victim, the Qur'ān appears to avoid Isaac's name deliberately, preferring instead the mere statement that it was Abraham's son. In the same manner, the Qur'ān does not mention the name of Noah's son in the story of his drowning in the Flood (Q 11:42–43).[3] Nor does it mention Cain and Abel by name in the story of their deadly encounter; the Qur'ān merely states that they were Adam's two sons (Q 5:27–31). In all these cases, the Qur'ān prefers to indicate the kinship relation of the sons rather than to specify their names. In this manner the drama is globalized, implying that sons or brothers at large, the flesh of their fathers or brothers, are faced with life-or-death situations. In most of these cases it is the father who faces the greatest challenge, for he is about to lose one of his own

---

3 Commentators of the Qur'ān identify him with Canaan. For Noah's curse of Canaan, see Genesis 9:25. And see also Reynolds, "Noah's Lost Son", pp. 129–148, for a possible relationship between Noah's son and Ezekiel 14:13–20.

sons, whatever his name. But Isaac's name does not disappear completely. It is mentioned at the end of the story of the attempted sacrifice, in the verses in which God gives Abraham the good tidings about Isaac's future as a righteous prophet and then goes on to bless them both (Q 37:112–113).

In short, the intended victim in the Qur'ān is apparently Isaac. The attempted sacrifice of Abraham's son thus connects to the other Meccan verses in which Abraham makes the journey to his land of refuge, where, as we saw in the chapter "The Patriarchs in al-Shām", he is blessed with Isaac and Jacob. In these verses, too, Ishmael does not yet accompany Abraham. As we saw in the previous chapter, Ishmael's participation as Abraham's sole partner in building the Kaʿba occurs only in the Medinan *sūras*. It may perhaps be surmised that Ishmael's role in building the Kaʿba is the appropriate substitute which the Qur'ān proposes for Isaac's implied role in the Meccan version of the story of the attempted sacrifice.[4]

The traditions: The attempted sacrifice on the Rock in Bayt al-Maqdis

The first Muslims to arrive in al-Shām were aware of the qur'ānic story of the attempted sacrifice and associated it with the Rock (al-Ṣakhra) in Bayt al-Maqdis. In this they were inspired by the Jewish tradition which located the attempted sacrifice on the Temple Mount.[5] The Muslims thus did not accept the Samaritan identification of the site of attempted sacrifice with Mount Gerizim,[6] nor the Christian view, which placed the event at Golgotha, the site of the Crucifixion.[7]

The evidence for the identification of the Rock with the place of the attempted sacrifice is provided in a tradition attributed to Kaʿb al-Aḥbār (d. 32/652), the Jewish convert to Islam who was well versed in the holy Scriptures, and also to the Prophet's Companion, the scholar ʿAbdallāh b. ʿUmar (d. 73/692):

4 See above, Chapter 8.

5 According to Jewish tradition, Solomon's Temple was built on Mount Moriah (2 Chronicles 3:1); it was identified with the "land of Moriah" where the Binding took place on one of its mountains (Genesis 22:2, 9). This identification was interwoven into the story of the Binding itself, in a passage stating that the mountain of the Binding is the one that "to this day" is called "the mount of the Lord", i.e. the Temple Mount. See Genesis 22:14: "So Abraham called that place 'The Lord will provide'; as it is said to this day, 'On the mount of the Lord it will be provided.'"

6 On this location see Kalimi, "The Land of Moriah", p. 362.

7 Eliav, *God's Mountain*, p. 184; Peters, *Jerusalem and Mecca*, p. 86.

> Ka'b and ʿAbdallāh b. ʿUmar maintained that the story of the sacrificial animal was in al-Shām, on the Rock of Bayt al-Maqdis, as it is related in the Torah.[8]

Granted the Rock *per se* is rarely mentioned as the precise location of the attempted sacrifice in Muslim sources,[9] but the mere location of the attempted sacrifice appears frequently in Muslim commentaries on the qurʾānic verses relating to the event. The exegete Muqātil b. Sulaymān (d. 150/767) says:[10]

> "And We ransomed him with a mighty sacrifice" – in Bayt al-Maqdis. The ram's (*kabsh*) name was Razīn.[11] It was of the ibex (*waʿl*). It had grazed in Paradise for forty years before it was slaughtered.

Later commentators mention the same location.[12] Muqātil's legend about the ram that grazed in Paradise is repeated by other exegetes as well. They assert that it grazed for forty autumns before being sacrificed.[13] In addition to its grazing in Paradise, its unique appearance is also recorded in a tradition of the Kūfan exegete Saʿīd b. Jubayr (d. 95/713):[14]

> In the name of Saʿīd b. Jubayr – "And We ransomed him with a mighty sacrifice" – He said: The ram which Abraham slaughtered had grazed in Paradise for forty years. It was grayish, with a reddish wool-like pelt.

The description of the ram's unique appearance is designed to show that it was special, namely that it was created beforehand for Abraham's sacrifice. That is why Abraham did not hesitate to sacrifice it, something that he would not have done had it been a stray ram that did not belong to him. In that vein, Jewish midrash already states that Abraham's ram was "one of ten things that were created before sunset [*bein ha-shemashot*]".[15]

8 Maqdisī, *Muthīr al-gharām*, p. 271.
9 See Livne-Kafri, "The Navel of the Earth", p. 71.
10 Muqātil, *Tafsīr* (Q 37:107).
11 Another version: Jarīr. See Ibn Kathīr, *Tafsīr* (Q 37:107).
12 Samarqandī, *Tafsīr* (Q 37:102–107); Thaʿlabī, *al-Kashf wa-l-bayān* (Q 37:102–107); Māwardī, *Nukat* (Q 37:102–107); Ibn ʿAṭiyya, *Tafsīr* (Q 37:102–107); Abū Ḥayyān, *al-Baḥr al-muḥīṭ* (Q 37:102–107).
13 E.g. ʿAbd al-Razzāq, *Tafsīr* (Q 37:103 [no. 2539]). See also Bashear, "Abraham's Sacrifice", p. 260.
14 Ṭabarī, *Tafsīr* (Q 37:107).
15 Midrash Tanḥuma (Warsaw), Genesis, Parashat Wayyera 23.

The ram's horns between Jerusalem and Mecca

Apart from the exegetical traditions, there is evidence of a concrete symbol of the attempted sacrifice, namely the horns of the ram that was given to Abraham instead of the son he intended to sacrifice. Thus we read:

> On a chain in the center of the Dome over the Rock there were a precious stone [*durra yatīma*], the two horns of Abraham's ram and the crown of the king of Persia [*Kisrā*]. They hung there in the days of ʿAbd al-Malik b. Marwān, and when the caliphate came into the hands of the Banū Hāshim, they transferred them to the Kaʿba.[16]

It here follows that the builders of the Dome of the Rock retained the pre-Islamic Jewish significance of the site on which it was constructed, that is, as the place of the Binding. To symbolize it they were able to present the ram's horns which they hung for all to see. However, the fact that eventually the ʿAbbāsids (the Banū Hāshim) moved the horns to the Kaʿba testifies to their sensitivity to the status of the shrine in Arabia and to their desire to make it a worthwhile competitor to the Dome of the Rock, and to present it as the true location of Abraham's attempted sacrifice. Let us examine this tendency more closely.

According to the available traditions, the ram's horns were hung in the Kaʿba not only since the ʿAbbāsid period, but already in pre-Islamic times.[17] One such tradition, transmitted by the Meccan scholar Ibn Abī Najīḥ (d. 131/748) in his father's name, relates that one day the Quraysh gathered at the Kaʿba and reminisced about its history since pre-Islamic days and about the renovations which they had made in it. Among other things, they recalled the following:

> The two horns of the ram that Abraham, the friend of the Raḥmān [Allāh], sacrificed, hung in [the Kaʿba], on the wall opposite the entrance. They would anoint them with balm whenever they anointed the Kaʿba itself.[18]

A tradition on the authority of the Medinan ʿIkrima (d. 105/723) relates that on the day on which Mecca fell into the victorious Muḥammad's hands (in the year 8/630), he entered the Kaʿba where he found the pair of horns that had been preserved among the other valuables consigned there by the Quraysh.[19] Another tradition contains the report of ʿUthmān b. Ṭalḥa, one of the Kaʿba's gatekeepers,

---

16 Wāsiṭī, *Faḍāʾil*, pp. 75–76 (no. 122). See also Minhājī, *Itḥāf al-akhiṣṣā*, I, p. 244; Mujīr al-Dīn, *al-Uns al-jalīl*, I, p. 275. See further, Busse, "The Sanctity of Jerusalem", p. 460; Elad, *Medieval Jerusalem*, p. 52; *idem*, "ʿAbd al-Malik and the Dome of the Rock", p. 182; *idem*, "The Temple Mount", p. 83; *idem*, "The Status of Jerusalem", p. 42; Bashear, "Abraham's Sacrifice", p. 275.

17 See also Rubin, "Ḥanīfiyya and Kaʿba", pp. 104, 118.

18 Azraqī, *Akhbār Makka*, p. 106.

19 *Ibid.*, p. 114.

from whom Muḥammad received its keys after having entered Mecca as victor. ʿUthmān relates that when the Prophet came out of the Kaʿba he summoned him and said: "In the House I saw the ram's horns and forgot to instruct you to cover them with a piece of cloth, for there should be nothing that would distract the worshippers' attention". ʿUthmān then adds that this was the ram by which Abraham's son Ishmael was redeemed.[20] Ibn Jurayj (d. 150/767), another Meccan transmitter, reports that an old woman of Mecca told him that she had seen the horns, which were reddish in color, like clay (*mughra*).[21] The Kūfan scholar ʿĀmir al-Shaʿbī (d. 103/721) claims, too, that he saw the ram's horns in the Kaʿba.[22] However, it is also related that when ʿAbdallāh b. al-Zubayr tore down the Kaʿba in order to rebuild it (in the year 64/683), the two horns were found on one of the walls, wrapped in rags (*mishaq*), and when they took hold of them they disintegrated, so desiccated were they.[23] In contrast to all these traditions, according to which the horns were inside the Kaʿba, a declaration attributed to Ibn ʿAbbās maintains that at the beginning of Islam the ram's head hung by its horns next to the Kaʿba's drainpipe, until it shriveled and disintegrated.[24]

The attempted sacrifice at Minā

As for the exact location in Mecca that was identified as the site of the attempted sacrifice, it may be assumed that it was the Kaʿba, where the ram's horns were kept. In addition, there is a tradition to the effect that Abraham sacrificed the ram on the stone named Maqām Ibrāhīm.[25] We shall return to this stone below.[26] It would appear that associating the stone with Abraham's attempted sacrifice is but an attempt to enhance the sanctity of the Kaʿba's environs, against the background of the tension between this and the other precincts that play a part in the pilgrimage rites.[27] Indeed, most of the relevant traditions locate the attempted sacrifice in another place, a few kilometers to the east of the Kaʿba, at a site at which the rites of the Feast of the Sacrifice (the 10th of the month of Dhū l-ḥijja)

20 *Ibid.*, p. 156.
21 *Loc. cit.*
22 Ṭabarī, *Tafsīr* (Q 37:107).
23 Azraqī, *Akhbār Makka*, p. 156. See also Elad, *Medieval Jerusalem*, p. 52.
24 Ṭabarī, *Tafsīr* (Q 37:107). On the various traditions about the horns of the ram see also Bashear, "Abraham's Sacrifice", pp. 273–275.
25 E.g. Ṭabarī, *Tafsīr* (Q 37:107). See also Bashear, "Abraham's Sacrifice", p. 268.
26 See below, Chapter 12.
27 On this competition cf. Rubin, "The Kaʿba", pp. 118–127

are performed to this day. The name of that place is Minā. The exegete Mujāhid b. Jabr (d. 104/722) notes that the animal given to Abraham was sacrificed at Minā, in the area where the animals are slaughtered for the feast (*al-manḥar*).[28] Another tradition transmitted by Saʿīd b. Jubayr (d. 95/713) similarly says:

> The rock at Minā, at the foot of Mount Thabīr, is the rock on which Abraham, peace be upon him, sacrificed the [victim] which ransomed his son Isaac.[29]

In a more extensive version of this tradition, Ibn Jubayr says that Abraham slaughtered "Isaac's ransom" on a rock at the foot of Mount Thabīr and adds that "this is the ram which Adam's son, peace be upon him, sacrificed and [God] accepted it from him. The ram was stored [*makhzūn*] until Isaac was ransomed with it. Adam's second son offered a sacrifice from the fruits of the field and [God] did not accept it from him".[30] This version, in which it is Isaac who was the intended sacrifice, is closer to the biblical account, although it does locate the event in Arabia. Isaac's name is retained here, as well as a connection to the midrashic conception which considers the ram's sacrifice to be part of a series of sacrifices, beginning with Adam or, in our case, with his son Abel,[31] who, unlike Abraham's son, did not have the good fortune of being ransomed by the sacrificial ram.[32]

The insertion of Isaac's name in Ibn Jubayr's version is based on the idea that is reflected in the following tradition:[33]

> In the name of Saʿīd b. Jubayr, he said: When Abraham saw in the dream the commandment to sacrifice Isaac, he took him on a month's journey during a single morning (*ghadāt*), until he brought him to the sacrificial site at Minā. When God released him from the duty of sacrifice and instructed him to slaughter the ram, he slaughtered it and took [Isaac back to al-Shām] on a month's journey during one evening [*rawḥa*]. The valleys and the mountains were folded up for him.

---

28 Ṭabarī, *Tafsīr* (Q 37:107).

29 Azraqī, *Akhbār Makka*, p. 200. See also Māwardī, *Nukat* (Q 37:105); Ibn Abī Ḥātim, *Tafsīr* (Q 37:102–107); Ibn Kathīr, *Tafsīr* (Q 37:102–107). See also Firestone, "Abraham's Son", pp. 122–124.

30 Azraqī, *Akhbār Makka*, p. 401; Ibn Abī Ḥātim, *Tafsīr* (Q 37:107); Ibn Kathīr, *Tafsīr* (Q 37:107). See also Bashear, "Abraham's Sacrifice", p. 254. And see Genesis 4:3–5 "(3) In the course of time Cain brought to the Lord an offering of the fruit of the ground, (4) and Abel for his part brought of the firstlings of his flock, their fat portions. And the Lord had regard for Abel and his offering, (5) but for Cain and his offering he had no regard. So Cain was very angry, and his countenance fell".

31 Minor Tractates, Aboth d'Rabbi Nathan, Chapter 1 (I, pp. 13–14 [17b-18a]): "The bullock which Adam offered, the bull which Noah offered, and the ram which our father Abraham offered on the altar instead of his son, were all beasts whose horns came into being before their hoofs as it is stated, [18a] *and Abraham lifted up his eyes, and looked, and behold behind him a ram caught*".

32 Cf. also Rubin, "The Kaʿba", p. 118, note 142.

33 Thaʿlabī, *al-Kashf wa-l-bayān* (Q 37:102–107). See also Suyūṭī, *al-Durr al-manthūr* (Q 37:102–107).

The miracle of travelling back and forth between two distant places in unnatural speed is employed here to preserve Isaac's presence also in the Arab environment of the attempted sacrifice.

The location of the attempted sacrifice on the rock at the foot of Mount Thabīr was retained over generations. Evidence for this is provided in a report according to which Lubāba bint ʿAlī, the daughter of ʿAbdallāh b. ʿAbbās (d. 68/687) built the "Mosque of the Ram" (*Masjid al-kabsh*) on this rock.[34] This report once again reveals the ʿAbbāsid involvement in protecting the pre-Islamic sanctity of Mecca and its environs as against the growing sanctity of Bayt al-Maqdis.

Three rocks thus compete over the virtue of being the site of the attempted sacrifice. One is the Rock within the Dome of the Rock, which preserves the Jewish location of Isaac's Binding, while the two others are in Arabia, one next to the Kaʿba (Maqām Ibrāhīm) and the other at Minā.[35] The two latter sites pit Ishmael against Isaac, although Isaacs's name has also survived in the traditions that locate the attempted sacrifice at Minā. The association of Ishmael's name with the idea that the attempted sacrifice occurred in Arabia reflects the majority view in Islam and is based on the idea that this son of Abraham somehow arrived in Mecca.

Sozomen

Here we must add that the Arabs were apparently aware already in pre-Islamic times of their connection to Ishmael's legacy. This is, at least, the impression one gets from his image among the Arabs as Sozomen describes in his book. This fifth-century historian of the Church (active circa 440 CE) depicts Ishmael as having bequeathed a system of laws and customs to his progeny. These laws and customs were forgotten in the course of time, under the influence of neighboring pagan nations, until a group of Ishmaelites came into contact with Jews, from whom they learned anew about their own origins. They reverted to their ancient customs, which were similar to those of the Jews before Moses received the Law.[36]

Had Sozomen written this account in the seventh century, one might have thought that he was describing the Arabs called *ḥanīf*s, who according to Muslim sources rejected their pagan environment and already before Muḥammad sought Abraham's monotheistic faith. A prominent *ḥanīf* was the Meccan Zayd b.

34 Azraqī, *Akhbār Makka*, p. 401. See also Bashear, "Abraham's Sacrifice", p. 268.
35 According to one of the traditions, the rock at Minā was called Uqayṣir. See Azraqī, *Akhbār Makka*, p. 401; Bashear, "Abraham's Sacrifice", p. 268.
36 Sozomen, *Ecclesiastical History*, pp. 309–310 (VI 38).

ʿAmr b. Nufayl, who is said to have guided Muḥammad himself to the right path.[37] However, the fact that Sozomen lived in the fifth century proves that in his day there already existed an Abrahamic-Ishmaelite monotheism among Arab tribes, who abandoned their pagan ways under the influence of their Jewish neighbors.[38]

To Sozomen's testimony one may add an even older one: Josephus' description of the custom of circumcision among Jews and Arabs. In his words, "The Arabs defer the ceremony [of circumcision] to the thirteenth year, because Ishmael, the founder of their race, born of Abraham's concubine, was circumcised at that age".[39]

From all of the above it is perhaps possible to surmise that the ram's horns of Abraham and Ishmael could have actually been hung in the pre-Islamic Kaʿba, as described in Arab sources. To this we may add the stone of Maqām Ibrāhīm, which also testifies to the pre-Islamic roots of the Kaʿba's connection to Abraham and Ishmael.[40] However, even if these are historical testimonies, the very preservation and dissemination of traditions concerning the ram's horns in the Kaʿba were designed to serve an urgent apologetic need, namely, to challenge the status of the Rock in Bayt al-Maqdis as the site of Abraham's attempted sacrifice. These traditions were aimed at preventing the equilibrium between the two regions of the sanctity space from being tilted in favor of al-Shām.

Arabs and non-Arabs

Lastly, it should be pointed out that beyond the inner tension within the Jerusalem-Mecca sanctity space, the issue of the identity of the son who was the intended sacrifice was also at the heart of the tensions between Arabs and non-Arabs in early Muslim society. Indeed, in view of the absence of the name of Abraham's son in the qurʾānic account of the attempted sacrifice, exegetes were divided into two camps: those who maintained that the intended sacrifice was Isaac,[41] and those who maintained that it was Ishmael.[42] Those who argued for Isaac represented circles of non-Arab origin (both Jews and Christians) in the

---

37 See Rubin, "Ḥanīfiyya and Kaʿba", pp. 99–103; Lecker, "Zayd b. ʿAmr".

38 See more about the significance of Sozomen's evidence in Rubin, "Ḥanīfiyya and Kaʿba", p. 99, note 68; Cook M., *Muhammad*, p. 81.

39 Josephus, *Jewish antiquities*, p. 107. And see Rubin, "Ḥanīfiyya and Kaʿba", p. 104.

40 See below, Chapter 12.

41 Mujāhid, *Tafsīr* (Q 37:101); Muqātil, *Tafsīr* (Q 37:101); Ṭabarī, *Tafsīr* (Q 37:107).

42 E.g. Mujāhid, *Tafsīr* (Q 37:101); ʿAbd al-Razzāq, *Tafsīr* (Q 37:103 [nos. 2531, 2540]); Ṭabarī, *Tafsīr* (Q 37:107). And see Firestone, "Abraham's Son", pp. 115–116, 125–128.

society of the first Islamic era. They suffered under the overbearing attitude of the Arabs towards them. By enhancing the status of Isaac as the intended sacrifice, a claim also supported by the testimony of the Hebrew Bible, they wished to improve their own status vis-à-vis the Arabs, who boasted of their Arab-Ishmaelite origins.[43] Matters went so far that a tradition was disseminated in the name of the Meccan preacher ʿUbayd b. ʿUmayr (d. 68/687) to the effect that the intended sacrifice was Isaac and that the entire event took place in al-Shām rather than in Arabia.[44] This was also Kaʿb al-Aḥbār's view, according to one tradition ascribed to him.[45] It may thus be said that the struggle over which location witnessed the scene of the attempted sacrifice never completely ceased, although the Feast of the Sacrifice, which takes place during the pilgrimage season to Mecca (at Minā), commemorates the Arab-Ishmaelite version of the attempted sacrifice.

Beside the issue of Abraham's attempted sacrifice, those who championed Mecca's status in the Jerusalem-Mecca sanctity space also saw to the dissemination of traditions which broaden the city's connection to other prophets, far and beyond the figures of Abraham and Ishmael. More on this in the next chapter.

---

43 See Goldziher, *Muslim Studies*, I, pp. 135–136.
44 ʿAbd al-Razzāq, *Tafsīr* (Q 37:103 [no. 2531]).
45 *Ibid.* (no. 2540).

10 The Kaʿba and the Prophets

> The transfer of the glory of "the land of the prophets" from Jerusalem to Mecca is not limited to Abraham and Ishmael. Several traditions extend the list of prophets who visited Mecca on some occasion in their lives, from Adam to the Children of Israel.

As seen in previous chapters, the Qurʾān promotes the Abrahamic-Ishmaelite sanctity of Mecca and the Kaʿba on the basis of pre-Islamic models appropriated from Jerusalem and Hebron. Mecca has thus become an appropriate arena for the appearance of Muḥammad, the Arabian prophet and Ishmael's descendant, through whom the divine plan of redemption will be fully accomplished in the community of believers. His expected emergence is mentioned in Abraham's and Ishmael's joint prayer upon completing the construction of the Kaʿba.[1]

After the Prophet's death, as Islam spread beyond the Arabian Peninsula, the need arose to preserve and promote Mecca as a fit place for prophetic activity, especially in light of the rising Islamic sanctity of Jerusalem, the ancient abode of prophets. In this city the Dome of the Rock was eventually constructed which threatened to overshadow the status of Mecca as a pilgrimage destination.[2] That is why the traditions that extol the virtues of Mecca highlight mainly its merit as a pilgrimage destination for all prophets.

Adam in Mecca

The first prophet is Adam. In contrast to the traditions discussed in the chapter "The Patriarchs in al-Shām" above, which locate his grave between Hebron and Jerusalem, there is a tradition in which Adam's grave is said to be in a cave on Mount Abū Qubays, overlooking the Kaʿba. Another version places the grave in the mosque of al-Khayf at Minā.[3] As seen in the previous chapter, Minā is the sacred site, a few kilometers to the east of the Kaʿba, where the rites of the Feast of the Sacrifice, commemorating Abraham's attempted sacrifice of his son, take place.

The idea that Adam is buried in Mecca would seem to imply that he came there as a pilgrim. Indeed, Ibn Isḥāq (d. 150/768), whose book on the life of Muḥammad begins with a survey of human history from its very beginning, relates:

---

1 See above, Chapter 8.

2 See above, Chapter 2.

3 Masʿūdī, *Murūj*, I, p. 38; Yaʿqūbī, *Taʾrīkh*, I, p. 17. On the other hand, some traditions locate the tombs of Adam and Noah at al-Kūfa, the Shīʿī holy city where the tomb of ʿAlī is also found. See Kister, "Sanctity Joint and Divided", p. 36.

https://doi.org/10.1515/9783111222318-011

> I was informed that Adam, peace be upon him, had touched all the corners [of the Ka'ba] before Abraham. Isaac and Sarah made the pilgrimage to [the Ka'ba] from al-Shām.[4]

It is thus indicated that Adam performed the rite of the *ṭawāf*, the circumambulation around the Ka'ba, and touched its four corners, as required. Sarah and Isaac, are unequivocally identified with al-Shām and the Cave of the Patriarchs, where they are buried. The idea of having them go on pilgrimage to Mecca is also aimed at presenting the shrine in Arabia as a destination no less elevated than Bayt al-Maqdis.

The tradition according to which Adam performed the *ṭawāf* around the Ka'ba is based on the belief that a primordial form of this shrine existed, as implied in Q 3:96, in which the Ka'ba is defined as "The first House established for the people".[5] Indeed, the exegete Qatāda (d. 117/735) explains that "the first House" is "the one which Allāh placed on earth, and Adam and all the people after him performed the *ṭawāf* around it".[6]

The Ka'ba from Adam to Abraham

Not only did Adam perform the *ṭawāf* around the primordial Ka'ba, every generation after him visited it. In Mujāhid's words, "Ever since God sent Adam, peace be upon him, down to the earth, [God's] House has not ceased to be adored and sanctified; the nations and the communities passed it on from one generation to the next [*tatanāsakhuhu al-umam wa-l-milal*], one nation after another and one community after another. The angels made the pilgrimage to it before Adam".[7] Even during the Flood, when God took the primordial Ka'ba up to heaven and left only its foundations on earth, the *ṭawāf* did not cease: Noah's Ark, which contained the survivors of the Flood, circled the site of the Ka'ba seven times.[8]

Further details about the generations between Adam and Abraham are provided by Ibn Isḥāq, who quotes 'Urwa b. al-Zubayr (d. 94/713):

> The Ka'ba was placed for Adam, who worshipped Allāh in it. After him Noah made the pilgrimage to the Holy House, and then the Flood came. The Ka'ba survived in the form of a red hill (*rabwa ḥamrā'*) whose location was known. Then Allāh sent Hūd to the people of 'Ād. He was busy with his people and therefore did not perform the pilgrimage to Mecca.

---

4 Azraqī, *Akhbār Makka*, p. 34.
5 See below, Chapter 12.
6 'Abd al-Razzāq, *Tafsīr* (Q 3:96)
7 Azraqī, *Akhbār Makka*, pp. 20–21.
8 'Abd al-Razzāq, *Tafsīr* (Q 22:26 [no. 1913]).

> Ṣāliḥ, who was sent to Thamūd, was also busy with them and did not perform the pilgrimage. Then Allāh showed Abraham the way to it [Q 22:26]; he made the pilgrimage, the rites were made known to him, and he declared the duty to visit the Holy House. Since then Allāh did not send even one prophet who did not make the pilgrimage to that House.[9]

Hūd and Ṣāliḥ were prophets whose activities among their respective nations, ʿĀd and Thamūd, are described in the Qur'ān. Their nations rejected them, and as punishment terrible catastrophes were inflicted on them, in which they perished. The statement that they never made the pilgrimage to Mecca preserves the idea that Abraham was the first to have reestablished the performance of the *ḥajj* since the Flood.

The number of prophets who came on pilgrimage to Mecca

Other traditions inflate the number of prophets who performed the pilgrimage. Mujāhid states that "seventy-five prophets performed the *ḥajj*; all circumambulated the House [the Ka'ba] and prayed in the mosque at Minā".[10] The prophets' prayers at Minā do much to enhance the sanctity of the mosque of al-Khayf there. In fact, this mosque occasionally replaces the al-Aqṣā Mosque in lists of the three most sacred mosques in the Jerusalem-Mecca sanctity space.[11]

Ibn Isḥāq, too, quotes numbers, this time on the authority of Ibn ʿAbbās, a Medinan scholar and the founder of qur'ānic exegesis, who belonged to the generation of the Prophet's Companions: "Seventy prophets walked along the ravine of al-Rawḥā' as pilgrims. They wore woolen garments and harnessed their camels with ropes of fiber. And in the mosque of al-Khayf seventy prophets prayed".[12] The ravine of al-Rawḥā' is on the way leading from Medina to Mecca. The prophets' simple attire symbolizes their devotion to the worship of God.

Al-Rawḥā' is also the place through which Moses passed on his way to perform the *ḥajj*. Mujāhid says:

> The prophet Moses made the pilgrimage riding on a red camel. He passed through al-Rawḥā' wearing two thin white garments, one on his loins and the other on his shoulder. He circumambulated the House and then circled al-Ṣafā and al-Marwa. When he was between

9 Azraqī, *Akhbār Makka*, p. 38.
10 *Ibid.*, pp. 34–35.
11 Kister, "Three Mosques", p. 183–184
12 Azraqī, *Akhbār Makka*, p. 38.

> al-Ṣafā and al-Marwa, he heard a voice from heaven saying: 'At your service [*labbayka*], my servant. I am with you'. Then Moses prostrated himself.[13]

Moses comes attired in the accustomed garb of pilgrims. His prostration is reminiscent of a similar event in the Qur'ān (Q 7:143), in which God appears to Moses and the latter "fell down swooning". In the present tradition the scene is duplicated in the Arabian environment of Mecca and the Kaʿba, imbuing this region with the distinctive aura of a land of prophetic revelation. Furthermore, God here expresses his submission to Moses through the *talbiya*, the call *labbayka*, which expresses absolute subservience. The pilgrims usually chant this call (*labbayka llāhumma labbayka*) on the way to Mecca as an expression of their submission to God, while here Allāh himself pronounces the *talbiya* in Moses' honor.

Al-Ṣafā and al-Marwa are two hills in the Kaʿba's vicinity whose sanctity is associated with the story of Hagar and Ishmael. At the end of their journey they ran out of water. Hagar runs between the two hills in search of water when Gabriel strikes the ground with his heel and shows her the Zamzam well which has broken through the surface.[14] In another tradition Gabriel teaches Moses how to move between al-Ṣafā and al-Marwa,[15] thus honoring Moses in the same way that Gabriel honored Abraham, who was guided by this angel on the path to the pilgrimage sites.

The Children of Israel in Mecca

Another location on the road to Mecca is Dhū Ṭuwā, a name that is mentioned in the description of the journey of the Children of Israel, who, like Moses, made the pilgrimage to Mecca: "When the nation [tribe] of the Children of Israel made its way to Mecca and arrived at Dhū Ṭuwā, all those belonging to that nation took off their shoes, due to the great reverence in which they held this holy place".[16]

---

13 Azraqī, *Akhbār Makka*, p. 35. See also Rubin, "The Kaʿba", p. 127; *idem*, *Between Bible and Qur'an*, pp. 36–46.
14 See Rubin, "The Kaʿba", pp. 122–127.
15 Azraqī, *Akhbār Makka*, p. 38.
16 Azraqī, *Akhbār Makka*, p. 361.

Jesus and Mecca

Jesus, too, made the pilgrimage to Mecca, as related by Muḥammad himself:

> In the ravine of al-Rawḥāʾ . . . seventy prophets passed on red she-camels harnessed with fiber ropes, wearing cloaks and pronouncing various *talbiya* formulas. Among them was Jonah son of Amittai [Yūnus b. Mattā], who declared: 'At your service [*labbayka*], oh dispeller of grief [*farrāj al-karib*], at your service'. Moses said: 'At your service, I am your servant, at your service.' [The transmitter] said: Jesus' *talbiya* will be: 'At your service, I am your servant, son of your servant girl [Mary], daughter of your two servants [Joachim and Anne], at your service.'[17]

The phrasing ascribed to Jesus is consistent with his image in the Qurʾān as a flesh-and-blood figure, rather than a son of God.[18] He is supposed to utter the *talbiya* when he comes to redeem the world in the Latter Days. This is made clear in the following tradition of the Prophet as reported by his Companion Abū Hurayra:

> Jesus son of Mary will descend [from heaven], kill the pig and remove the cross. The people will gather to pray under his leadership, money will be given until it will not be accepted anymore, and he will abolish the *kharāj* tax. He will come to al-Rawḥāʾ, whence he will leave for the *ḥajj* or the *ʿumra*, or both together.[19]

The bounty that will accompany Jesus' arrival will create a situation in which people will want to pay for what they purchase, but no one will want to accept the money, because it will be so plentiful. Taxes will be abolished, since they will have become unnecessary. In other versions Jesus will also defeat the false Messiah, al-Dajjāl, in addition to destroying typical Christian foods and symbols. To all this, the tradition just quoted adds Jesus' pilgrimage. In this way, he is made an adherent of the sanctity of Mecca and the Kaʿba. This devotion will coexist with his profound association with al-Shām, where he lived all his life, where he died, and where he is expected to reveal himself again at the end of days.[20]

Mecca as a refuge for prophets

The pilgrimage of the prophets is made not only for ritual purposes, but at times also in order to find shelter and safety from persecution. As we saw in a preceding chapter ("The Patriarchs in al-Shām"), Abraham and Lot found shelter in "the

---

17 Azraqī, *Akhbār Makka*, pp. 38–39. See also Kister, "Sanctity Joint and Divided", p. 53.
18 On the history of the various *talbiya* versions see Kister, "On a Monotheistic Aspect".
19 Aḥmad b. Ḥanbal, *Musnad*, II, p. 290.
20 See above, Chapter 5.

land that We had blessed", that is, al-Shām (Q 21:71). Furthermore, there are traditions about places in that land which sheltered prophets from their persecutors. Thus Ramla, for example, was the place where the prophet Ṣāliḥ sought refuge from his unbelieving people (Thamūd).[21]

On the other hand, there is a tradition of Ibn ʿAbbās according to which, in the verse about the refuge of Abraham and Lot, the blessed land is Mecca, and a reference is made to Ishmael's arrival at the House. Ibn ʿAbbās argues that the Kaʿba is described in the Qurʾān (Q 3:96) as "blessed" (*mubārak*).[22] Therefore according to Ibn ʿAbbās, the Kaʿba, too, may fit the description of "the land that We had blessed".

Other traditions amplify the number of prophets who found refuge in Mecca. Seventy, seventy-five or even ninety-nine prophets, according to these traditions, escaped to Mecca and were buried in the *ḥijr*.[23] This is a sacred precinct in the courtyard opposite the Kaʿba. Its boundaries are the Black Stone, the stone known as Maqām Ibrāhīm,[24] and the Zamzam well. One of the traditions is traced back to the Prophet:

> Every one of the prophets whose people perished [because it had rejected the prophets] made his way to Mecca, where he worshipped God together with the (few) who came with him, until he died. Noah died there, as well as Hūd, Ṣāliḥ and Shuʿayb. Their graves are in the area between Zamzam and the *ḥijr*.[25]

As noted above, some traditions maintain that Hūd and Ṣāliḥ did not come to Mecca, because they were busy with their own peoples. But this is not the case in the traditions discussed here. A particularly detailed account is provided by Wahb b. Munabbih (d. 110/728) who specialized in the biographies of the prophets. He relates that Ṣāliḥ, Hūd and Shuʿayb convinced the believers in their respective communities to flee with them from the unbelievers and to seek refuge in Mecca. They performed the pilgrimage, remained there for the rest of their lives, and were buried there. Their graves are located to the west of the Kaʿba.[26] Another report stresses that Hūd's grave is in Mecca, rather than in al-Shām, as some others claim.[27]

---

21 Kister, "Sanctity Joint and Divided", p. 21.
22 Ṭabarī, *Tafsīr* (Q 21:71).
23 Azraqī, *Akhbār Makka*, p. 34. See also Rubin, "The Kaʿba", pp. 109–111.
24 See below, Chapter 12.
25 Azraqī, *Akhbār Makka*, p. 34. See also Kister, "Sanctity Joint and Divided", p. 54.
26 Azraqī, *Akhbār Makka*, p. 39.
27 Kister, "Sanctity Joint and Divided", p. 23.

Medina and the prophets

Medina, too, could boast of a relationship with several prophets, first and foremost with Muḥammad. One tradition tells of the believers' uncertainty with respect to the most appropriate place in which to bury the Prophet. Some proposed Bayt al-Maqdis, because it was the "burial place of the prophets" (*madfan al-anbiyā'*). However, the choice eventually fell on Medina, on the advice of Abū Bakr.[28] Medina was thus considered superior to the earlier burial site of the prophets.

Apart from Muḥammad, Jesus, too, was annexed to Medina's glory. This is seen in a tradition that says that when he descends from heaven, he will perform a *hijra* to Medina and will live there until his death. Then he will be buried next to the tombs of Abū Bakr and 'Umar.[29]

Shared sanctity of the land of the prophets

To conclude, we note that a distinction is continually made between prophets who were buried in Mecca and those buried in Bayt al-Maqdis. Thus, the exegete Muqātil b. Sulaymān says:

> In the Holy Mosque, between Zamzam and the Corner [of the Black Stone], there are the graves of seventy prophets, among them Hūd, Ṣāliḥ and Ishmael. But the graves of Adam, Abraham, Isaac, Jacob and Joseph are in Bayt al-Maqdis.[30]

This is a harmonizing tradition that provides the two contenders within the Jerusalem-Mecca sanctity space with equal shares in the merit of hosting the prophets' graves.

The Jerusalem-Mecca sanctity space is not only the place where God sends His prophets in order to disseminate the true faith and so to implement the divine plan of redemption. This space also contains the abode of God Himself. With respect to this belief too, we see a movement of sanctity patterns from al-Shām to Mecca and the Ka'ba, an issue to which the next four chapters are devoted.

---

28 Haythamī, *Ṣawā'iq*, I, p. 86. The tradition is quoted in Kister, "A Comment on the Antiquity", p. 186.
29 See above, Chapter 5.
30 Azraqī, *Akhbār Makka*, p. 39.

Part Five: **Land of the Temple**

11 Solomon's Temple

Qur'ānic Meccan verses describe how Solomon's Temple was built with the aid of devils and demons. The interest the Qur'ān shows in this event is yet another sign of its identification with the Jewish vision of redemption. Extra-qur'ānic traditions associate Solomon's Temple with the construction of the Dome of the Rock and present it as a fulfillment of the messianic vision of the Torah (*al-Tawrāt*). The Jewish aspect of a redemption fulfilled thanks to the "Kingdom of Ishmael" is revealed in *The Secrets of Rabbi Simon ben Yoḥay.*

Al-Shām is the abode not only of God's chosen, but also of God himself. The builder of God's Temple in al-Shām was Solomon, the memory of whose project has been preserved in traditions elaborating on the Dome of the Rock's sanctity. The construction of Solomon's Temple is mentioned in the Qur'ān. In what follows the relevant verses are examined, and then the traditions that associate the Temple with the Dome of the Rock.

Solomon and the blessed land

Meccan verses describe the Temple's construction by Solomon and the part taken by devils (*shayāṭīn*) in the project. The Qur'ān mentions their aid in the course of the description of Solomon's mighty kingdom, the like of which was not given to any mortal. It is symbolized, among other things, by two gifts which God granted the king at the latter's request (Q 38:35–38):

> (35) He said: 'My Lord, forgive me, and give me a kingdom such as may not befall anyone after me; surely you are the all-giver.' (36) So We subjected to him the wind, that ran at his commandment, softly, wherever he might light on, (37) and the devils (*wa-l-shayāṭīn*), every builder and diver (38) and others also, coupled in fetters.

In this passage the Qur'ān retells a biblical account of how God rewarded Solomon when the Temple's construction was complete. In the biblical version, after Solomon has completed the construction of the Temple and the royal palace, God tells him, among other things: ". . . Then I will establish your royal throne over Israel forever, as I promised your father David, saying, 'There shall not fail you a successor on the throne of Israel'" (1 Kings 9:1–5). In another passage (1 Kings 3:5–14), God tells Solomon that he may request whatever he likes ("Ask what I should give you") and grants him much more than he asks for.

In the qur'ānic passage cited above, God's grace consists of two gifts: The wind's submission to Solomon's commands, and the recruitment of devils to work for him. In yet another qur'ānic version, the wind connects Solomon to the blessed land (Q 21: 81–82):

https://doi.org/10.1515/9783111222318-012

> (81) And to Solomon the wind (*al-rīḥ*), strongly blowing, that ran at his command unto the land that We had blessed; and We had knowledge of everything; (82) and of the devils some dived for him and did other work besides; and We were watching over them.

In contrast to Muḥammad, who arrives at the blessed location in a nocturnal journey (Q 17:1), Solomon is taken there by the wind. Exegetes explain that the wind took Solomon and his people wherever he wanted and then returned him to his home in al-Shām.[1] The wind's submission to Solomon's will is mentioned in a Jewish midrash:

> Solomon made use of the spirits [*ruḥōt*] and sent them to India from where they brought him water with which to water [the pepper-plant] here [in the Land of Israel] . . .[2]

In this midrash the wind brings much-needed rain to the Holy Land from India. The statement in the Qur'ān that the wind carried Solomon to "the blessed land" (*al-arḍ allatī bāraknā fīhā*) creates a link with the journeys of Abraham and the Children of Israel to the same land, as well as to Muḥammad's nocturnal journey there.[3]

The labor of the demons for Solomon

The second gift which God grants Solomon, in response to the latter's request, is the recruitment of devils (*shayāṭīn*) or demons (*jinn*) to work for him. The toil of the *jinn* is described in detail in the following passage (Q 34:12–13):

> (12) And to Solomon the wind; its morning course was a month's journey, and its evening course was a month's journey. And We made the fount of molten brass to flow for him. And of the *jinn*, some worked before him by the leave of his Lord; and such of them as swerved away from our commandment, We would let them taste the chastisement of the Blaze; (13) fashioning for him whatsoever he would — prayer niches, statues, porringers like water-troughs, and anchored cooking-pots. 'Labor, O House of David, in thankfulness; for few indeed are those that are thankful among my servants.'

The Qur'ān does not elaborate on the function of the things which the *jinn* made for Solomon in their work on land and sea. However, we do know from Jewish and Christian sources that God gave Solomon dominion over the demons, who

---

1 Ṭabarī, *Tafsīr* (Q 21:81).

2 Midrash Rabbah, VIII, p. 55 (Ecclesiastes Rabbah 2:5).

3 Regarding Abraham's journey, see above, Chapter 6. On the journey of the Children of Israel, as well as of Muḥammad himself, see above, Chapter 1.

also helped him to erect the Temple.[4] Thus we read in The Song of Songs Rabbah:

> Huna said in the name of R. joseph: All assist the king; all the more then do all assist for the glory of the King of Kings, the Holy One, blessed be He, even spirits, even demons, even ministering angels.[5]

Furthermore, in one of the Jewish Apocrypha, The Testament of Solomon, the demons who help construct the Temple are engaged in cutting stones (2:5), spinning the hemp for the ropes (4:12), picking up stones and hurling them up to the heights of Temple (7:8), digging the foundations (8:12), cutting marble (10:10), carrying firewood (11:7), making bricks (12:5) and bringing water (18:42).[6] In the Talmud Bavli it is related that Ashmedai, king of the demons, was forced to provide Solomon with the *shamīr* (an extraordinary kind of material or a creature that could split rocks) in order to cut the stones for the Temple.[7]

In light of all this, it may be assumed that in the above qur'ānic passage (Q 34:12–13), too, the works which the *jinn* performed for Solomon included help in the Temple's construction. Indeed, the "prayer niches" (Arabic: *maḥārīb;* sing. *miḥrāb*) which the *jinn* built for him were apparently small chapels in the Temple which were parallel to the oratories in Christian sites (see also Q 3:37, 39; 19:11). The statues (*tamāthīl*) are reminiscent of those that are described in 1 Kings 7:29 ("lions, oxen and cherubim"). The "fount of molten brass" (*'ayn al-qiṭr*) seems to allude to the numerous bronze artifacts prepared for the Temple (1 Kings 7).

The qur'ānic passage under discussion ends with God addressing the entire House of David urging them to labor "in thankfulness", that is, for God's sake. This is yet another hint that the activity in question is the construction of the Temple.

Later in the same *sūra*, the Qur'ān again mentions the *jinn*'s work for Solomon (Q 34:14):

---

4 See Sasson, *A King and Layman*, pp. 129–130 (I thank Dr. Amir Lerner for drawing my attention to this book).

5 Midrash Rabbah, IX, p. 3 (The Song of Songs Rabbah 1: 5). See also *Pesikta Rabbati*, I, p. 310 (Piska 15): "Before Solomon sinned, fearlessly he ruled even over demons, saying *I got me . . . Adam's progeny, demons and she-demons* (Eccles. 2:8), that is, demons of both kinds" (reference from Amir Lerner).

6 Sasson, *A King and Layman*, p. 131.

7 Talmud Bavli, Gittin 68a-b. See Sasson, *A King and Layman*, p. 130.

> And when We decreed that he should die, naught indicated to them that he was dead but the beast of the earth devouring his staff; and when he fell down, the *jinn* saw clearly that, had they only known the unseen, they would not have continued in the humbling chastisement.

The "chastisement" is the *jinn*'s hard labor for Solomon which they continued, not knowing that he had died in the meantime. Only when Solomon's body fell, releasing the staff on which he leaned did they cease their labors.[8] Muslim exegetes explain that when Solomon's time came, there were still twelve months of work left, and so he asked God to hide the fact of his death from the *jinn* for this period of time; God acquiesced, and the *jinn* completed their work.[9] In midrashic sources, however, it is related that twelve months passed from the completion of the Temple until it was inaugurated, and that the structure remained closed during that time.[10]

In sum, the increased attention the Qur'ān pays to Solomon and his Temple is yet further proof of its identification with the Jewish vision of messianic redemption on the Temple Mount in Jerusalem.

Solomon's Temple and the Dome of the Rock

The first Muslims who came to al-Shām were not only familiar with the story of Solomon's journey to the blessed land and the help he received from the *jinn* but were also aware of the messianic vision of rebuilding the Temple that had stood on the Temple Mount before its destruction. Indeed, when they first came to Jerusalem, in the reign of caliph ʿUmar b. al-Khaṭṭāb (ruled 13–23/634–644), they immediately exposed the Rock, perhaps even with the help of some Jews.[11] Christian sources tell of a supposed attempt by Jews, as early as the year 18/639, to rebuild the "Temple of Solomon" under Muslim auspices.[12] Whether this was true or not,

8 See also Talmud Bavli, Sanhedrin 20b: "Resh Lakish said: At first, Solomon reigned over the higher beings . . . Afterwards, [having sinned,] he reigned [only] over the lower . . . But eventually his reign was restricted to Israel . . . Later, his reign was confined to Jerusalem alone . . . And still later he reigned only over his couch . . . And finally, he reigned only over his staff . . . ".

9 Māwardī, *Nukat* (Q 34:14).

10 *Pesikta Rabbati*, I, p. 125 (Piska 6): "The same sort of thing happened to Solomon. He finished the work of the Temple in the month of Marheshvan: *And in the eleventh year, in the month of Bul . . . was the House finished* (I Kings 6:38) . . . But because the Temple stayed locked up for twelve months, everyone was sneering at Solomon . . . ". See also Sasson, *A King and Layman*, pp. 78–79.

11 Gil, "The Jewish Community", p. 136.

12 Leder, "Attitude", p. 70.

the Muslims eventually constructed the Dome of the Rock on the Temple Mount.[13] It was built by the Umayyad caliph ʿAbd al-Malik b. Marwān (d. 86/705) who completed it in the year 72/691.[14] Traditions about the Dome of the Rock illuminate its place in the messianic vision and highlight its relation to David and Solomon. This supports the hypothesis of some modern scholars that ʿAbd al-Malik did indeed intend to rebuild Solomon's Temple.[15] One of the earliest such traditions is quoted by al-Ṭabarī (d. 310/923), in the name of Wahb b. Munabbih (d. 110/728) who was well known for his knowledge of the lives of the prophets as recounted in the Bible:

> David saw the angels putting their drawn swords back into their sheaths and ascending from the Rock heavenward on a golden ladder. Then David said: This is the place fit for building a mosque (*masjid*). David wanted to begin to build it, but Allāh revealed to him the following: 'This is a hallowed house (*bayt muqaddas*) and your hands are anointed with blood. Therefore, not you will build it, but one of your sons. I will make him king after you and call him Solomon, and keep him far from bloodshed. When Solomon became king, he built it and honored it.[16]

This tradition shifts to the Rock a retold version of the story in 1 Chronicles 21, in which David sees an angel holding a drawn sword. The angel has come to punish Israel after Satan incited David to count the people. David sees the angel by the threshing floor of Ornan the Jebusite, "standing between earth and heaven, and in his hand a drawn sword stretched out over Jerusalem" (1 Chronicles 21:15–16). Subsequently the angel commands David to build an altar on Ornan's threshing floor; this is also the place where Solomon will in future erect the Temple.[17]

In Wahb's version just quoted, a golden ladder stands on the Rock and the angels ascend to heaven on it. The fact that they ascend with sheathed swords reflects the angel's departure after God had accepted David's plea.[18] The ladder

13 See above, Chapter 2.

14 See Gil, *History of Palestine*, pp. 92–98. However, some scholars hold that 72 AH was the year of the founding of the edifice not of its completion. On the various views concerning the time of the completion of the construction work see Milwright, *The Dome of the Rock*, pp. 42–43.

15 Sharon, "The Praises of Jerusalem", p. 63. For more details, see Elad, "The Status of Jerusalem", pp. 53–55. Also see a survey of the various scholarly opinions concerning the reasons and aims of the building in Elad, *Medieval Jerusalem*, pp. 161–163; Levy-Rubin, "The Dome of the Rock", pp. 442–443.

16 Ṭabarī, *Taʾrīkh*, I, p. 485 (Brill: I, p. 572)

17 2 Chronicles 3:1: 1 Solomon began to build the house of the Lord in Jerusalem on Mount Moriah, where the Lord had appeared to his father David, at the place that David had designated, on the threshing floor of Ornan the Jebusite.

18 2 Samuel 24:16–17.

evokes Jacob's ladder in the Book of Genesis as well as the role of the Rock as the place from which God himself and Muḥammad ascended to heaven.[19]

Allāh's decision that Solomon rather than David would build the Temple reflects the biblical version of God's words to David.[20] However, in the version of Wahb's tradition recorded in Ibn ʿAsākir (d. 571/1175),[21] David is said to have laid the Temple's foundations (*qawāʿid*) with the intention of building it, but in the end it was Solomon who did.[22] In another version, on the authority of the Prophet's contemporary Ubayy b. Kaʿb, Allāh addresses David directly:

> Build me a house. [David] said: My Lord, in what place in the land? [Allāh] said: In the place where you will see the angel drawing his sword. Then David saw an angel standing on the Rock, holding a sword.[23]

These versions shape ʿAbd al-Malik's Dome of the Rock in the image of David's and Solomon's Temple that was built on the same Rock.

The promise to Jacob and the Dome of the Rock

Muslim tradition connects the Temple that was constructed on the Rock not only with David and Solomon, but also with a messianic vision revealed already to one of the biblical Patriarchs, Jacob. A tradition recorded by Ibn Saʿd (d. 230/845) on the authority of Muḥammad b. Kaʿb al-Quraẓī (d. 117/735) reads:

> Allāh revealed to Jacob as follows: I will send from among your offspring kings and prophets, until I will send the Prophet, the man of the *ḥaram* [the sacred precinct of Mecca], whose nation will build the shrine [*haykal*] of Bayt al-Maqdis. He is the seal of the prophets and his name is Aḥmad.[24]

Here God brings Jacob the tidings that among his descendants there will be a line of kings and prophets whose ultimate mission will be accomplished through Muḥammad, here called Aḥmad. This is how he is already called in the Qurʾān, in Jesus' prophecy about him (Q 61:6). His designation as "seal of the prophets" is also based on the Qurʾān (Q 33:40). Apart from these qurʾānic allusions, this tradition

19 See above, Chapter 2.
20 1 Kings 8:16–19.
21 Ibn ʿAsākir, *Taʾrīkh Dimashq*, XVII, pp. 103–104.
22 *Ibid.*, p. 104.
23 Yāqūt, *Muʿjam al-buldān*, V, p. 167 (s.v. al-Maqdis).
24 Ibn Saʿd, *Ṭabaqāt*, I, p. 163. See also Rubin, *The Eye of the Beholder*, p. 25; Livne-Kafri, "A Note on Some Traditions", p. 82; Kister, "A Comment on the Antiquity", p. 185.

elaborates on the biblical scene in which Jacob is in Bethel and God changes his name from Jacob to Israel, telling him: ". . . a nation (*goy*) and a company of nations (*goyyīm*) shall come from you, and kings shall spring from you" (Genesis 35:11–12). The Islamic version of this promise focuses on Muḥammad's nation which will build the shrine (*haykal*) after him. The tradition thus expands the vision of redemption which now culminates with the construction of the Dome of the Rock. It also indirectly promotes the status of the Umayyad rulers, including ʿAbd al-Malik, as the bearers of the redemption vision and as those who made it a reality.[25]

God's promise to Jacob in Genesis 28 has its Islamic version, this time again in a tradition of Wahb b. Munabbih. Wahb describes Jacob's dream of the ladder on which the angels ascend and descend,[26] and then provides his expanded version of God's promise to Jacob on that occasion:

> . . . and Allāh revealed [to Jacob]: 'I am Allāh. There is no God except me, your God and the God of your fathers Abraham, Ishmael and Isaac. To you and your offspring after you I gave this holy land. I blessed you and them, and entrusted you with the book, wisdom and prophecy. I will be with you until you return to this place, and then you will make it a house (*bayt*) in which you and your seed will worship me.[27]

The statement that Jacob will build a house for the worship of God implies that the Dome of the Rock is the place which Jacob called "Bethel", where he took the stone that he put under his head and set it up as a pillar.[28] Ishmael's mention next to Isaac confirms the Ishmaelite identity of Abraham's seed.[29] This tradition thus stresses the Arab identity of those who implemented the vision of constructing the house of God.

King David and ʿAbd al-Malik

The Dome of the Rock fulfilled not only the divine promise to Jacob, but also the promise God gave directly to Jerusalem:

25 The self-image of the Umayyads as the heirs of the vision of generations of prophets also appears in a different context, in the letter of caliph al-Walīd II (d. 126/744) to the governors of the provinces in the Umayyad state. See Rubin, "Prophets and Caliphs", pp. 88–93.
26 Genesis 28:12–22.
27 Yāqūt, *Muʿjam al-buldān*, V, p. 167 (s.v. al-Maqdis). See also Maqdisī, *Muthīr al-gharām*, pp. 271–272.
28 Genesis 28:18–19.
29 See above, Chapter 7.

> [Rejoice] Jerusalem (*Īrūshalāyim*) – this is Bayt al-Maqdis and the Rock, and it is called the shrine [*al-haykal*] — I am sending you my servant ʿAbd al-Malik; he will build and embellish you. I will restore in Bayt al-Maqdis its first kingdom and will crown it with gold, silver and precious stones. I will send to you my creature and place my throne on the Rock. I am Allāh the Lord, and David is the king of the Children of Israel.[30]

This tradition is related on the authority of Kaʿb al-Aḥbār (d. 32/652), the Jew whom we met in previous chapters and who converted to Islam and became a prolific source of information concerning holy scriptures and the history of the people of Israel. The tradition weaves the sanctity of the Dome of the Rock into the words that God addressed directly to the holy city which here is called by its biblical Hebrew name, *Īrūshalāyim*. ʿAbd al-Malik appears here as Allāh's servant, who will build the shrine (*al-haykal*). This role also has a biblical precedent, this time in the prophecy of Zechariah, who tells of a person who will build God's Temple (Zechariah 6:12–13):[31]

> (12) Say to him: Thus says the Lord of hosts: Here is a man whose name is Branch [צֶמַח]: for he shall branch out in his place, and he shall build the temple of the Lord. (13) It is he that shall build the temple of the Lord; he shall bear royal honor, and shall sit upon his throne and rule. There shall be a priest by his throne, with peaceful understanding between the two of them.

The passage apparently refers to Zerubbabel who will rebuild the destroyed Temple. The Jewish Sages noted that the numerical value of the letters of the Hebrew word for "branch" — צֶמַח (*ẓemaḥ*) — was 138, equal to the numerical value of the Hebrew word for "comforter" — מְנַחֵם (*menaḥem*) — mentioned in Lamentations 1:17 ("Zion stretches out her hands, but there is no one to comfort her [אֵין מְנַחֵם לָהּ]"). The tidings about the man called צֶמַח thus also predict the coming of the מְנַחֵם.[32] In the Islamic version of Kaʿb al-Aḥbār, the person called צֶמַח who will build the Temple is none other than ʿAbd al-Malik.

The tradition we just examined places King David, "the king of the Children of Israel", next to ʿAbd al-Malik. The presence of the former enhances the messianic

---

30 Ibn al-Murajjā, *Faḍā'il*, pp. 63–64 (no. 50). The tradition is quoted in Livne-Kafri, "A Note on Some Traditions", pp. 82–83; *idem*, *Selected Essays*, p. 46. A shortened and distorted version is found in Wāsiṭī, *Faḍā'il*, p. 86 (no. 138). See also Elad, *Medieval Jerusalem*, pp. 162–163; *idem*, "The Temple Mount, p. 76; *idem*, "The Status of Jerusalem", p. 55; Sharon, "The Praises of Jerusalem", p. 57; Rubin, *Between Bible and Qur'an*, pp. 19–20; Levy-Rubin, "The Dome of the Rock", p. 455.
31 See also Zechariah 3:8.
32 Talmud Yerushalmi, I, p. 211 (Berakhot 2:4): "Rabbi Joshua ben Levi said: His name is Ẓemaḥ. Rabbi Yudan, the son of Rabbi Aivu, said: His name is Menaḥem. Ḥanina the son of Rabbi Abbahu said: They is no disagreement here since the numerical value of one is the numerical value of the other. Ẓemaḥ is equal to Menaḥem".

significance of ʿAbd al-Malik's deed, as if the Dome of the Rock were the reconstructed Temple that marks the redemption of the Israelites who will return to their land with David, the King Messiah.

A similar role is assigned to David in yet another tradition of Wahb b. Munabbih in which Allāh addresses the Rock and predicts the coming of David, riding on his mount. Allāh himself will place His throne on the Rock and will gather all humans there.[33] The placing of God's throne on the Rock also hints at the renewed edifice of the Temple erected by ʿAbd al-Malik, although his name is not mentioned here. Only the name of David has remained, which preserves the sense of the future messianic redemption.

The idea of God's throne standing on earth already appears in the Hebrew Bible.[34] Of particular relevance to our discussion is the following passage from Zechariah 2:10–11 [14–15]), in which God addresses Jerusalem:

> (10) Sing and rejoice, O daughter of Zion! For lo, I will come and dwell in your midst, says the Lord. (11) Many nations shall join themselves to the Lord on that day, and shall be my people; and I will dwell in your midst. . .

This prophecy predicts that the nations will come to Jerusalem when God himself will come and dwell there. In the present Islamic version, the Rock is the site of God's throne and the place where the redeemed will gather, together with David who will be riding his mount. As we already saw above, the Rock is also the place where God will pass judgment on those who will be revived on the Day of Resurrection.[35]

To sum up, the traditions just examined reveal aspects of the Dome of the Rock's Islamic sanctity as associated with the rebuilt Temple and the biblical visions of Jerusalem's messianic future. In these traditions the Muslim nation which the Umayyad rulers represent is the one that implements the redemption plan which God announced in the Jewish and Christian Scriptures.

The Jewish angle

Not only the Muslims in al-Shām saw themselves as the implementers of the messianic vision, the Jews, too, saw the Muslims as redeemers. This is evinced in Jewish texts composed towards the end of the Umayyad period, that is, towards the

33 Abū Nuʿaym, *Ḥilyat al-awliyāʾ*, IV, p. 66.
34 Ezekiel 43:7 He said to me: Mortal, this is the place of my throne and the place for the soles of my feet, where I will reside among the people of Israel forever.
35 See above, Chapter 4.

middle of the eighth century CE. These texts present Muḥammad and Islam as bearers of the tidings of redemption. No doubt their authors joyfully accepted what they heard the Muslims claiming about themselves. A text which shows this most clearly is a treatise entitled *The Secrets of Rabbi Simon ben Yoḥay.*[36] It contains a vision revealed to Rabbi Simon by the angel Metatron, using models taken from the vision of Balaam (Numbers 24). Here is what we read near the beginning, when the angel reveals to Rabbi Simon the appearance of Islam in the Land of Israel:

> When he saw the kingdom of Ishmael that was coming, he began to say: 'Was it not enough, what the wicked kingdom of Edom did to us, but we must have the kingdom of Ishmael too'? At once Metatron the prince of the countenance answered and said: 'Do not fear, son of man, for the Holy One, blessed be he, only brings the kingdom of Ishmael in order to save you from this wickedness. He raises up over them a prophet according to his will and will conquer the land for them and they will come and restore it in greatness and there will be great terror between them and the sons of Esau.[37]

Muḥammad is here perceived as a prophet sent at God's behest, and the Islamic conquest of Palestine is explicitly viewed as deliverance from the Byzantine Christians who had ruled the land until the Muslims came. A subsequent passage in the *Secrets* adds furthermore:

> The second king who arises from Ishmael will be a lover of Israel; he restores their breaches and the breaches of the temple. He hews Mount Moriah and makes it all straight, and builds a mosque there on the temple rock, as it is said: ". . . your nest is set in the rock" (Numbers 24:21). He makes war against the sons of Esau and kills his armies and takes many captives from them, and he will die in peace and with great honor.[38]

According to Bernard Lewis,[39] the "second king" is Muʿāwiya, to whom the author of *The Secrets* also attributes acts which were carried out before his time, during the caliphate of the second caliph, ʿUmar b. al-Khaṭṭāb. Whatever the identity of this Muslim ruler, he is clearly praised as a friend of the Jews, who carried out building and cleaning projects on the Temple Mount, and, in particular, erected a mosque there. The passage delineates a Muslim-Jewish alliance, fed no doubt by enmity towards their common enemy, the Children of Esau, namely, the Byzantine Empire.

---

36 Jellinek, *Bet Ha-Midrasch*, III, pp. 78–82. The text was studied extensively in Lewis, "Apocalyptic Vision". See also Hoyland, *Seeing Islam*, pp. 308–312; Gil, *History of Palestine*, pp. 61–63; Sharon, "The Praises of Jerusalem", pp. 63–64.
37 Jellinek, *Bet Ha-Midrasch*, III, p. 78. The English translation is based on Lewis, "Apocalyptic Vision", pp. 321–322.
38 Jellinek, *Bet Ha-Midrasch*, III, p. 79; Lewis, "Apocalyptic Vision", pp. 324–325.
39 Lewis, "Apocalyptic Vision", p. 328.

The Temple and the prophets at large

The traditions which Muslims continued to disseminate over the generations preserve the association of the Dome of the Rock with Solomon, as well as with all other prophets. They add details concerning the permission which God gave to Solomon to make any request he wanted. One such tradition, transmitted in the name of Muḥammad himself, relates that when Solomon had completed the Temple's construction, he asked Allāh for wisdom as great as God's, and for a kingship the likes of which will never be possessed by anyone after him. Allāh acceded to his request.[40] Other traditions reassert the Temple Mount's position in the redemption plan and concurrently highlight its connection with all prophets. Thus a tradition of Ibn ʿAbbās says about the Temple:

> . . . It was the prophets who built it and the prophets who dwelled in it. There is no handbreadth (*shibr*) in it where a prophet did not pray or an angel did not stay.[41]

It follows that the site's sanctity originates in its role as the locus of prophetic activity throughout the generations.

Prayer niches in Solomon's Temple

The Temple Mount's relationship to the prophets is especially noticeable in traditions about their prayer niches (*maḥārīb*) there which, as we saw above, are mentioned in the Qurʾān in connection with the labors of the *jinn* for Solomon.[42] According to one version, the Temple which Solomon built had six thousand prayer niches, equal to the number of prophets descended from Israel. Above them was Muḥammad's niche, the highest of them all. The list of the other high niches includes those of Adam, Seth, Idrīs (Enoch), Noah, Hūd, Ṣāliḥ, Shem, Abraham, Ishmael, Isaac, Jacob, and then those of Jacob's twelve sons, as well as the niches of David, Solomon, Jesus, Zechariah and John.[43]

---

40 Yāqūt, *Muʿjam al-buldān*, V, p. 166 (s.v. al-Maqdis).

41 *Ibid.*, p. 167.

42 Q 34:13.

43 Ibn al-Murajjā, *Faḍāʾil*, pp. 146–147. And see a comprehensive survey of the reports about the prayer niches in Elad, "Seven *miḥrābs*".

Edifices in Bayt al-Maqdis from David's and Solomon's days

Some traditions about the role of David and Solomon in the Temple's construction contain folkloristic stories about Solomon. These will not be treated here.[44] Instead, let us cite some traditions about sites which the Muslims identified as remnants from the times of David and Solomon. Thus, for example, Yāqūt (d. 626/1229) reports that al-Masjid al-Aqṣā is located in the eastern part of the city and faces the *qibla*, that is, south, and that "its foundation (*asās*) is the work of David, peace be on him . . . ".[45] Yāqūt further mentions a structure on the Temple Mount called David's Dome, located next to the Dome of the Miʿrāj.[46]

The names of David and other prophets appear in a list given by Yāqūt of the eight iron gates of Bayt al-Maqdis, among them the Zion gate, the gate of Jeremiah's cell and the gate of the *miḥrāb* (prayer niche) of David.[47] Another list of twenty (!) gates of al-Masjid al-Aqṣā contains, among others, the gate of the Prophet (Muḥammad), the gate of the *miḥrāb* of Mary, the gate of the pool of the Children of Israel, the gate of the tribes (Jacob's twelve sons), the gate of Abraham and the gate of David.[48] Yāqūt also preserved for us a list of the city's water cisterns, including the cistern of the Children of Israel and the cistern of Solomon.[49]

The connection between the buildings on the Muslim Temple Mount and Solomon's Temple is clearly delineated in a folkloristic story describing the Rock's size in Solomon's days. The Rock is said to have been twelve cubits high. Above it is a wooden dome eighteen miles high, on top of which a golden deer is mounted. Between its eyes there is a red pearl which casts light for a distance of three days' travel. Its light enables women on the other side of the Jordan river to weave at night. In the morning and in the evening, the dome casts a shadow for a distance of three days' travel, and shelters the inhabitants of the Jordan valley from the sun. Yāqūt does not fail to remark that this story is further from the truth than it is from heaven.[50] Remnants of the building projects of the kings were identified

---

44 See also Schwarzbaum, *Folkloristic Aspects*, pp. 16–25.
45 Yāqūt, *Muʿjam al-buldān*, V, pp. 168, 169 (s.v. al-Maqdis). See also *ibid.*, p. 169.
46 *Ibid.*, p. 168.
47 *Ibid.*, p. 169.
48 *Ibid.*, p. 170. See also Busse, "The Sanctity of Jerusalem", p. 466; Elad, "The Status of Jerusalem", p. 52.
49 Yāqūt, *Muʿjam al-buldān*, V, pp. 168, 169 (s.v. al-Maqdis).
50 *Ibid.*, I, p. 520 (s.v. Bayt Rāma). See also Wāsiṭī, *Faḍāʾil*, p. 84; Busse, "The Sanctity of Jerusalem", p. 458; Sharon, "The Praises of Jerusalem", p. 61; Livne-Kafri, "The Navel of the Earth", p. 59.

not only in Jerusalem, but also in Hebron. Yāqūt reports that some say that the fortress of Hebron was built on foundations laid by Solomon.[51]

The glory of Solomon's Temple as embodied in the Dome of the Rock doubtlessly constitutes one of the major aspects of the Islamic sanctity of Jerusalem; it is hinted at already in the Qur'ān, in the description of the *jinn*'s labors for Solomon. But a transfer of the virtue of "the land of the Temple" from Jerusalem to Mecca can be discerned already in the Qur'ān itself, in passages signaling the Qur'ān's abandonment of the Jewish vision of messianic redemption. More on this in the next chapter.

51 Yāqūt, *Muʿjam al-buldān*, II, p. 387 (s.v. al-Khalīl).

12 “The first House established for the people”

As part of the polemic with Judaism and the abandonment of the Jewish vision of messianic redemption, the Qur’ān identifies in the Medinan *sūra*s the Kaʿba as a House (*bayt*), i.e. temple, that preceded the one in Jerusalem. This idea is supported by the image of Abraham who is said to have frequented Mecca and established the pilgrimage to it. Abraham’s relationship to the Kaʿba is also reflected in pre-Islamic poetic verses about Abraham’s footprints preserved on a sacred stone in Mecca. The Qur’ān’s interest in highlighting the primordial existence of the Abrahamic Kaʿba is one aspect of the shaping of this shrine’s image as a proper arena for Muḥammad’s emergence, the Arabian Messenger who is descended from Abraham and Ishmael.

In contrast to the qur’ānic Meccan verses that allude to the wondrous building of Solomon’s Temple, the Medinan verses place the Kaʿba as the primary shrine, thanks to Abraham who established it many generations before Solomon. The idea that the Kaʿba is more ancient than Solomon’s Temple is yet another aspect of the tendency to transfer sanctity patterns from al-Shām to Mecca and the Kaʿba. This process coincides with the abandonment in the Medinan verses of the Jewish vision of messianic redemption evinced in the Meccan verses. Explicit renunciation of their redemption dreams is perhaps expressed in Q 4:53: “Or have they [the Jews] a share in the Kingdom (*al-mulk*)? If that is so, they do not give the people a single date-spot”. This verse seems to mean that the Jews will never achieve the Kingdom that they have been dreaming of, in which case they would have kept on preventing others from sharing their fortunes. Perhaps even some disappointment is reflected here with regard to the Jews’ refusal to finance Muḥammad’s campaigns.

The first-House passage

The idea of the primordial existence of the Abrahamic Kaʿba is clearly present in a Medinan passage that runs as follows:

Q 3:96–97:

> (96) The first House established for the people was that at Bakka, blessed, and a guidance to all beings. (97) Therein are clear signs — Maqām Ibrāhīm . . .

This passage contains a twofold definition of the Kaʿba. Firstly, it is the first House (*bayt*), i.e. a shrine that served as a pilgrimage destination where the people

https://doi.org/10.1515/9783111222318-013

would worship God. It is located in Mecca, or Bakka, as it is called in this verse.[1] Secondly, it is Maqām Ibrāhīm that forms part of "the clear signs". This passage is preceded by verses which declare that the teachings of Abraham and Jacob predated the teachings of the Torah (of Moses). They also call on the believers to follow the religion of Abraham, who was a *ḥanīf* (Q 3:93–95). The passage cited above intensifies the polemics against the Jews and highlights the primordial existence of the Kaʿba that predated any other pilgrimage destination.

The primordial existence of the *bayt* in Mecca is further demonstrated in its second definition, namely, its status as Maqām Ibrāhīm, i.e. Abraham's standing-place. There he stood and prayed. This image of Abraham is already described in a Jewish midrash (Talmud Bavli, Berachoth 6b):

> Whosoever has a fixed place (*maqōm*) for his prayer has the God of Abraham as his helper. And when he dies, people will say of him: Where is the pious man, where is the humble man, one of the disciples of our father Abraham! – How do we know that our father Abraham had a fixed place [for his prayer]? For it is written: And Abraham got up early in the morning to the place where he had stood. [Gen. 19: 27] And 'standing' means nothing else but prayer. For it is said: Then stood up Phinehas and prayed [Psalms 106: 30].[2]

Abraham's standing in prayer at a place called Maqām Ibrāhīm is also implied in the Qurʾān itself, in another Medinan verse (Q 2:125):

> . . . Take to yourselves the Maqām Ibrāhīm for a place of prayer.

The believers are here urged to make for themselves a place of prayer (*muṣallā*) at a site where Abraham already prayed in the past. The passage that follows this verse deals with Abraham's relationship to the Kaʿba and his building activities there together with Ishmael (Q 2:125–129).[3] This sequence implies that the prayer alluded to in the phrase Maqām Ibrāhīm is closely associated with the scene of the Kaʿba's construction and its establishment as a pilgrimage center. Indeed, in the final clause of the first-House passage, the Qurʾān confirms the preferential standing of that House as a pilgrimage destination (Q 3:97):

> . . . It is the duty of the people towards God to come on pilgrimage to the House, if one is able to make one's way there. As for the unbeliever, God is all-sufficient nor needs any being.

---

1 Commentators on the Qurʾān explain that the form *Bakka* is derived from the Arabic root *b-k-k*, which means crushing. Accordingly, they explain that it denotes the crowds of pilgrims who are pushing each other around the Kaʿba. See various additional explanations in Azraqī, *Akhbār Makka*, pp. 196–198.

2 See Speyer, *Die biblischen Erzählungen*, pp. 161–162.

3 See above, Chapter 8.

In another verse the primordial existence of the Kaʿba as a place of pilgrimage is again associated with Abraham, this time in the commandment that God gives him (Q 22:27):

> And proclaim among the people the pilgrimage, and they shall come unto you on foot and upon every lean beast, they shall come from every deep ravine.

To sum up, Abraham's figure is used in the first-House passage, as well as elsewhere, to support the idea that the Kaʿba as pilgrimage destination predated any other site of this nature. This contention constitutes an implied reproof of the Jews, whose Temple was established only in the days of Solomon.

The biblical model: "exalted from the beginning"

The polemical intent of the first-House passage is sharpened when compared with the following biblical verse (Jeremiah 17:12):

> O glorious throne, exalted from the beginning (מָרוֹם מֵרִאשׁוֹן), the place of our sanctuary (מְקוֹם מִקְדָּשֵׁנוּ).

Just like the first-House passage, the verse in Jeremiah speaks about primordial existence and a "place", *maqōm*. For Jeremiah the primordiality is that of God's throne which is glorious and has been exalted since the beginning of the world. The "place" is that of the Temple. The combination of these two components conveys the idea that the site of the Temple on the Temple Mount is also the site of God's throne and has been exalted since earliest times. In the Jewish midrash this verse serves as the basis for the perception that the Temple was one of the first things ever created. Thus, for example, in the Talmud Bavli (Nedarim 39b) we read:

> Seven things were created before the world, viz., the Torah, repentance, the Garden of Eden, Gehenna, the Throne of Glory, the Temple, and the name of the Messiah. . . The Temple, as it is written, A glorious high throne from the beginning is the place of our Sanctuary. The name of the Messiah, as it is written, His name [sc. of the Messiah] shall endure for ever [Psalms 72: 17].[4]

---

4 In a version appearing in Genesis Rabbah, composed in Palestine during the fifth or the sixth century, God promises His people four things (Midrash Rabbah, II, p. 562 [Genesis Rabbah 63:8]: 1. To reveal Himself to 2. To avenge what Esau [Rome] 3. To rebuild the Temple for them 4. To bring them the royal Messiah. Each promise is based on a biblical verse containing the word "first". The promise to rebuild the Temple is based on Jer. 17:12 in which the Temple is 'on high from the first' [מָרוֹם מֵרִאשׁוֹן – מְקוֹם מִקְדָּשֵׁנוּ].

The Qur'ān reconstructs this combined pattern of primordial existence and place:

	Primordial existence	Place
Jeremiah 17:12	exalted from the beginning	*maqōm* of our sanctuary
Q 3:96–97	The first House established for the people	Maqām Ibrāhīm

Despite the identical pattern, the level of primordiality is different. Jeremiah and the midrash refer to the heavenly, preexistent, Temple, whereas in the Qur'ān the primordial existence is in the terrestrial sense — a site on earth to which people come as pilgrims. In this capacity, the terrestrial House in Mecca predates the terrestrial Temple that was constructed only in the days of Solomon, in contrast to the Kaʿba, where Abraham prayed and which he established as a pilgrimage site.

Tafsīr of the first-House passage: Maqām Ibrāhīm and the pilgrimage

The observation that the qur'ānic first-House passage declares the chronological supremacy of the Abrahamic Kaʿba over that of Solomon's Temple is corroborated by a number of exegetes. This is, for example, what al-Zajjāj (d. 311/924) says:

> As for the construction [of the first House], there is no doubt that it was Abraham who built it. God, may he be exalted, said: "And when Abraham, and Ishmael with him, raised up the foundations of the House" [Q 2:127] . . . As for the Temple [*al-maqdis*], it was built by Solomon.[5]

Al-Rāzī (d. 607/1210) expands on this matter:

> The nations are all agreed that the builder of this House was al-Khalīl [Abraham], peace be upon him, and that the builder of the Temple was Solomon, peace be upon him. There is no doubt that al-Khalīl is of a higher grade and more exalted than Solomon, peace be upon him. Therefore, from this aspect, the Kaʿba deserves to be more honored than the Temple [*ashraf min Bayt al-Maqdis*].[6]

Other traditions anchor the first-House passage in a Jewish-Muslim polemic. A tradition of the Meccan Ibn Jurayj (d. 150/767) relates that the passage was revealed to the Prophet after a dispute that broke out between Jews and Muslims. The Jews claimed that Bayt al-Maqdis was superior to the Kaʿba, for the former

5 Zajjāj, *Maʿānī l-Qur'ān* (Q 3:96).
6 Rāzī, *Tafsīr* (Q 3:96).

was the destination of the prophets' *hijra* (*muhājar al-anbiyā'*) and the location of the Holy Land (*al-arḍ al-muqaddasa*). In response, the passage concerning the first House and Maqām Ibrāhīm was revealed, and the Prophet explained that the virtues enumerated in this passage were unique to the Kaʿba, "and are not in Bayt al-Maqdis".[7] In other words, everything necessary for implementing the plan of redemption is already in place in Mecca, the site of the first House and where Abraham found a place for himself and his progeny, a long time before Solomon's Temple was built.

In the texts examined so far, Abraham is portrayed as the founder of the pilgrimage to Mecca, and as such he is also the first pilgrim there. The same notion comes up in a tradition by Ibn Isḥāq (d. 150/768) who composed a biography of the Prophet and anchored it in the history of the prophets of all ages. Extensive quotes about the history of the prophets from Ibn Isḥāq's book were preserved not only in al-Ṭabarī's (d. 310/923) history, but also in al-Azraqī's (d. 222/837) history of Mecca. I will quote from the latter. Ibn Isḥāq reports that Abraham would make the pilgrimage to the House, that is, the Kaʿba, every year, mounted on al-Burāq, "and since then all prophets and nations made the pilgrimage".[8] Abraham's journey to the Kaʿba is described in a pattern parallel to that of the Prophet's journey to al-Masjid al-Aqṣā. Both move between the two regions of the sanctity space and both ride the same mount, al-Burāq, but in opposite directions. The reversal of the direction preserves the status of the Holy Mosque (al-Masjid al-Ḥarām) in Mecca not only as a point of departure (for Muḥammad's journey) but also as a destination (for Abraham's journey). The connection of al-Burāq to Abraham appears also in a tradition quoted in a commentary on Q 17:1, the verse about the Prophet's nocturnal journey. When Gabriel was about to take Muḥammad on the journey to al-Masjid al-Aqṣā, he presented al-Burāq to him and said: "Ascend and ride, for this is Abraham's mount, on whose back he would visit the Holy House".[9] Furthermore, according to Ibn Isḥāq, "Allāh commanded Abraham to perform the *ḥajj* and to establish it for the people. [Allāh] showed him the rites of the House [the Kaʿba] and determined for him its rules and commandments. On the day on which Abraham was instructed about this, he was in Bayt al-Maqdis which is in Īliyā'".[10] This is another way in which the tradition preserves Mecca's status as a destination to which even those who reside in Bayt al-Maqdis are not exempt from the duty to come as pilgrims.

7 Azraqī, *Akhbār Makka*, pp. 39–40.
8 Azraqī, *Akhbār Makka*, p. 34. See also Kister, "Sanctity Joint and Divided", pp. 53, 56, 58.
9 Thaʿlabī, *al-Kashf wa-l-bayān* (Q 17:1).
10 Azraqī, *Akhbār Makka*, p. 37.

The stone of Maqām Ibrāhīm

Another aspect of the significance of the qur'ānic phrase Maqām Ibrāhīm is revealed in the following line of poetry, ascribed to the Prophet's uncle, Abū Ṭālib:

وَمَوْطِىءِ إبراهيمَ في الصَّخْرِ رَطْبَةٌ / على قَدَمَيْه حافِياً غَيْرَ ناعِلِ[11]

By Abraham's footprint in the rock [when still] damp[12]/
[Standing] on both feet, bare, without sandals

The group of verses in which this line appears mentions a series of pre-Islamic places of worship in Mecca and its surroundings which served as stations on the pilgrimage path.[13] This line alludes to a legend concerning Abraham's footprints on a certain stone, without giving any details about the circumstances in which they were made. But the very fact that Abraham's footprints are mentioned in pre-Islamic poetry describing sacred sites in Mecca constitutes further evidence for the antiquity of the relationship between Abraham and the Kaʿba; it is also consistent with the testimony of Sozomen concerning the ideas of pre-Islamic Arabs about their forefather Ishmael.[14]

Against the background of the pre-Islamic myth about Abraham's footprints, it may be assumed that the qur'ānic phrase Maqām Ibrāhīm alludes not only to Abraham's standing in prayer, but also to a specific stone on which his footprints were to be seen. This comes out also in the words of the Meccan exegete Mujāhid b. Jabr (d. 104/722). Explaining the meaning of the "clear signs" which in the first-House passage are said to include the Maqām Ibrāhīm, he says: "The traces of Abraham's two feet [*athar qadamayhi*] on the [stone of the] *Maqām* are a clear sign".[15]

The myth of Abraham's footprints on the stone gave rise to traditions about the circumstances in which he stood on it. According to one version, Abraham stood there as he declared the duty to perform the pilgrimage (Q 22:27). This, too, is transmitted in the name of the exegete Mujāhid:

> Abraham, peace be upon him, stood on this [stone of the] Maqām and said: O people, answer the call of your Lord. [Mujāhid] said: They said: At your service, God, at your service.

---

11 Ibn Hishām, *Sīra*, I, p. 292.

12 The syntactic structure of the verse is vague. I translated following the traditions saying that God softened the rock under Abraham's feet. A different understanding is implied in Guillaume, *The Life of Muhammad*, p. 123: "By Abraham's footprint in the rock still fresh".

13 Rubin, "Ḥanīfiyya and Kaʿba", p. 106. And See above, Chapter 1.

14 See above, Chapter 9.

15 Ṭabarī, *Tafsīr* (Q 3:97).

> [Mujāhid] said: Whoever has made the pilgrimage from then to this day is counted among those who heeded the call of Abraham, peace be upon him.[16]

As seen above (in the Chapter "The Kaʿba and the prophets"), the formula "At your service, God" (*labbayka llāhumma*) is the *talbiya* invocation pronounced by pilgrims on their way to Mecca. Other traditions add that after Abraham finished his announcement of the *ḥajj*, his footprints remained in the stone as a sign for the people.[17]

Some traditions connect Abraham's footprints with his standing on the stone when building the Kaʿba together with his son Ishmael.[18] The exegete Ibn ʿAṭiyya (d. 546/1151) explains:

> Among the signs [mentioned in the first-House passage] is the stone of the *Maqām*. Abraham stood on it as he raised up the foundations of the House, when the structure was already too high for him. Then, whenever the wall became higher, the stone raised him in the air. He continued building while standing on it; Ishmael would hand him the bricks and the clay, until he finished the wall. Then Allāh, since he wanted to immortalize this as a sign for the dwellers of the world, softened the stone and Abraham's feet sank into it, as if they were within clay. These sublime tracks [*al-athar al-ʿaẓīm*] remained impressed in the stone to this day.[19]

Yet another version is transmitted on the authority of Ibn ʿAbbās, according to which Ishmael carried the bricks for building the Kaʿba on his back and handed them to Abraham. When the walls became too high, Ishmael placed the stone of the Maqām where Abraham worked, so he could stand on it and continue building the wall. The stone is thus called Maqām Ibrāhīm, because Abraham stood on it.[20]

To complete the picture, we note that other traditions maintain that Abraham's footprints were left on the stone after he placed his feet on it and lowered his head towards Ishmael's wife or mother so that she could wash his hair while he remained sitting on his mount (he did not dismount, because that is what he had promised his wife Sarah).[21] In this legend there is no standing on the stone; the connection of the stone to the scene of washing the hair thus would appear to be of a secondary nature. The likely aim of the connection was to exalt Ishmael's

16 Azraqī, *Akhbār Makka*, p. 272. See also Kister, "Maqām Ibrāhīm", p. 480.
17 Azraqī, *Akhbār Makka*, pp. 34, 272, 273.
18 See above, Chapter 8.
19 Ibn ʿAṭiyya, *Tafsīr* (Q 3:97).
20 Azraqī, *Akhbār Makka*, p. 26. See also *ibid.*, pp. 274–275. And see Kister, "Maqām Ibrāhīm", pp. 479–480.
21 E.g. Zamakhsharī, *Kashshāf* (Q 3:96); Rāzī, *Tafsīr* (Q 3:96). See also Kister, "Maqām Ibrāhīm", p. 480.

wife or mother and praise her for the hospitality she showed.[22] Furthermore, some contemporary scholars maintain that Maqām Ibrāhīm is the site of Abraham's attempted sacrifice of his son.[23] However, this does not fully explain the meaning of "standing" inherent in the word *maqām*.

We have thus seen that thanks to the Abrahamic sanctity of the Kaʿba the Qurʾān was able to shape its image as the first temple on earth, one that predated Solomon's Temple. This argument fits in with the polemic against the Jews that is reflected throughout the Medinan *sūras*. The polemic originated in the disappointment with the Jews who refused to recognize the Arabian prophet as the harbinger of their salvation as well as to help him financially. Furthermore, as the first Muslims came to Jerusalem not long after the Prophet's death, and in light of the permanence of Jerusalem's Islamic sanctity, especially thanks to the Umayyads, pro-Maccan traditions were disseminated with a view to expanding the Kaʿba's primordial existence and to anchor it in the Creation. More on this in the next chapter.

22 But see a different explanation of the episode in Schussman, "Abraham's Visits", pp. 339–340.
23 See Sinai, *Fortschreibung*, p. 142; Neuwirth, *Der Koran als Text*, p. 647.

13 The First House in Creation

Post-qur'ānic tradition endeavors to maintain the supremacy of the Kaʿba vis-à-vis the Temple in Jerusalem by shaping its image as a primordial shrine that preceded the Temple in the process of the Creation. This attempt is discerned in further interpretations of the first-House passage (Q 3:96–97). These traditions even present the Kaʿba as the origin of the Creation. In addition, they turn the construction of the Kaʿba by Abraham and Ishmael into a link in the history of the Kaʿba's building which began with Adam.

Inspired by the Jewish idea about the Foundation Stone [Hebrew, *Even ha-Shtiyya*] being the origin of the Creation, the first Muslims who came to al-Shām soon applied the idea to the Rock (al-Ṣakhra) on the Temple Mount.[1] This eventually prompted the partisans of the glory of Mecca and the Kaʿba to elaborate on the latter's antiquity and to place its origins at a time preceding that of the primordial shrine in Bayt al-Maqdis.

The Kaʿba and the Creation

To begin with, in a series of traditions that interpret the first-House passage (Q 3:96–97), the House, i.e. the Kaʿba, is presented as the origin of the Creation. Thus, the exegete Mujāhid (d. 104/722) explains:

> Allāh created the House two thousand years before all the earth, at a time when God's throne was on the water. At that time, the House was still in a state of white foam [*zibda*] that floated on the water. Then the earth was pulled and stretched [*duḥiyat*] from the place underneath it.[2]

According to this interpretation, the significance of the Kaʿba as "first" is absolute and not limited to its role as the first shrine to be placed for the people on earth, as a straightforward reading of the qur'ānic text would imply.

Other traditions in which the Kaʿba is presented as the origin of the Creation appear in commentaries on the title "Mother of Towns" (*umm al-qurā*) which the Qur'ān bestows on Mecca (Q 6:92):

1 See above, Chapter 2.
2 Ṭabarī, *Tafsīr* (Q 3:96).

https://doi.org/10.1515/9783111222318-014

> This is a book We have sent down, blessed and confirming that which was before it, and for you to warn the Mother of Towns and those around it.

The exegete Muqātil b. Sulaymān (d. 150/767) explains that the title Mother of Towns means that the entire earth "was pulled and stretched [*duḥiyat*] from the place underneath the Kaʿba".[3] This interpretation accords with the fact that the Prophet is sent to warn "those around (*ḥawla*) it", that is, the Kaʿba is in the center. A more extensive tradition in the name of Ibn ʿAbbās describes in detail how the world was created from the Mother of Towns:

> When the throne had hovered over the water, before Allāh created the heaven and the earth, he sent a whistling wind (*rīḥ haffāfa*) that struck the water and exposed a soft block of snow (*khashafa*) in the place (intended for) this House, that looked like a dome. He then pulled and stretched the earth from underneath it. The earth wobbled again and again, so he stabilized it by means of mountains which he set on it like pegs [see, for example, Q 16:15]. The first mountain set on it was Abū Qubays. That is why Mecca was called Mother of Towns.[4]

The description of the primordial form of the Kaʿba as a dome (*qubba*) may reflect a model of sanctity appropriated from the Dome of the Rock, or an earlier dome-like structure on the Temple Mount. Be that as it may, traditions indicate that as early as the time of Muʿāwiya b. Abī Sufyān (d. 60/680), the first Umayyad caliph, there was a structure there which may even have been identified as al-Masjid al-Aqṣā.[5]

Other traditions, not within the domain of Qurʾān exegesis, describe a sequence of primordial creations in which the Kaʿba precedes Bayt al-Maqdis in time. In one such tradition, ʿĀʾisha, the Prophet's wife, relates that the Prophet declared:

> God had created Mecca and surrounded it with angels, a thousand years before he created any bit of the entire earth. Then he joined Medina [to Mecca] and to Medina he joined Bayt al-Maqdis. Then he created the entire earth at once, after a thousand years.[6]

---

3 Muqātil, *Tafsīr* (Q 6:92). See also Ṭabarī, *Tafsīr* (Q 6:92). Cf. Livne-Kafri, "The Navel of the Earth", pp. 50–51. But according to other interpretations, the title Umm al-Qurā means that Mecca is the most important among the cities in Arabia, or serves as the central crossroad in it. See e.g. Māwardī, *Nukat* (Q 6:92).

4 Azraqī, *Akhbār Makka*, p. 3–4.

5 Elad, *Medieval Jerusalem*, p. 33; *idem*, "The Temple Mount", pp. 63–70.

6 Wāsiṭī, *Faḍāʾil*, p. 16 (no. 18). See also Daylamī, *Firdaws*, II, p. 185 (no. 2928); Ibn al-Murajjā, *Faḍāʾil*, p. 10 (no. 2); Samhūdī, *Wafāʾ*, I, p. 117; Busse, "The Sanctity of Jerusalem", p. 463; Livne-Kafri, "The Navel of the Earth", p. 51.

This version makes not only the creation of Mecca but that of Medina as well, older than that of Bayt al-Maqdis, which has thus been downgraded to third place in the order of creation. The extent to which this order is determined by local patriotism can be seen in yet another version, in which Mecca was first to be created, then Medina, then Bayt al-Maqdis, and then the mosque of al-Kūfa.[7] Not only is Bayt al-Maqdis moved down from first place here, but al-Kūfa, a city holy to Shīʿīs, has also been included in the sequence of primordial creations.

The Kaʿba predated al-Masjid al-Aqṣā by forty years

Some traditions which deal with the construction of the terrestrial Kaʿba also refer to a primordial existence of the shrine. In one of them the Prophet's Companion Abū Dharr relates:

> I asked the Prophet: O Messenger of Allāh, which mosque was established (*wuḍiʿa*) first? He said: The Holy Mosque [al-Masjid al-Ḥarām]. – And then which one? He said: The Farthest Mosque [al-Masjid al-Aqṣā]. I said: How much time separates them? He said: Forty years.[8]

This tradition found its way into several canonical *ḥadīth* collections including that of al-Bukhārī (d. 256/869) — a sign that Muslim scholars accepted it as completely reliable.[9] This tradition detaches the foundation of the shrines in Mecca and Jerusalem from Abraham and Solomon respectively. The Kaʿba is still older, but now the chronological difference has been reduced to forty years. Forty is a well-known typological figure; it occurs often, for example, in descriptions of the stages in which a divine plan is implemented. Accordingly, forty years is the time in which God dwelled on the Rock at Bayt al-Maqdis before He ascended to heaven in the middle of the process of Creation.[10] An eminent holy mountain in Syria (Qāsiyūn) will survive forty years after the end of the world as a reward for its compliance with God's command to give up its shade and blessing in favor of the "mountain of Bayt al-Maqdis" (*Jabal Bayt al-Maqdis*).[11] The forty years that according to the Prophet elapsed between the creation of the Kaʿba and that of al-Masjid al-Aqṣā are thus meant to signal an appropriate and solemn period of time separating two stages in God's preordained plan.

7 Kister, "Three Mosques", p. 191; Livne-Kafri, "The Navel of the Earth", p. 51.
8 Ṭabarī, *Tafsīr* (Q 3:96). See Busse, "The Sanctity of Jerusalem", p. 463; Livne-Kafri, "The Navel of the Earth", p. 52.
9 Bukhārī, *Ṣaḥīḥ*, IV, p. 177 (*Aḥādīth al-anbiyāʾ* [60]); Ibn Māja, *Sunan*, I, no. 753.
10 Wāsiṭī, *Faḍāʾil*, p. 70 (no. 113); Kister, "Three Mosques", p. 195.
11 Kister, "Sanctity Joint and Divided", p. 26.

Muslim scholars have noted that the forty-years tradition detaches the beginning of the construction of the two shrines from the figures of Abraham and Solomon. Accordingly, the exegete al-Qurṭubī (d. 671/1273) states that according to some, Abraham and Solomon only renewed (*jaddadā*) what others before them had founded. He adds the possibility that it was Adam who built the primordial Ka'ba, and that forty years later some of his descendants founded Bayt al-Maqdis.[12] Another tradition maintains that Adam himself built the two shrines. The tradition appears in the *Kitāb al-tījān*, in Ibn Hishām's (d. 218/833) recension, and is recorded on the authority of Wahb b. Munabbih (d. 110/728), a transmitter of numerous traditions about the prophets. Wahb relates that after Adam built the House (the Ka'ba), God commanded him to go to the sacred city (*al-balad al-muqaddas*), namely, Bayt al-Maqdis, where Gabriel showed him how to build the Temple. He built the Temple and performed the prescribed rites there. The direction of prayer (*qibla*) from the Temple was the Holy Mosque (in Mecca).[13] It is thus implied that the Ka'ba constituted the primordial direction of prayer, thus depriving Bayt al-Maqdis of this virtue as well.

Al-Bukhārī's commentator, Ibn Ḥajar al-'Asqalānī (d. 852/1449) adds more details about the original builders of al-Masjid al-Aqṣā, in his comments on the forty-years tradition. He quotes traditions to the effect that "the first to have founded [*assasa*] al-Masjid al-Aqṣā was Adam, peace be upon him, and some say, the angels, and some say, Shem son of Noah, peace be upon him, and some say, Jacob, peace be upon him".[14] Shem son of Noah is mentioned in a tradition of Ka'b al-Aḥbār as having erected the Temple's earliest foundation (*al-asās*), on which David and Solomon constructed their building.[15] This is probably a reflection of the midrashic identification of Shem son of Noah with the ancient king of Jerusalem, Melchizedek king of Salem, who was "priest of God Most High", as described in Genesis 14:18.[16] Indeed, another version states that after Noah had left the Ark, Melchizedek "the sage" (*al-ḥabr*) built the Temple over Adam's grave (in Bayt al-Maqdis). This had taken place before Abraham reached the Promised Land (*arḍ al-maw'id*) in the land of al-Shām. Melchizedek was guided by God to

12 Qurṭubī, *Aḥkām al-Qur'ān* (Q 3:96).
13 Ibn Hishām, *Tījān*, pp. 21–22. See also Ibn Ḥajar, *Fatḥ al-bārī*, VI, p. 291.
14 Ibn Ḥajar, *Fatḥ al-bārī*, VI, p. 291. See also Livne-Kafri, "The Navel of the Earth", p. 70. On Jacob's status as the founder of al-Masjid al-Aqṣā, see above, Chapter 11.
15 Ibn al-Jawzī, *Ta'rīkh Bayt al-Maqdis*, pp. 36–37. see also Ibn al-Murajjā, *Faḍā'il*, p. 17 (no. 9); Ibn Shaddād, *al-A'lāq al-khaṭīra*, pp. 187–188; Minhājī, *Itḥāf al-akhiṣṣā*, I, p. 8. See also Livne-Kafri, "The Navel of the Earth", pp. 67, 70.
16 Schwarzbaum, *Folkloristic Aspects*, p. 16 (with references to Midrashic sources).

Adam's grave.[17] There is clearly a trend here to establish Jerusalem as an ancient shrine, much older than the Kaʿba built by Abraham. This made it even more urgent to evoke the typological forty-years tradition which allows the Kaʿba to repossess the glory of chronological primacy.

Abraham's Kaʿba and Adam

In contrast to traditions that detach the foundation of the Kaʿba and al-Masjid al-Aqṣā from Abraham and Solomon respectively, there are others which attempt to preserve Abraham's status as the builder of the first shrine on earth. Thus the exegete Ibn ʿAṭiyya (d. 546/1151) states that the Prophet's declaration about the forty years that separate the construction of the Kaʿba from that of al-Masjid al-Aqṣā implies that both shrines were established by Abraham himself (*min waḍʿ Ibrāhīm jamīʿan*). Ibn ʿAṭiyya adds that this explanation refutes al-Zajjāj's explanation of the first-House passage (see the previous chapter), in which he speaks of Abraham as builder of the Kaʿba and of Solomon as builder of the Temple. If just forty years separate the two shrines, Solomon could not have been the first who built the Temple; he only renewed (*jaddada*) what Abraham had built.[18]

Abraham is not only presented as the builder of both the Kaʿba and al-Masjid al-Aqṣā, but his building activities also have a direct connection to Adam, as we learn, for example, in the following tradition of Wahb b. Munabbih:

> When Allāh, may he be exalted, sent his friend Abraham to build him the House, Abraham sought the first foundation [*al-asās al-awwal*] which Adam's sons had laid on the spot where stood the tent [*al-khayma*] built of a precious stone.[19] Allāh had lowered it for Adam from the tents of Paradise in order to console him [for having expelled him from Paradise]. It was placed for him in Mecca, where the future holy House would stand. Abraham continued to dig until he reached the foundations [*al-qawāʿid*] laid by Adam's sons where the tent had stood.[20]

Ibn Isḥāq (d. 150/768), who begins his book on the life of Muḥammad with a history of previous prophets, relates that Abraham and Ishmael together dug until they reached the foundation built by Adam (*asās Ādam al-awwal*). The foundation

17 Ibn Shaddād, *al-Aʿlāq al-khaṭīra*, p. 187.
18 Ibn ʿAṭiyya, *Tafsīr* (Q 3:96). See also Abū Ḥayyān, *al-Baḥr al-muḥīṭ* (Q 3:96).
19 On the tent (*khayma*) that was sent down to Adam see also Azraqī, *Akhbār Makka*, p. 8, in a further tradition of Wahb b. Munabbih.
20 Azraqī, *Akhbār Makka*, pp. 27–28.

contained such huge stones that even thirty men were unable to lift them. Abraham then built the Kaʿba on Adam's foundation.[21]

The direct link between Abraham and Adam can also be discerned in another tradition by Wahb b. Munabbih which relates what God told Adam after he descended to earth. Among other things, God told him about the House he had chosen for himself, one that was superior to any other, namely the Kaʿba, which would be called Allāh's House. God would put it in the most superior territory which he had chosen for himself on the day he created heaven and earth. God would make it "the first House established for the people", and the people would make pilgrimage to it, "on foot and upon every lean beast, they shall come from every deep ravine" (Q 22:27). All people will visit it, "nation after nation, generation after generation, prophet after prophet, until the time will come of a prophet of the sons of Adam who will be the seal of the prophets [Muḥammad]. Before that prophet there will be another, who will give his name to the House and to whom all of its glory will be dedicated; that will be Abraham, for whom God will raise the foundations of the House . . .".[22]

Similar tidings were heard by Hagar from the angel Gabriel when Abraham brought her to Mecca, as related by Ibn Isḥāq. An angel showed her the House which was at the time just a red hill of mud (*rabwa ḥamrāʾ madara*), and said to her: "This is the first House established for the people on earth [Q 3:96]. It is the ancient House [Q 22:29] of God. Know that Abraham and Ishmael will raise it for the people".[23]

The link between the Kaʿba built by Abraham and what was built by Adam is reflected in numerous traditions about its ancient foundations. One of many examples is the following, reported by ʿAbdallāh b. Abī Ziyād:[24]

> When Allāh, may he be exalted, brought down Adam, peace be upon him, from Paradise, he said: O Adam, build me a House [on earth] opposite [*bi-ḥidhāʾ*] my House in heaven, where you and your descendants will worship me, as the angels worship me around my throne. Then the angels descended to Adam and he dug until he reached the seventh [and deepest layer of] earth. Then the angels cast rocks [into the pit and filled it] until they reached the level of the ground. Adam had taken [with him from heaven] a precious stone [*yāqūta*], red and hollow, with four white corners, which he placed above the foundation stones. The precious stone remained thus until the Flood came, and then Allāh, may he be praised and exalted, raised it to heaven.[25]

21 *Ibid.*, pp. 30–31.

22 *Ibid.*, pp. 15–17.

23 *Ibid.*, p. 23. See also *Ibid.*, p. 24, in the version of Ibn ʿAbbās.

24 Perhaps this is ʿAbdallāh b. al-Ḥakam b. Abī Ziyād al-Qaṭawānī (d. 255/869).

25 Azraqī, *Akhbār Makka*, p. 12.

This tradition traces back to Adam the foundations which the Qur'ān mentions in connection with Abraham and Ishmael. The foundations are said to have been laid by angels who filled in with stones a pit as deep as the seventh earth. This was the depth of the ancient foundations according to the exegete Mujāhid.[26] The Kaʿba built by Adam, says this tradition, was located opposite the heavenly House where the angels worship God. This is al-Bayt al-Maʿmūr, "the Inhabited House" (Q 52:4). Other traditions tell us that were al-Bayt al-Maʿmūr to fall to the earth, it would land on the Kaʿba.[27]

The caliph ʿUmar b. al-Khaṭṭāb heard a similar story from Kaʿb al-Aḥbār who related that Allāh, when he brought Adam down to earth, also sent down a hollow precious stone that became a shrine where God was worshipped and around which the people circumambulated. The angels who had descended with Adam built the shrine's foundations with rocks. Kaʿb added that when the Flood came Allāh lifted the building to heaven, leaving only its foundations.[28]

It is worth noting that Adam's association with the foundations of the Kaʿba reappears in a tradition about ʿAbdallāh b. al-Zubayr (d. 73/692), the ruler of Mecca. He renovated the Kaʿba after it had been damaged by fire when the Umayyads besieged the city. The builders dug and found huge stones, as large as camels. They could not be moved, and the people were convinced that these belonged to the building constructed by Adam.[29]

Other traditions praise the virtues of the foundations of Adam's and Abraham's Kaʿba. A tradition of Ibn ʿAbbās tells what happened when Adam came to Mecca:

> Gabriel struck the ground with his wings and exposed foundations [*uss*] planted in the lowest [the seventh] earth. The angels cast rocks inside, each weighing so much that only thirty men could lift one. He built [the House] of five mountains: Mount Lebanon, the Mount of Olives, Mount Sinai, Mount al-Jūdī and Mount Ḥirā'. [He built upon the deep foundation] until he reached the level of the ground. Ibn ʿAbbās said: The first who established [*assasa*] the House, prayed in it and circumambulated it was Adam, peace be upon him . . .[30]

The five mountains whose rocks Adam used to raise the foundation laid by the angels represent the sanctity space in its entirety: Mount Lebanon, the Mount of Olives and Mount Sinai represent al-Shām, Mount al-Jūdī is where Noah's Ark

---

26 Ṭabarī, *Tafsīr* (Q 2:127). See also Azraqī, *Akhbār Makka*, p. 4.
27 Muqātil, *Tafsīr* (Q 22:26); Azraqī, *Akhbār Makka*, p. 7.
28 Azraqī, *Akhbār Makka*, p. 10.
29 *Ibid.*, pp. 10–11.
30 *Ibid.*, p. 7. See also Ṭabarī, *Tafsīr* (Q 2:127); Ibn al-Jawzī, *Zād al-masīr* (Q 2:127). Cf. also Busse, "Jerusalem and Mecca", p. 241.

came to rest, and Mount Ḥirāʾ is in Mecca; on the latter Muḥammad secluded himself until his first revelation. In other words, the entire sanctity space converged on the foundation of the Kaʿba.

Not only Adam, but also Abraham is presented as having used the rocks of the five mountains. It is related that "when Abraham built the House, Ishmael helped him and the angels passed the rocks from Ishmael [to Abraham]". The rocks in question were from these five mountains.[31] According to other versions there were seven mountains whose rocks the angels passed to Abraham, but their names are not given.[32]

Of all the mountains in al-Shām, the sanctity of Mount Sinai that spread into Arabia is occasionally highlighted. Thus, in one story, Mount Sinai is said to have been torn asunder when the Torah was given there to Moses. It split into seven mountains which flew southward from al-Shām. Five of them landed in the Ḥijāz and two in Yemen. The mountains in the Ḥijāz are Uḥud, Thabīr, Ḥirāʾ, Thawr and Wariqān, all within the confines of Mecca and Medina.[33]

On the other hand, some versions highlight the virtue of Mount Ḥirāʾ. They maintain that this was the only mountain from which the foundation stones were taken for the structure which Abraham and Ishmael built.[34] This marks the superior standing of a mountain inside Mecca compared with those outside it.

The transfer of sanctity from other parts of the sanctity space to Mecca is also reflected in traditions about Abraham's prayer at the Kaʿba.[35] In the qurʾānic version of his prayer he asks, among other things (Q 2:126):

> And when Abraham said, 'My Lord, make this a land secure, and provide its people with fruits, such of them as believe in God and the Last Day.'

One tradition about this prayer, reported by some family members of the Prophet's Companion Jubayr b. Muṭʿim (d. 58/677), relates that when Abraham prayed for the wellbeing of the people of Mecca, Allāh transferred the land of Ṭāʾif from al-Shām and put it in its place [in the Ḥijāz], as a source of livelihood for Mecca.[36] This implies that Mecca and its environs absorbed the sanctity of al-Shām, part of whose earth was moved to Arabia. Since all this happened thanks to Abraham's prayer, it is he himself who became the conduit whereby al-Shām's sanctity was

31 Samarqandī, *Tafsīr* (Q 2:127).
32 Azraqī, *Akhbār Makka*, p. 20.
33 Suyūṭī, *al-Durr al-manthūr* (Q 7:143); Kister, "Sanctity Joint and Divided", pp. 19–20.
34 Huwwārī, *Tafsīr* (Q 2:127). See also Ṭabarī, *Tafsīr* (Q 2:127); Thaʿlabī, *al-Kashf wa-l-bayān* (Q 2:127); Zamakhsharī, *Kashshāf* (Q 2:127); Qurṭubī, *Aḥkām al-Qurʾān* (Q 2:127).
35 See above, Chapter 8.
36 Azraqī, *Akhbār Makka*, p. 41. See also Kister, "Sanctity Joint and Divided", p. 35.

moved to Arabia. Here, too, we see the post-qur'ānic attempt to uphold Mecca's status and to ensure it a sanctity that was not of a lesser degree than that of al-Shām.

Here we conclude our survey of the competition between Solomon's Temple and the Kaʿba which began in the Qur'ān, in the Medinan passage that calls the Kaʿba "the first House". Another aspect of the contest between the two shrines is reflected in the issue of the direction of prayer, also mentioned in a Medinan *sūra*. In this case, too, the issue involves a polemic with the Jews. More on this in the next chapter.

14 The direction of prayer (*qibla*) within the sanctity space

Medinan verses state that the Kaʿba is the binding *qibla*. In doing so, the Qurʾān reflects the fervent desire of the believers to return to the holy places in Mecca which they had been prevented from visiting after the *hijra*. Aside from that, this *qibla* marks the abandonment of the Jewish direction of prayer as well as the growth of the non-Jewish and non-Christian Islamic self-image. These occurrences take place against the background of the changing qurʾānic attitude towards the aspirations of the Jews for redemption in their holy land. In traditions that were disseminated after the Muslims arrived in al-Shām, a clear effort can be discerned to uphold the status of the Kaʿba as *qibla*. This became necessary due to the rising sanctity of the Rock in Bayt al-Maqdis which threatened the status of Mecca as the sole direction of prayer. These traditions trace the beginning of the establishment of the Kaʿba as *qibla* back to the days of the prophets of yore. However, the Rock, too, retained its standing as a direction of prayer, at least among some circles.

The coexistence of two ritual centers within the same sanctity space gave rise to a struggle over the direction of prayer (*qibla*). This takes us back to the tension, discerned in the Qurʾān, between Solomon's and Abraham's shrines. Solomon's Temple in Jerusalem was the ancient Jewish direction of prayer, already in the days of Solomon himself. In the prayer he says after the Temple's construction has been completed, one of his wishes is (1 Kings 8:30):

> Hear the plea of your servant and of your people Israel when they pray toward this place.

In this manner, Solomon who stands in prayer inside the Temple, defines this place as the people of Israel's direction of prayer.[1] As for the Kaʿba, however, we saw in previous chapters that the Qurʾān in a Medinan verse defines this shrine as Maqām Ibrāhīm (Q 3:97), implying that the Abrahamic shrine was more ancient than that of Solomon.[2] We also saw that the description of the Kaʿba as Maqām Ibrāhīm is associated with the idea that Abraham already prayed there, after having completed the construction of the Kaʿba (Q 2:127–129).[3] The place where Abraham prayed is also meant to be the place where the believers pray (Q 2:125).

---

1 Cf. Peters, *Jerusalem and Mecca*, p. 7. In the following generations, the Sages decided that the Temple Mount was to be the direction of prayer, instead of the Temple that had been destroyed long ago. See Eliav, *God's Mountain*, pp. 203–204.

2 See above, Chapter 12.

3 See above, Chapter 8.

https://doi.org/10.1515/9783111222318-015

The Kaʿba as *qibla*: The qurʾānic data

The *sūra* that delineates Abraham's relationship to the Kaʿba and its construction goes on to state that the Kaʿba or, more exactly, the "Holy Mosque" (al-Masjid al-Ḥarām) in which it is situated, is the proper direction of prayer (Q 2:142–150):

> (142) The fools among the people will say, 'What has turned them from the direction they were facing in their prayers aforetime?' Say: 'To God belong the East and the West; he guides whomsoever he will to a straight path.' (143) Thus We appointed you a midmost nation that you might be witnesses to the people, and that the Messenger might be a witness to you; and We did not appoint the direction you were facing, except that We might know who followed the Messenger from him who turned on his heels — though it were a grave thing save for those whom God has guided; but God would never leave your faith to waste – truly, God is all-gentle with the people, all-compassionate. (144) We have seen you turning your face about in the heaven; now We will surely turn you to a direction that shall satisfy you. Turn your face towards the Holy Mosque; and wherever you are, turn your faces towards it. Those who have been given the Book know it is the truth from their Lord; God is not heedless of the things they do. (145) Yet if you should bring to those that have been given the Book every sign, they will not follow your direction; you are not a follower of their direction, neither are they followers of one another's direction. If you follow their caprices, after the knowledge that has come to you, then you will surely be among the evildoers (146) whom We have given the Book, and they recognize it as they recognize their sons, even though there is a party of them conceal the truth and that wittingly. (147) The truth comes from your Lord; then be not among the doubters. (148) Every one has a direction to which to turn; so be you forward in good works. Wherever you may be, God will bring you all together; surely God is powerful over everything. (149) From whatsoever place you issue, turn your face towards the Holy Mosque; it is the truth from your Lord. God is not heedless of the things you do. (150) From whatsoever place you issue, turn your face towards the Holy Mosque; and wherever you may be, turn your faces towards it, that the people may not have any argument against you, excepting the evildoers of them; and fear you them not, but fear you me; and that I may perfect my blessing upon you, and that haply so you may be guided.[4]

This passage uses the direction of prayer as a means for elevating Mecca to the rank of the primary destination within the sanctity space. At the same time, a dissociation is implied here from the prayer customs of "the fools", namely, "those who have been given the Book", that is, the Jews. The latter express their consternation at the fact that Muḥammad has changed his previous direction of prayer. Thus the command to face the Holy Mosque in Mecca constitutes indeed an act of detachment from prayer in the direction of Jerusalem, the direction in which the Jews prayed.

---

4 On these verses cf. also Rubin, "Between Arabia and the Holy Land", pp. 349–350; Friedmann, "Pillars of Islam", pp. 264–266.

The observation that the *qibla* verses are meant to shift the direction of prayer from Jerusalem to Mecca is supported by traditions that explain that these verses represent the earliest case in the Qurʾān where a law is abrogated by a later one, in a process known as *al-nāsikh wa-l-mansūkh*. The abrogated law is prayer in the direction of Bayt al-Maqdis.[5] The Qurʾān justifies the change with the argument that the People of the Book "recognize it as they recognize their sons". This seems to mean that in their own Scriptures the Jews can find the assertion that Muḥammad is the true prophet whose coming was announced by God. They should therefore join him, thereby complying with their own holy Scriptures.

However, although the *qibla* verses mark the abandonment of the direction of prayer of the People of the Book, it would seem that there was a more direct reason for the change. This we learn from the fact that the Holy Mosque in Mecca is often mentioned in verses where God condemns the unbelievers of the Quraysh for their refusal to allow the Prophet, who was in Medina, free access to Mecca and the Kaʿba:

Q 2:217:

> They will question you concerning the holy month, and fighting in it. Say: 'Fighting in it is a heinous thing, but to bar people from God's way, and to spead disbelief in him, and the Holy Mosque, and to expel its people from it — that is more heinous in God's sight; and persecution is more heinous than slaying.' . . .

Q 5:2:

> . . . Let not detestation for a people who barred you from the Holy Mosque move you to commit aggression. . .

Q 8:34:

> But what have they now, that God should not chastise them, when they are barring people from the Holy Mosque, not being its protectors? Its only protectors are the godfearing; but most of them know not.

Q 22:25:

> Those who disbelieve, and bar people from God's way and the Holy Mosque that We have appointed equal unto people, alike him who cleaves to it and the tent-dweller, and whosoever purposes to violate it wrongly, We shall let him taste a painful chastisement.

5 E.g. Qurṭubī, *Aḥkām al-Qurʾān* (Q 2:142).

Q 48:25:

> They are the ones who disbelieved, and barred you from the Holy Mosque and the offering, detained so as not to reach its place of sacrifice. If it had not been for certain men believers and certain women believers whom you knew not, lest you should trample them, and there befall you guilt unwittingly on their account (that God may admit into his mercy whom he will), had they been separated clearly, then We would have chastised the unbelievers among them with a painful chastisement.

The great anger Muslims felt at being denied access to the Kaʿba makes it easier to understand why the Holy Mosque was fixed as the direction of prayer. It symbolized the Muslims' devotion to the Kaʿba and their desire to return to it, as if it were a yearned-for Promised Land. This yearning is expressed in a dream in which God promises the Prophet that he will eventually enter Mecca with the believers and perform the rites of the *ḥajj* (Q 48:27):

> God has indeed fulfilled the vision he vouchsafed to his Messenger truly: 'You shall enter the Holy Mosque, if God wills it, in security, your heads shaved, your hair cut short, not fearing.' He knew what you knew not, and appointed ere that a nigh *fatḥ*.

This verse seems to shed more light on the reason why the Muslims are instructed to face the Holy Mosque whenever they pray.

The tradition: Circumstances of the change of *qibla*

Extra-qur'ānic traditions expand on the history of the first *qibla* and the circumstances under which it was abandoned. First, a number of traditions relate that at the beginning of the Muslim presence in Medina, the mosques of the Muslims, including that of Muḥammad himself, faced Bayt al-Maqdis or al-Shām.[6] For example, here is a tradition which appears in Ibn Shabba's (d. 262/876) book on the history of Medina:

> The Prophet came to Qubā' [in Medina], where his Companions had already built a mosque before, in which they faced Bayt al-Maqdis in prayer. When the Prophet came to it, he prayed with them and changed nothing in the mosque.[7]

The circumstances under which the Prophet changed the direction of prayer from Bayt al-Maqdis to the Kaʿba are described in traditions that do not all agree

6 Rubin, "Between Arabia and the Holy Land", pp. 351–353.
7 Ibn Shabba, *Ta'rīkh al-Madīna*, I, p. 51.

as to the immediate cause of the change. They all make an effort to justify this change which could be construed as reflecting a lack of consistency on God's part. The reasons for the change are given in the following tradition recorded by the exegete Muqātil b. Sulaymān (d. 150/767):

> When [the Prophet] emigrated to Medina on the second day of the month of Rabīʿ al-Awwal, he was instructed to pray in the direction of Bayt al-Maqdis, in order that the People of the Book do not denounce him as a liar for praying toward a different *qibla* than their own, especially since they found his description [as a true prophet] in the Torah. So the Prophet and his Companions faced Bayt al-Maqdis in prayer from the time he came to Medina, for seventeen months. The Anṣār [residents of Medina] had prayed in the direction of Bayt al-Maqdis two years before the Prophet's *hijra*. For the Prophet, the Kaʿba was the more beloved of the two *qiblas* [*aḥabb al-qiblatayn*], and he therefore said to Gabriel: 'I wish that my Lord would divert me from the *qibla* of the Jews to another'. Gabriel said: 'I am but a servant, like you. I have nothing of my own. Ask it of your Lord'. Gabriel ascended to heaven and the Prophet began to gaze for a long time heavenward, in the hope that Gabriel would bring him what he requested. Then in the month of Rajab, during the first [noon] prayer, two months before the Battle of Badr, Allāh revealed the verse: "We have seen you turning your face about in the heavens; now We will surely turn you to a direction that shall satisfy you. Turn your face towards the Holy Mosque; and wherever you are, turn your faces towards it". [Q 2:144].[8]

This tradition explains Muḥammad's praying in the direction of Bayt al-Maqdis as nothing more than a tactic designed to preserve Jewish support for Muḥammad as the redeeming prophet whose appearance is predicted in the Torah. Muḥammad is presented, however, as eventually having come to prefer the true *qibla*, namely the Kaʿba. Other traditions also describe the disappointment of the Jews at this change, although they never intended to actually recognize Muḥammad as a prophet.[9]

Beyond the immediate circumstances, the change of *qibla* towards the Kaʿba is perceived as a solemn occasion, dictated to Muḥammad from on high by the angel Gabriel. Thus al-Khargūshī (d. 406/1015) reports:

> It is related that Gabriel descended from heaven and removed [*rafaʿa*] all the mountains and buildings between [the Prophet] and Mecca. Thus it happened that when the Prophet was in the middle of the midday prayer and had already finished part of it, Gabriel signaled to the Prophet to turn towards the drain [*miʾzāb*] of the House [the Kaʿba], and the Prophet saw it.[10]

8 Muqātil, *Tafsīr* (Q 2:142–144).

9 Ibn Hishām, *Sīra*, II, pp. 198–199.

10 Khargūshī, *Sharaf al-Muṣṭafā*, II, p. 401. See also Rubin, "The Direction of Prayer", pp. 17–18.

After Muḥammad: Renewed tension between the two *qiblas*

In spite of the qur'ānic establishment of the Holy Mosque in Mecca as the final, obligatory *qibla*, when the first Muslims arrived in Jerusalem, the sanctity of the Temple Mount, al-Masjid al-Aqṣā, the destination of Muḥammad's nocturnal journey, was renewed. This process culminated in the construction of the Dome of the Rock which was believed to have been the spot from which Muḥammad ascended to heaven. This belief was promoted by the Umayyad caliphs, who built the Dome.[11] Furthermore, it would appear that, in the mind of the believers, the *qibla* did not remain restricted to Mecca, as determined by the Qur'ān, but occasionally returned to Bayt al-Maqdis. Evidence for this is a tradition disseminated in the name of al-Zuhrī (d. 124/742):

> Since Adam descended to earth, Allāh did not send any prophet without having ordained the Rock of Bayt al-Maqdis as a *qibla* for him.[12]

It here follows that facing Bayt al-Maqdis in prayer is in line with the legacy of the prophets whom Allāh sent in every generation to disseminate Islam. From a practical point of view, it is known that the first Muslims outside of Arabia were in the habit of taking over existing houses of prayer, especially churches, and conducting prayers there. Initially the direction of prayer in such places (toward the east) was retained, probably out of technical reasons, not due to a conscious desire to retain the *qibla* of Bayt al-Maqdis. Indeed, the direction of prayer was eventually updated towards the Ka'ba.[13]

The accidental or intentional renewal of the status of Bayt al-Maqdis as *qibla* provoked resistance on the part of circles that feared for the qur'ānic legacy of the faith. Their objection is reflected in reports about accusations against 'Abd al-Malik, for example, by his rival, the ruler of Mecca 'Abdallāh b. al-Zubayr. The latter claimed that, by building the Dome of the Rock, 'Abd al-Malik diverted the rites of the *ḥajj* from Mecca to the *qibla* of the Children of Israel.[14] If we take into

---

11 See above, Chapter 2.

12 Wāsiṭī, *Faḍā'il*, p. 51 (no. 78). See also Mujīr al-Dīn, *al-Uns al-jalīl*, I, p. 193; Ibn al-Murajjā, *Faḍā'il*, p. 98 (no. 99); Minhājī, *Itḥāf al-akhiṣṣā*, I, p. 177, II, p. 10. Cf. Kister, "Sanctity Joint and Divided", p. 52; Rubin, "The Direction of Prayer", p. 23.

13 Suliman Bashear's opinion that the first Muslims in the occupied countries did not yet have one exclusively binding direction of prayer (the Ka'ba) is unlikely. Even traditions describing cases in which the Prophet does not descend from his riding beast and prays the voluntary prayer in the direction the beast is headed (including east), do not necessarily indicate that the Ka'ba was not yet the official *qibla*. Bashear, "*Qibla Musharriqa*", p. 269. See also Rubin, "The Direction of Prayer", pp. 19–20.

14 See Elad, *Medieval Jerusalem*, p. 54; *idem*, "The Status of Jerusalem", p. 40.

account the possibility that the builders of the Dome of the Rock intended to reconstruct Solomon's Temple,[15] then the intention of making it into a shrine towards which one would pray cannot be ruled out, just as Solomon established his Temple as the direction of prayer (see above). Whether or not such an intention was behind the construction of the Dome of the Rock, this is how it was perceived by those who feared for the standing of the Kaʿba. A particularly acerbic formulation of such fears is that of the Qur'ān exegete Muqātil b. Sulaymān, who declares that facing Bayt al-Maqdis in prayer, after its abrogation in the Qur'ān, constitutes straying from the straight path (*ḍalāla*).[16]

The clearest effort to defend the status of the Kaʿba as the binding direction of prayer is revealed in a group of traditions that describe a purported dialogue between the caliph ʿUmar b. al-Khaṭṭāb (ruled 13–23/634–644), during whose rule Jerusalem fell under Muslim rule, and the converted Jew Kaʿb al-Aḥbār. The various versions of these traditions are familiar to scholars,[17] but a further look at them seems to be in order, so as to clarify the tendency which they reflect. The event which they describe takes place when ʿUmar arrives together with Kaʿb al-Aḥbār at the precinct of al-Masjid al-Aqṣā, on the Temple Mount. ʿUmar wants to establish a place of prayer there, or an actual mosque where the Muslims will be able to pray in the usual way, that is, in the direction of the qur'ānic *qibla*, Mecca and the Kaʿba. ʿUmar asks Kaʿb for his opinion on where inside the enclosure of al-Masjid al-Aqṣā he should locate the place of prayer. Here is what Kaʿb proposed, according to one version we possess (it appears in the *ḥadīth* collection of Aḥmad b. Ḥanbal (d. 241/856)):

> In the name of ʿUbayd b. Ādam, he said: I heard ʿUmar b. al-Khaṭṭāb say to Kaʿb: 'Where, in your opinion, should I pray'? [Kaʿb] said: 'If you listen to me, you should pray behind the Rock, and then all of al-Quds will be before you'. ʿUmar said: 'Your conduct resembles [*ḍāhayta*] the ways of the Jews. I will not do so, but will pray in the place where God's Messenger prayed'. Then [ʿUmar] moved forward in the direction of the *qibla* and prayed. Then he came, took off his cloak and swept the rubbish, and the people also swept.[18]

Kaʿb's advice to ʿUmar to pray "behind" the Rock, means that when he prays in the direction of the usual *qibla*, namely towards Mecca, he should do so at a

15 See above, Chapter 11.

16 Muqātil, *Tafsīr* (Q 2:150): . . .*fa-inna l-ṣalāta qibala Bayt al-Maqdis baʿda mā nusikhat al-ṣalātu ilayhi ḍalāla.*

17 See the sources and studies quoted in Elad, *Medieval Jerusalem*, pp. 30–31, 157–158; *idem*, "The Temple Mount", p. 63; *idem*, "The Status of Jerusalem", p. 51; Rubin, "Between Arabia and the Holy Land", pp. 355–356. See also Gil, *History of Palestine*, pp. 65–66.

18 Aḥmad b. Ḥanbal, *Musnad*, I, p. 38. Cf. Busse, "The Sanctity of Jerusalem", p. 457; Rubin, "Between Arabia and the Holy Land", pp. 355–356.

location where he would not only face Mecca, but the Rock as well. Since the Kaʿba lies to the south of Jerusalem, he would have to stand north of the Rock, so as to face both the Rock and Mecca at the same time. Kaʿb explains that the reason for his suggestion is that if ʿUmar accepts it, all of al-Quds will be in front of him. This is, by the way, one of the earliest occurrences of the name al-Quds for the city, which is usually called Bayt al-Maqdis.[19] Kaʿb, the Jewish convert to Islam, tries through his proposal to uphold the status of Bayt al-Maqdis as a legitimate direction of prayer. But ʿUmar for his part decides to stand at the spot where, in his view, Muḥammad already stood in prayer when he was in al-Masjid al-Aqṣā. He therefore moves forward leaving the Rock behind him, thus facing only the Kaʿba.

The image of ʿUmar depicted here is of someone who, on the one hand, established the Temple Mount as a sacred Muslim shrine identified with the site where the Prophet had already prayed upon arriving at al-Masjid al-Aqṣā, and, on the other hand, preserved the status of the Kaʿba as the sole *qibla*.

In another version, transmitted in the name of Rajāʾ b. Ḥaywa (d. 112/730), ʿUmar gives the following explanation for his decision:

> We will locate the *qibla* [of al-Masjid al-Aqṣā] on its front [*ṣadr*], just as Allāh's Messenger located the *qibla* of our mosques on their front.[20]

Al-Masjid al-Aqṣā's "front" is of course its south side, the side that faces Mecca. In order to emphasize his decision, ʿUmar also tells Kaʿb: "We were not commanded [to face] the Rock, but [only] the Kaʿba". Another version of the same conversation appears in Abū ʿUbayd's (d. 224/838) *Kitāb al-amwāl*; there Kaʿb formulates his proposal to ʿUmar as follows:

> Fix [the *qibla*] behind the Rock, and so you will combine the two *qiblas*, that of Moses and that of Muḥammad.[21]

Here Kaʿb argues that his proposal to combine the *qibla* of the Rock with that of Mecca is consistent with the direction of prayer adopted by Moses, a prophet and a Muslim in every respect. But ʿUmar rejects this suggestion as an unseemly imitation of Jewish ways. For ʿUmar, there is no essential difference between Moses and the Jews, and the only valid *qibla*, as far as he is concerned, is the one adopted by Muḥammad who stood south of the Rock, facing Mecca. ʿUmar adds that "the best part of mosques is their front side". Once again, in the case of the

---

19 On this tradition see Goitein, *Studies*, p. 140; *idem*, "Arabic Names", p. 65.

20 Ṭabarī, *Taʾrīkh*, III, p. 611 (Brill: I, p. 2408). See also Rubin, "Between Arabia and the Holy Land", pp. 349–351.

21 Abū ʿUbayd, *Amwāl*, p. 73 (no. 430). See also Kister, "Sanctity Joint and Divided", p. 57.

confines of al-Masjid al-Aqṣā, the front part is to the south, which was therefore chosen as the place of prayer.[22]

The testimony of al-Farazdaq

In addition to the dialogue between Kaʿb and ʿUmar, evidence for the Muslim mobilization for preserving the *qibla* of the Kaʿba as against the sanctity of the Dome of the Rock also comes from additional literary sources, including poetry. Of special interest are some poetic verses composed by the poet al-Farazdaq (d. 114/732) who lived in the Umayyad period. Here is one of them:[23]

وَبَيْتانِ بَيْتُ اللهِ نَحْنُ وُلاتُهُ   وَبَيْتٌ بِأَعْلَى إيلياءَ مُشَرَّفُ

Two houses there are, Allāh's house whose possessors are we /
And a house on the height of Īliyā', venerable

The "two houses" are the two shrines, the Kaʿba in Mecca and the Temple on the summit of Īliyā' or Jerusalem. In al-Farazdaq's time the Dome of the Rock was already in existence. The fact that the two shrines are mentioned in tandem testifies to a sanctity space that is perceived to encompass both. The poet boasts of the Arabs' control over them (he belonged to the northern Arab tribe of Tamīm), thus hinting at the idea that the Arabs were chosen by Allāh over all others who did not have the fortune of possessing shrines of such sanctity. However, despite their equal merit, other verses by this poet signal a tendency to prefer one of them over the other:[24]

وَرِثْنا عَنْ خَليلِ اللهِ بَيْتًا   يَطِيبُ لِلصَّلاةِ وَلِلطُّهورِ

هُوَ البَيْتُ الذي مِنْ كُلِّ وَجْهٍ   إلَيْهِ وُجوهُ أصْحابِ القُبورِ

From Allāh's friend we inherited a House/ fit for prayer and purification
It is the House to which from all sides / the faces of the grave dwellers are turned

Allāh's friend (*khalīl*) is Abraham, who is thus named in the Qur'ān (Q 4:125). The poet is proud of the Arabs, offspring of Ishmael, and declares that it is they who preserve Abraham's heritage as embodied in the House, i.e. the Kaʿba, which Arabs have bequeathed from one generation to the next. Implied here is the superiority of the Kaʿba to the Temple in Īliyā' thanks to its status as *qibla*, the direction of

22 See more about the objection in the following generations to prayer towards the Rock in Gil, *History of Palestine*, pp. 101–103.
23 Farazdaq, *Dīwān*, II, p. 32 line 9. See also Kister, "Three Mosques", p. 182.
24 Farazdaq, *Dīwān*, I, p. 283 lines 9–10.

prayer. The poet notes that not only the living face it in prayer, but the dead as well. This is a reference to the custom of burying the dead and turning their bodies towards Mecca. Here, again, we thus have evidence for the preservation of the ancient sanctity of the Kaʿba vis-à-vis that of Jerusalem.

The antiquity of the Kaʿba as *qibla*

Some of the traditions which were designed to defend the *qibla* of the Kaʿba maintain that, while the commandment to face the Holy Mosque in prayer was revealed to the Prophet in a Medinan *sūra*, he himself used to pray in the direction of Mecca even when the direction of prayer was still towards al-Shām, that is, before the *hijra*. One such tradition is recorded in the *sīra* of Ibn Isḥāq (d. 150/768), in the version of Yūnus b. Bukayr (d. 199/815):

> Allāh's Messenger prayed in Mecca and his *qibla* was towards al-Shām, but when he prayed he did so against the two corners [of the Kaʿba], that of the Black Stone and the southern corner. As he was standing there, the Kaʿba was between him and al-Shām.[25]

Muḥammad thus faced not only Bayt al-Maqdis but the Kaʿba as well. The same practice of the Prophet is also reported in Ibn Hishām's (d. 218/833) version, who adds two framework stories (one about Abū Jahl and another about ʿUmar b. al-Khaṭṭāb), according to which the Prophet enjoyed divine protection as he prayed facing at the same time both the Kaʿba and al-Shām.[26]

Some traditions associate the status of the Kaʿba as the binding *qibla* with the pre-Islamic Abrahamic heritage. One of them is recorded in al-Azraqī's (d. circa 250/864) book on the history of Mecca. It is quoted from al-Wāqidī (d. 207/822), an expert on Muḥammad's biography, and related on the authority of the Prophet's Companion Abū Saʿīd al-Khudrī (d. 65/685). The latter heard the details from ʿAbdallāh b. Salām, a Jew who believed in Muḥammad and converted to Islam. Ibn Salām explains how Abraham's footprints came to be on the stone known as Maqām Ibrāhīm:[27]

> When Abraham was ordered to announce the duty of the *ḥajj*, he stood on the stone of the) Maqām. Then the Maqām rose, until it became a mountain, the highest one, that overlooked the area below it. [Abraham] said: 'O people, obey the call of your Lord'. The people replied

25 Yūnus b. Bukayr, *al-Siyar wa-l-maghāzī*, p. 200. See more in Rubin, "The Kaʿba", p. 104, note 29. Cf. also Busse, "Jerusalem and Mecca", p. 242.
26 Ibn Hishām, *Sīra*, I, pp. 319, 372; Rubin, "Between Arabia and the Holy Land", pp. 350–351.
27 See above, Chapter 12.

to him, saying: ‘At your service, God’. The imprint of his feet [*athar qadamayhi*] was left [on the Maqām] in accordance with God’s will. [Abraham] looked to his right and to his left and said: ‘Obey your Lord’s call’. When he finished, he was instructed to make of the Maqām a *qibla*. Since then he would face it in prayer, standing before the door [of the Kaʿba]. The stone remained the *qibla* as long as God wished. Afterwards Ishmael would pray towards [the Maqām] in front of the door of the Kaʿba. Then there was Allāh’s Messenger, who was instructed to pray towards Bayt al-Maqdis. He faced it in prayer before he made the *hijra* and afterwards. Then God wished to turn him towards the *qibla* with which he was pleased for himself and for his prophets. Since then [the Prophet] faced [the Kaʿba’s] drain in prayer, as long as he was in Medina. Then he came to Mecca, and there he prayed facing the Maqām, as long as he stayed in Mecca.[28]

This tradition links the time of the imprint of Abraham’s feet on the Maqām Ibrāhīm to his declaration of the commandment to perform the *ḥajj* (Q 22:27). The tradition implies that, although Muḥammad may have prayed towards Bayt al-Maqdis at some stage, for reasons which this tradition does not explain, the *qibla* which both he and God always preferred was the Kaʿba, the direction in which Abraham and Ishmael had prayed.

The idea that Abraham prayed towards the Kaʿba is also reflected in words ascribed to Zayd b. ʿAmr b. Nufayl, a pre-Islamic *ḥanīf* and adherent of the Abrahamic faith, who is said to have instructed Muḥammad on ritual matters:

Ibn Isḥāq said: A member of Zayd b. ʿAmr b. Nufayl’s family told me that Zayd, when standing in the Mosque, facing the Kaʿba, would say: ‘At your service[, Lord], in devotion to your worship and in subservience’. [He also said]:

عُذتُ بما عاذ به إبراهِمْ　　مستقبل القبلة وهو قائمْ

I shall seek shelter where Abraham sought shelter / as he turned towards the *qibla* while standing[29]

Even if they were meant to glorify the figure of Zayd and to promote the status of the Kaʿba within the sanctity space, the historical value of these words should not be dismissed out of hand, since the people of Mecca were aware of Abraham’s and Ishmael’s religious heritage even before the advent of Muḥammad.[30] It is also possible that the mention of Abraham’s “standing” constitutes yet another intimation of the pre-Islamic idea of Maqām Ibrāhīm as a place where Abraham left his footprints.[31]

28 Azraqī, *Akhbār Makka*, p. 273. Cf. Kister, “Maqām Ibrāhīm”, p. 480.
29 Ibn Hishām, *Sīra*, I, p. 245. See also Rubin, “Ḥanīfiyya and Kaʿba”, pp. 101–103.
30 See above, Chapter 9.
31 See above, Chapter 12.

In the same vein, other traditions foster the idea that the Kaʿba was the shrine towards which not only Abraham and Ishmael turned, but all the other prophets as well.[32] A number of such traditions can be found in commentaries on a verse in which God commands the Jews in Egypt, "and make your houses a direction for people to pray to (*qibla*)" (Q 10:87). Several exegetes explained this command as an instruction for Moses and the Children of Israel to face the Kaʿba in prayer and to make their mosques point towards it.[33] To these we may add traditions which present the Kaʿba as the *qibla* of the prophets of all generations, including Moses.[34] Furthermore, as maintained in the commentaries on the first-House verse (Q 3:96), at the time of the primordial creation of the Kaʿba, God determined that the House would be built on that spot and decided that it would be the people's *qibla*.[35]

Not only did the Kaʿba come to enjoy the status of the earliest *qibla* on earth, the very idea of praying towards Bayt al-Maqdis was presented as a deviation from the true *sunna*, which guided all the prophets since the very beginning. This is implied in a tradition on the authority of Muḥammad b. Kaʿb al-Quraẓī (d. 117/735):

> No prophet ever disputed with another prophet over the *qibla* or the *sunna*, except that Allāh's Messenger prayed in the direction of Bayt al-Maqdis for sixteen months after having arrived in Medina. Then he pronounced the following verse: "He has laid down for you as religion that He charged Noah with" [Q 42:13].[36]

This account means that by ceasing to face Bayt al-Maqdis in prayer sixteen months after the *hijra*, the Prophet and the believers returned to the ways of all the prophets, that is, to face the Kaʿba.

The sanctity of the two *qiblas*

In addition to the traditions concerning the antiquity of the *qibla* of the Kaʿba, there was also an explicit prohibition on those who prayed in al-Masjid al-Aqṣā to combine the two *qiblas*.[37] Still, the Rock's *qibla* was never completely abandoned.

---

32 Rubin, "The Direction of Prayer", pp. 25–27.
33 Muqātil, *Tafsīr* (Q 10:87). See also Rubin, "Between Arabia and the Holy Land", pp. 354–355.
34 Kister, "Sanctity Joint and Divided", pp. 54, 57.
35 Azraqī, *Akhbār Makka*, p. 40.
36 Ibn Saʿd, *Ṭabaqāt*, I, p. 243. See also Rubin, "The Direction of Prayer", pp. 23–24, with a different explanation of the meaning of the tradition.
37 See Kister, "Three Mosques", p. 194.

For example, the geographer Yāqūt (d. 626/1229) tells of a Muslim by the name of Abū ʿAlī al-Awaqī, whom he met in Bayt al-Maqdis. He was a pious ascetic, a recluse who used to face al-Masjid al-Aqṣā in prayer.[38] Another example can be found in the following story related by the scholar al-Fuḍayl b. ʿIyāḍ (d. 187/803):

> When the *qibla* was turned towards the Kaʿba the Rock said: 'My God, I was the *qibla* for your creatures until you sent the best of your creatures as prophet, and then you shifted their *qibla* away from me. [God] said: 'Rejoice, for I shall place my throne on you, and will in the future gather [*ḥāshir*] to you my creatures, pass judgment over you, and over you shall resurrect [*wa-nāshir*] my creatures'.[39]

The Rock's elevated status is preserved here, despite the change of *qibla* to the Kaʿba. The memory of the Rock's status as *qibla* was preserved in a tradition ascribed to the Prophet, one that is quite common in *ḥadīth* collections. In it, the Prophet is said to have forbidden the believers to relieve themselves in the direction of either of the two *qiblas*.[40]

This concludes the chapters on the status of the sanctity space as the Land of the Temple — Solomon's Temple in al-Shām and the Kaʿba in Arabia. This also concludes our discussion of the five aspects of sanctity that enfold the space which al-Shām and Arabia share. In order to complete the picture, we will in the next chapter examine a number of qurʾānic verses that shed further light on the change—already discussed in previous chapters—of the attitude of the Qurʾān towards the Jewish vision of redemption. This change takes place concurrently with the move of the center of gravity from al-Shām to Arabia, as can be seen in the transition from the Meccan to the Medinan *sūras*.

---

38 Yāqūt, *Muʿjam al-buldān*, I, p. 283 (s.v. Awah). See also Rubin, "Between Arabia and the Holy Land", p. 357.
39 Yāqūt, *Muʿjam al-buldān*, V, p. 167 (s.v. al-Maqdis). See also Busse, "The Sanctity of Jerusalem", p. 456.
40 Aḥmad b. Ḥanbal, *Musnad*, V, p. 430.

Part Six: **The Messianic Vision Inverted**

15 Romans (al-Rūm), Jews and Muslims

The Qurʾān's departure from the vision of the redemption of the Jews in their holy land is reflected not only in the Medinan verses examined in the preceding chapters, but also in a number of Medinan passages that deal with the martial aspect of the qurʾānic message. One of these, which opens *Sūrat al-Rūm* (30), deals with the military confrontation between Persian and Roman [= Byzantine] armies in "the nearest part of the land", that is, Palestine. The passage expresses hope for a Byzantine victory, after their defeat at the hands of the Persians. The Byzantines' anticipated victory is presented as a sign of the completion of God's plan that will bring joy to the believers in Arabia. The joy is almost certainly due to the fact that the Persians were perceived as the patrons of the Jews in Jerusalem, having permitted them to resume their worship on the Temple Mount after they had occupied Jerusalem in 614. The imminent Persian defeat that would bring joy to the believers seems to refer to the renewal of Byzantine control of Jerusalem in the year 628. The same negative attitude towards the Jews is reflected in Medinan *sūra*s that deal with Muḥammad's victories in the Arabian region of the sanctity space. These victories are presented as the completion of God's plan of redemption, whose agents are the Muslims who are overcoming their Jewish opponents and the idolaters. The Jews were thus excluded from the ancient redemption vision concerning which they were once considered by the Muslims potential partners. In exegetical traditions the chronological proximity between the victories in Arabia and the events in Palestine were perceived as signs of God's hand which was guiding the direction of the redemption plan in both regions of the sanctity space.

The transfer of sanctity patterns from Jerusalem to Mecca, as signaled in the qurʾānic Medinan *sūra*s, runs parallel with the Muslim renunciation of the Jewish vision of messianic redemption in the Land of Israel. This vision was dealt with above in connection with Muḥammad's nocturnal journey and the Qurʾān's identification with the Jewish messianic hopes for redemption that grew in view of the Persian takeover of Jerusalem in 614 (Chapter 1). A number of Medinan passages that deal with the martial aspect of the qurʾānic message provide further evidence as to the end of the Qurʾān's identification with these hopes. A detailed examination of those passages makes it possible to complete the picture of both the sanctity space and the accomplishment of the redemption plan in the two regions of that space, al-Shām and Arabia.

The Roman victory and the inversion of the messianic vision

We begin with a unique passage that has no counterpart in any other part of the Qurʾān (Q 30:1–5):

https://doi.org/10.1515/9783111222318-016

> (1) *Alif Lām Mīm* (2) The Rūm have been vanquished (3) in the nearest part of the land; and, after their vanquishing, they shall be the victors (4) in a few years. To God belongs the command before and after, and on that day the believers shall rejoice (5) in God's help; God helps whomsoever He decides to help and He is the all-mighty, the all-compassionate.

This is the only passage in the Qur'ān that mentions al-Rūm (Romans), i.e. the Byzantines, and their defeat in "the nearest part of the land" (*adnā l-arḍ*). A number of Muslim exegetes have explained that this phrase refers to al-Urdunn and Filasṭīn, that is, al-Shām.[1] If this is so, then the defeat of the Rūm seems to be the loss of Jerusalem to the Persian forces in 614. The Byzantine setback in Jerusalem was preceded by a series of losses in other regions, including the defeat in al-Shām itself, in Adhri'āt (Daraa, in southern Syria) in 613.[2] In fact, exegetes mention the name Adhri'āt as the place where the great confrontation between the two powers in "the nearest part of the land" occurred.[3] It is thus possible that the defeat of the Rūm in "the nearest part of the land" refers not only to the loss of Jerusalem, but to the loss of al-Shām entirely.

Regarding the Qur'ān's reference to the expected turn of events and victory of the Rūm, scholars are agreed that the Qur'ān is speaking about the victory over the Persians at Ctesiphon, the Persian capital, which fell in 628.[4] However, Ctesiphon is in Mesopotamia, and it is more likely that "the nearest part of the land" mentioned in the *sūra* under discussion is not only the site of the Rūm's defeat but also that of their imminent triumph. It is thus more likely that the Qur'ān here refers to the Byzantine victory in Jerusalem, which also occurred in 628. Two years later the Byzantine Emperor Heraclius made a triumphal entry into the city, which had been recovered for Christendom.[5]

The course of events is explained succinctly by the exegete al-Ṭabrisī (d. 548/1153): "Bayt al-Maqdis [Jerusalem] was [as dear] to the Rūm as the Ka'ba was to the Muslims, and the Persians expelled them from it".[6] Here the exegete reveals the Muslims' awareness of the sanctity of Jerusalem for Christians, which he compares to the sanctity of Mecca for Muslims. Subsequently he explains that the future rejoicing of the believers over the Rūm's victory is due not only to the Byzantines' renewed takeover of Bayt al-Maqdis, but also—and mainly— to the believers' hatred of the Persians who had occupied it.[7] It is for this reason that the exegete adds a

1 Muqātil, *Tafsīr* (Q 30:2).
2 Bowersock, *Empires*, p. 62.
3 E.g. Ṭabarī, *Tafsīr* (Q 30:2).
4 Bowersock, *Empires*, p. 62.
5 E.g. Kaegi, *Byzantium*, pp. 26–33; Gil, *History of Palestine*, pp. 5–7.
6 Ṭabrisī, *Majma' al-bayān* (Q 30:2–3).
7 *Ibid.* (Q 30:4–5).

description of the return of Bayt al-Maqdis into the hands of the Rūm (in the year 628) and the triumphal entry of Heraclius, "King of the Rūm" (in 630).[8]

In the above discussion of Muḥammad's nocturnal journey (Chapter 1), I pointed out that, in the wake of the Persian occupation of Jerusalem in 614, the Jews were granted freedom of movement in the city and on the Temple Mount, a development which amplified Jewish hopes for messianic redemption. It was against this background that I conjectured that Muḥammad's vision of a nocturnal journey to this site precisely when it was under Persian rule expresses identification with Jewish messianic hopes fostered by the Persian presence. Muḥammad in his nocturnal journey is like Moses who took the Children of Israel out of Egypt on a nocturnal journey to their Promised Land. However, in the passage before us that opens *Sūrat al-Rūm*, which is later than the passage of Muḥammad's nocturnal journey (Q 17:1), the situation has been reversed: God promises a Roman victory over the Persians, after the latter's temporary triumph. Indeed, the passage continues with God's promise that the believers will rejoice with the Rūm's victory. Furthermore (Q 30:6),

> The promise of God! God fails not his promise, but most people do not know it.

The qur'ānic endorsement of the anticipated victory of the Rūm over the Persians —the protectors of the Jews in Jerusalem—signals a departure from the Jewish messianic vision of redemption, after the Jews of Medina refused to recognize Muḥammad as a true prophet. But the hope the Qur'ān expresses for the completion of God's promise that would bring joy to the believers is also a sign of the general messianic atmosphere which engulfed the entire region in the wake of the continuous confrontation between the Persian and the Byzantine empires.[9] However, the Qur'ān no longer includes the Jews in this vision.

The chronology of the Rūm passage

Sūrat al-Rūm (30) belongs to the late Meccan period, i.e. much earlier than the date of the final victory of the Romans over the Persians in 628 and the triumphant entrance of Heraclius to Jerusalem in 630. Therefore, the opening passage

8 *Loc. cit.*

9 On the connection between the messianic atmosphere and the Rūm passage see Heilo, *Eastern Rome*, pp. 21–22; Shoemaker, "The Reign of God", pp. 537–538. Cf. also Kaegi, *Heraclius*, pp. 78–80, 96, 205–208.

of Q 30 might be taken as either a prophecy that came true, or as a later retrospective vision in which actual events have been remolded as an apocalyptic forecast. This literary phenomenon is known, for example, from Jewish *piyyutim* (sacred poetry) of the early seventh century (e.g., the one called "On That Day") that might perhaps be understood as alluding to the Byzantine campaign against the Persians in Palestine.[10] The latter option is to be preferred, in which case, the qur'ānic apocalyptic forecast was built into a Meccan *sūra* in order to enhance the prophecy's impact. However, Qur'ān exegetes, as could be expected, reject the idea that this passage was revealed after the Byzantine victory, and instead view it as a Meccan text that demonstrates Muḥammad's prophetic powers.[11]

There is an alternative variant reading (*qirā'a*) of this passage, based on the perception that it was indeed revealed only after the victory of the Rūm.[12] This reading can be found, for example, in al-Ṭabarī's *Tafsīr* (italics mine):

> (2) The Rūm *have been victorious* (*ghalabat*) (3) in the nearest part of the land; but, after their victory, they *shall be vanquished* (*sa-yughlabūn*) (4) in a few years . . .[13]

Al-Ṭabarī explains that this reading means that, after the victory of the Rūm over the Persians, the Muslims will vanquish the former. Other exegetes add more details and explain that according to this reading the Muslim victory in the days of the second caliph ʿUmar b. al-Khaṭṭāb (ruled 13–23/634–644) was the event that would make the believers rejoice.[14]

The clash with the Jews of Medina: The *ḥashr* of the Naḍīr

The Byzantines' recovery and their defeat of the Persians who had protected the Jews in Jerusalem were evident even before the definitive victory of the Romans in 628. As for the Jews, they had already been expelled from Jerusalem in 617.[15] Therefore it is feasible to suppose that in due course the undermining of the status of the Jews in Jerusalem would inspire the idea that in Arabia, too, God would surely help

10 Sivan H., "From Byzantine to Persian Jerusalem", especially pp. 287–289, 294–298, 301–303. But see a more sceptical view with regard to the dating of "On That Day" in Hoyland, *Seeing Islam*, pp. 319–320.
11 Ibn ʿAṭiyya, *Tafsīr* (Q 30:6).
12 On the various ways in which this passage was interpreted see El-Cheikh, "*Sūrat al-Rūm*".
13 Ṭabarī, *Tafsīr* (Q 30:3).
14 Abū Ḥayyān, *al-Baḥr al-muḥīṭ* (Q 30:4).
15 See above, Chapter 1.

His believers in confronting the Jews who did not accept Muḥammad as the harbinger of redemption. Whether or not this reasoning is valid, the qur'ānic verses which deal with Muḥammad's campaign against the Jews of Medina clearly reflect the idea of divine assistance in accordance with an ancient redemption plan. The first significant clash with the Jews mentioned in the Qur'ān is described in the following passage (Q 59:2):

> It is He who expelled (*akhraja*) from their habitations the unbelievers among the People of the Book at the first mustering (*awwal al-ḥashr*). You did not think that they would go forth, and they thought that their fortresses would defend them against God; then God came upon them from whence they had not reckoned, and he cast terror into their hearts . . .

The acting power in this passage—as everywhere in the Qur'ān—is God who implements the redemption planned for His believers in Arabia. As part of this plan He expels the People of the Book from their habitations. Exegetical traditions tell us that the expelled were the Jews of the tribe of al-Naḍīr who were banished in the year 4/625.[16] The Qur'ān calls their expulsion *awwal al-ḥashr*, the "first" *ḥashr*, or perhaps, the "beginning" of the *ḥashr*. In the immediate context of the verse, the word *ḥashr* means "expulsion", but, as we saw above,[17] the basic meaning of the root *ḥ-sh-r* in the Qur'ān is "to gather". This is the meaning of the word when the Qur'ān describes the gathering of the resurrected dead who are taken from the grave to face God's judgment. It is therefore possible that in the verse at hand, too, the word *ḥashr* is connected to the process of resurrection. This is, at least, the approach taken in some exegetical traditions. The exegete Muqātil b. Sulaymān (d. 150/767) explains that the "first" *ḥashr* refers to the actual war against al-Naḍīr in Medina, after which a second *ḥashr* will come, that of the Resurrection. The *ḥashr* will begin with the Jews' expulsion from Medina towards al-Shām and Adhri'āt.[18] Similarly, 'Ikrima (d. 105/723), a member of the circle of Ibn 'Abbās, the father of Qur'ān exegesis, explains:

> The place towards which the [resurrected] people will be led together [*maḥshar al-nās*] will be al-Shām, and the first who were gathered [*ḥushira*] from this nation were al-Naḍīr.[19]

The exegete Ibn al-'Arabī (d. 543/1148) provides a more detailed clarification:

16 On the expulsion of al-Naḍīr see Lecker, *Muḥammad and the Jews*, pp. 135–156.
17 See above, Chapter 4.
18 E.g. Muqātil, *Tafsīr* (Q 59:2).
19 Nu'aym b. Ḥammād, *Fitan*, p. 425.

> The *ḥashr* has a first, middle and last [stage]. The first stage is the *ḥashr* of al-Naḍīr, the middle stage is the *ḥashr* of [the Jews of] Khaybar, and the last stage is the *ḥashr* on the Day of Resurrection [*yawm al-qiyāma*].[20]

According to these interpretations, the first *ḥashr* which took place when al-Naḍīr was expelled started the process of the ingathering of the people towards al-Shām, which would reach its ultimate goal on the Day of Resurrection.[21] In light of these explanations, it may well be that the Qur'ān labels the expulsion of al-Naḍīr "the first *ḥashr*" to suggest that, since they in any case are striving to be resurrected in al-Shām (more specifically, on the Mount of Olives),[22] they should be rather happy with their expulsion, as it gets them closer to their longed-for destination. The cynical scorn with which this Medinan *sūra* opens marks a deterioration in the Qur'ān's approach to Jewish eschatological aspirations.

The defeat of Qurayẓa

A clash with another Jewish tribe is described in the following Medinan passage (Q 33:25–27):

> (25) And God sent back those that were unbelievers in their rage, and they attained no good; God spared the believers from fighting. Surely God is omnipotent, all-mighty. (26) And He brought down those of the People of the Book who supported them from their fortresses and cast terror in their hearts; some you slew, some you made captive. (27) And he bequeathed upon you their lands, their habitations, and their possessions, and a land you never trod. God is powerful over everything.

The fact that this passage mentions the People of the Book in association with their fortresses, indicates that these are the Jews of Medina who possessed fortifications behind which they could seek shelter when necessary. The fortresses are also mentioned in the passage about al-Naḍīr quoted above.[23] Furthermore, there is no reason to reject the interpretations that maintain that this passage describes the fate of the Medinan Jews of the tribe of Qurayẓa who helped the unbelievers

---

20 Qurṭubī, *Aḥkām al-Qur'ān* (Q 59:2).
21 See also the explanations of the *Ḥadīth* commentator Ibn Ḥajar al-'Asqalānī (d. 852/1449). He cites another example of expulsion from al-Shām even before the Resurrection. It happened to the Umayyads who were driven out by 'Abdāllah b. al-Zubayr from Medina towards Syria. See Ibn Ḥajar, *Fatḥ al-bārī*, XI, p. 326 [On Bukhārī, *Ṣaḥīḥ*, *Riqāq* (81:45)].
22 See above, Chapter 4.
23 Lecker, *Muḥammad and the Jews*, p. 31.

in the Battle of the Trench, al-Khandaq (5/627).[24] The passage tells of the slaying of members of the tribe, an event described in detail in *sīra* sources. The passage also emphasizes God's grace who bequeathed the estates of the People of the Book to the believers, while promising them another inheritance in "a land you never trod". This formulation would seem to refer to territory outside Medina. Some exegetes maintain that it might be the Jewish colony in Khaybar (150 km. north of Medina), which fell in the year 6/628. Other commentators suggest that the land not yet conquered stands for all the territories which the Muslims are about to occupy in the course of time, including the lands of the Persians and the Rūm.[25] As seen above, the same interpretation was read into the Rūm passage (Q 30:2–7).

At any rate, the verse in question tells us that the promised redemption of the Muslims will take place in a region they will inherit that lies beyond the present bounds of the community of believers. The redemption which takes place here involves the defeat of the Jews, an idea which accords with the Rūm passage in which a similar tone is noticeable which is represented by joy at the Persians' defeat.

The victories in Arabia and the concept of *fatḥ*

One word used in the Qur'ān in the context of the struggle with the Jews and other enemies is *fatḥ*. It is a complex term which can be illuminated in light of the following passages. One of them runs as follows (Q 5:51–52):

> (51) O believers, take not Jews and Christians as friends; they are friends of each other. Whoso of you makes them his friends is one of them. God guides not the people of the evildoers. (52) Yet you see those in whose hearts is sickness vying with one another to come to them, saying, 'We fear lest a turn of fortune should smite us.' But it may be that God will bring *fatḥ*, or some commandment from him, and then they will find themselves, for that they kept secret within them, remorseful.

The anti-Jewish and anti-Christian context of the idea of *fatḥ* comes out clearly here. Both groups are accused of plotting against the Muslims, and in retaliation the Qur'ān threatens them with a *fatḥ* that Allāh will grant the believers and which will cause the Jews and the Christians remorse. The word here clearly

24 Ṭabarī, *Tafsīr* (Q 33:26). See also Lecker, *Muḥammad and the Jews*, p. 157–177; Shnizer, "The Figure of Muḥammad", p. 53.
25 Ṭabarī, *Tafsīr* (Q 33:27).

denotes an aspect of redemption in which Allāh will tip the scales in favor of the believers.

Fatḥ versus Quraysh

However, the concept of *fatḥ* more often appears in the context of the struggle against Arab idolaters. This can be seen in a Meccan passage (Q 32:28–29):

> (28) They also say, 'When shall be this *fatḥ*, if you speak truly?' (29) Say: 'On the day of the *fatḥ* their faith shall not profit the unbelievers, nor shall they be respited.'

Here the "Day of *fatḥ*" denotes the time when Allāh will tip the scales in favor of the believers. In all likelihood, the reference is to the Day of Judgment, when all people will be judged according to their deeds in this world; however, since the verse gives no precise time, it can also be interpreted as a promise that the unbelievers will be defeated on earth. Some exegetes who adopt this interpretation mention in this context Muḥammad's victory over his enemies of the Quraysh at the Battle of Badr which took place in the year 2/624, two years after Muḥammad's *hijra* from Mecca to Medina. In this battle the Muslims defeated the army of unbelievers that came from Mecca to protect a caravan of Meccan merchants making its way back from Syria. Other exegetes link this verse with the day of Muḥammad's triumphant entry into Mecca (8/630).[26] Since the *sūra* in which this verse appears belongs to the Meccan period, clearly the interpretations read into it a prediction of events on earth that did not yet happen. At any rate, here, too, we see the typical blurring of the boundaries between this world and the next, the two spheres in each of which God's plan of redemption for his Prophet and his believers may be accomplished.

"A nigh *fatḥ*"

A number of verses contain the phrase "a nigh *fatḥ*" (*fatḥ qarīb*). For example, Q 61:10–13 reads:

> (10) O believers, shall I direct you to a commerce that shall deliver you from a painful chastisement? (11) You shall believe in God and His Messenger, and struggle in the way of God with your possessions and your selves. That is better for you, did you but know. (12) He will forgive you your sins and admit you into gardens underneath which rivers flow, and to

26 On the various likely interpretations see e.g. Ṭabarī, *Tafsīr* (Q 32:29).

goodly dwelling-places in gardens of Eden; that is the mighty triumph; (13) and other things you love, victory (*naṣr*) from God and a nigh *fatḥ*. Good tidings to the believers!

The peak of the redemption promised here will come in Paradise, but that will be in addition to a "nigh" *fatḥ*. The exegetes who were already aware of the Muslim conquests outside of Arabia explained that the reference here is to these conquests or at least to Muḥammad's takeover of Mecca.[27] Whichever the case, the promise of redemption encompasses both this world and the world to come.

A nigh *fatḥ* is also referred to, more than once, in Q 48:27:

God has indeed fulfilled the vision he vouchsafed to his Messenger truly: 'You shall enter the Holy Mosque, if God wills it, in security, your heads shaved, your hair cut short, not fearing.' He knew what you knew not, and appointed ere that a nigh *fatḥ*.

This passage, as we saw above,[28] is in line with several other verses in which God condemns the unbelievers among the Quraysh for having denied the Prophet and his followers, who left Mecca for Medina in the *hijra* (622 CE), free access to the Kaʿba in order to perform the *ḥajj* rites. Mecca thus became an object of longing for the believers who had been barred from it. In the above verse the Holy Mosque (al-Masjid al-Ḥarām) in Mecca is elevated to the position of a local Promised Land which Muḥammad and his followers will enter and perform there the pilgrimage rites, all according to God's promise given to the Prophet in a dream.

Exegetes of the Qurʾān associate the Prophet's promised entry into Mecca with a well-known chapter in Muḥammad's life. They quote traditions to the effect that the Prophet dreamt that he and his Companions entered Mecca and performed the *ḥajj* rites. The dream inspired them to make the journey to Mecca, but the troops of the Quraysh stopped them at the city's outskirts, in a place called al-Ḥudaybiyya (in the year 6/628). The two sides held talks which resulted in the agreement known as the Ḥudaybiyya Treaty. One article in this treaty stipulated that Muḥammad and his followers would be allowed to enter Mecca as pilgrims in the following year. This did indeed happen (in the year 7/629). According to the qurʾānic formulation, these events fulfil a divine promise given to Muḥammad in a dream.

In the above qurʾānic verse the promise that God gives Muḥammad contains two stages: After the longed-for entry into al-Masjid al-Ḥarām, the believers are promised a nigh *fatḥ*. The exegetes explain that this refers to the fall of the Jewish colony in Khaybar which the Prophet attacked in the year 6/628, immediately

---

27 E.g. Ibn al-Jawzī, *Zād al-masīr* (Q 61:13).
28 See above, Chapter 14.

after signing the Ḥudaybiyya Treaty.[29] Indeed, it appears that this agreement presented the Prophet with an opportunity to deal with Khaybar.[30]

A "nigh *fatḥ*" is also promised in the following passage in the same *sūra* (Q 48:18–21):

> (18) God was well pleased with the believers when they were swearing fealty to you under the tree, and He knew what was in their hearts, so he sent down the *sakīna* upon them, and rewarded them with a nigh *fatḥ* (19) and many spoils to take; and God is ever all-mighty, all-wise. (20) God has promised you many spoils to take; these He has hastened to you, and has restrained the hands of people from you, and that it may be a sign to the believers, and to guide you on a straight path, (21) and other spoils you were not able to take; God had encompassed them already. God is powerful over everything.

Here, too, the *fatḥ* in question has been linked by exegetes to the events at Ḥudaybiyya and Khaybar. The passage opens with an oath of allegiance under a tree; exegetes explain that the event in question was a renewal of the believers' allegiance to the Prophet at Ḥudaybiyya, under an ancient acacia tree (*samura*). In recompense, Allāh promises the believers a "nigh *fatḥ*". According to the exegetes, this is an allusion to the plentiful spoils which would fall into the believers' hands at Khaybar.[31] Furthermore, God then promises the believers even more: "other spoils you were not able to take; God has encompassed them already". Some have explained that this is a reference to the imminent conquest of Mecca which occurred in 8/630. Other commentators expand the vision's span and maintain that this refers to all the spoils which the Muslims will in future take from the unbelievers wherever they may be, including the spoils of Persia and Byzantium.[32] Although here, too, exegetes engage in a backward projection of the defeat of the Persians and the Rūm, which in fact happened only after Muḥammad's death, it is not out of the question that the Qur'ān in this case expresses the hope that spoils will come from beyond the Arabian Peninsula, from kingdoms already engaged in unending mutual attrition.

29 E.g. Ṭabarī, *Tafsīr* (Q 48:27).

30 On the series of the Ḥudaybiyya-Khaybar events see Lecker, "The Ḥudaybiyya Treaty". Lecker draws attention to reports about a defense pact between the Quraysh and the Jews of Khaybar which was annulled by the Ḥudaybiyya Treaty. See also Shnizer, "The Figure of Muḥammad", pp. 53–54.

31 Ṭabarī, *Tafsīr* (Q 48:18).

32 Ṭabarī, *Tafsīr* (Q 48:21, and 48:20).

Simultaneous Byzantine and Muslim victories

The beginning of the *sūra* under discussion here, Q 48, contains yet another mention of *fatḥ*, this time as something that has already been achieved (Q 48:1–3):

> (1) Surely We have given you a manifest *fatḥ*, (2) that God may forgive you your former and your latter sins, and complete His blessing upon you, and guide you on a straight path, (3) and that God may assist you with abundant help.

Here, too, exegetes identify *fatḥ* with the Ḥudaybiyya Treaty and its results. The Kūfan scholar ʿĀmir al-Shaʿbī (d. 103/721) says:

> The verse "Surely We have given you a manifest *fatḥ*" was revealed after al-Ḥudaybiyya. [God] forgave him his first and last sins; [The believers] renewed their pledge of satisfaction [*mubāyaʿat al-riḍwān*- Q 48:18]; [the believers] were fed with the dates of Khaybar [in the year 6/628]; the Rūm had the upper hand over the Persians (Fāris); the believers rejoiced in the fulfilment of the words of the book of God; the People of the Book overcame the Majūs (Magians).[33]

Here the commentator is clearly aware of the chronological correlation between Muḥammad's victories in Arabia and the Persian defeat in Palestine. The Rūm are presented as a People of the Book, i.e. Christians whose monotheism is better than the Zoroastrianism of the Persians, the Majūs.

The same awareness of the parallel chronology is implied in commentaries on the Rūm passage (Q 30:2–7) which maintain that the victory of the Rūm in "the nearest part of the land" greatly bolstered the believers' morale during their confrontation with Quraysh at Ḥudaybiyya.[34] Furthermore, some traditions report that the victory of the Rūm occurred simultaneously with Muḥammad's victory in the Battle of Badr:

> From Abū Saʿīd. He said: on the day of the Battle of Badr, the Rūm overcame Persia. This brought joy to the believers' hearts, because [the Rūm] were of the People of the Book. Then Allāh revealed the verses "*Alif Lām Mīm*. The Rūm have been vanquished [*ghulibat*]". [Abū Saʿīd] said: They had been defeated before [Badr]. He then continued reading until he came to the sentence, "and on that day the believers shall rejoice in God's help".[35]

---

33 ʿAbd al-Razzāq, *Tafsīr* (Q 48:1). See also Ṭabarī, *Tafsīr* (Q 48:1); Ibn al-Jawzī, *Zād al-masīr* (Q 48:1).

34 E.g. Muqātil, *Tafsīr* (Q 30:4); Fīrūzābādī, *Tanwīr al-miqbās* (Q 30:4); Ṭabarī, *Tafsīr* (Q 30:4); Ibn al-Jawzī, *Zād al-masīr* (Q 30:4).

35 Ṭabarī, *Tafsīr* (Q 30:2). See also Mubārakfūrī, *Tuḥfat al-aḥwadhī*, VIII, pp. 255–256 (no. 4004) (= Tirmidhī, *Sunan*, *Qirāʾāt* [43]: *Q* 30).

According to this comment, the believers' joy at the victory of the Rūm came about at the time of the Muslims' victory at Badr. The chronology (i.e. the Byzantine victory in 628) was unhesitatingly subordinated to the idea of the redemption that supposedly took place in 624, simultaneously in Arabia and in al-Shām. Another possibility is that the interpretation echoes the victories of the Emperor Heraclius over the Persians in other provinces (Anatolia, Armenia) before 628.[36]

In the following Medinan verse, which appears in another *sūra*, *fatḥ* is also a terrestrial event that has already taken place (Q 57:10):

> How is it with you, that you expend not in the way of God, and to God belongs the inheritance of the heavens and the earth? Not equal is he among you who spent, and who fought before the *fatḥ*; those are mightier in rank than they who spent and fought afterwards; and unto each God has promised the reward most fair; and God is aware of the things you do.

There are those who maintain that *fatḥ* here refers to Muḥammad's triumphal entry into Mecca (in the year 8/630), or the Ḥudaybiyya Treaty that preceded the fall of Khaybar and that proclaimed the armistice, whose benefits to Muḥammad were discussed above. Whatever the event to which the verse refers, it clearly marks the last opportunity to be numbered among the veterans of Islam, with the attendant prestige and greater share in the spoils of war which this status confers.

The *fatḥ* is fully achieved in Q 110:

> (1) When comes the help of God, and the *fatḥ*, (2) and you see people entering God's religion in throngs, (3) then proclaim the praise of your Lord, and seek His forgiveness; for He turns again unto people.

Here *fatḥ* refers to an event which marks the Islamic definitive triumph, a most solemn occasion that makes it imperative to thank and praise God. According to the exegetes, this event was the Prophet's triumphant entry into Mecca. The *fatḥ* is mentioned here together with *naṣr*, i.e. "victory". The latter appears also in the Rūm passage (Q 30:2–7) which contains a redemption vision as part of the divine plan promised the believers. It may be added that the verb *naṣara* is also used to describe the same kind of divine succor, once in the Battle of Badr (Q 3:123) and again in the believers' victory at Ḥunayn in the year 8/630 (Q 9:25). These cases all

36 Bowersock, *Empires*, pp. 55–56. Lecker points to the proximity in time between the beginning of Heraclius's renewed military campaign against the Persians in 622 and Muḥammad's *hijra* that year to Medina. Lecker says that the Byzantines and their Ghassānid protégés had encouraged the people of Medina to give the Prophet shelter in their city. See Lecker, "Ghassānids and Byzantines", p. 277.

reflect the wide scope of a redemption plan which encompasses all the Islamic victories, in Arabia and elsewhere.

From persecuted in Mecca to triumphant in Medina

The idea that the redemption plan encompasses the victories already achieved in Arabia, or those which would be achieved there in future, is also reflected in traditions dealing with yet another significant Medinan verse (Q 8:26):

> (26) And remember when you were few and abased in the land, and were fearful that the people would snatch you away; but He gave you refuge, and confirmed you with His help, and provided you with the good things, that haply you might be thankful.

This verse highlights the change in the Muslims' fortunes, as they were transformed from a persecuted minority in Mecca to victors in Medina. In the wake of this transformation the believers ceased to fear "the people" who had threatened to uproot them. The exegetes associate this process with the great redemption plan that encompasses the entire region. A tradition transmitted in the name of Wahb b. Munabbih (d. 110/728), one of the earliest transmitters of traditions about the history of the prophets, states that "the people" who no longer terrify the believers are the Persians,[37] or even the Persians and the Rūm together.[38] A similar interpretation is offered in the name of the exegete Qatāda (d. 117/735), who explains this verse as follows:

> [The believers] were trapped between two lions, Qayṣar [the emperor of the Rūm] and Kisrā [the Persian king], and were fearful lest the people would uproot them. These were the Persians and the Rūm and the Arabs who dwelled around Mecca.[39]

Some exegetes do not include the Persians and the Rūm in "the people" whom the believers no longer feared, arguing that their defeat did not occur until after the Prophet's death, when Islam expanded beyond Arabia, during the caliphate of ʿUmar b. al-Khaṭṭāb.[40] At any rate, M.J. Kister observes, in his examination of the exegetical traditions concerning the Persians and the Byzantines, that they reflect the rivalry between the two empires over the control of the regions of the Arab Peninsula at the end of the sixth century and the beginning of the seventh. He notes that the traditions bring out the impact of this rivalry on the life of the communities

37 ʿAbd al-Razzāq, *Tafsīr* (Q 8:26).
38 Ṭabarī, *Tafsīr* (Q 8:26); Thaʿlabī, *al-Kashf wa-l-bayān* (Q 8:26).
39 Samarqandī, *Tafsīr* (Q 8:26). See also Thaʿlabī, *al-Kashf wa-l-bayān* (Q 8:26).
40 Ibn ʿAṭiyya, *Tafsīr* (Q 8:26); Abū Ḥayyān, *al-Baḥr al-muḥīṭ* (Q 8:26).

in the Peninsula. The struggle between the two empires, in which the two vassal kingdoms of al-Ḥīra and Ghassān took an active part, was closely watched by the unbelievers and Muslims.[41]

One may therefore surmise that in the verse before us the Qurān not only celebrates the redemption achieved as a result of the believers' victory over their oppressors in Arabia, but also the decline in the power of the two mutually hostile kingdoms that intimidated the entire region. Differently put, it may well be that, as in passages discussed above, the Qur'ān here, too, views the defeat of the unbelievers in Arabia as presaging Muslim victories beyond Arabia, in lands controlled by the tottering empires.

The conquest of al-Shām in the wake of the Children of Israel

Traditions that describe the first stages in the Muslim expansion into al-Shām consistently promote the idea that Muslim successes on the battlefields outside of Arabia were part of an ancient redemption plan that was already hinted at in the Qur'ān. One such tradition concerns the following qur'ānic verse (Q 24:55):

> God has promised those of you who believe and do righteous deeds that He will surely make you successors in the land, even as He made those who were before them successors, and that He will surely establish their religion for them that He has approved for them . . .

A number of Muslim exegetes explain that "those who were before them" are the Children of Israel, to whom Allāh bequeathed al-Shām.[42] It is related, possibly in the spirit of this interpretation, that a Muslim general declaimed this verse to his troops on the eve of the Battle of al-Yarmūk (15/636).[43] The Muslim victory in this key battle at the gates of al-Shām was thus perceived as a reenactment of the bequeathing of this land to the Children of Israel. One commentary states that the verse constitutes a promise to the believers that Muḥammad will occupy Mecca.[44] This is yet another sign of the idea that al-Shām and Arabia belong to the same sanctity space.

---

41 Kister, "Al-Ḥīra", pp. 143–144.

42 E.g. Māwardī, *Nukat* (Q 24:55). An explicit promise to the Israelites to bequeath to them the land of their enemies is given in Q 7:129.

43 My attention to this report was drawn by Avraham Hakim. And see Hakim, "Biblical Annunciation", pp. 138–139.

44 Māwardī, *Nukat* (Q 24:55).

The association between the Children of Israel and the triumphant Muslims in al-Shām can be seen in a tradition about the capture of Jerusalem (ca. 17/638) also revolving around a qur'ānic verse. This tradition relates that on the morning of the battle, the Muslim commanders recited to their troops the verse in which Moses says to the Children of Israel: "My people, enter the Holy Land [*al-arḍ al-muqaddasa*] which God has prescribed for you, and do not turn back [Q 5:21]".[45]

Muḥammad and al-Shām

Finally, let us look at some traditions which are not centered on qur'ānic verses, but which also reflect the broad horizons of the redemption plan. One of these appears in the early biography (*sīra*) of Muḥammad composed by Ibn Isḥāq (d. 150/768):

> Allāh's Messenger sent Usāma b. Zayd b. Ḥāritha to al-Shām and ordered him to lead the cavalry into the territory of al-Balqā' and al-Dārūm, in the land of Filasṭīn. The people equipped themselves, and with Usāma also went the first *muhājirūn* [those who had returned from the first *hijra* to Abyssinia].[46]

This report deals with the Prophet's actions in the year 10/632, shortly before his death in Medina. It ascribes to him the explicit intention of undertaking a campaign beyond the northern border of the Ḥijāz. The destination which Ibn Isḥāq mentions within al-Shām is Palestine (*Filasṭīn*), and within it the territory between al-Balqā' in Transjordan and al-Dārūm, a town near the Mediterranean Sea, south of Gaza.[47] If one accepts this tradition at face value, then it complements the impression given by the Qur'ān itself that the vision of redemption encompasses not only Arabia, but al-Shām as well.

In another tradition we find Muḥammad near the border of al-Shām, during the Muslim campaign at Tabūk, one of the Prophet's last campaigns (9/630). In Tabūk there was a garrison of Byzantine troops, or troops belonging to the Ghassānid kingdom, a vassal state of Byzantium. Not all the Muslims in Medina were happy to take part in this campaign, because of the hardships involved in such an extended journey. Q 9 contains quite a few verses devoted to the difficulties

45 Wāqidī, *Futūḥ al-Shām*, I, p. 14.

46 Ibn Hishām, *Sīra*, IV, p. 291.

47 Perhaps this is Kefar Darom which is mentioned in Talmud Bavli, Sotah 20b. Al-Dārūm was actually captured in 13/634. See Yāqūt, *Mu'jam al-buldān*, II, p. 424 (s.v. al-Dārūm). And see *loc. cit.*, verses by the contemporary poet Ziyād b. Ḥanẓala describing the assault of the Muslim cavalry on the troops of the Rūm in the area.

which the Prophet encountered in financing and recruiting soldiers for the campaign. The tradition runs as follows:

> Allāh's Messenger stood in the mountain pass [*thaniyya*] of Tabūk and said: Everything that is on that side is al-Shām – and pointed in the direction of al-Shām with his hand – and everything which is on this side is Yemen – and pointed in the direction of Medina with his hand.[48]

This all-encompassing division into two regions, Yemen and al-Shām, instead of the more specific delineation of the Ḥijāz on the one hand and Palestine on the other,[49] conveys a message of Muslim ownership over all of Arabia, including Yemen, and all of Syria and Palestine. That is why the Prophet's declaration is given in the mountain pass that links the two regions which were to become one unit under the banner of Islam.[50]

48 Shāfiʿī, *Umm*, I, p. 189; Ibn ʿAsākir, *Taʾrīkh Dimashq*, I, p. 196. For the various versions of Muḥammad's declaration in Tabūk, see Bashear, "Yemen in Early Islam", pp. 345–350.
49 The sources usually refer to the border line that separates al-Shām — or rather, Palestine — and northern Ḥijāz, which runs through Wādī al-Qurā. See Lecker, "Zuhrī", pp. 58–61.
50 For more details about Muḥammad's interest in Syria and the campaigns to northern Ḥijāz and southern Palestine, see Abu-Qorah, *The Hebrew Conquest*, pp. 195–200; Donner, *The Early Islamic Conquests*, pp. 96–109.

Summary

Throughout the book, aspects of the Islamic sanctity of Jerusalem and al-Shām at large are displayed under five major headings: (1) Navel of the Earth; (2) Land of Redemption; (3) Land of Resurrection; (4) Land of the Prophets; (5) Land of the Temple. The qurʾānic roots of these aspects have been pointed out, followed by an examination of the movement of the sanctity patterns from Jerusalem to Mecca, and also to Medina. In some of the five themes, this movement can already be discerned in the Qurʾān itself, while in others it first appears in extra-qurʾānic traditions disseminated during the early period of the Muslim presence in al-Shām.

Transition of sanctity patterns in the Qurʾān

As for the Qurʾān, the movement of the sanctity patterns and the change of balance in favor of Mecca is reflected in Medinan *sūras*, where the transition is associated with the changing attitude towards the Jewish vision of redemption in Jerusalem. The positive attitude towards this vision is preserved in earlier passages, Meccan verses which date from the period before the Muslim disappointment with the Jews who refused to accept Muḥammad as the bearer of their yearned-for redemption.

Thus, Chapter 1, which is placed under the heading "Navel of the Earth", contains a study of a vision that opens a Meccan *sūra* (17), in which the Prophet experiences a nocturnal journey from Mecca to al-Masjid al-Aqṣā, i.e. the Temple Mount in Jerusalem. Heavenly visions are revealed to him in that place which, being at the navel of the earth, is situated in the middle of the "blessed" ground that surrounds it. It is suggested that the nocturnal journey signals identification with the Jewish messianic vision of redemption in Jerusalem. This suggestion is based on the fact that the Children of Israel's exodus from Egypt is also described in the Qurʾān as a nocturnal journey towards the same "blessed" destination as that of Muḥammad's nocturnal journey. Aside from this, the vision of Muḥammad's journey takes place at a time of burgeoning Jewish hopes for redemption in Jerusalem, under the auspices of the Persians who wrested the city from the Byzantines in 614.

Another passage in the same Meccan *sūra* is discussed in Chapter 3, placed under the heading "Land of Redemption" (Q 17:104). In this passage the Qurʾān identifies yet again with the Jewish vision of redemption. In it God promises the Children of Israel to bring them gathered together in the Latter Days (*waʿd al-ākhira*). This promise seems to allude to the hopes of the Jews for messianic redemption in their holy land. This hope is reflected in Jewish messianic texts which describe the return of the displaced Jews from exile in the Latter Days.

https://doi.org/10.1515/9783111222318-017

Under the heading "Land of Resurrection", Chapter 4 contains a study of Meccan passages which fashion the events of the Day of Resurrection on the model of biblical apocalyptic visions. The latter revolve around the redemption of Israel and God's descent to judge the nations gathered in Jerusalem in the Latter Days. However, in the qur'ānic remolding, the redemption of Israel in Jerusalem is transformed into a universal gathering of all resurrected people on the Day of Judgment. The Qur'ān does not specify the location of the place of resurrection, but the mere employment of Jewish apocalyptic materials and their reshaping as the Resurrection testifies to the disguised presence of the Jewish idea of messianic redemption in Jerusalem.

Under the heading "Land of the Prophets", Meccan verses are discussed in Chapter 6, in which the identification of the Qur'ān with the Jewish vision of redemption can be seen more directly. These are verses about Abraham's journey to the blessed land and his being blessed there with Isaac and Jacob. The destination of his journey is identical to the Children of Israel's destination in their nocturnal exodus from Egypt, as well as to Muḥammad's destination on his nocturnal journey.

Under the heading "Land of the Temple", I examine in Chapter 11 Meccan passages that reflect an identification of the Qur'ān with the Jewish redemption vision. They depict the help which demons provided to Solomon in the construction of the Temple. In these depictions Solomon himself is carried to the blessed land that was also the destination of Abraham, the Children of Israel, and Muḥammad himself.

Aside from these Meccan passages, there are the Medinan ones in which the transition of sanctity patterns from Jerusalem to Mecca is discerned quite clearly. These passages are dealt with in the chapters arranged under the heading "Land of the Prophets". In Chapter 7 Medinan passages about Abraham are discussed which highlight the Ishmaelite identity of his offspring and display a sharply polemic attitude towards the Jews and the Christians, who refused to accept Muḥammad as bearer of redemption and so betrayed the true Abrahamic heritage. In Chapter 8, the Medinan passages are examined which produce a direct link between Abraham, Ishmael, and the building of the Kaʿba. The evidence in the Book of Jubilee is brought in order to shed more light on the origin of the link between Abraham and the Kaʿba as described in the Meccan, and more explicitly, Medinan *sūra*s.

More Medinan verses are studied in the chapters arranged under the heading "Land of the Temple". While Meccan *sūra*s focus on Solomon and the demons who worked for him, in the Medinan passages discussed in Chapter 12 the focus is on the Kaʿba, which is given the epithets "the first House" and "the *Maqām* of Abraham". These descriptions are designed to demonstrate that the Abrahamic Kaʿba is more ancient than Solomon's Temple. The same transition from Solomon's Temple to the Kaʿba can be seen in verses discussed in Chapter 14, which abandon the direction of prayer (*qibla*) used by the People of the Book and shift it to the Holy Mosque encompassing the Kaʿba.

From all of the above we may conclude that the attention given in Medinan *sūras* to Mecca and the Kaʿba is aimed at shaping their image as an appropriate arena for the appearance of Muḥammad, and at promoting the Ishmaelite identity of the community of believers.

Transition of sanctity patterns in the *ḥadīth*

As for the extra-qurʾānic traditions, they, as a rule, came into being after the Muslim expansion outside of Arabia, when the Muslims realized that their own faith had become one of the world's principal religions. The same applies to traditions about the sanctity of Jerusalem which date back to the first stages of the Islamic control over Palestine. These traditions appropriated Jewish and Christian models of sanctity and applied them to Islamic Jerusalem and to al-Shām as a whole. The process of Islamization of these places was needed to establish the presence of the Muslims in the lands of the Jews and the Christians. But the first Muslims in Palestine also preserved in their minds the memory of the Qurʾān which had given them the energy to break out of Arabia in the first place. The combined memory of the Qurʾān and the newly-appropriated Jewish and Christian sanctity models are reflected in the earliest Muslim traditions about Jerusalem and al-Shām.

Under the heading "Navel of the Earth", traditions are discussed in Chapters 1–2 which evince the revival of the memory of Muḥammad's nocturnal journey to al-Masjid al-Aqṣā and elaborate on the circumstances of this journey as well as on its connection to other prophets. The traditions also describe the Prophet's miraculous ascent to heaven from the Temple Mount.

Under the heading "Land of Redemption", exegetical traditions are examined in Chapter 3 which illuminate the connection between the qurʾānic "promise of the Latter Days" (*waʿd al-ākhira*) and the myth of the expected return of the ten Israelite tribes who dwell beyond the river Sambaṭyon. These traditions seem to corroborate the initial qurʾānic identification with the Jewish vision of redemption. Some traditions associate "the promise of the Latter Days" with the Islamic apocalyptic future and predict that the returning tribes of Israel will cooperate with the Muslims in the conquest of Constantinople.

Under the heading "Land of Resurrection", traditions are studied in Chapter 4, which further develop the relationship between the qurʾānic depictions of the Resurrection and the Rock on the Temple Mount, shaping it as the site where the resurrected will gather.

Under the heading "Land of the Prophets", traditions are discussed in Chapter 6 which expand on the relationship of the prophets with al-Shām, which is hinted at already in the Qur'ān. They highlight the tombs of the prophets located in that land as well as various aspects of their prophetic activity there. These traditions also emphasize the duty of the believers to go to al-Shām on the path taken by the prophets in order to defend it.

Under the heading "Land of the Temple", traditions are examined in Chapter 11 which promote the connection of Solomon's Temple to the Dome of the Rock, which is also in keeping with the spirit of the Jewish messianic vision.

When the first Islamic traditions about Jerusalem were created, traditions about Mecca and the Ka'ba hardly existed. The first Muslims outside of Arabia did keep the memory of the qur'ānic verses about Mecca and the Ka'ba, but the need to revive them within traditions that elaborated on the sanctity and history of those places only emerged when the Arabian self-image of the Muslims had to be fostered in the face of the increasing role of non-Muslims in the Islamic state that eventually spread beyond the initial borders of Syria and Iraq. More specifically, in view of the growing sanctity of Jerusalem which reached its apex with the construction of the Dome of the Rock, there arose the fear lest the sanctity of the Arabian shrine—deeply ingrained in the pre-Islamic Arab heritage and in the Qur'ān itself—would lose prestige. Fear for the status of Mecca and the Ka'ba can be clearly discerned in traditions which transfer the sanctity patterns from Jerusalem to Arabia.

Accordingly, under the heading "Navel of the Earth", traditions are pointed out in Chapter 2, in which the Prophet is said to have ascended to heaven directly from Mecca, which according to this depiction is located at the navel of the earth.

Under the heading "Land of Resurrection", traditions are noted in Chapter 5 which rather confer on Mecca and Medina the merit of being the land of Resurrection.

Under the heading "Land of the Prophets", traditions are shown in Chapter 9 which transfer this title to Mecca and the Ka'ba. Some of these traditions elaborate on the qur'ānic relationship of Abraham and Ishmael to the Ka'ba, transfer the location of Abraham's attempted sacrifice of his son to Mecca, and make Ishmael the main focus of that event. In this they contrast both with traditions that locate the attempted sacrifice in Jerusalem and with the qur'ānic version itself, as it appears in a Meccan *sūra*. There the affair takes place in al-Shām and the intended victim is Isaac, although he is not mentioned there by name. In Chapter 10, traditions are pointed out which extend the association of Mecca and Medina with prophets other than Abraham and Ishmael.

Under the heading "Land of the Temple", traditions are pointed out in Chapter 12 which revolve around qur'ānic verses that pose the Abrahamic Ka'ba as a counterweight to Solomon's Temple. These traditions expand on the idea that the Abrahamic

Kaʿba is more ancient than Solomon's. In Chapter 13, traditions are surveyed which enhance the idea of the primordial creation of the Kaʿba. In Chapter 14, traditions are examined which describe the circumstances under which the direction of prayer was changed from Jerusalem to the Holy Mosque in Mecca, and confirm the standing of the Kaʿba as the final *qibla*.

Under the heading "The Messianic Vision Inverted", Chapter 15 gets back to events discussed in Chapter 1, that took place in Palestine following the Persian takeover of Jerusalem in 614 which was terminated in 628 with the Byzantine recapture of the city. This chapter expands on the correlation between the events in Palestine and the events within Arabia that took place after the *hijra*. The latter are dealt with in Medinan passages referring to Muḥammad's victories over the Quraysh as well as over the Jews. These passages signal a departure from the Jewish vision of redemption and emphasize its application to Muslims only.

The transfer of sanctity patterns from Jerusalem to Mecca as evinced in the traditions before us never diminished the status of Jerusalem. The traditions in praise of this Jewish-Christian holy city that had come under the rule of Islam were preserved over generations, just as were the traditions in praise of Mecca and Medina. Yet one can hardly speak about an equilibrium in the importance of these two foci of sanctity. Political circumstances, such as the Umayyad interests on the one hand, and the interests of their opponents on the other, engendered attempts to raise the prestige of one of these foci of sanctity at the expense of the other. The rivalry is reflected mainly in the value ascribed to prayer in each of these places, a value that differs from one tradition to another.[1] Jerusalem's status in Islam has been preserved to this day, independently of the undisputed sanctity of Mecca and the Kaʿba. Traditions that foster Jerusalem's status as a sacred city continue to appear in the writings of Muslim thinkers to this day. These writings have been analyzed by several scholars,[2] and lie beyond the scope of the present work.

1 See mainly Kister, "Three Mosques".
2 See especially Reiter, *From Jerusalem to Mecca*.

Bibliography

ʿAbd al-Razzāq, *Muṣannaf* = ʿAbd al-Razzāq b. Hammām al-Ṣanʿānī. *Al-Muṣannaf*. Ed. Ḥabīb al-Raḥmān al-Aʿẓamī. 11 vols. Beirut: al-Maktab al-Islāmī, 1970.

ʿAbd al-Razzāq, *Tafsīr* = ʿAbd al-Razzāq b. Hammām al-Ṣanʿānī. *Tafsīr al-Qurʾān*. Ed. Muṣṭafā Muslim Muḥammad. 3 vols. Riyad: Maktabat al-Rushd, 1989.

Abot de Rabbi Nathan Version B = *The Fathers According to Rabbi Nathan (Abot de Rabbi Nathan Version B)*, A translation and Commentary by Anthony J. Saldarini. Leiden 1975.

Abū Dāwūd, *Sunan* = Abū Dāwūd, *al-Sunan*. 2 vols. Cairo: Muṣṭafā al-Bābī al-Ḥalabī, 1952.

Abū Ḥayyān, *al-Baḥr al-muḥīṭ* = Abū Ḥayyān, Muḥammad b. Yūsuf. *Al-Baḥr al-muḥīṭ fī l-tafsīr*. Ed. Zuhayr Jaʿīd. 10 vols. Dār al-Fikr: Beirut 1992.

Abū Nuʿaym, *Ḥilyat al-awliyāʾ* = Abū Nuʿaym, Aḥmad b. ʿAbdallāh al-Iṣbahānī. *Ḥilyat al-awliyāʾ wa-ṭabaqāt al-aṣfiyāʾ*. 10 vols. Cairo 1938, repr. Beirut 1967.

Abū ʿUbayd, *Amwāl* = Abū ʿUbayd, al-Qāsim b. Sallām. *Kitāb al-amwāl*, Beirut 1981.

Abu-Qorah, *The Hebrew Conquest* = Osamah A. Abu-Qorah, *A Structural Comparison of the Hebrew Conquest and the Arab Conquest of Southern Syria: Trans-Jordan and Palestine*, University of California, Los Angeles: ProQuest Dissertations Publishing, 1989.

Aḥmad b. Ḥanbal, *ʿIlal* = Aḥmad b. Ḥanbal. *Al-ʿIlal wa-maʿrifat al-rijāl*. Ed. Waṣiyyullāh b. Muḥammad ʿAbbās, Riyad–Beirut 1988.

Aḥmad b. Ḥanbal, *Musnad* = Aḥmad b. Ḥanbal. *Al-Musnad*. 6 vols. Beirut: al-Maktab al-Islāmī, 1978.

Ambros, *A Concise Dictionary* = Arne A. Ambros, *A Concise Dictionary of Koranic Arabic*, Wiesbaden 2004.

Apocalypse of Abraham = "The Apocalypse of Abraham: Translated by R. Rubinkiewicz", in James H. Charlesworth (ed.), *The Old Testament Pseudepigrapha*, London 1983, I, pp. 689–705.

Apocalypse of Ezra = "The Fourth Book of Ezra: A New Translation and Introduction by B.M. Metzger", in James H. Charlesworth (ed.), *The Old Testament Pseudepigrapha*, London 1983, I, pp. 517–559.

Arazi, "Matériaux" = Albert Arazi, "Matériaux pour l'étude du conflit de préséance entre la Mekke et Médine", *Jerusalem Studies in Arabic and Islam* 5 (1984), pp. 177–235.

Ashtor, "Arabic Book" = Eliyahu Ashtor, "An Arabic Book on the 'Merits of Jerusalem'", *Tarbiẕ* 30/2 (1961), pp. 209–214. [Hebrew]

Avi-Yonah, *Rome and Byzantium* = Michael Avi-Yonah, *In the Days of Rome and Byzantium*, Jerusalem 1980. [Hebrew]

ʿAyyāshī, *Tafsīr* = Muḥammad b. Masʿūd al-ʿAyyāshī. *Al-Tafsīr*. Ed. Hāshim al-Rasūlī al-Maḥallātī. 2 vols. Beirut 1991.

Azraqī, *Akhbār Makka* = Abū l-Walīd al-Azraqī, *Akhbār Makka*. In F. Wüstenfeld (ed.), *Die Chroniken der Stadt Mekka*, Göttingen, 1858, repr. Beirut n.d., vol. I.

Balādhurī, *Ansāb* = al-Balādhurī, Aḥmad b. Yaḥyā. *Jumal min ansāb al-ashrāf*. Ed. Suhayl Zakkār and Riyāḍ Ziriklī. 13 vols. Beirut: Dār al-Fikr, 1996.

Baras, "The Persian Conquest" = Zvi Baras, "The Persian Conquest and the Late Byzantine Rule", in Zvi Baras and others (eds.) *Eretz Israel: From the Destruction of the Second Temple to the Muslim Conquest* (Vol. 1 Jerusalem 1982), pp. 300–349. [Hebrew]

Bashear, "Abraham's Sacrifice" = Suliman Bashear, "Abraham's Sacrifice of his Son and Related Issues", *Der Islam* 67 (1990), pp. 243–277.

Bashear, *"Qibla Musharriqa"* = Suliman Bashear, *"Qibla Musharriqa and Early Muslim Prayer in Churches", The Muslim World* 81 (1991), pp. 267–282.

https://doi.org/10.1515/9783111222318-018

Bashear, "Yemen in Early Islam" = Suliman Bashear, "Yemen in Early Islam: An Examination of Non-Tribal Traditions", *Arabica* 36 (1989), pp. 327–361.

Beck, "Die Gestalt des Abraham" = Edmund Beck, "Die Gestalt des Abraham am Wendepunkt der Entwicklung Muhammeds", *Le Muséon* 65 (1952), pp. 73–94.

Bereshit Rabbati = Ch. Albek (ed.), *Midrash Bereshit Rabbati*. Jerusalem 1940.

Borrmans, "Resurrection"= Maurice Borrmans, "Resurrection", *Encyclopaedia of the Qur'ān*. Consulted online on 15.01.21. http://dx.doi.org/10.1163/1875-3922_q3_EQSIM_00356

Bowersock, *Empires* = Glen W. Bowersock, *Empires in Collision in Late Antiquity*, Massachusetts 2012.

Bukhārī, *Ṣaḥīḥ* = Muḥammad b. Ismāʿīl al-Bukhārī. *Al-Ṣaḥīḥ*. 9 vols. Beirut: Dār Iḥyāʾ al-Turāth al-ʿArabī, n.d.

Busse, "Jerusalem and Mecca" = Heribert Busse, "Jerusalem and Mecca, the Temple and the Kaaba: An Account of their Interrelation in Islamic Times", in Moshe Sharon (ed.), *The Holy Land in History and Thought: Papers submitted to the International Conference on the Relations between the Holy* Land *and the World outside It*, Johannesburg 1986 (Brill Archive 1988), pp. 236–246.

Busse, "The Destruction of the Temple" = Heribert Busse, "The Destruction of the Temple and its Reconstruction in the Light of Muslim Exegesis of Sūra 17: 2–8", *Jerusalem Studies in Arabic and Islam* 20 (1996), pp. 1–17.

Busse, "The Sanctity of Jerusalem" = Heribert Busse, "The Sanctity of Jerusalem in Islam", *Judaism* 17 (1968), pp. 441–468.

Cook M., *Muhammad* = Michael Cook, *Muhammad*, Oxford 1983.

Cook, "Dajjāl" = David Cook, "Dajjāl", in: *Encyclopaedia of Islam, THREE*. Consulted online on 15.01.21. http://dx.doi.org/10.1163/1573-3912_ei3_COM_25826

Cook, *Muslim Apocalyptic* = David Cook, *Studies in Muslim Apocalyptic*, Princeton, N.J.: The Darwin Press, 2002.

Crone and Cook, *Hagarism* = Patricia Crone, Michael Cook. *Hagarism: The Making of the Islamic World*. Cambridge 1977.

Crone, "Problems in Sura 53" = Patricia Crone, "Problems in Sura 53", *Bulletin of the School of Oriental and African Studies* 78 (2015), pp. 15–23.

Dan, "Palaestina Salutaris" = Yaron Dan, "Palaestina Salutaris (Tertia) and its Capital", *Israel Exploration Journal* 32 (1982), pp. 134–137.

Dānī, *Fitan* = al-Dānī, Abū ʿAmr ʿUthmān b. Saʿīd. *Al-Sunan al-wārida fī l-fitan wa-ghawāʾilihā wa-l-sāʿa wa-ashrāṭihā*. Ed. Riḍāʾullāh al-Mubārakfūrī. 6 vols. Riyad, 1995.

Daylamī, *Firdaws* = al-Daylamī, Abū Shujāʿ. *Al-Firdaws bi-maʾthūr al-khiṭāb*. Ed. al-Saʿīd b. Basyūnī Zaghlūl. 5 vols. Beirut 1986.

Donner, *The Early Islamic Conquests* = Fred McGraw Donner, *The Early Islamic Conquests*, Princeton 1981.

Drory, "A History of Early Islam" = Joseph Drory, "A History of Early Islam", in Meir M. Bar-Asher and Meir Hatina (eds.), *Islam: History, Religion, Culture* (Jerusalem 2017), pp. 57–86. [Hebrew]

Eisenstein, *Ozar Midrashim* = Judah David Eisenstein, *Ozar Midrashim*. New York 1915. Consulted online on 15.01.21. https://www.otzar.org/wotzar/book.aspx?15692

Elad, "ʿAbd al-Malik and the Dome of the Rock" = Amikam Elad, "Abd al-Malik and the Dome of the Rock: A Further Examination of the Muslim Sources", *Jerusalem Studies in Arabic and Islam* 35 (2008), pp. 167–226.

Elad, "An Early Arabic Source" = Amikam Elad, "An Early Arabic Source Concerning the Markets of Jerusalem", *Cathedra* 24 (1982), 31–40 [Hebrew]

Elad, *Medieval Jerusalem* = Amikam Elad, *Medieval Jerusalem and Islamic Worship: Holy Places, Ceremonies, Pilgrimage*, Leiden 1999.

Elad, "Seven *miḥrābs*" = Amikam Elad, "Al-Masjid al-Aqṣā during the Umawī Period: Seven *miḥrābs* with Seven Domes", *Jerusalem Studies in Arabic and Islam* 49 (2020), pp. 339–432.
Elad, "The Coastal Cities" = Amikam Elad, "The Coastal Cities of Palestine during the Early Middle Ages", *The Jerusalem Cathedra* 2 (1982), pp. 146–167.
Elad, "The Status of Jerusalem" = Amikam Elad, "The Status of Jerusalem in the Umayyad Period", *Ha-Mizrah ha-Haddash* 44 (2004), pp. 17–68. [Hebrew]
Elad, "The Temple Mount" = Amikam Elad, "The Temple Mount in the Early Islamic Period", in Yitzhak Reiter (ed.), *Sovereignty of God and Man: Sanctity and Political Centrality on the Temple Mount*, Jerusalem 2001, pp. 57–109 [Hebrew]
El-Cheikh, "*Sūrat al-Rūm*" = Nadia Maria El-Cheikh, "*Sūrat al-Rūm*: A Study of the Exegetical Literature", *Journal of the American Oriental Society* 118 (1998), pp. 356–364.
Eliav, *God's Mountain* = Yaron Z. Eliav, *God's Mountain: The Temple Mount in Time, Place, and Memory*. Baltimore: Johns Hopkins University Press, 2005.
Ende, "Baqīʿ al-Gharqad" = Werner Ende, "Baqīʿ al-Gharqad", in: *Encyclopaedia of Islam, THREE*. Consulted online on 15.01.21. http://dx.doi.org/10.1163/1573-3912_ei3_COM_23494
Epstein, *Works* = Abraham Epstein, *The Works of Abraham Epstein*. Collected and prepared for publication by Abraham Meir Habermann. Jerusalem 1950. [Hebrew]
Even-Shmuel, *Midrashei Geula* = Yehuda Even-Shmuel, *Midrashei Geula*. Jerusalem 2017. [Hebrew]
Fākihī, *Akhbār Makka* = Muḥammad b. Isḥāq al-Fākihī, *Akhbār Makka*. Ed. ʿAbd al-Malik b. Duhaysh. 6 vols. Mecca 1986–1988.
Farazdaq, *Dīwān* = Hammām b. Ghālib al-Farazdaq. *Dīwān*. 2 vols. Dār Ṣādir li-l-Ṭibāʿa wa-l-Nashr, Beirut 1960.
Firestone, "Abraham's Son" = Reuven Firestone, "Abraham's Son as the Intended Sacrifice (*al-Dhabīḥ*, Qurʾān 37: 99–113): Issues in Qurʾānic Exegesis", *Journal of Semitic Studies* 34 (1989), pp. 95–131.
Fīrūzābādī, *Tanwīr al-miqbās* = Muḥammad b. Yaʿqūb al-Fīrūzābādī, *Tanwīr al-miqbās min tafsīr Ibn ʿAbbās*, Beirut 2006.
Friedmann, "Pillars of Islam" = Yohanan Friedmann, "The Pillars of Islam", in Meir M. Bar-Asher and Meir Hatina (eds.), *Islam: History, Religion, Culture* (Jerusalem 2017), pp. 250–280. [Hebrew]
Gil, *History of Palestine* = Moshe Gil, *A History of Palestine, 634–1099*. Cambridge 1992.
Gil, "Political History" = Moshe Gil, "Political History of Jerusalem in the early Islamic Period", in Joshua Prawer (ed.), *The History of Jerusalem: The Early Islamic Period (638–1099)*, Jerusalem 1987, pp. 1–31. [Hebrew]
Gil, "The Apocalypse of Zerubbabel" = Moshe Gil, "The Apocalypse of Zerubbabel in Judaeo-Arabic", *Revue des études juives* 165 (2006), pp. 1–98.
Gil, "The Jewish Community" = Moshe Gil, "The Jewish Community," in Joshua Prawer (ed.), *The History of Jerusalem: The Early Islamic Period (638–1099)*, Jerusalem 1987, pp. 133–162. [Hebrew]
Goitein, "Arabic Names" = S.D. Goitein, "On the Arabic Names of Jerusalem", *Minha Lihuda* [Jerusalem 1950], pp. 62–66 [Hebrew]
Goitein, "Sanctity" = S.D. Goitein, "The Sanctity of Palestine in Muslim Piety", *Yediot* 12 (1946), pp. 120–126. [Hebrew]
Goitein, *Studies* = S.D. Goitein, *Studies in Islamic History and Institutions*, Leiden 1966, pp. 135–148.
Goldziher, *Muslim Studies* = Ignaz Goldziher, *Muslim Studies (Muhammedanische Studien)*, ed. and trans. S.M. Stern and C.R. Barber, London 1967–1971.
Grabar, *The Dome of the Rock* = Oleg Grabar, *The Dome of the Rock*, Cambridge, Massachusetts/London 2006.
Grabar, "The Meaning of the Dome of the Rock" = Oleg Grabar, "The Meaning of the Dome of the Rock", in Derek Hopwood (ed.), *Studies in Arab History: The Antonius Lectures, 1978–87*, New York 1990, pp. 151–163.

Grabar, "The Umayyad Dome of the Rock" = Oleg Grabar, "The Umayyad Dome of the Rock in Jerusalem", *Ars Orientalis* 3 (1959), pp. 33–62.

Grossmann E., *The Concepts of ribāṭ* = Elimelech Grossmann, *The Concepts of ribāṭ and thughūr in the Early Islamic Tradition and in the Contemporary* Research, *their Role in the Confrontation with the Byzantines, the Visigoths and the Franks during the First Three Centuries AH*. Thesis Submitted for the Degree "Master of Arts", Tel Aviv University, Tel Aviv 2017.

Grossmann, "Jerusalem in the Jewish Apocalypse" = Abraham Grossmann, "Jerusalem in the Jewish Apocalypse of the Early Middle Ages ", in Joshua Prawer (ed.), *The History of Jerusalem: The Early Islamic Period (638–1099)*, (Jerusalem 1987), pp. 236–248. [Hebrew]

Guillaume, *The Life of Muhammad* = Alfred Guillaume, *The Life of Muhammad: A Translation of Ibn Isḥāq's Sīrat Rasūl Allāh*, Oxford 1974.

Hakim, "Biblical Annunciation" = Avraham Hakim, "The Biblical Annunciation Made to ʿUmar b. al-Khaṭṭāb: The Religious Legitimation of the Early Islamic Conquests", *Jerusalem Studies in Arabic and Islam* 42 (2015), pp. 129–150.

Ḥākim, *Mustadrak* = al-Ḥākim Muḥammad b. ʿAbdallāh al-Naysābūrī. *al-Mustadrak ʿalā l- Ṣaḥīḥayn*. 4 vols. Hyderabad 1342/1923.

Hasson, "Jerusalem in the Muslim Perspective" = Yizhak Hasson, "Jerusalem in the Muslim Perspective: The Qurʾān and the Tradition Literature", in Joshua Prawer (ed.), *The History of Jerusalem: The Early Islamic Period (638–1099)*, Jerusalem 1987, pp. 283–313. [Hebrew]

Hasson, "Last Judgment" = Isaac Hasson, "Last Judgment", *Encyclopaedia of the Qurʾān*. Consulted online on 15.01.21. http://dx.doi.org/10.1163/1875-3922_q3_EQCOM_00105

Havel, "Jerusalem" = Boris Havel,. "Jerusalem in Early Islamic Tradition", *Miscellanea Hadriatica et Mediterranea* [MHM] 5 (2018), pp. 113–179.

Hawting, "Zamzam" = Gerald R. Hawting, "The Disappearance and Rediscovery of Zamzam and the Well of the Kaʿba", *Bulletin of the School of Oriental and African Studies* 43 (1980), 44–54.

Haythamī, *Majmaʿ al-zawāʾid* = al-Haythamī, Nūr al-Dīn. *Majmaʿ al-zawāʾid wa-manbaʿ al-fawāʾid*. 10 vols. Repr. Beirut 1987.

Haythamī, *Ṣawāʿiq* = al-Haythamī, Abū l-ʿAbbās Aḥmad b. Ḥajar. *Al-Ṣawāʿiq al-muḥriqa ʿalā ahl al-rafḍ wa-l-ḍullāl wa-l-zandaqa*. Ed. ʿAbd al-Raḥmān b. ʿAbdallāh al-Turkī, Kāmil Muḥammad al-Kharrāṭ, Beitut 1997.

Heilo, *Eastern Rome* = Olof Heilo, *Eastern Rome and the Rise of Islam: History and Prophecy*, London and New York: Routledge, 2016.

Himmelfarb, "Sefer Zerubbabel" = "Sefer Zerubbabel", Introduction and translation by Martha Himmelfarb, in David Stern, Mark Jay Mirsky (eds.), *Rabbinic Fantasies*, New Haven 1990, pp. 67–90.

Hirschberg, "The Place of Jerusalem" = H.Z. Hirschberg "The Place of Jerusalem in the Muslim World", *Jerusalem: A Quarterly for the Study of Jerusalem and its History* 2 (1949) pp. 65–70. [Hebrew]

Hoffman, "Intercession" = Valerie J. Hoffman, "Intercession", *Encyclopaedia of the Qurʾān*. Consulted online on 15.01.21. http://dx.doi.org/10.1163/1875-3922_q3_EQCOM_00097

Horovitz, "Muhammeds Himmelfahrt" = Josef Horovitz, "Muhammeds Himmelfahrt", *Der Islam* 9 (1918), pp. 159–183.

Horowitz, "The Vengeance of the Jews" = Elliott Horowitz, "'The Vengeance of the Jews was Stronger than their Avarice': Modern Historians and the Persian Conquest of Jerusalem in 614", *Jewish Social Studies*, New Series, 4, 2 (1998), pp. 1–39.

Hoyland, *Seeing Islam* = Robert G. Hoyland, *Seeing Islam as Others Saw It: a Study and Evaluation of Christian, Jewish and Zoroastrian Writings on Early Islam*, Princeton 1997.

Huwwārī, *Tafsīr* = Hūd b. Muḥakkam al-Huwwārī, *Tafsīr kitāb Allāh al-ʿAzīz*. Ed. Belḥāj Sharīfī. 4 vols. Beirut: Dār al-Gharb al-Islāmī, 1990.

Ibn Abī Ḥātim, *Tafsīr* = Ibn Abī Ḥātim,ʿAbd al-Raḥmān b. Muḥammad. *Tafsīr al-Qurʾān al-ʿaẓīm*. Ed. Asʿad Muḥammad al-Ṭayyib. 10 vols. Mecca-Riyad: Maktabat Nizār Muṣṭafā al-Bāz, 1997

Ibn Abī Shayba, *Muṣannaf* = Ibn Abī Shayba, ʿAbdallāh b. Muḥammad. *Al-Muṣannaf fī l-aḥādīth wa-l-āthār*. Ed. ʿAbd al-Khāliq al-Afghānī. 15 vols. Bombay, 1979–1983.

Ibn al-Ḍurays, *Faḍāʾil al-Qurʾān* = Ibn al-Ḍurays, Muḥammad b. Ayyūb. *Faḍāʾil al-Qurʾān*. Ed. Ghazwat Budayr. Damascus: Dār al-Fikr, 1987.

Ibn al-Faqīh, *Buldān* = Ibn al-Faqīh, Aḥmad b. Muḥammad al-Hamadhānī. *Kitāb al-buldān*. Ed. Yūsuf al-Hādī, Beirut 1996.

Ibn al-Jawzī, *Taʾrīkh Bayt al-Maqdis* = Ibn al-Jawzī, Abū l-Faraj ʿAbd al-Raḥmān. *Taʾrīkh Bayt al-Maqdis*. Ed. Muḥammad Zenhom, Muḥammad ʿAzb, Cairo 2001.

Ibn al-Jawzī, *Zād al-masīr* = Ibn al-Jawzī, Abū l-Faraj ʿAbd al-Raḥmān. *Zād al-masīr fī ʿilm al-tafsīr*. 9 vols. Beirut: al-Maktab al-Islāmī, 1984.

Ibn al-Murajjā, *Faḍāʾil* = Ibn al-Murajjā, Abū l-Maʿālī b. Ibrāhīm al-Maqdisī. *Faḍāʾil Bayt al-Maqdis wa-l-Khalīl wa-faḍāʾil al-Shām*. Ed. Ofer Livne–Kafri. Shfaram, 1995.

Ibn ʿAsākir, *Taʾrīkh Dimashq* = Ibn ʿAsākir, Abū l-Qāsim ʿAlī b. al-Ḥasan. *Taʾrīkh madīnat Dimashq*. Ed. ʿUmar b. Gharāma al-ʿAmrawī. 80 vols. Beirut: Dār al-Fikr, 1415/1995-1421/2000.

Ibn ʿAṭiyya, *Tafsīr* = Ibn ʿAṭiyya, Abū Muḥammad ʿAbd al-Ḥaqq. *Al-Muḥarrar al-wajīz fī tafsīr al-kitāb al-ʿazīz*. 16 vols. Rabat: Wizārat al-Awqāf wa-l-shuʾūn al-Islāmiyya, 1975–1991.

Ibn Ḥajar, *Fatḥ al-bārī* = Ibn Ḥajar, Shihāb al-Dīn Aḥmad al-ʿAsqalānī. *Fatḥ al-bārī sharḥ Ṣaḥīḥ al-Bukhārī*. 13 vols. Cairo 1892, repr. Beirut n.d.

Ibn Hishām, *Sīra* = Ibn Hishām, ʿAbd al-Malik. *Al-Sīra al-nabawiyya*. Ed. Muṣṭafā al-Saqqā, Ibrāhīm al-Abyārī, and ʿAbd al-Ḥafīẓ Shalabī. 4 vols. Beirut: Dār Iḥyāʾ al-Turāth al-ʿArabī, 1971.

Ibn Hishām, *Tījān* = Ibn Hishām, ʿAbd al-Malik. *Al-Tījān fī mulūk Ḥimyar*. Sanʿāʾ 1929, repr. 1979.

Ibn Kathīr, *al-Nihāya fī l-fitan* = Ibn Kathīr Ismāʿīl b. ʿUmar. *Al-nihāya fī l-fitan wa-l-malāḥim*. Ed. Aḥmad ʿAbd al-Shāfī, Beirut: Dār al-Kutub al-ʿIlmiyya, 1988.

Ibn Kathīr, *Tafsīr* = Ibn Kathīr Ismāʿīl b. ʿUmar. *Tafsīr al-Qurʾān al-aẓīm*. 4 vols. Cairo: Dār al-Fikr, n.d.

Ibn Māja, *Sunan* = Ibn Māja, Muḥammad b. Yazīd. *Al-Sunan*. Ed. Muḥammad ʿAbd al-Bāqī. 2 vols. Cairo: Dār Iḥyāʾ al-Kutub al-ʿArabiyya, 1952.

Ibn Qutayba, *Mukhtalif al-ḥadīth* = Ibn Qutayba, ʿAbdallāh b. Muslim. *Taʾwīl mukhtalif al-ḥadīth*. Ed. Muḥammad Zuhrī al-Najjār, Beirut 1972.

Ibn Saʿd, *Ṭabaqāt* = Ibn Saʿd. *Kitāb al-ṭabaqāt*. 8 vols. Beirut: Dār Ṣādir-Dār Bayrūt, 1960.

Ibn Shabba, *Taʾrīkh al-Madīna* = Ibn Shabba, Abū Zayd ʿUmar. *Taʾrīkh al-Madīna al-Munawwara*. Ed. Fahīm Muḥammad Shaltūt. 4 vols. Mecca, 1979.

Ibn Shaddād, *al-Aʿlāq al-khaṭīra* = Ibn Shaddād, Abū Muḥammad b. ʿAlī. *Al-Aʿlāq al-khaṭīra fī dhikr umarāʾ al-Shām wa-l-Jazīra*, vol. 3: *Taʾrīkh Lubnān wa-l-Urdunn wa-Filasṭīn*. Ed. Sāmī al-Dahhān, Damascus, 1962.

Irshai, "Chronography and Apocalypse" = Oded Irshai, "'When you see the Kingdoms fighting each other, look for the feet of the Messiah': Chronography and Apocalypse in Late Antiquity", in Yehuda Even-Shmuel, *Midrashei Geula* (Jerusalem 2017), pp. i-li. [Hebrew]

Ish-Shalom, "The Cave of Machpela" = Michael Ish-Shalom. "The Cave of Machpela and the Sepulchre of Moses", *Tarbiẓ* 41/2 (1972), pp. 203–210. [Hebrew]

Jellinek, *Bet Ha-Midrasch* = Adolph Jellinek. *Bet Ha-Midrasch*. Jerusalem 1938 [Hebrew]

Josephus, *Jewish antiquities* = Henry St. John Thackeray (trans.), *Josephus in Nine Volumes*. IV: *Jewish antiquities*, books I-IV. Repr. London 1978.

Jubilees = VanderKam, *Jubilees*.

Kaegi, *Byzantium* = Walter E. Kaegi, *Byzantium and the Early Islamic Conquests*, Cambridge 1992.
Kaegi, *Heraclius* = Walter E. Kaegi, *Heraclius: Emperor of Byzantium*, Cambridge 2003.
Kalimi, "The Land of Moriah" = Isaac Kalimi, "The Land of Moriah, Mount Moriah, and the Site of Solomon's Temple in Biblical Historiography", *Harvard Theological Review* 83 (1990), pp. 345–362.
Kessler, "'Abd al-Malik's Inscription" = Christel Kessler, "'Abd al-Malik's Inscription in the Dome of the Rock: A Reconsideration", *Journal of the Royal Asiatic Society* 1 (1970), pp. 2–14.
Khargūshī, *Sharaf al-Muṣṭafā* = al-Khargūshī, Abū Saʿd ʿAbd al-Malik b. Abī ʿUthmān. *Sharaf al-Muṣṭafā*. Ed. Nabīl al-Ghamrī. 6 vols. Mecca: Dār al-Bashā'ir al-Islāmiyya, 2003.
Khaṭīb al-Baghdādī, *Taʾrīkh Baghdād* = Al-Khaṭīb al-Baghdādī, Aḥmad b. ʿAlī. *Taʾrīkh Baghdād*. Ed. Muḥammad Saʿīd al-ʿUrfī and Muḥammad Ḥāmid al-Fiqī. 14 vols. Cairo *ca.* 1932, repr. Beirut n.d.
Kister, "A Comment on the Antiquity" = Meir J. Kister, "A Comment on the Antiquity of Traditions Praising Jerusalem", *The Jerusalem Cathedra* 1981, Jerusalem: Yad Itzhak Ben Zvi, 1981, pp. 185–186.
Kister, "Al-Ḥīra" = Meir J. Kister, "Al-Ḥīra: Some Notes on its Relations with Arabia", *Arabica* 15 (1968), pp. 143–169.
Kister, "Maqām Ibrāhīm" = Meir J. Kister, "Maqām Ibrāhīm: A stone with an Inscription", *Le Muséon* 84 (1971), pp. 477–491.
Kister, "Mecca and Tamīm" = Meir J. Kister, "Mecca and Tamīm", *Journal of the Economic and Social History of the Orient* 8 (1965), pp. 113–63.
Kister, "On a Monotheistic Aspect" = Meir J. Kister, "On a Monotheistic Aspect of a Jāhiliyya Practice", *Jerusalem Studies in Arabic and Islam* 2 (1980), pp. 33–58.
Kister, "Sanctity Joint and Divided" = Meir J. Kister, "Sanctity Joint and Divided: On Holy Places in the Islamic Tradition", *Jerusalem Studies in Arabic and Islam* 20 (1996), pp. 18–65.
Kister, "Three Mosques" = Meir J. Kister, "'You Shall Only Set Out for Three Mosques': a Study of an Early Tradition", *Le Muséon* 82 (1969), pp. 173–196.
Landau-Tasseron, "Ḥadīth" = Ella Landau–Tasseron, "Ḥadīth", in Meir M. Bar-Asher and Meir Hatina (eds.), *Islam: History, Religion, Culture*, Jerusalem 2017, pp. 191–219. [Hebrew]
Lassner, *Medieval Jerusalem* = Jacob Lassner, *Medieval Jerusalem: Forgoing an Islamic City in spaces Sacred to Christians and Jews*, Ann Arbor 2017.
Lazarus-Yafeh, *Intertwined Worlds* = Hava Lazarus-Yafeh, *Intertwined Worlds: Medieval Islam and Bible Criticism*, Princeton 1992.
Lazarus-Yafe, "Jerusalem and Mecca" = Hava Lazarus-Yafe, "Jerusalem and Mecca", *Judaism* 46 (1997), pp. 197–205.
Lecker, "Abū Mālik" = Michael Lecker, "Abū Mālik ʿAbdallāh b. Sām of Kinda: A Jewish Convert to Islam", *Der Islam* 71 (1994), pp. 280–282.
Lecker, "Ghassānids and Byzantines" = Michael Lecker, "Were the Ghassānids and the Byzantines behind Muḥammad's Hijra?", in Denis Genequand and Christian Robin (eds.), *Les Jafnides, des rois arabes au service de Byzance* (VIe siècle de l'ère chrétienne), Paris 2015, pp. 268–286.
Lecker, *Muḥammad and the Jews* = Michael Lecker, *Muḥammad and the Jews*. Jerusalem 2014. [Hebrew]
Lecker, "The Exilarch's Dams" = Michael Lecker, "The Exilarch's Dams", In Elinoar Bareket, Yoram Erder, Meira Polliack, (eds.), *Yad Moshe: Studies in the History of the Jews in Muslim Lands in Memory of Moshe Gil* [Teʿuda XXIX 2018], pp. 15–26. [Hebrew]
Lecker, "The Ḥudaybiyya Treaty" = Michael Lecker, "The Ḥudaybiyya Treaty and the Expedition against Khaybar", *Jerusalem Studies in Arabic and Islam* 5 (1984), pp. 1–12. [repr. in *idem*, *Jews and Arabs in Pre- and Early Islamic Arabia*, Variorum Collected Studies Series, Aldershot, 1998, XI]

Lecker, "Zayd b. ʿAmr" = Michael Lecker, "Zayd b. ʿAmr", in: *Encyclopaedia of Islam, Second Edition*, Edited by: P. Bearman, Th. Bianquis, C.E. Bosworth, E. van Donzel, W.P. Heinrichs. Consulted online on 24 January 2021. http://dx.doi.org/10.1163/1573-3912_islam_SIM_8138

Lecker, "Zuhrī" = Michael Lecker, "Biographical Notes on Ibn Shihāb al-Zuhrī", *Journal of Semitic Studies* 41 (1996), pp. 21–63.

Leder, "Attitude" = Stefan Leder, "The Attitude of the Population, Especially the Jews, towards the Arab-Islamic Conquest of Bilād al-Shām and the Question of their Role therein", *Die Welt des Orients* 18 (1987), pp. 64–71.

Leemhuis, "Apocalypse" = Frederik Leemhuis, "Apocalypse", *Encyclopaedia of the Qurʾān*. Consulted online on 15.01.21. http://dx.doi.org/10.1163/1875-3922_q3_EQCOM_00014

Levy-Rubin, "The Dome of the Rock" = Milka Levy-Rubin, "Why was the Dome of the Rock Built? A New Perspective on a Long-discussed Question", *Bulletin of the School of Oriental and African Studies* 80 (2017), pp. 441–464.

Lewis, "Apocalyptic Vision" = Bernard Lewis, "An Apocalyptic Vision of Islamic History", *Bulletin of the School of Oriental and African Studies* 13 (1950), pp. 308–338.

Lewis, "Palestine" = Bernard Lewis, "Palestine: On the History and Geography of a Name", *The International History Review* 2/1 (1980), pp. 1–12.

Licht, *Apocalypse of Ezra* = Jacob Licht, *The Apocalypse of Ezra: Translation, Annotation and Introduction*. Jerusalem 1968. [Hebrew]

Livne-Kafri, "A Note on Some Traditions" = Ofer Livne-Kafri, "A Note on Some Traditions of *Faḍāʾil al-Quds*", *Jerusalem Studies in Arabic and Islam* 14 (1991), pp. 71–83.

Livne-Kafri, "Christian Attitudes" = Ofer Livne-Kafri, "Christian Attitudes Reflected in the Muslim Literature in Praise of Jerusalem", *Proche-Orient Chrétien* 54 (2004). pp. 347–375.

Livne-Kafri, "In Praise of Jerusalem" = Ofer Livne-Kafri, "The Muslim Traditions in Praise of Jerusalem (*faḍāʾil al-Quds*): Diversity and Complexity", *Annali* 58 (1998), pp. 165–192.

Livne-Kafri, "Jerusalem in Early Islam" = Ofer Livne-Kafri, "Jerusalem in Early Islam: The Eschatological Aspect", *Arabica* 53 (2006), pp. 382–403.

Livne-Kafri, "The Navel of the Earth" = Ofer Livne-Kafri, "Jerusalem: The Navel of the Earth in Muslim Tradition", *Der Islam* 84/1 (2007), pp. 46–72.

Livne-Kafri, *Selected Essays* = Ofer Livne-Kafri, *Jerusalem in Early Islam: Selected Essays*, Jerusalem 2000. [Hebrew]

Mandel, "'Birah'" = Pinchas Mandel, "'Birah' as an Architectural Term in Rabbinic Literature", *Tarbiz* 61 (1992), pp. 195–217. [Hebrew]

Maqdisī, *Muthīr al-gharām* = al-Maqdisī, Shihāb al-Dīn. *Muthīr al-gharām ilā ziyārat al-Quds wa-l-Shām*. Ed. Aḥmad al-Khaṭīmī, Beirut: Dār al-Jīl, 1994.

Masʿūdī, *Murūj* = al-Masʿūdī, ʿAlī b. al-Ḥusayn. *Murūj al-dhahab*. Ed, M. M. ʿAbd al-Ḥamīd. 4 vols. Cairo 1965.

Māwardī, *Nukat* = al-Māwardī, ʿAlī b. Muḥammad. *Al-Nukat wa-l-ʿuyūn fī tafsīr al-Qurʾān*. Ed. ʿAbd al-Maqṣūd b. ʿAbd al-Raḥīm. 6 vols. Beirut: Dār al-Kutub al-ʿIlmiyya, 1992.

Midrash Rabbah = Midrash Rabba. Translated into English with Notes, Glossary and Indices under the Editorship of H. Freedman and Maurice Simon, London 1939.

Midrash Tanḥuma (Warsaw) = Midrash Tanḥuma, Warsaw 1875.

Midrash Tanḥuma (Buber) = Midrash Tanḥuma. Ed. S. Buber, Wilna 1885.

Midrash Zuta = Salomon Buber (ed.), *Midrash Zuta on Song of Solomon, the Book of Ruth, Lamentations, and Ecclesiastes*, Wilna 1921. [Hebrew]

Milwright, *The Dome of the Rock* = Marcus Milwright, *The Dome of the Rock and its Umayyad Mosaic Inscriptions*, Edinburgh: Edinburgh University Press, 2016.

Minhājī, *Ithāf al-akhiṣṣā* = al-Minhājī, Abū ʿAbdallāh Muḥammad b. Shihāb al-Dīn. *Ithāf al-akhiṣṣā bi-faḍāʾil al-masjid al-aqṣā*. Ed. Aḥmad Ramaḍān Aḥmad. 2 vols. Cairo 1982.

Minor Tractates = *The Minor Tractates of the Talmud (Massektoth Ḳeṭanoth)*, Translated into English with Notes, Glossary and Indices under the Editorship of A. Cohen. 2 vols. London 1971.

Mubārakfūrī, *Tuḥfat al-aḥwadhī* = al-Mubārakfūrī, ʿAbd al-Raḥmān, *Tuḥfat al-aḥwadhī sharḥ Jāmiʿ al-Tirmidhī*. Ed. ʿAbd al-Raḥmān Muḥammad ʿUthmān. 10 vols. Cairo: Dār al-Fikr, 1979.

Muḥibb al-Dīn, *Qirā* = Muḥibb al-Dīn al-Ṭabarī, *al-Qirā li-qāṣid Umm al-Qurā*. Ed. Muṣṭafā al-Saqqā. Cairo 1970.

Mujāhid, *Tafsīr* = Mujāhid b. Jabr. *Al-Tafsīr*. Ed. ʿAbd al-Raḥmān al-Sūratī. 2 vols. Beirut: al-Manshūrāt al-ʿIlmiyya, n.d.

Mujīr al-Dīn, *al-Uns al-jalīl* = Mujīr al-Dīn al-Ḥanbalī. *Al-Uns al-jalīl bi-Taʾrīkh al-Quds wa-l-Khalīl*. 2 vols. Beirut 1973.

Muqātil, *Addendum* = Muqātil b. Sulaymān, *Addendum to the tafsīr on Q 17: 1*, in Muqātil, *Tafsīr*, II, pp. 51–515 (editor's note).

Muqātil, *Tafsīr* = Muqātil b. Sulaymān, *Tafsīr al-Qurʾān*. Ed. ʿAbdallāh Maḥmūd Shiḥāta. 5 vols. Cairo: al-Hayʾa l-Miṣriyya al-ʿĀmma li-l-Kitāb, 1979.

Muslim, *Ṣaḥīḥ* = Muslim b. al-Ḥajjāj. *Al-Ṣaḥīḥ*. 8 vols. Cairo: Maktabat Muḥammad ʿAlī Ṣubayḥ n.d.

Myers, *The Ituraeans* = E.A. Myers, *The Ituraeans and the Roman Near East: Reassessing the Sources*, Cambridge 2010.

Nasāʾī, *Sunan* = al-Nasāʾī, Aḥmad b. Shuʿayb. *Al-Sunan al-ṣughrā*. Ed. ʿAbd al-Fattāḥ Abū Ghudda. Aleppo 1986.

Neuwirth, *Der Koran als Text* = Angelica Neuwirth, *Der Koran als Text der Spätantike: Ein Europäischer Zugang*, Berlin 2010.

Newman, "Dating Sefer Zerubavel" = Hillel Newman, "Dating Sefer Zerubavel: Dehistoricizing and Rehistoricizing a Jewish Apocalypse of Late Antiquity", *Adamantius* 19 (2013), pp. 324–336.

Newman, "Methodological and Historical Criticism" = Hillel Newman, "*Midrashei Geula* by Yehuda Even-Shmuel: Methodological and Historical Criticism", in Yehuda Even-Shmuel, *Midrashei Geula* (Jerusalem 2017), pp. lii-xciv. [Hebrew]

Nöldeke – Schwally, *Geschichte des Qorans* = Theodor Nöldeke, *Geschichte des Qorans*, zweite Auflage, bearbeitet von F. Schwally, Hildesheim–New York 1970.

Nuʿaym b. Ḥammād, *Fitan* = Nuʿaym b. Ḥammād. *Kitāb al-fitan*. Ed. Majdī b. Manṣūr b. Sayyid al-Shūrā. Beirut: Dār al-Kutub al-ʿIlmiyya, 1997.

Oppenheimer/Lecker, "Boundaries of Babylonia" = Aharon Oppenheimer and M. Lecker, "Lineage Boundaries of Babylonia", *Zion* – Jubilee Volume (1935–1985), pp. 173–187. [Hebrew]

Paret, *Der Koran: Kommentar und Konkordanz* = Rudi Paret, *Der Koran: Kommentar und Konkordanz*, Stuttgart: Verlag W. Kohlhammer, 1971.

Peshiṭta (Deuteronomy) = *The Syriac Peshiṭta Bible with English Translation*. Deuteronomy. Translation by Carmel McCarthy; text prepared by George A. Kiraz, Joseph Bali, NJ, 2013.

Pesikta Rabbati = William G. Braude (trans.), *Pesikta Rabbati; Discourses for Feasts, Fasts, and Special Sabbaths*. 2 vols. New Haven and London 1968.

Peters, *Jerusalem and Mecca* = Francis E. Peters, *Jerusalem and Mecca: The Typology of the Holy City in the Near East*, New York 1986.

Qummī, *Tafsīr* = ʿAlī b. Ibrāhīm al-Qummī, *al-Tafsīr*. 2 vols. Beirut: Muʾassasat al-Aʿlā li-l-Maṭbūʿāt, 1991.

Qurṭubī, *Aḥkām al-Qurʾān* = Muḥammad b. Aḥmad al-Qurṭubī, *al-Jāmiʿ li-aḥkām al-Qurʾān*. 20 vols. Cairo: Dār al-Kātib al-ʿArabī, 1967.

Rāzī, *Tafsīr* = Fakhr al-Dīn Abū ʿAbdallāh Muḥammad b. ʿUmar al-Rāzī, *al-Tafsīr al-kabīr*. 32 vols. Tehran: Dār al-Kutub al-ʿIlmiyya, n.d.

Reeves, "Jewish Apocalyptic" = John C. Reeves, "Jewish Apocalyptic Lore in Early Islam: Reconsidering the Figure of Kaʿb al-Aḥbār", in John Ashton (ed.), *Revealed Wisdom: Studies in Apocalyptic in Honour of Christopher Rowland*, Leiden: Brill, 2014, pp. 200–216.

Reeves, "Sefer Zerubbabel" = John C. Reeves, "Sefer Zerubbabel: The Prophetic Vision of Zerubbabel ben Shealtiel", in Richard Bauckham, James R. Davila, and Alexander Panayotov, (eds.), *Old Testament Pseudepigrapha: More Noncanonical Scriptures*, Volume 1, Grand Rapids, Mich.: William B. Eerdmans, 2013, pp. 448–466.

Reeves, *Trajectories* = John C. Reeves (ed.), *Trajectories in Near Eastern Apocalyptic: A Postrabbinic Jewish Apocalypse Reader*, Leiden: Brill, 2006.

Reiter, *From Jerusalem to Mecca* = Yitzhak Reiter. *From Jerusalem to Mecca and Back: The Islamic Consolidation of Jerusalem*. Jerusalem 2005. [Hebrew].

Reiter, "The Third in Sanctity" = Yitzhak Reiter, "The Third in Sanctity, the First in Politics: al-Ḥaram al-Sharīf in the Eyes of the Muslims", in Yitzhak Reiter (ed.), *Sovereignty of God and Man: Sanctity and Political Centrality on the Temple Mount*, Jerusalem 2001, pp. 155–179. [Hebrew]

Reynolds, "Noah's Lost Son" = Gabriel Said Reynolds, "Noah's Lost Son in the Qurʾān", *Arabica* 64 (2017), pp. 129–148.

Robinson, Ch., *Abd al-Malik* = Chase F. Robinson, *Abd al-Malik*, Oxford: Oneworld, 2005.

Robinson, "Antichrist" = Neal Robinson, "Antichrist", *Encyclopaedia of the Qurʾān*. Consulted online on 15.01.21. http://dx.doi.org/10.1163/1875-3922_q3_EQCOM_00013

Robinson, *Discovering the Qurʾān* = Neal Robinson, *Discovering the Qurʾān: A Contemporary Approach to a Veiled Text*, Second Edition, Washington: Georgetown University Press, 2003.

Rubin Z., "History of Jerusalem" = Zeev Rubin, "History of Jerusalem in the Byzantine Period", in Eli Schiller (ed.), *History of Jerusalem from the Destruction of the Second Temple to the Uthmanic Period*, Jerusalem [*Ariel* 83–84] 1992, pp. 15–44. [Hebrew]

Rubin, *Between Bible and Qur'an* = Uri Rubin, *Between Bible and Qur'an: The Children of Israel and the Islamic Self-Image*, Princeton: The Darwin Press, 1999.

Rubin, "Between Arabia and the Holy Land" = Uri Rubin, "Between Arabia and the Holy Land: A Mecca-Jerusalem Axis of Sanctity", *Jerusalem Studies in Arabic and Islam* 34 (2008), pp. 345–362.

Rubin, "Children of Israel" = Uri Rubin, "Children of Israel", in: *Encyclopaedia of Islam, THREE*. Consulted online on 15.01.21. http://dx.doi.org/10.1163/1573-3912_ei3_COM_24398

Rubin, "Ḥanīfiyya and Kaʿba" = Uri Rubin, "Ḥanīfiyya and Kaʿba: An Inquiry into the Arabian Pre-Islamic Background of Dīn Ibrāhīm", *Jerusalem Studies in Arabic and Islam* 13 (1990), pp. 85–112.

Rubin, *Muḥammad the Prophet* = Uri Rubin, *Muḥammad the Prophet in the Early Literature of Ḥadīth*. Thesis submitted for the degree "Doctor of Philosophy", Tel Aviv University, Tel Aviv 1976. [Hebrew]

Rubin, *The Eye of the Beholder* = Uri Rubin, *The Eye of the Beholder: The Life of Muḥammad as Viewed by the Early Muslims* (a Textual Analysis), Princeton: The Darwin Press, 1995.

Rubin, "Muḥammad's Night Journey" = Uri Rubin, "Muḥammad's Night Journey (*isrāʾ*) to al-Masjid al-Aqsa: Aspects of the Earliest Origins of the Islamic Sanctity of Jerusalem", *al-Qantara* 29 (2008), pp. 147–165.

Rubin, "Prophets and Caliphs" = Uri Rubin, "Prophets and Caliphs: The Biblical Foundations of the Umayyad Authority", Herbert Berg (ed.), *Method and Theology in the Study of Islamic Origins*, Leiden 2003, pp. 88–93.

Rubin, "The Direction of Prayer" = Uri Rubin, "The Direction of Prayer in Islam: On the History of a Conflict Between Rituals", *Historia: Journal of the Historical Society of Israel* 6 (2000), pp. 5–29. [Hebrew]

Rubin, "The Īlāf of Quraysh" = Uri Rubin, "The Īlāf of Quraysh: A Study of *Sūra* CVI", *Arabica* 31 (1984), pp. 165–188.

Rubin, "The Kaʿba" = Uri Rubin, "The Kaʿba: Aspects of its Ritual Functions", *Jerusalem Studies in Arabic and Islam* 8 (1986), pp. 97–131.
Rubin, "The Promised Land" = Uri Rubin, "The Promised Land and the End of Days in the Qurʾān and the Early Muslim Tradition", In Elinoar Bareket, Yoram Erder, Meira Polliack, (eds.), *Yad Moshe: Studies in the History of the Jews in Muslim Lands in Memory of Moshe Gil* [Teʿuda XXIX 2018], pp. 329–351. [Hebrew]
Sadan, "The Tomb of Moses" = Yosef Sadan, "The Tomb of Moses (*Maqām Nabī Mūsā*): Rivalry between Religions as to their Respective Holy Places", *Hamizrah Hehadash* 28 (1979), pp. 22–38. [Hebrew]
Ṣadūq, *ʿIlal* = al-Shaykh al-Ṣadūq Abū Jaʿfar Muḥammad b. ʿAlī b. al-Ḥusayn b. Bābawayhi al-Qummī, *ʿIlal al-sharāʾiʿ*, Najaf 1385/1966.
Safrai, "Jerusalem and the Jews" = Shmuel Safrai, "Jerusalem and the Jews from Constantine to the Muslim Conquest"., in Yoram Tsafrir and Shmuel Safrai (eds.), *The History of Jerusalem: The Roman and Byzantine Periods (70-638 CE)*, Jerusalem 1999, pp. 251–258. [Hebrew]
Samarqandī, *Tafsīr* = Abū l-Layth Naṣr b. Muḥammad al-Samarqandī, *Tafsīr al-Qurʾān*. Ed. ʿAlī Muʿawwaḍ, ʿĀdil ʿAbd al-Mawjūd, and Zakariyyā al-Nawtī. 3 vols. Beirut: Dār al-Kutub al-ʿIlmiyya, 1993.
Samhūdī, *Wafāʾ* = al-Samhūdī, Nūr al-Dīn ʿAlī b. Aḥmad. *Wafāʾ al-wafā bi-akhbār dār al-Muṣṭafā*. Ed. Muḥammad Muḥyī l-Dīn ʿAbd al-Ḥamīd, Beirut 1984.
Sasson, *A King and Layman* = Gilad Sasson, *A King and Layman: The Sages' Attitude towards King Solomon*, Tel Aviv 2013. [Hebrew]
Schussman, "Abraham's Visits" = Aviva Schussman, "Abraham's Visits to Ishmael: The Jewish Origin and Orientation", *Tarbiz* 49 (1980), pp. 325–345. [Hebrew]
Schwarzbaum, *Folkloristic Aspects* = Haim Schwarzbaum, *The Folkloristic Aspects of Judaism and Islam*, Tel Aviv 1975. [Hebrew]
Shāfiʿī, *Umm* = Muḥammad b. Idrīs al-Shāfiʿī, *al-Umm*. 8 vols. Beirut: Dār al-Maʿrifa, 1990.
Sharon, "Shape of the Holy"= Moshe Sharon, "Shape of the Holy", *Studia Orientalia* 107 (2009), pp. 283–310.
Sharon, "The Cities of the Holy Land" = Moshe Sharon, "The Cities of the Holy Land under Islamic Rule", *Cathedra* 40 (1986), pp. 83–120. [Hebrew]
Sharon, "The Praises of Jerusalem" = Moshe Sharon, "'The Praises of Jerusalem' as a Source for the Early History of Islam", *Bibliotheca Orientalis* 49 (1992), pp. 56–67.
Shnizer, "The Figure of Muḥammad" = Aliza Shnizer, "The Figure of Muḥammad and Key Events of his Biography", in Meir M. Bar-Asher and Meir Hatina (eds.), *Islam: History, Religion, Culture* (Jerusalem 2017), pp. 30–56. [Hebrew]
Shnizer, *The Qurʾān* = Aliza Shnizer. *The Qurʾān: Aspects of its Sacredness according to Early Islamic Tradition*. Thesis submitted for the degree "Doctor of Philosophy", Tel Aviv University, Tel Aviv 2003. [Hebrew]
Shoemaker, "The Reign of God" = Stephen J. Shoemaker, "'The Reign of God Has Come': Eschatology and Empire in Late Antiquity and Early Islam", *Arabica* 61 (2014), pp. 514–558.
Silverstein, "Hāmān" = Adam Silverstein, "Hāmān's transition from the Jāhiliyya to Islam", *Jerusalem Studies in Arabic and Islam* 34 (2008), pp. 285–308.
Sinai, *Fortschreibung* = Nicolai Sinai, *Fortschreibung und Auslegung: Studien zur frühen Koraninterpretation*, Wiesbaden 2009.

Sinai, "Inheriting Egypt" = Nicolai Sinai, "Inheriting Egypt: The Israelites and the Exodus in the Meccan Qur'ān", in Majid Daneshgar and Walid A. Salih (eds.), *Islamic Studies Today: Essays in Honor of Andrew Rippin*, Leiden–Boston 2017, pp. 198–214.

Sivan H., "From Byzantine to Persian Jerusalem" = Hagith Sivan, "From Byzantine to Persian Jerusalem: Jewish Perspectives and Jewish/Christian Polemic", *Greek Roman and Byzantine Studies* 41 (2000), pp. 277–306.

Sivan, "*Faḍā'il al-Quds*" = Emanuel Sivan, "The Beginnings of the *Faḍā'il al-Quds* Literature", *Israel Oriental Studies* 1 (1971), pp. 263–271.

Sivan, *Political Myths* = Emanuel Sivan, *Arab Political Myths*. Tel Aviv 1988. [Hebrew]

Smith, "Eschatology"= Jane I. Smith, "Eschatology", *Encyclopaedia of the Qur'ān*. Consulted online on 15.01.21. https://referenceworks.brillonline.com/entries/encyclopaedia-of-the-quran/eschatology-EQCOM_00055?s.num=0&s.f.s2_parent=s.f.book.encyclopaedia-of-the-quran&s.q=eschatology

Sozomen, *Ecclesiastical History* = *The Ecclesiastical History of Sozomen*. Translated from the Greek by Eduard Walford, London 1855.

Speyer, *Die biblischen Erzählungen* = Heinrich Speyer, *Die biblischen Erzählungen im Qoran*, Hildesheim/New York City/Zürich: Georg Olms Verlag, reprint Hildesheim 2013.

Stemberger, "Jerusalem in the Early Seventh Century" = Günter Stemberger, "Jerusalem in the Early Seventh Century: Hopes and Aspirations of Christians and Jews", in Lee I. Levine (ed.), *Jerusalem: Its Sanctity and Centrality to Judaism, Christianity, and Islam*, New York 1999, pp. 260–272.

Suhaylī, *al-Rawḍ al-unuf* = ʿAbd al-Raḥmān b. ʿAbdallāh al-Suhaylī, *al-Rawḍ al-unuf*. Ed. ʿAbd al-Ra'ūf Saʿd. 4 vols. Cairo 1971.

Suyūṭī, *al-Durr al-manthūr* = Jalāl al-Dīn al-Suyūṭī, *'al-Durr al-manthūr fī l-tafsīr bi-l-ma'thūr*. 6 vols. Cairo: Būlāq, 1869, repr. Beirut: Dār al-Maʿrifa, n.d.

Suyūṭī, *La'āli'* = Jalāl al-Dīn al-Suyūṭī, *al-la'āli'al-maṣnūʿa fī l-aḥādīth al-mawḍūʿa*. 2 vols. Cairo 1933.

Ṭabarī, *Tafsīr* = Muḥammad b. Jarīr al-Ṭabarī, *Jāmiʿ al-bayān fī tafsīr al-Qur'ān*. 30 vols. Cairo: Būlāq, 1323/1905, repr. Beirut 1972.

Ṭabarī, *Ta'rīkh* = Muḥammad b. Jarīr al-Ṭabarī, *Ta'rīkh al-rusul wa-l-mulūk*. Ed. Muḥammad Abū l-Faḍl Ibrāhīm. 10 vols. Repr. Cairo 1987 Ed. M.J. De Goeje *et al.* 15 vols. Leiden 1879–1901.

Ṭabrisī, *Majmaʿ al-bayān* = al-Faḍl b. al-Ḥasan al-Ṭabrisī, *Majmaʿ al-bayān fī tafsīr al-Qur'ān*. 30 vols. Beirut: Dār al-Fikr, 1957.

Talmud Bavli = Halakhah.com by Tzvee Zahavy: *Full Text of the English Babylonian Talmud*. Consulted online on 15.01.21. http://halakhah.com/

Talmud Yerushalmi = *The Jerusalem Talmud*: Edition, Translation, and Commentary by Heinrich W. Guggenheimer. Berlin/New York: de Gruyter: 1999–2001.

Targum Pseudo-Jonathan = J. W. Etheridge, *The Targums of Onkelos and Jonathan ben Uzziel on the Pentateuch*. New York 1968.

Tesei, "Cosmological Notions" = Tommaso Tesei, "Some Cosmological Notions from Late Antiquity in Q 18: 60–65:The Quran in Light of Its Cultural Context", *Journal of the American Oriental Society* 135 (2015), pp. 19–32.

Testament of Levi = "Testaments of the Twelve Patriarchs: A New Translation and Introduction by H.C. Kee – Testament of Levi", in James H. Charlesworth (ed.), *The Old Testament Pseudepigrapha*, London 1983, I, pp. 788–795.

Testament of Moses = "Testament of Moses: A new Translation and Introduction by J. Priest", in James H. Charlesworth (ed.), *The Old Testament Pseudepigrapha*, London 1983, I, pp. 919–934.

Testament of Solomon = "Testament of Solomon: A New Translation and Introduction by D. C. Duling", in James H. Charlesworth (ed.), *The Old Testament Pseudepigrapha*, London 1983, I, pp. 935–987.

Thaʿlabī, *al-Kashf wa-l-bayān* = Abū Isḥāq Aḥmad b. Muḥammad al-Thaʿlabī, *al-Kashf wa-l-bayān ʿan tafsīr āy al-Qurʾān*. Ed. Abū Muḥammad b. ʿĀshūr and Naẓīr al-Sāʿidī. 10 vols. Beirut: Dār Iḥyāʾ al-Turāth al-ʿArabī, 2002.

Tsafrir, "The Provinces in Palestine" = Yoram Tsafrir, "The Provinces in Palestine: Names, Borders and Administrative Districts", in Zvi Baras and others (eds.), *Eretz Israel: From the Destruction of the Second Temple to the Muslim Conquest*, Vol. 1 Jerusalem 1982, pp. 350–386. [Hebrew]

Ulmer, *Pesiqta Rabbati* = Rivka Ulmer, *Pesiqta Rabbati: A Synoptic Edition of Pesiqta Rabbati Based upon All Extant Hebrew Manuscripts and the Editio Princeps*. 3 vols. Atlanta 1997–2002.

van Ess, "ʿAbd al-Malik and the Dome of the Rock" = Josef Van Ess, "ʿAbd al-Malik and the Dome of the Rock: An Analysis of Some Texts", in Julian Raby and Jeremy Johns, (eds.), *Bayt al-Maqdis: ʿAbd al-Malik's Jerusalem*, Vol. I, Oxford: Oxford University Press, 1992, pp. 89–103.

van Ess, "Vision and Ascension" = Josef van Ess, "Vision and Ascension: *Sūrat al-Najm* and its Relationship with Muḥammad's *miʿrāj*", *Journal of Qurʾanic Studies* 1 (1999), 47–62.

van Ruiten, "Abraham's Last Day" = Jacques van Ruiten, "Abraham's Last Day According to the *Book of Jubilees* (Jub. 22: 1–23:8)", in *Rewritten Biblical Figures*, ed. Erkki Koskenniemi and Pekka Lindqvist; Studies in Rewritten Bible 3; Vinona Lake, 2010, pp. 57–88.

VanderKam, *Jubilees* = James C. VanderKam, *Jubilees: A Commentary on the Book of Jubilees*. Edited by Sidnie White Crawford, Minneapolis 2018.

Wāḥidī, *Wasīṭ* = al-Wāḥidī, ʿAlī b. Aḥmad. *Al-Wasīṭ fī tafsīr al-Qurʾān al-majīd*. Ed. ʿĀdil Aḥmad ʿAbd al-Mawjūd *et al.* 4 vols. Beirut: Dār al-Kutub al-ʿIlmiyya, 1994.

Wansbrough, *Quranic Studies* = John Wansbrough, *Quranic Studies*, Oxford 1977.

Wāqidī, *Futūḥ al-Shām* = al-Wāqidī (Ps.-). *Futūḥ al-Shām*. Cairo 1949, repr. Beirut n.d.

Wāqidī, *Maghāzī* = al-Wāqidī, Muḥammad b. ʿUmar. *Kitāb al-maghāzī*. Ed. Marsden Jones. 3 vols. London: Oxford University Press, 1966.

Wāsiṭī, *Faḍāʾil* = al-Wāsiṭī, Muḥammad b. Aḥmad. *Faḍāʾil al-bayt al-muqaddas*. Ed. Isaac Hasson. Jerusalem: Institute of Asian and African Studies, 1979.

Wensinck, *The Navel of the Earth* = Arent Jan Wensinck, *The Ideas of the Western Semites Concerning the Navel of the Earth* (*Verhandelingen der Koninlijke Akademie van Wetenschappen te Amsterdam*, Afdeeling Letterkunde, Nieuwe Reeks 17 n.1), Amsterdam 1917.

Werman, *Jubilees* = Cana Werman, *The Book of Jubilees: Introduction, Translation, and Interpretation*. Jerusalem 2015. [Hebrew]

Wertheimer, *Batei Midrashos* = Solomon Aaron, and Abraham Joseph, Wertheimer (eds.). *Batei Midrashos*, Jerusalem 1955. [Hebrew]

Whelan, "Forgotten Witness" = Estelle Whelan, "Forgotten Witness: Evidence for the Early Codification of the Qurʾān", *Journal of the American Oriental Society* 118 (1998), pp. 1–14.

Witztum, "The Foundations of the House" = Joseph Witztum, "The Foundations of the House (Q 2: 127)", *Bulletin of the School of Oriental and African Studies* 72 (2009), pp. 25–40.

Witztum, "The Qurʾān and Qurʾānic Research" = Joseph Witztum. "The Qurʾān and Qurʾānic Research", in Meir M. Bar-Asher and Meir Hatina (eds.), *Islam: History, Religion, Culture*, Jerusalem 2017, pp. 135–167. [Hebrew]

Yaʿqūbī, *Taʾrīkh* = al-Yaʿqūbī, Aḥmad b. Abī Yaʿqūb. *Al-Taʾrīkh*. 2 vols. Beirut: Dār Ṣādir, 1960.

Yāqūt, *Muʿjam al-buldān* = Yāqūt al-Ḥamawī. *Muʿjam al-buldān*. 5 vols. Beirut: Dār Ṣādir, 1957.

Yassif, *The Book of Memory* = Eli Yassif (ed.), *The Book of Memory, that is The Chronicles of Jerahme'el*, Tel Aviv 2001. [Hebrew]

Yūnus b. Bukayr, *al-Siyar wa-l-maghāzī* = *Kitāb al-siyar wa-l-maghāzī li-Muḥammad b. Isḥāq*. Ed. S. Zakkār, Damascus, Dār al-Fikr, 1978.

Zajjāj, *Maʿānī l-Qurʾān* = al-Zajjāj, Abū Isḥāq. *Maʿānī l-Qurʾān wa-iʿrābuhu*. Ed. ʿAbd al-Jalīl Shalabī. 5 vols. Beirut: ʿĀlam al-Kutub, 1988.

Zamakhsharī, *Kashshāf* = al-Zamakhsharī, Jārullāh Maḥmūd b. ʿUmar. *Al-Kashshāf ʿan ḥaqāʾiq al-tanzīl*. 4 vols. Cairo: Dār al-Fikr, 1977.

Zamakhsharī, *Rabīʿ al-abrār* = al-Zamakhsharī, Jārullāh Maḥmūd b. ʿUmar. *Rabīʿ al-abrār wa-nuṣūṣ al-akhyār*. Beirut 1992.

Index

ʿAbbāsids 6, 142, 145
ʿAbd al-Malik b. Marwān 10, 26, 33, 77, 80, 161–165, 192
ʿAbd al-Razzāq 70, 125
ʿAbdallāh b. ʿAbbās 56, 145
ʿAbdallāh b. Abī Ziyād 183
ʿAbdallāh b. al-Zubayr 26, 87, 143, 184, 192
ʿAbdallāh b. Masʿūd 75
ʿAbdallāh b. Salām 16, 106, 108, 196
ʿAbdallāh b. ʿUmar 89, 140
Abel 139, 144
Abū ʿAbdallāh (Jaʿfar al-Ṣādiq) 90
Abū ʿAlī al-Awaqī 199
Abū Bakr 88–89, 154
Abū Dharr 180
Abū Dāwūd 35
Abū Hurayra 34, 103, 152
Abū Jahl 196
Abū Mālik al-Quraẓī 76
Abū Saʿīd al-Khudrī 196
Abū Ṭālib 15, 23, 175
Abū ʿUbayd 194
–*Kitāb al-amwāl* 194
ʿĀd 150
Adam 3, 32, 91, 104, 139, 144, 148–149, 167, 178, 181–186
Adhriʿāt 204, 207
Aḥmad b. Ḥanbal 85, 193
ʿĀʾisha 31, 179
ʿAlī b. Abī Ṭālib 72, 74
ʿĀmir al-Shaʿbī 143, 213
Amoraim 18
Anas b. Mālik 22, 30
al-Aqṣā Mosque 150
Arberry, J. 8
Ashkelon (ʿAsqalān) 72–73, 87–88, 93, 108
Ashmedai 159
ʿAṭāʾ al-Khurāsānī 5
al-Azraqī 2, 31, 174

Balaam 166
Bāniqyā 87
Banū Salima (of the Khazraj) 88
Baqīʿ al-Gharqad 69, 86–89
Battles
– Battle of Ajnādayn 23
– Battle of Badr 95, 210, 213–214
– Battle of Tabūk 90, 217
– Battle of the Trench, al-Khandaq 209
– Battle of Uḥud 86–88
– Battle of Yarmūk 216–217
al-Bayt al-Maʿmūr 184
Bayt al-Maqdis 5, 9, 15–16, 22–23, 25–27, 29, 31–36, 55, 68–73, 77, 86, 90, 94, 102–104, 111–113
Bible, the Hebrew 40, 51, 66, 68, 99, 119, 130–131, 134, 147, 165 *see also* Torah, the
Black Stone, the 31–32, 91–92, 94, 153
Book of Zerubbabel 19, 47–51, 56, 66
al-Bukhārī 35, 85–86, 180–181
al-Burāq 22, 29, 35, 174
Busse, Heribert 1
Byzantium/Byzantines 18–20, 23–24, 29, 47, 57, 59, 99, 106, 108, 111, 166, 203–219, 223

Constantinople 29, 57–59, 113, 221
Cook, Michael 6
Crone, Patricia 6
Ctesiphon 2

al-Dajjāl/al-masīḥ al-dajjāl 56, 85, 113, 152
Damascus 72, 80, 93, 106–107
David 3, 157, 161–165, 167–168, 181
Day of Judgment, the 63, 72–73, 75–77, 79, 89, 91, 94–95, 210, 220
Day of Resurrection, the 52–53, 63, 68–69, 71, 73, 76–77, 79, 81–82, 84, 89, 91–95, 165, 208, 220
demons (*jinn*) 158–160, 167, 169, 220
devils 157–158
dispute
– with Christianity 114, 135, 209, 220
– with Judaism 114, 135, 173, 220
Drory, Joseph 1

Egypt 20–21, 36, 40, 43, 45, 50, 100, 105, 108, 111–112, 198, 205, 219–220
– Exodus from 20–21, 40, 100, 205, 219–220

https://doi.org/10.1515/9783111222318-019

Elad, Amikam 1–2
Esau 111, 134
Exilarch, the 72, 87
– son of 87
Ezekiel 17
Ezra the Scribe 53–56

Fakhr al-Dīn al-Rāzī 45, 173
al-Fākihī 31
fatḥ 209–212
– nigh *fatḥ* (*fatḥ qarīb*) 210–212
Feast of the Sacrifice 143, 147–148
Filasṭīn 8–9, 101, 106, 111
Flood, the 104, 139, 149–150, 184
Foundation Stone (Hebrew: *Even ha-Shtiyya*) 27, 178
al-Farazdaq 195–196
al-Fuḍayl b. ʿIyāḍ 199

Gabriel 22, 28–29, 77, 103, 151, 174, 181, 183, 191
Ghassān 216–217
Gil, Moshe 70
Gog and Magog 86
Goitein, S.D. 2, 5, 9

ḥadīth 3–4, 7–8, 35, 89, 180, 193, 199, 221–223
Hagar 119, 151, 183
Haggai 105
ḥajj 15, 16, 33, 35, 93, 124, 126, 150, 174, 176, 190, 192, 197, 211
Haman 42
ḥanīf 116, 145, 171, 197
ḥaram 91–93, 124, 162
al-Ḥasan [al-Baṣrī?] 70
ḥashr 69, 84, 88, 206–208
Hasson, Yitzhak 1–2, 27
Hebron 73, 103–104, 121, 127, 130, 134–135, 148, 169
Heraclius 204, 205, 214
Ḥijāz 1, 185, 217–218
hijra 6, 22, 26, 89, 101, 109–111, 154, 187, 196, 198, 210–211, 223
Homs (Ḥimṣ) 59, 72, 112
Hūd 150, 153, 167
Ḥudaybiyya 211–214
Ḥudhayfa b. al-Yamān 32

Ibn ʿAbbās 64, 90, 101, 124, 143, 150, 153, 176, 179, 184, 207
Ibn Abī Najīḥ 142
Ibn al-ʿArabī 207
Ibn ʿAsākir 104, 162
Ibn ʿAṭiyya 176, 182
Ibn Ḥajar al-ʿAsqalānī 36, 181
Ibn Hishām 15, 181, 196
Ibn Isḥāq 15, 23, 36, 148–150, 174, 182–183, 196, 217
Ibn al-Jawzī 86
Ibn Jurayj 143, 173
Ibn Qutayba 32
Ibn Saʿd 31, 162
Ibn Salām 17
Ibn Shabba 190
Ibn Shihāb al-Zuhrī 26
Ibn Taymiyya 104
Ibn al-Zubayr 29
Ibrāhīm b. Abī ʿAbla al-Maqdisī 69
idolaters 116, 129, 132, 203, 210
iḥrām 35
ʿIkrima 142, 207
Īliyāʾ 9, 13, 23–24, 174, 195
Isrāfīl 77–78
Ishmael/Ishmaelite 113–137, 140, 143, 145–148, 151, 163, 167, 170, 175–176, 178, 182–186, 197–198, 220–222

Jaʿfar al-Ṣādiq 90 *see also* Abū ʿAbdallāh
Jehoshafat 76
Jeremiah 168
Jerusalem-Mecca sanctity space 3–4, 8, 13, 16, 33–34, 83–87, 93, 138, 146–147, 150, 154, 174, 184–185, 187–199, 203
Jesus 4, 22, 29, 56, 70, 79, 81–82, 84–85, 89, 102, 105, 113, 115, 118, 151, 154, 162, 167
Jewish messianic vision 99, 101, 113, 205, 219, 222
Jewish vision of redemption 39, 63, 120, 157, 199, 219–221, 223
jihād 108, 111

John the Baptist 44, 167
Joseph 42, 100, 103–104
Josephus 146
Joshua 56
Jubayr b. Muṭʿim 185

Kaʿb al-Aḥbār 28, 34, 57, 59, 70–72, 77, 94, 102, 106–107, 112, 140, 147, 164, 181, 184, 193–195
al-Kalbī 54
al-Khargūshī 191
Khaybar 47, 207, 209, 211–212, 214
al-Khayf 33, 148, 150
Kister, M.J. 4–5, 215–216
Kitāb al-tījān 181
Koraḥ, congregation of 48–49, 51, 66
al-Kūfa 74, 87, 95, 180

lafīf 47, 51–52
Latin 54–55
Latter Days, the 20, 39–60, 63, 66, 68
Lewis, Bernard 166
Livne-Kafri, Ofer 1–2, 78
Lot 84, 99–100, 107, 110, 152–153

Mahdī, the 59–60
Malachi 105
Mālik b. Ṣaʿṣaʿa 35
Māmillā (Mamilla) 70
al-Marwa 90, 151
Mary 113, 168
al-Masjid al-Aqṣā 1, 9–10, 13–25, 32–33, 35, 40, 55, 85, 102, 168, 174, 179–182, 192–194, 198, 219
al-Masjid al-Ḥarām 13, 33, 174, 180, 188, 211
al-Māwardī 52
Maymūna 34, 73
Melchizedek 3, 181
Midrash Rabbah
- I, 346 (Genesis Rabbah 42:16) 19
- I, 491 (Genesis Rabbah 56:1) 122
- II,634 (Genesis Rabbah 69:7 78
- VIII, 55 (Ecclesiastes Rabbah 2:5) 158
- IX, 3 (The Song of Songs Rabbah 1:5) 159
Midrash Tanḥuma 141

miḥrāb 159, 167–168
Minā 15, 33, 143–145, 147–148, 150
al-Minhājī 69
Mishna 42
Moses 9, 21–22, 27, 39, 41, 43, 48, 50, 58, 79, 81, 99, 102, 106–107, 115, 118, 150–151, 171, 185, 194, 198, 205, 217
- Sons of 58
"Mother of Towns" (*umm al-qurā*) 178–179
Mount Abū Qubays 91, 148
Mount Ḥirāʾ 185
Mount al-Jūdī 184
Mount Lebanon 105, 184
Mount Moriah 122
Mount of Olives, the 29, 49, 66–70, 105–106, 184, 208
Mount Sinai 22, 85, 105, 107, 118, 184–185
Mount Thabīr 145
Muʿāwiya b. Abī Sufyān 74, 111, 166, 179
muhājir/muhājirūn 89, 92–93, 110
Muḥammad b. Kaʿb al-Quraẓī 162, 198
mujāhid/mujāhidūn 66, 69, 91, 101, 107
Mujāhid b. Jabr 144, 150, 175, 178, 184
Mujīr al-Dīn al-Ḥanbalī 69, 104
Muqātil b. Sulaymān 5, 23, 27, 33, 53–56, 64, 70, 75, 77–78, 86, 94, 110–111, 118, 141, 154, 179, 191, 193, 207

Banū al-Naḍīr 206–208
al-nāsikh wa-l-mansūkh 189
Nawf al-Bikālī 77
Nehemiah Ben Ḥushiel 19
Noah 104, 117, 139, 149, 167, 181, 184
- Noah's Ark 149, 184
Nuʿaym b. Ḥammād 57

Patriarchs, the Three 99–120
- Patriarchs, the Four (Abraham, Isaac, Jacob, and Ishmael) 114–120
- Cave of the Patriarchs (Hebrew: מערת המכפלה) 99, 102–104, 149
- Abraham/Abrahamic/Abram 3, 9, 21, 40, 84, 95, 99–104, 107, 111–153, 167–168, 170–178, 180–188, 195–198, 220, 222
- Abraham's covenant 116–118, 120

- *al-Khalīl* 99, 103, 195
- Maqām Ibrāhīm ("Abraham's standing place") 31–33, 91, 143, 146, 153, 158, 171, 173–177, 187, 196–197, 220
- Isaac 99–104, 114–115, 119–121, 123–125, 127, 130, 132, 138, 139, 140, 142, 144–146, 149, 163, 167, 220, 222
- Binding of 124–125, 130, 138, 142, 145
-Jacob 3, 58, 99–104, 114–115, 120–121, 127, 131–135, 140, 161– 163, 167–168, 170, 181, 220
Persia/Persians 18–19, 47, 203–219, 223
Pesikta Rabbati 67, 160
Pharaoh 21, 40–45, 50
Pirkei Mashiach 49
polemic with/against Judaism/the Jews 135, 170, 173, 177, 186, 220
Promised Land, the 20, 39, 56–57, 59, 72, 99, 101, 111–112, 119

Qatāda b. Di'āma 59, 65, 84–85, 107, 110, 149, 215
Qazwīn 93, 95
qibla 168, 181, 187–199, 221, 223
al-Quds 69, 193–194
Quraysh 16, 30, 132, 142, 189, 210–213, 223
Banū Qurayẓa 208–209
al-Qurṭubī 16, 181

Rābi'a bint Ismā'īl al-'Adawiyya 69
Rajā' b. Ḥaywa 194
Ramla 73, 153
Rebecca/Rebekah 127, 134
Reiter, Yitzhak 2–3
ribāṭ 73, 106–108, 111
Rome, Romans (al-Rūm) 18, 59, 111, 113, 203–219, 223 *see also* Byzantium/Byzantines

Sa'd b. Abī Waqqāṣ 92–93
al-Ṣafā 90, 151
Ṣafwān b. 'Amr 59
al-sāhira 63–66, 69, 90
Sa'īd b. Jubayr 141, 144
al-Ṣakhra 10, 23, 27, 76, 80, 104, 140, 178
Ṣāliḥ 150, 153, 167
al-Samarqandī 121
Sambaṭyon 56, 58, 221
sanctity patterns, transfer/transition/movement of 4, 84, 90, 95, 154, 170, 203, 219–223
Sarah 100, 103, 119, 149, 176
Ṣa'ṣa'a b. Ṣūḥān 74
Satan (Iblīs) 105, 161
Sde Boker inscription 78
shafā'a 81–82
shamir, the 159
Sharon, Moshe 11, 78–79
Sheba 21
Shem 181
Shī'īs 71, 87, 90, 180
Shu'ayb 153
Simon ben Yoḥay, The secrets of 157, 166
Solomon 3, 9, 21, 34, 103, 126, 134, 157–170, 172–174, 176–177, 180–182, 186–187, 193, 199, 220, 222–223
Solomon's Temple 157–170, 173–174, 177, 186–187, 193, 199–220, 222–223
Sozomen 145–146, 175
Ṣūfīs 69, 87, 105
sunna 198
Syria 1, 4, 8, 72, 104, 106–107, 112, 180, 204, 210
Syriac 54–55
al-Suddī 54
al-Suhaylī 15

al-Ṭabarī 30, 52, 161, 174, 206
al-Ṭabrisī 204
Tabūk 90
tafsīr 5, 7–8, 23, 33, 52, 56, 69–70, 86, 94, 111, 121, 173–174, 206
Ṭā'if 185
talbiya 94, 151–152, 176
Talmud Bavli 18, 67, 114, 159, 171, 172
Talmud Yerushalmi 50
ṭawāf 92, 123, 149
al-Tha'labī 102
Thamūd 150, 153
al-Tirmidhī 89
Torah, the 22, 28, 51, 77, 79, 87–88, 102, 103, 112, 115, 119, 157, 171, 184–185, 191 *see also* Bible, the Hebrew

ʿUbayd b. ʿUmayr 147
Ubayy b. Kaʿb 27, 162
ʿUmar b. al-Khaṭṭāb 33, 59, 72, 88–89, 105, 107, 154, 160, 166, 184, 193–196, 206, 215
Umayyads 1–2, 26, 30, 35, 74, 99, 111, 163, 165, 177, 179, 184, 192, 195, 223
Umm Hāniʾ 23
umma 53, 58, 82–83, 116, 128, 131
al-Urdunn 8, 106–107, 204
ʿUrwa b. al-Zubayr 149
ʿUthmān b. Ṭalḥa 142–143

waʿd al-ākhira 39, 44–47, 50–53, 55–57, 60, 221
Wahb b. Munabbih 69–70, 109, 153, 161–163, 165, 181–183, 215
Wansbrough, John 6
al-Wāqidī 31, 196
al-Wāsiṭī 2
Werman, Cana 133–134

Yaḥyā b. ʿAbdallāh b. Ṣayfī 92
al-Yaʿqūbī 26, 29
Yāqūt 76, 168–169, 199
Yemen 107, 185, 218
Yūnus b. Bukayr 196

al-Zajjāj 173, 182
al-Zamakhsharī 125
Zamzam well 31, 151, 153
Zayd b. ʿAmr b. Nufayl 145–146, 197
Zechariah 66, 105, 164, 165, 167
Zerubbabel 164
Ziyād b. Ḥanẓala 23
al-Zuhrī 26, 33, 192

Verses from the Hebrew Bible

I Chronicles
- 21 161
- 21:15–16 161

Deuteronomy
- 26:5 115
- 29:28 [27] 55
- 33:10 58

Exodus
- 1:15–21 41
- 12:31 121

Ezekiel
- 8:1–4 17–18
- 37:12 67

Genesis
- 11:27–29 115
- 11:31 100
- 12 118
- 12:1–2 138–139
- 12:9 122
- 12:13 117
- 13:14–15 40
- 14:18 181
- 15:18 111
- 17:18–20 131
- 18:10 119
- 21:10 19
- 21:13 131
- 22:2 139
- 22:3, 4, 9, 14 122
- 27:28–29 131–132
- 28:12–22 163
- 35:11–12 163

Isaiah
- 27:13 66, 68
- 40:3–4 66
- 52:7 50
- 65:17 64

Jeremiah
- 17:12 172–173
- 31:31–33 [30–32] 119

Joel
- 3 [4]:1–2 76
- 3 [4]:18 48

Joshua
- 2:1 48

1 Kings
- 3:5–14 157
- 7 159
- 7:29 159
- 8:30 187
- 8:65 112
- 9:1–5 126, 157

Lamentations
- 1:17 164

Numbers
- 13–14 48
- 16:31–32 48
- 24 166

Psalms
- 50:5 50
- 71:20 50
- 72:17 172
- 106:30 171
- 126:4 122
- 137:5 109

Zechariah
- 2:10–11 [14–15] 165
- 14:3–4 49, 66
- 6:12–13 164

Verses from the Jewish Apocrypha
Apocalypse of Ezra (= 4 Ezra) 53–56
- 39–50 54–55

Book of Jubilees
- 22 127–137
- 22:24 134
- 29:16–17, 19 124
- 31:5–6 134
- 32:22 133
- 36:12 134
- 36:20 134
- 37–38 134
- 46 43
- 46:16 42

Testament of Moses
- 9:2 44

Testament of Solomon
- 2:5 159
- 4:12 159
- 7:8 159
- 8:12 159
- 10:10 159

Verses from the New Testament
Acts
- 3:25–26 118

1 Corinthians
- 15:52 68

Epistle to the
- Galatians
  - 3:15–17 118
  - 3:26–29 118
  - 4:30 119

Hebrews
- 7:25 82
- 8:9–10 119
- 8:13 119

Revelation
- 18:1 75–76
- 21:1–3 64–65

Romans
- 8:34 82

Verses from the Qur'ān
Q 2:65 111
Q 2:89 51
Q 2:101 51
Q 2:124 117–118
Q 2:125 123, 171, 187
Q 2:125–129 171
Q 2:126 124, 185
Q 2:126–129 127–129

Q 2:127 121, 124
Q 2:127–128 125
Q 2:127–129 187
Q 2:129 126
Q 2:130–132 117
Q 2:133 114
Q 2:136 115
Q 2:140 115
Q 2:142–150 188
Q 2:144 191
Q 2:217 189
Q 2:255 82
Q 3:26 215
Q 3:37, 39 159
Q 3:55 105
Q 3:64 116
Q 3:65–68 115
Q 3:84 115
Q 3:93–95 171
Q 3:96 149, 183, 198
Q 3:96–97 170, 173, 178
Q 3:97 171, 187
Q 3:110 82
Q 3:123 214
Q 4:53 170
Q 4:75 40
Q 4:97–98 40
Q 4:125 103,195
Q 4:158 105
Q 4:163 115
Q 5:2 189
Q 5:14 120
Q 5:21 217
Q 5:27–31 139
Q 5:51–52 209
Q 5:60 111
Q 6:73 65
Q 6:75–79 122
Q 6:92 178
Q 7:75 40
Q 7:128–129 41
Q 7:130–133 40
Q 7:136 40
Q 7:137 9, 21, 40, 102
Q 7:138 40
Q 7:143 151
Q 7:159 53, 56, 58
Q 7:172 92
Q 8:26 40
Q 8:34 189
Q 9 217
Q 9:25 214
Q 9:103 82
Q 10:3 82
Q 10:87 198
Q 11:42–43 139
Q 11:69–71 100
Q 12:6, 38 100
Q 14:35–40 123, 127–129
Q 14:48 64
Q 16:120 116
Q 17:1 1, 8–9, 35, 40, 55, 102, 158, 174, 205
Q 17:4–7 43
Q 17:76 45
Q 17:103–104 45
Q 17:104 20, 39, 45–47, 50–53, 56–57
Q 17:105–109 51
Q 17:111 81
Q 18:47 63
Q 18:63 27
Q 19:11 159
Q 19:41–48 100
Q 19:49–50 100, 138
Q 20:77 21
Q 20:105–108 64
Q 20:109 82
Q 21:51–70 101
Q 21:71 9, 21, 84, 107, 110
Q 21:71–73 100, 138
Q 21:81 9, 21
Q 21:81–82 157
Q 22:25 189
Q 22:26 121, 125
Q 22:27 172, 175, 183, 197
Q 22:29 183
Q 24:55 216
Q 26:52 21
Q 26:57–66 42
Q 28:4–6 41
Q 28:57 124
Q 29:26 110
Q 29:26–27 101, 138
Q 29:67 124
Q 30:1–5 203

Q 30:2–7 209, 213–214
Q 30:6 205
Q 30:14 77
Q 30:43 77
Q 32:4 82
Q 32:28–29 210
Q 33:25–27 208
Q 33:40 162
Q 33:56 81
Q 34:12–13 158–159
Q 34:14 159–160
Q 34:18 21
Q 34:23 82
Q 35:9 64
Q 37:99 110
Q 37:99–101 138
Q 37:102–113 139
Q 37:112–113 140
Q 37:113 117
Q 38:35 34
Q 38:35–38 157
Q 39:44 82
Q 39:68–69 75
Q 43:45 23
Q 44:23–28 43
Q 47:15 54
Q 47:19 82
Q 48:1–3 213
Q 48:18–21 212
Q 48:25 190
Q 48:27 190, 211
Q 50:41 79
Q 50:41–44 78
Q 52:4 184
Q 53:9 36
Q 53:13–18 17
Q 53:26 82
Q 54:6 79
Q 57:10 214
Q 57:26 117
Q 59:2 207
Q 61:6 162
Q 61:10–13 210
Q 67:15 64
Q 68:42 75
Q 79:6–14 65
Q 93:4 46
Q 110:1, 3 214

www.ingramcontent.com/pod-product-compliance
Lightning Source LLC
Chambersburg PA
CBHW020227170426
43201CB00007B/337